DEH313
Social Sciences/School of Education/Institute of Educational Techno
An Interfaculty Third Level Course

PRINCIPLES OF SOCIAL AND EDUCATIONAL RESEARCH

BLOCK 3

UNIT 11
ASKING QUESTIONS
Michael Wilson

UNIT 12
OBSERVATIONAL RESEARCH
Peter Foster

UNIT 13
DOCUMENTARY SOURCES, STATISTICAL RECORDS AND DATA BASES
Ruth Finnegan and Ray Thomas

UNIT 14
WHAT IS DONE WITH DATA?
Betty Swift

UNIT 15
EXTRACTING AND PRESENTING STATISTICS
Roger Sapsford

UNIT 16
THE POLITICS OF OPERATIONALIZATION
Roger Sapsford and Pamela Abbott

The Open University

DEH313 Course Team

Roger Sapsford, Senior Lecturer in Research Methods, Faculty of Social Sciences, and Course Team Chair

Michele Aylard, Course Secretary, Psychology

Andrew Bertie, Academic Computing Services

Judith Calder, Deputy Director, Institute of Educational Technology

Tim Clark, Research Fellow, School of Management

Jack Clegg, Producer, Audio-visual Services

Stephen Clift, Editor, Social Sciences

Sarah Crompton, Graphic Designer

Ruth Finnegan, Professor in Comparative Social Institutions, Faculty of Social Sciences

Adam Gawronski, Academic Computing Services

Martyn Hammersley, Reader in Educational and Social Research, School of Education

Fiona Harris, Editor, Social Sciences

Kevin McConway, Senior Lecturer in Statistics, Faculty of Mathematics

Ann Macfarlane, Secretary, School of Education

Sheila Peace, Lecturer, Department of Health and Social Welfare, Institute of Health, Welfare and Community Education

David Scott-Macnab, Editor, Social Sciences

Paul Smith, Media Librarian

Keith Stribley, Course Manager, Faculty of Social Sciences

Betty Swift, Lecturer in Research Methods, Institute of Educational Technology

Ray Thomas, Senior Lecturer in Applied Social Sciences, Faculty of Social Sciences

Pat Vasiliou, Discipline Secretary, Psychology

Steve Wilkinson, Producer, BBC

Michael Wilson, Senior Lecturer in Social Sciences, Faculty of Social Sciences

Consultant Authors

Pamela Abbott, Principal Lecturer in Sociology and Social Policy, University of Plymouth

David Boulton, Lecturer, Faculty of Community Studies and Education, Manchester Polytechnic

Peter Foster, Senior Lecturer in Education, Crewe and Alsager College of Higher Education

Victor Jupp, Principal Lecturer in Sociology, Polytechnic of Newcastle upon Tyne

William Schofield, Lecturer, Department of Experimental Psychology, University of Cambridge

External Assessor

Robert Burgess, Professor of Sociology, University of Warwick

Advisory Panel

Peter Aggleton, Senior Lecturer in Policy and Management in Education, Goldsmiths' College, University of London

Jeanette James, Consultant Psychologist and Open University Tutor

Elizabeth Murphy, Lecturer in Social Science, University of Nottingham

The Open University
Walton Hall, Milton Keynes
MK7 6AA

First published 1993. Reprinted 1995

Copyright © 1993 The Open University

All rights reserved. No part of this publication may be reproduced, stored in a retrieval system or transmitted, in any form or by any means, without written permission from the publisher or a licence from the Copyright Licensing Agency Limited. Details of such licences (for reprographic reproduction) may be obtained from the Copyright Licensing Agency Ltd of 90 Tottenham Court Road, London WC1P 9HE.

Edited, designed and typeset by the Open University.

Printed in the United Kingdom by the Alden Press, Oxford

ISBN 0 7492 0155 X

This text forms part of an Open University Third Level Course. If you would like a copy of *Studying with the Open University*, please write to the Central Enquiry Service, P.O. Box 200, The Open University, Walton Hall, Milton Keynes MK7 6YZ, United Kingdom. If you have not already enrolled on the course and would like to buy this or other Open University material, please write to Open University Educational Enterprises Ltd, 12 Cofferidge Close, Stony Stratford, Milton Keynes MK11 1BY, United Kingdom.

1.2

UNIT 11 ASKING QUESTIONS

Prepared for the Course Team by Michael Wilson

CONTENTS

Associated study materials		4
1	**Introduction**	5
	1.1 Variety of interview and questionnaire methods	5
	1.2 Procedural/structural factors	6
	1.3 Contextual factors	7
	1.4 Comparison of methods of asking questions	9
2	**Highly structured methods**	9
	2.1 Interviewer schedules	10
	2.2 Open-ended questions in standardized interview schedules	13
	2.3 Self-administered questionnaires	14
	2.4 Piloting	14
	Appropriate language	16
	Prompting	16
	Ordering of questions	17
	Discrimination	18
	2.5 The importance of piloting	20
3	**Asking more complex questions using highly structured methods**	**20**
	3.1 Factual questions	21
	3.2 Retrospective questions and diaries	22
	3.3 Composite measurement	22
4	**Unstructured methods of asking questions**	**25**
	4.1 Less structured methods	26
	4.2 Unstructured methods of interviewing: a research example	26
	4.3 Interviewer control in unstructured interviews	29
5	**Conclusion: validity and degrees of structuring**	**30**
Answers to activities		33
References		35

ASSOCIATED STUDY MATERIALS

There is one major activity associated with this unit, which is a critical examination of part of the DEH313 Video-cassette. I suggest that you watch the sections entitled: 'A relatively unstructured interview (life history)' and 'A relatively structured interview' before starting to read the unit. At two points in the text (Activities 5 and 7) you will find specific questions about these interviews; to answer them you will need to watch the video again.

1 INTRODUCTION

Empirical social science requires, by definition, the collection of original data in one form or another in order to describe phenomena or to underpin explanations of how social or behavioural events are produced. This block of the course is concerned with the different ways in which data are collected by social scientists. This unit is particularly concerned with methods of data collection which involve interviewing or questioning individuals. There are other methods of data collection and later units in this block will deal with them.

Social scientists use a wide range of techniques to collect their data, not all of them involve 'asking questions' of respondents or informants. Structured observational methods, for example, require the systematic observation of behaviour (including verbal behaviour) but without direct questioning of the observed. Participant observation may involve asking questions, but in a different sort of way from the techniques dealt with in this unit — the questions arise naturally in the course of observation rather than as part of a more explicit researcher's role (though participant observers often do employ more formal interview methods as well). Observational methods of gathering data for research purposes are dealt with in Unit 12. However, there is a great deal of diversity even within research whose main data come from asking questions.

1.1 VARIETY OF INTERVIEW AND QUESTIONNAIRE METHODS

The techniques of data collection which this unit discusses are the following:

1 Face-to-face interviews where an *interview schedule* is used: a standard one for each respondent, in which the questions have the same wording, are asked in the same order, and where the ability of the interviewer to vary the wording of the question or the order in which they are asked is strictly limited.

2 The telephone interview. A variant on the face-to-face interview using a schedule is the one conducted on the telephone; an increasingly common choice of data-collection method because of its speed and comparative cheapness. It is much favoured by market researchers. Telephone interviews are, of course, not 'face-to-face' and some of the non-verbal cues which affect the interaction between interviewer and respondent are missing — body-language, for example — but in terms of a personal and social interaction between respondent and interviewer they have much in common with truly 'face-to-face' interviews.

3 Postal questionnaires, with which most people are familiar because of their wide-spread commercial use to collect market information. Here, the respondent is asked to read the questions and to answer either by ringing or ticking one of the 'answer boxes' provided; or less likely, to write in their own 'free response' to a question.

4 Face-to-face interviews which are in a *free format*; that is they are conducted, approximately, like natural conversations between two people. They are often tape recorded for a later full analysis; although the interviewer may take continuous and contemporaneous notes — this is difficult to do whilst at the same time concentrating on the management of the interview. Note taking can also be more obtrusive than tape recording. Although 'naturalistic', interviews such as these are managed to a large extent by the interviewer, who sets the agenda of questions, probes more deeply into issues of interest with supplementary questions and records the answers and the discussion. They do not use standardized schedules like methods 1, 2 and 3 but the interviewer will use a list of topics even if the wording of specific questions is not standardized.

I shall use certain dimensions throughout this unit in order to clarify the similarities and differences between the methods of asking questions which I have just listed. Let me first introduce these dimensions briefly; throughout the unit I shall give examples of different methods of data collection and show how they may be compared along the three dimensions used here, which are: *procedural*, *contextual*, and *structural*. Two of these dimensions are closely linked, the procedural and the structural, and although they may be distinguished conceptually, it is useful to deal with them together. The reason for this close linkage will become clear as you read through the next section.

1.2 PROCEDURAL/STRUCTURAL FACTORS

The first dimension on which methods of data collection may be compared is that of the *procedures* which are employed. At one extreme of the dimension, or continuum of procedures, lie the social science methods which try to imitate those of the natural sciences: the positivistic methods of investigation which seek to reproduce the *controls* over variables which the exact or natural sciences hold to be their particular strength. An important set of issues, from the social scientist's point of view, is concerned with the reaction of human subjects to the knowledge that they are being investigated — and in this respect human subjects differ most markedly from the inanimate objects of natural science investigations. Simply to know that one is a research subject can change the subject's expressions of beliefs and attitudes, not to mention behaviour, in a way which can produce results which are artificial and of only a poor application to the natural world of human interaction. The experiment, discussed in Unit 6, is the purest case of adopting natural science methods in the human sciences. The strengths of the experiment are that it controls extraneous variables which might explain the occurrence or size of the effect under study. For example, the words which the experimenter uses to instruct (or manipulate) the subject are carefully laid down, as are the methods of measuring the changes in performance of the subject in the experiment. Methods of measurement are also closely prescribed, as is the context of the experiment — in a laboratory, for example, with great care being taken that subjects do not talk to one another and so risk biasing the results. The object of the experiment is that a 'manipulation' or treatment is given to the experimental subjects but not to the matched control group who, ideally, have the same characteristics as the experimental group but who do not receive the experimental treatment. Differences between the experimental and the control groups can therefore be attributed to the experimental treatment and not to *extraneous* variables which are controlled by the rigid procedures of the experiment.

At the other extreme of the procedural dimension, lies the *naturalistic* interview between researcher and respondent. This takes the form of a conversational type of interaction between investigator and respondent. Obviously, the respondent usually knows that the interview is a research one but the form of the questions follows a natural line through the respondent's replies, which are recorded in full for later analysis, rather than being summarily reduced to a 'measurement' or series of measurements. The ideal in the naturalistic or unstructured interview is to approximate the 'feeling' of the unforced conversations of everyday life. The naturalism of this sort of interview means that many extraneous variables which might well change the information being collected, are uncontrolled. Other people, such as partners, friends or children may be present and may well join in the interview and have an effect on what the respondent says, although the interviewer will try to avoid this if at all possible. The settings of the interviews are everyday ones such as the respondent's home or workplace — not the laboratory. Above all, the questions asked and the wording used are not closely prescribed but are 'situational' in order to maintain naturalism. In terms of procedures, then, the naturalistic interview is at the opposite end of the spectrum from the experiment.

This is the most important dimension on which methods of data collection may be compared. The comparison is one of *highly structured* and *less structured* methods, because all methods of data collection entail *some* degree of structure.

A highly structured method of asking questions is one in which the procedures of data collection are carefully laid down so that individual interviewers are required not to depart from them in any way. Questions, for example, are worded in the same way and should be asked as written (in interview schedules and questionnaires), in the same order, and the responses should be categorized according to the *response categories* which the research designer has provided. Often the respondent does not follow the procedures of the interviewer and will ask for clarification of a question's meaning or will give a response which is not easily categorized. In these cases the interviewer is provided with *prompts* which allow subsidiary information to be given but which, again, follow a set routine; that is, even the prompts are highly structured and minimize the opportunities for the interview to move towards an agenda of interest which is determined by the respondent rather than the researcher, whether wholly or partly. Highly structured methods also discourage the interviewer or data collector from departing from the design for data collection which the researcher has laid down. Certain types of laboratory experiment (in which the interaction between subject and researcher is prescribed in detail) represent a highly structured method of data collection. So do postal questionnaires, in which each respondent receives a copy of the same questionnaire and is expected to complete it in the same order, following the same questions. As we shall see in Section 2, there is little control over the way in which a respondent completes a postal questionnaire but the principle remains the same — an invariant structure for eliciting information, preferably information given by the respondent and not by someone else!

Less structured methods of data collection include the naturalistic or unstructured interview. Here the questions are not asked in an invariant order (although *some* agenda of questions or topics is determined by the interviewer) and the phrasing of each question can be varied according to what has gone before, what the interviewer has already found out, and according to the respondent's understanding. That is, the interview appears less artificial, more natural, and more resembling a conversation between equal participants. The idea of prompts in the structured sense is unnecessary because supplementary questions can be put according to the replies received, in a way which does not interfere with the natural flow of conversation.

There are advantages and disadvantages to both highly structured and less structured methods; in no sense is it true to say that one is to be preferred to the other or that one is more objective than the other. The examples in Sections 2–4 show how the range of methods of asking questions proceed and they also give the opportunity for a detailed comparison between methods of different degrees of structure.

1.3 CONTEXTUAL FACTORS

The contextual dimension of data collection includes a number of issues and is, perhaps, less of a single dimension of comparison than the procedural and structural ones, but the effect of context on responses is sometimes a critical one.

Firstly, the terms on which the interview has been agreed to is important. What status does the interviewer claim (often implicitly rather than explicitly) to ask questions about the respondent's personal beliefs, opinions or status? What, in other words, is the legitimacy of the interviewer? At one extreme of this comparison lies the market research interview, conducted in the street or (more commonly nowadays) over the telephone. Although small rewards for co-operation are frequently offered (small sums of money, free samples or gift vouchers) there is little in it for the respondent. At the other end of the spectrum lies a request to take part in 'scholarly' research which may be of little direct use to the respondent but which enlists a sense of altruism as a motivation.

The context of interviewing affects *response rates* (see Unit 8) greatly. Market research interviews often achieve a response rate of less than 50 per cent, mainly through refusals rather than failure to contact selected respondents. But 'scholarly' research also often fails to achieve good response rates. Morton Williams (1990) argues that good response rates are most difficult to obtain in surveys of the general public on topics not directly relevant to their lives. For example Van Dijk *et al.* (1990) in a large scale study of the experience of crime in seventeen countries, conducted over the telephone, achieved response rates of only 45 per cent to 60 per cent. An example which shows how the right context can greatly improve response rates is a study of patient satisfaction with referrals from a large group family practice to out-patient departments of local hospitals (Harrington and Wilson, work in progress) in which the patients' perception that the results will be of use to them is leading to response rates of nearly 100 per cent.

Another important aspect of context is the perception of the interviewer's characteristics by the respondent, i.e. the way in which the respondent will *ascribe* beliefs and opinions to the interviewer on the basis of visible characteristics such as accent and dress (perceived social class), ethnic origin, or gender. Ascribed characteristics (or the perception of them) can affect the replies which are received so that interviewers with different ascribed characteristics will receive different replies to the same questions.

This is known as *inter-interviewer variability* and its source lies in the respondents' 'reading' of the characteristics of the interviewer. An experiment (a British one) in which an actor, alternately using a middle-class and a working-class persona (using changes of accent and of dress), approached subjects at a railway station asking for directions, showed how the subjects' perceptions of the 'interviewer' changed their responses (Sissons, 1970). Subjects were chosen randomly so that selection biases were controlled. The different ratings of 'helpfulness' which were received, depending on whether the working-class or the middle-class persona was presented, varied significantly in favour of the middle-class persona.

Similarly, differences in ethnicity between respondent and interviewer can also change responses. In a study of British people of Jamaican origins, Goodman (cited in Wilson, 1979) asked questions about Jamaican women's fertility aspirations — that is, the number of children which they would like to have. Goodman was white and he became concerned during field work that the responses which he obtained would be biased in a downwards direction because of a perception by Jamaican women that high fertility aspirations would be regarded very negatively by whites (the research was conducted shortly after Britain tightened immigration controls in a general climate of anti-black and anti-immigrant political demands). To check the bias produced by using a white (and male) interviewer, a team of Jamaican women interviewers was trained to use the same highly-structured questionnaire on another, but similar, sample to that which Goodman had initially used. The difference between the two samples in terms of their desired family size showed that Goodman received responses which significantly under-represented the fertility aspirations of the Jamaican women when compared to those obtained by similar interviews which were carried out by black, female interviewers.

In general, any ascribed characteristic of the interviewer (that is, one which is relatively unalterable, such as skin colour or accent) can bias the responses obtained in any sort of interview. The best practice to minimize this sort of interviewer bias is to match the ascribed characteristics of interviewers with respondents (so that blacks interview blacks, women interview women, and middle- or working-class people interview their class equals).

Finally, under 'context', the power relations between interviewer and respondent are important. Perceptions that the interviewer is in a position to influence (for bad or for good) the respondent's life chances in a direct way (rather than as a member of a group) can alter the nature of the responses or even the willingness to take part. Simkin's study of the psychological well-being of the long-term unemployed recruited a suitable sample through the local Job Centre (Simkin, 1992). She acknowledges the problems which this caused and the likelihood that she, as researcher, would be associated with the Job Centre regime and particularly with the government's 'availability for work' tests which seek to disqualify people from unemployment benefit (which is not means-tested and is paid at a higher rate than Income Support) if for any reason they are not immediately available to work — through mental ill-health, for example.

1.4 COMPARISON OF METHODS OF ASKING QUESTIONS

It is probably clear to you that the three dimensions of comparison of data-collection methods are not entirely clear-cut or exclusive. In particular, methods which embody a high degree of structure are also ones in which the procedures for data collection are closely specified. Nevertheless, structure and procedure can be distinguished, and will be in the remainder of this unit.

The term 'unstructured' interview is also a bit of a misnomer because a completely unstructured interview is impossible.

Why is it impossible for an interview to be completely unstructured?

Natural conversations have a structure; unstructured interviews also have a structure — often not quite the same structure as that of natural conversations. An interview conducted in an unstructured style still contains a degree of control of the interview process by the interviewer to introduce topics as she or he sees fit and to exercise control of the whole process. The fact that the interview is more naturalistic (i.e. it reflects better the normal rules of conversations such as 'turn-taking') should not disguise the issue that the interviewer has a focus (or series of foci) for what is being asked. Thus the term 'less structured' methods of data collection is preferable to 'unstructured' and one should think of the dimension of structure as a *variable*, ranging from highly to less structured methods.

These introductory dimensions on which to classify ways of asking questions will become clear as we look at specific examples, and in so doing I shall raise other issues of how the critical reader of research should look for 'good practice' in data collection, whatever the degree of structure, or the different contexts in which data are collected, or how closely the procedures are specified. There is no one best way of collecting data; the method chosen depends on the nature of the research questions which are posed and the specific questions which it is desired to ask of the respondents. The aim of all methods is to obtain valid and reliable data — true answers to questions, not distorted by the methods of collection or prone to chance fluctuation — which can be used as the basis for credible conclusions. The methods differ, however, in how they guard against threats to validity and what price the researchers are prepared to pay, in terms of potential invalidity in one area, to strengthen their claim to validity in another.

2 HIGHLY STRUCTURED METHODS

Different forms of structure occur in all methods of data collection, but most strongly in what I describe in the introduction as highly structured forms of asking questions. There are two main highly structured forms of asking questions: the self-administered questionnaire and the interview schedule. Although they have many points in common, the interviewer-administered schedule allows for more control over the interview situation than does the self-administered questionnaire which is either sent by post or administered to a group such as a class in a school. The interview schedule should be used by a *trained* interviewer in order to ensure that it is applied in a standardized way, as we shall see. The self-administered questionnaire is, by definition, controlled by the respondent who is untrained, and it therefore calls for a more sophisticated layout and preparation than one which can be 'corrected' by a trained interviewer in the course of the interview. This is particularly true if the schedule/questionnaire is at all complicated by *routing* instructions such as 'If you answered "yes" to question 14 go to question 16', or what American social scientists call 'skip questions'. A trained and experienced interviewer will be less confused by such 'skip questions' than a once-only recipient of a questionnaire.

2.1 INTERVIEWER SCHEDULES

Here is an example of a question from a highly structured interview schedule used in the experience of crime study cited in Section 1.3.

> Interviewer (reading from the schedule):
>> I now want to ask you about crimes you or your household may have experienced in the past five years. It is sometimes difficult to remember such incidents so I will read these questions slowly and I would like you to think carefully about them.
>>
>> In the past five years have you or other members of your household had any of their cars/vans/trucks stolen? Please take your time to think about this.
>
> Respondent:
>> Er ... let me think ... yes Uwe had his car taken when was that ... '85 no '86 I think ... he got it back soon after but the bastards had smashed in the bonnet. Is that what you want?
>
> Interviewer:
>> Thank you.

(Van Dijk *et al.*, 1990)

There are a number of points to note about this schedule and this question, taken from an interview schedule for an international survey of victims of crime carried out in 1988/1989. A standardized interview schedule was used in seventeen countries and the respondents were contacted by telephone, using a method of random dialling of phone numbers (thus generating a random sample of private numbers, excluding business numbers). The schedule was, of course, translated into the appropriate language; the example interview above was originally conducted in German.

How would you characterize the behaviour of the interviewer in this excerpt? What effect do you think it had on the respondent?

Notice firstly the interviewer's reply to 'Is that what you want?' which was the neutral (i.e. unbiased) response of 'Thank you'. The interviewer has been trained to be non-directive and non-judgemental in what is said to queries raised by the respondent. (The whole point of asking standardized questions in a standardized way is to obtain the *respondent's* answer, not one suggested by the interviewer.) The date of 1985/1986 (dates of the survey were 1988/1989) clearly fits the timespan which the interviewer asked for, but he or she did not want to influence the willingness of the respondent to answer further questions by either over-enthusing about the response obtained or sounding negative if the reply had not fitted into it. A suitable prompt or follow-up question might well have been in this case: 'Has there been anything more recent?' It must also be said that the interviewer's scripted 'Thank you' might have sounded rather artificial and wooden, and in this sense the naturalness of the less structured interview might well be less off-putting than the limited range of scripted responses or prompts which the interviewer can make in the context of a formal interview schedule; this 'artificiality' is held to be one of the weaknesses of the standardized interview schedule.

If a respondent is nervous about the interview, cold or wooden replies may well intensify his or her reluctance to continue. Interviewers, after training and experience, are encouraged to adopt a positive tone of voice and to smile or nod, whatever the reply, as a way of encouraging the respondent. Such non-verbal behaviour is just as much a prompt as a spoken follow-up question. Both sorts of prompting, i.e. verbal and non-verbal, introduce a variation in the social interaction between interviewer and respondent which is far from fully controlled and may introduce an unknown source of *bias* into the recorded responses. But prompting of different sorts is essential to any well-conducted interview and the effects which it, and certain characteristics of the interviewer, may have on the respondents' replies has to be regarded as a source of *response error*.

Response error covers systematic biases which may affect the responses collected by an interviewer. Systematic bias, as opposed to random bias, is when distortions of the respondent's opinions or beliefs tend to occur in one direction only. For example, *social desirability* responding occurs when answers are altered to show the respondent in a desirable light with respect to the interviewer, including the views which the respondent ascribes to the interviewer on the basis of external characteristics such as social class or gender. This can only be discounted or controlled for by a careful matching of interviewers to respondents so that discrepancies of social class, ethnicity and gender are minimized. *Acquiescence* responding is where the respondent is tempted to answer favourably no matter what the question. It should be obvious that social desirability and acquiescence overlap and reinforce each other as sources of response bias. The former can be controlled by careful matching of the characteristics of interviewers to their sample of respondents and the latter by careful phrasing of questions so that they do not seem to invite one sort of response rather than another, but this is not always easy and needs careful *piloting* (see Section 2.4). For further details of response bias, see Miller and Wilson (1983).

All this leaves the interviewer, using a *standardized* schedule and the researcher who designed it, in something of a dilemma. On the one hand he or she wishes to make the interview appear as natural as possible by encouraging the respondent to take part in a 'conversation', although a highly controlled and directed one (which is what is partly meant by a *standardized* method of data collection). On the other hand, the interviewer must be sensitive to the respondent's understanding of the questions asked and be willing to elaborate or prompt in order to ensure that this understanding is genuine. To ensure the latter, it is essential that prompts are used, both of the verbal and non-verbal sorts.

This leads to a paradox. Interviewers *must* probe or prompt to ensure a full understanding of a question, but even if they follow the 'best practice' in non-directive prompts and non-directive body language, prompts of any sort mean that a different question has been asked of the respondent, because they answer to different depths of understanding. But the essential feature of standardized methods of data collection is that each respondent is asked the same question, carrying the same meaning, so that responses are comparable across the sample. In an ideal sense, these are difficult principles to reconcile. In practice, given the variability and idiosyncrasies of a team of interviewers, reconciliation of these principles is impossible.

It may be thought that the paradox may be overcome by using one interviewer for all respondents. But no one individual interviewer can hope to present himself or herself in exactly the same way to each respondent. They will change with each different encounter and so will the necessary prompts, if they are to avoid the wooden artificiality which I noted above as a defect of the standardized method of interviewing. If the interviewer is inflexible then she or he will either prejudice the continuation of the interview or bias the responses which are obtained.

In summary, the ideal standardized interview schedule consists of the following:

1. The same questions should be asked of every respondent, using the same wording. This is standardization of the questions. The context and procedures of the method of asking questions should also be standardized, by the interviewer introducing the research purposes in the same way and by using the same format for approaching the respondents.

2. There is an assumption that all respondents will understand the question in the same way. If they do not appear to understand the question as asked and want clarification then the prompts or subsidiary information which the interviewer gives should be non-directive, i.e. they should not indicate the sort of answer which is desirable and, no matter what the response (however irrelevant it may be), the respondent should not feel that they have made a 'mistake' in any way. Prompting is usually necessary in a standardized schedule for many respondents because, no matter how well the questions are *piloted* (see Section 2.4), a standard question will be interpreted differently by different respondents. The paradox is that if no prompts are allowed then different respondents will respond to what they perceive to be different questions. If one does prompt, one cannot be sure that the respondents have replied to the *same* question.

3. Almost as a corollary of the last point, the respondent should feel motivated to continue to answer further questions; this is partly a matter of context, partly a matter of the length of the interview schedule (measured by the average time to complete the interview), and partly a question of how well the interviewer maintains a motivation to continue the interview.

4. The interviewer (or a coder working after the event[1]) should be able to categorize the responses to any question into a set of mutually exclusive and exhaustive categories. In the crime study example above (Van Dijk *et al.*, 1990) the answer categories were threefold: 'Yes', 'No', 'Don't know'. This is as simple a categorization as possible, many are far more complicated, but note how the interviewer has to decide if the date of the crime fits the five-year period which the designers have decreed. If it did not he or she has only a limited range of prompts to use in order to clarify the matter without embarrassing the respondent and jeopardizing continued co-operation.

5. A less simple categorization of responses (and one more commonly used) is a Likert scale — named after its inventor, R. Likert. Here the responses are coded by the interviewer, in the field, to one of five or seven categories; again using mutually exclusive and exhaustive categories. Typical Likert categories are:

> Strongly agree
>
> Agree
>
> Neither agree nor disagree
>
> Disagree
>
> Strongly disagree
>
> (with a particular statement).

This is a five-fold Likert categorization. Seven-fold categorizations will use three categories on either side of the 'neutral' category of 'Neither agree nor disagree'. The language used for the categories will fit the sense of the question and may invite agreement with a given statement or ask for responses to a question which the interviewer has to code into a specific category. An example is an American study of the people's view of the police as a public service:

---

[1] A coder is one of the research team who classifies verbatim responses, which have been recorded by the interviewer, into one of a set of codes. The questions which need this sort of *post hoc* coding are known as open-ended or uncoded questions. They are 'coded' but not by the interviewer in the field (see Section 2.2). Coding is discussed further in Unit 14.

> How would you rate the overall quality of police services in your neighbourhood? Remember, we mean the two or three blocks around your home. Are they outstanding, good, adequate, inadequate, or very poor?
>
> (Zeller and Carmines, 1980)

This is, of course, a five-fold Likert scale with the response categories tailored to the sense of the question. What it does not cover is those who could not or would not give a codeable response, and such replies have to be categorized as 'Don't know'. The research designer hopes to keep such replies to a minimum because they are not susceptible to an easy analysis, by not being codeable to one of the predetermined categories. Avoiding uncodeable categories depends both on the questions being phrased in a way which is understood by respondents and upon questions which connect with the concerns of the respondent — in a word, which have salient meaning to them. *Salience* means that the questions and the issues to which they refer have a connection with the respondents' experiences and are relevant to them. Piloting is one way, and the most important one, of assessing both the meaning and the salience of specific questions to respondents.

2.2 OPEN-ENDED QUESTIONS IN STANDARDIZED INTERVIEW SCHEDULES

Some schedules use open-ended (uncoded) questions in which the respondent's reply is written down by the interviewer to be classified later into one of a set of codes. There are rarely more than a few of these in any particular schedule because of the extra work involved in the data-collection process, but they do have an important advantage.

ACTIVITY 1

List the advantages and disadvantages of this kind of question.

Uncoded questions allow the researcher to search the full range of responses obtained before reducing replies to a set of categories, and the 'translation' of replies to coded categories can be done by the researcher in the office rather than by the interviewer in the field. This means that open-ended questions do not constrain the respondent's beliefs or opinions to pre-determined categories as fully standardized methods of data collection must do. Although it is not so apparent with interview schedules as it is in self-administered questionnaires, the respondent can also see that his or her reply is being taken down fully rather than summarily reduced to a tick in a box and the sense that their responses are not constrained can help to improve the naturalism of this method. However, the interviewer has to be relied upon to extract the relevant material from what may be a long response and to discard the irrelevant, and replies to open-ended questions can rarely be taken down truly verbatim; the potential for bias introduced by the interviewer is considerable. Another disadvantage to *post hoc* coding (sometimes called office coding as opposed to field coding by the interviewer) is that it increases the time and cost of the questionnaire survey. Many investigators prefer to avoid using open-ended questions; they are liable to introduce an unknown degree of interviewer bias and to vitiate the advantage of highly structured methods of data collection — standardization, and speed and ease of numerical analysis of the results. Unit 14 discusses how open-ended responses are coded in the office.

2.3 SELF-ADMINISTERED QUESTIONNAIRES

Questionnaires are just as much highly structured methods of data collection as are interview schedules. Their chief advantage over interviewer-led methods is that they are cheap, particularly if they can be group-administered. Even postal questionnaires are much cheaper than the use of interviewer schedules, and it is far quicker to conduct an investigation by questionnaire than by any other highly structured data collection method.

Their response rates are, however, usually low, unless they engage the respondents' interests or the investigation is perceived to be of direct value to the respondent — as was the case with the patient-satisfaction survey cited in Section 1.3. The critical reader should always look to see what the response rate was for an investigation and also whether any information is given on the characteristics of those who did *not* respond so that some assessment of the representativeness of the sample obtained may be made. This, of course, is desirable whatever the method of data collection, but it is a point particularly important in questionnaire investigations because of low response rates.

Both closed and open-ended questions may be used in questionnaires, but where interview schedules may introduce some degree of interviewer bias in the recording of responses or the use of prompts or the interaction between the interviewer and the respondent, different sorts of bias may arise in the use of self-completed questionnaires. Fundamentally, the investigator has no control over the conditions in which the data are elicited. It may not be the required respondent who actually completes the questionnaire, it may be a group or family effort, and the questionnaire may be completed in any order that the respondent likes — despite the careful ordering of the questions which the designer may have selected. The degree of literacy of the respondents must also be carefully considered when evaluating the use of questionnaires. For example, and it is an extreme one, I once received a research proposal which wanted to survey a sample of functional illiterates by means of a postal questionnaire! Completing a questionnaire in a manner satisfactory to the researcher is a lot to ask of many respondents, and *piloting* of drafts of questionnaires on samples which are representative of the target population is essential (see below) both to gauge the length of time which it takes and to investigate whether the questions are properly understood by the respondent.

2.4 PILOTING

A pilot investigation is a small-scale trial before the main investigation, intended to assess the adequacy of the research design and of the instruments to be used for data collection; piloting the data-collection instruments is essential, whether interviewer schedules or questionnaires are used. (One purpose of piloting is to assess whether the chosen methods of sampling are adequate to meet design requirements but, since this was the subject of Unit 8, I will not discuss it further here.)

An important purpose of a pilot is to devise a set of codes or response categories for each question which will cover, as comprehensively as possible, the full range of responses which may be given in reply to the question in the main investigation. For this to work effectively, the pilot sample must be representative of the variety of individuals which the main study is intended to cover. Representativeness is difficult to guarantee with the small samples which pilot studies necessarily use. It is better to construct a purposive sample for a pilot study so that the full range of individuals and their possible responses is covered, as far as the range can be known in advance of the study. Purposive or theoretical samples such as these can be contrasted with probability samples (see Unit 8) in which the random selection of individuals in large numbers gives a reasonable assurance that the sample represents the population accurately. Pilot investigations do not attempt to represent, in the statistical sense, the correct proportions of different types of individuals in the population because the purpose is not to estimate the true proportions of such types, but to cover the entire range of replies which might be given to any of the possible questions in the first draft of a questionnaire or schedule. By covering the full range of replies, the researcher is then in a position to work out a set of codes or response categories which embraces the entire range of responses which might be given. This is a counsel of perfection and, no matter how good the pilot, responses may turn up in the main study which have not been anticipated in the pilot results.

The response category of 'Other (specify) ... ' is often included in the codes for closed questions as a way of avoiding a complete foreclosure of the researcher's or the interviewer's options when unexpected and difficult-to-code responses are obtained — even after the pilot results seem to show that the set of response categories is adequate and the main investigation has gone ahead. If the interviewer has (correctly) dealt with a difficult response, it can be treated like a response to an open-ended question; thus it can be dealt with in the office rather than coded crudely in the field. The office coder has a number of possibilities: an 'Other' response may be coded into one of the existing categories because it can reasonably (and at leisure!) be seen that it was not really an 'Other'; a new code or category can be devised if an 'Other' response is found to be common; or there will remain genuine oddities which are truly 'Others' and are left as such. The objective is to reduce the 'Other' category to as few as possible because they are difficult to analyse and usually end up as missing values. This means that 'odd' responses tend to become lost in highly structured methods of investigation.

There are other aims besides the devising of comprehensive coding frames for specific questions when piloting questionnaires and interview schedules. These other aims have to do with the overall design of the instrument rather than with specific questions, except for points 2 and 5 in the list below.

These other aims represent criteria for an instrument which works effectively as a highly structured method of data collection. The aims include:

1 Do the respondents understand the question as initially phrased? This is a matter of using appropriate language according to the sort of research population one is dealing with. Interviewing a sample from a population of young working-class people will require rather different language from that required when interviewing a sample from a population of young graduates.

2 Are the potential respondents able to think of the whole range of possible responses to any particular question or do they need a particular type of prompting?

3 Does the interview schedule or questionnaire take too long to complete so that pilot respondents are showing signs of impatience?

4 What is the best order for the questions? If questions which are sensitive appear too early this might jeopardize gaining the information required or even the completion of the interview itself.

5 Do the questions *discriminate* effectively between different respondents? Investigations which simply seek to *describe* the frequency of occurrence of particular characteristics in a sample of a population do not need to discriminate in their questions. Investigations which are *explanatory* in purpose, however, do need to discriminate; that is questions should 'spread' the respondents across the response categories. Consider, for example, a Likert type question which asks medical general practitioners to record their response to a series of statements to do with mentally disturbed patients, such as: 'Neurotic patients, by and large, tend to be ungrateful for the trouble taken with their treatment', using a standard set of five response categories ranging from 'Strongly agree' to 'Strongly disagree'. If the sample of general practitioners had overwhelmingly answered 'Strongly agree' or overwhelmingly 'Strongly disagree' this particular question would have shown no discrimination and would have been useless in explaining how different types of general practitioner responded to mental illness (Shepherd *et al.*, 1966). Explanations in highly structured methods of data collection (which ask stan-

dardized questions and assign the answers to pre-determined response categories) rest upon correlations between variables. Variables are constructed from the responses to specific questions, and it is essential that respondents are 'spread' across the response categories, otherwise there will be no variation which can be correlated with the variation in responses to another question.

Each of these aims or purposes of the pilot will be discussed further.

Appropriate language

ACTIVITY 2

How, at the piloting stage, would you go about ensuring that the language of a questionnaire was comprehensible and natural for the respondents?

On the phrasing and language to be used in formulating the question, the pilot is particularly useful. It is common, in well-designed research, to have a two-phase pilot study. In the first phase, using the sort of theoretical sample I specified above — i.e. one covering the whole range of individual types which the main investigation is intended to sample — less structured methods are used. That is, more naturalistic interview methods, in which the interviewer has an agenda of general topics, phrased as broad questions, but not the invariant and specific questions of a finalized questionnaire. The replies can be tape recorded for later analysis and from them questions in the appropriate language can be drawn up and also an initial set of response categories or codes devised. In the second phase, using another sample drawn or constructed in the same way as the first phase, a more structured technique is used. This is where a draft of a questionnaire or schedule appears for the first time and it is administered (by interviewer or by self-completion by the respondent) in a similar way to the final instrument. How well the specific, rather than broad, questions are understood can be assessed, as can the length of the questionnaire or schedule — measured by how long it typically takes to complete (point 3 above).

Prompting

Point 2 in the criteria for an effective instrument of data collection raises something more subtle about responses to individual questions. Can the respondent be expected to articulate (or even to think of) the full range of possible responses to a particular question? For example, if the research investigation was concerned with the effect of certain stressful life-events on personal health, the investigator might ask the question (amongst others):

Have you experienced any stressful problems in the past year?

with a view to relating 'stress' to health status.

ACTIVITY 3

What are the problems of this kind of question, and how would you go about overcoming them?

The problems are that respondents may not realize that their experiences have been stressful, nor remember those which they prefer to forget. In this sort of case, a special type of prompt is often used, called a *show card*. This lists the full range of possibilities of responses for the respondent, who is asked to indicate which one or ones apply to him or her. An example is Slack's (1992) study of mental health and the unemployed. As part of the study, Slack wanted to know what 'life stressors' people had experienced during the course of the past year, in order to control for the effect of life stressors on any possible relationship between unemployment and mental health. It is unlikely that members of her sample would have systematically reviewed all the unpleasant possibilities which might have happened to them so a show card was used which listed a number of stressful events or experiences and the respondent was asked to say which ones had occurred to them. The list of life stressors could have been derived from a pilot investigation (and originally was) but Slack, legitimately, borrowed it from already published work.

> Having thought over the past year could you consider this list of problems which some people say they have had. Point to those, if any, which have caused you or your immediate family problems during the *last year*.
>
> (Slack, 1992)

The list of problems (possible responses) on the show card was:

Serious injury to yourself or your spouse requiring hospital treatment.

Serious mental or physical illness in yourself or your wife requiring hospital treatment.

Long-standing mental or physical ill health in yourself or your spouse which is managed by your family doctor.

Death of a friend, a close relative and/or a spouse. Please say which.

Break-up of the family.

Increase in arguments with spouse.

Rowing with neighbours.

Involvement in fights.

Jail sentence.

Minor convictions, e.g. speeding, drunkenness, fighting.

Unwanted pregnancy.

Problems related to alcohol or drugs.

Burglary/mugging.

Although a show card acts as a multiple prompt, it does carry the risk of biasing responses because it increases the likelihood of responses emerging which may not have occurred spontaneously. In this example, the possibility of answering 'No problems' was invited, but weakly:

> Point to those, *if any*, which have caused you ...
>
> (Ibid., my italics)

It is better to ask two separate questions — of which the first is a screening question which signals whether the interviewer is to proceed to the second, e.g. 'Have you had any problems in the past year?' — before using a show card like Slack's.

Ordering of questions

The ordering of the questions is a complex matter and one that is frequently badly handled. It is generally better to put demographic questions towards the end, if possible. By demographic I mean age, marital status, family relationships, occupation, etc. This is partly because they are uninteresting questions to the respondent and one wishes to engage their interest in the interview as soon as possible and partly because, being sensitive, they may be resented. Other topics/questions which should be regarded as sensitive include sexual orientation, health status (particularly mental health status), income, and professional and educational qualifications; such questions should not come near the beginning of an interview or a questionnaire. It is instructive, when reading published research reports, to relate response rates and refusals to the design of the questionnaire or schedule and particularly to the ordering of the questions (if the researcher gives enough information to allow a judgement to be made). Other factors affecting response rates, must of course, be taken into account.

A good questionnaire designer will also think carefully about what is essential to ask as well as the order in which to ask questions; does one need to know exact income, for example, or will an income bracket do just as well? If it would, then a show card containing income brackets can be given to respondents and their responses need only be A, B, C, etc. This is perceived as less intrusive than insisting on precise figures. However, it may be important in some circumstances to be exact about 'factual' questions such as income or age, and a show card with income brackets would be insufficient. For a further discussion on the difficulties of some 'factual' questions, see Section 3.1.

Discrimination

The piloting of individual questions needs to take account of the ability of a question to discriminate between respondents, but only for certain types of investigation.

ACTIVITY 4

For what kinds of research is it important that questions discriminate between respondents, and when might this not matter?

Descriptive investigations are aimed at the accurate estimation of the frequency in the population of certain responses and are unconcerned with 'spreading' the responses across the response categories. If, for example, 90 per cent of responses in a sample of the general British population classify themselves as white/European in response to a question about ethnic origin (as in the 1991 Census), this is not a problem; all the researcher and the critical reader are concerned with is whether the estimation is reasonably accurate. Explanatory investigations, on the other hand, are trying to relate differences on one variable (constructed from responses to specific questions) to differences on another variable. Here, the discriminatory power of a question does matter and the pilot should be testing it. A question which discriminates effectively will show a spread of responses across the answer categories. This is not necessarily an even spread, but one which shows a significant frequency of response in each category.

An example of a descriptive investigation is Mack and Lansley's (1985) study of the experience of poverty in the UK. They asked a number of questions of both poor people and non-poor people, amongst which were a number of questions referring to the experience of living on, or close to, the official poverty line (as defined by household income calculated by the Department of Social Security to be that of the minimum income of Supplementary Benefit). One of their questions concerned housing conditions:

> Here is a list of problems which some people say they experience in their homes. With regard to the house you live in now, which if any, have caused you problems in the past year?
>
> (Mack and Lansley, 1985)

Respondents are shown a card with the following 'problems' or response categories:

No problems.

Damp.

Poor heating.

Infestations, e.g. mice, rats, cockroaches.

No indoor toilet.

No indoor bath.

Broken windows.

Not enough rooms so that teenagers of opposite sexes have to share a bedroom.

Other problems (please specify).

By linking housing deprivation to income poverty Mack and Lansley showed that those on or near the Supplementary Benefit line (within 140 per cent of it, to be precise) experienced a disproportionate number of problems with their housing compared to those whose incomes were above the 140 per cent of Supplementary Benefit line. The Supplementary Benefit line was, at the time of the study, the official 'poverty line' in the UK; those on it, or worse, those below it, were 'poor'. Those above it were the 'non-poor'. Mack and Lansley showed that those with incomes up to 40 per cent above the Supplementary Benefit line experienced a disproportionate number of housing problems, an indication that the Supplementary Benefit line was set too low. From the point of view of discrimination between respondents in the sample the fact that the better-off reported 'No problems' in the above list in an overwhelming proportion is not a matter for criticism. Mack and Lansley's survey (using interviewers and standardized interviewer-schedules) was seeking to *describe* the differences in living conditions and experiences of the poor in the contemporary UK compared to the non-poor.

In contrast, explanatory investigations do require that questions should discriminate fairly evenly between different sorts of respondent. In the United States McIver *et al.* (in Zeller and Carmines, 1980) investigated the links between being a victim of crime, the type of neighbourhood the respondent lived in, and the respondent's perception of the quality of the police service which they received. This represents three important variables whose intercorrelations were vital to the investigation and to *explaining* the connection between experiencing crime personally and perceiving the quality of the local police service on a scale ranging from poor to good.

One of the questions which they asked (as mentioned above, Section 2.1), measuring perception of the quality of police service, was the following:

> How would you rate the overall quality of police services in your neighbourhood? Remember, we mean the two or three blocks around your home. Are they outstanding, good, adequate, inadequate, or very poor?
>
> (Zeller and Carmines, 1980)

Another question which they asked, again to do with the perceived quality of the police service, was:

> When the police are called to your neighbourhood, in your opinion do they arrive very rapidly, quickly enough, slowly, or very slowly, not at all?
>
> (Ibid.)

If responses across their sample had accumulated heavily on, say, 'adequate' in the first question or 'not at all' in the second question, then both questions would have failed to discriminate between respondents. Too many of the responses would have been alike and would have made it impossible to calculate useful correlations between 'perceived quality of police services' — the underlying variable which these two questions would help to measure — and other variables of importance such as 'criminal victimization'.

In general, when responses to a question are to form a variable for an explanatory analysis, the pilot must show that responses across the sample to a question are divided amongst the response categories — not necessarily evenly, but 'spread' to a sufficient extent to allow a useful analysis of the correlations between variables to occur. Questions which do not discriminate in this way should be eliminated from an instrument after the pilot stage has explored the adequacy of the interview schedule or the questionnaire.

2.5 THE IMPORTANCE OF PILOTING

When reading research based on highly structured data-collection methods, look critically for an account of how the data-collection instruments were piloted. Whether interview schedules or questionnaires were used, piloting should have been carried out and the process by which the questions in their final form were arrived at should be documented. Ideally, some account should also be given of how the respondents' co-operation was obtained (the 'research bargain') and how they reacted to the time which the interview, etc., took.

Unfortunately, this is likely to prove impossible to find in journal articles because pressure of space (and convention, as well) means that questionnaires are rarely printed with the substantive findings and analyses. Even books, where space is less of a problem, often omit an account of the methods employed in empirical work. Taking a modern empirical work at random from my bookshelves (Pahl's *Divisions of Labour*, 1984), I found no copy of the interview schedule used nor even what the actual questions were which were asked! Pahl was investigating formal and informal work and the division of labour within the household — a difficult area theoretically — and the omission of key methodological details is surprising.

3 ASKING MORE COMPLEX QUESTIONS USING HIGHLY STRUCTURED METHODS

Certain topics in data collection prove to be more difficult to gain valid and reliable information about than may appear at first sight. These include: retrospective questions where the respondent is asked to remember past behaviours and opinions; 'factual' information about such things as income and occupational career; and, most difficult of all, the scoring or measurement of 'attitudes' where a number of questions are used to place a respondent on a scale which represents a single continuum of an attitude or test of attainment for which any respondent has a score derived from a number of separate questions. The latter is a *composite measurement* which is composed of responses or scores from a number of discrete questions.

A continuum or a uni-dimensional scale assumes that there is a single property which is being measured. For example, the property of height is uni-dimensional; it is assumed that every member of a population may be placed on a particular point of the scale, ranging from low to high. However, social science concepts which denote 'properties' are more complex than physical properties such as height, weight, or temperature and each social science concept may represent a number of different dimensions. The main problem in composite measurement is to disentangle these different dimensions. For example, social class probably consists in most people's perceptions of two dimensions: occupational or status prestige on the one hand, and income level on the other. These two dimensions do not overlap perfectly (in fact, far from it) and this is reflected in the popular ideas of 'genteel poverty' and of 'nouveaux riches'. Section 3.3 shows how the responses to a set of related questions may be analysed to show two or more dimensions of an underlying attitude. The aim in analysis is to distinguish the different dimensions so that each can be seen as a single dimension.

3.1 FACTUAL QUESTIONS

Apparently simple, factual questions can be more difficult than at first appears. Oppenheim (1979) gives a good example of the difficulties which even the simplest question might hold, particularly if the researcher is vague as to why the question is being asked. Oppenheim's question was:

> Do you have a TV set?

Think about this question. What potential ambiguities do you identify?

Who, asks Oppenheim, is the 'you' in the question? Is it the respondent (i.e. are we asking if the respondent owns a set personally), the family, the parent(s) if a child is being asked, the landlord if it is a lodger who is the respondent? Are we interested in whether the TV set is owned or rented? Ambiguity is implicit in the word 'have'.

In this simple example, most of the problems can be solved by being clear about the purpose of asking the question and being clear about what details it is necessary to know. Some factual questions are more difficult but can be tackled by knowing clearly what is essential and what is not.

Income, for example, is notoriously difficult to estimate accurately. The *New Earnings Survey* (Department of Employment) is the main source on changes in earnings for a large number of occupations and is a primary source of reference for government, employers and trade unions. The questionnaire which generates the material is directed at employers and asks for gross earnings (before tax and National Insurance deductions) and for a division between standard earnings and overtime earnings. This is probably accurate and reliable because it accords with the way in which employers keep wage records — though there is doubt if small employers are as accurate or as reliable as larger employers with specialized departments for salaries and wages. However, a question about income directed at non-corporate respondents is a very different matter. Does one want gross or net income? If income fluctuates weekly or monthly, does the investigator want an estimate of the average (typical) income and, if so, over what past time period? Or, if the purpose of the investigation is *not* accurate estimation but only an approximate one, because the analysis will be seeking to correlate income with other variables, then very precise measurements are unimportant — an income bracket will do. All these considerations alter the criteria for assessing the adequacy of the questions used to obtain respondents' incomes. As for incomes, so for age (to the nearest year, to the nearest month — children are usually asked for exact dates of birth, adults for age last birthday) and for several other variables.

Occupational status appears to be straightforward but it is far from that, because the purpose in asking for a respondent's job is often to place him or her in a social class classification. Occupational labels such as teacher, engineer, or manager cover a wide status range, and it is impossible to locate an individual in a social class classification without knowing more about, for example, whether the job is one which requires the holder to supervise others (and if so, how many?) and what qualifications are needed to enter the occupation. The need for these further details means that prompts will have to be used. This is easier with schedules administered by an interviewer than with questionnaires (i.e. self-completion schedules) because the interviewer will immediately know which is a prompt and when it is needed. With questionnaires, great care is needed to keep the question clear and at the same time to get sufficient detail for the investigator's purposes. A cluttered and badly laid out questionnaire will risk confusing the respondent.

3.2 RETROSPECTIVE QUESTIONS AND DIARIES

Van Dijk *et al.*'s (1990) question (Section 2.1) which asks the respondent to think back over the past five years and remember if they suffered the theft of a motor vehicle is typical of the problems which can arise with retrospective questions. Is the respondent's memory accurate enough — leaving aside ambiguities in the question itself? With an interviewer, the situation can be better controlled and if the answer is clearly outside the time period asked for, a prompt can be used such as 'Has there been anything more recent?' This is much more difficult with self-completion questionnaires, and questions which ask for retrospection should be regarded with suspicion if they are used in self-administered questionnaires.

Accurate answers to questions which ask for periodical behaviour are equally difficult to ensure: not because the respondent is consciously trying to impress the interviewer (though that might be a problem with certain types of deviant behaviour) but because memory is very fallible. Even innocuous questions such as 'How often do you visit your dentist?', besides being vague as to the period which is referred to (i.e. recently, over the past five years), will also suffer from memory lapses.

If an accurate estimation of the frequency of a particular behaviour is an important objective of the investigation, a preferred method of data collection is the use of diaries. Coxon (1989) is conducting a study of male homosexual behaviour in which an important variable for his investigation is the number of different sexual partners his respondents have in a prescribed time period. He has devised a structured diary which each of his respondents is asked to complete daily using simple code language for where the encounter took place and the behaviour which occurred. Separate entries are required for each new partner. By collecting the completed diaries regularly, Coxon hopes to obtain an accurate count, amongst other information, of the frequency with which gay men take new partners. This would be difficult to obtain by conventional interviewing methods, where reliance on long-term memory would be very dubious.

3.3 COMPOSITE MEASUREMENT

At its simplest, the idea of 'measurement' in the social sciences is that a response to a question can be used as a means of classifying an individual. Where the question is a simple, factual one, this is relatively straightforward. For example, gender is measured in only two categories; occupational status can be measured more elaborately but, typically, six categories are used (from higher professional/managerial to unskilled manual). These classifications are derived from answers to single questions, although care has to be taken to make the question (and the response) precise enough (as I noted in Section 3.1).

When we wish to measure more complex and more abstract characteristics such as opinions, personality traits, or attitudes, however, relying on a single response will be problematic. It is possible to measure individual attitudes towards divorce, for example, by asking the single question 'Do you think that divorce should be made more difficult?' and classifying the responses into 'Yes' and 'No', but this seems crude. Even if the question (and the measurement) were made more sophisticated by putting the question in the form of a statement; 'Divorce is too easy today', and providing five Likert categories for the respondent to indicate the extent of their agreement or disagreement with it, we are still relying on a single response, albeit one which allows five categories of measurement rather than two.

Very abstract entities such as attitudes are *constructs* which are created by the process of investigation; they are not directly observable responses. What we can observe are the responses we obtain when we present the individual with statements or ask questions which will *indicate* whether or not the construct is present. With attitudes we conceive of the construct as being a continuum so that authoritarianism, for example, is measured on a scale running from very authoritarian at one extreme to not authoritarian at the other. The probability of accurately locating an individual on such a scale by means of a single question or statement is very low. Partly, this is due to inevitable problems of measurement error which is a general issue in all investigations, and partly it is because any single question will be a mixture of a 'true' indicator of the construct and error. Respondents may make idiosyncratic responses, particularly to opinion questions. The question above on divorce may be interpreted by some respondents, for example, as a question about the need for tougher laws generally, not just ones on divorce. Such responses, then, would be compounded of general attitudes towards the criminal justice system *and* specific attitudes towards divorce laws as such. In other words, the indicator (the response to the question) may be drawing on two different constructs, the first of which in this example would be 'error'.

Composite measures use batteries of indicators in order to achieve a single measurement of an underlying construct. By using multiple measurements, it is possible to disentangle the specific 'errors' in individual questions from what they indicate about the underlying construct. With a carefully chosen set of questions (often called items in composite measurement) more accurate measurements may be made.

The process of composite measurement usually commences with the assembly of a large pool of items or individual questions which seem, on the face of it, to measure the same theoretical construct. Considerable work is necessary to refine the initial item pool into a form which is short enough to be tolerated by respondents and which satisfies a number of statistical tests. The main requirement of such measures is that they should be single dimensions and items are selected for final inclusion partly on the basis of how strongly they contribute to a common factor underlying the pool of items. Given the resources needed to create a new composite measure, those which become established in the theoretical literature are widely used by other researchers. Examples of theoretical constructs for which standard composite measures are available include: authoritarianism, Machiavellism, and Eysenck's (1970) extroversion–introversion. These examples are all personality traits but composite measurement is also used for tests of attainment and for intelligence tests.

An example of a battery of indicators which has been tested for uni-dimensionality and which has been widely used in research is Eysenck's extroversion–introversion scale. Note that they are for self-completion and that the allowed responses are 'Yes' and 'No'.

> SELECTED ITEMS FROM EXTROVERSION/INTROVERSION SCALE
>
> Do you prefer action to planning for action?
>
> Do you like to play pranks upon others?
>
> Would you rate yourself a talkative individual?
>
> Are you inclined to be moody?
>
> Would you rate yourself as a tense or highly strung individual?
>
> Have you often felt listless and tired for no good reason?
>
> (Eysenck, 1970)

The example from Eysenck represents an elaborate, finished, product in which the single continuum of a theoretical construct has been statistically demonstrated. What the theoretical construct is, however, and how it is related to behaviour, is another and much more controversial matter. Eysenck has argued, for example, that criminals are disproportionately found to be highly extroverted and highly neurotic, measured on his extroversion–introversion scale and on another of his scales, neuroticism–stability. He also believes that personality traits are genetically determined and therefore innate.

To see how the responses to an initial pool of items or questions are used to test whether or not a single underlying attitude is being measured, let us look in more detail at McIver *et al.*'s study (in Zeller and Carmines, 1980) of the public's evaluation of the US police. Five questions were designed to elicit evaluation of the quality of police services:

> How would you rate the overall quality of police services in your neighbourhood? Remember, we mean the two or three blocks around your home. Are they outstanding, good, adequate, inadequate, or very poor?
>
> Do you think that your police department tries to provide the kind of services that people in your neighbourhood want? [Responses: 'Yes'/ 'No'.]
>
> When the police are called to your neighbourhood, in your opinion do they arrive very rapidly, quickly enough, slowly, or very slowly? [Also coded: 'Not at all'.]
>
> Policemen in your neighbourhood are generally courteous. Do you agree or disagree? Do you feel strongly about this?
>
> The police in your neighbourhood treat all citizens equally according to the law. Do you agree or disagree? Do you feel strongly about this?
>
> (Zeller and Carmines, 1980)

Responses to these five questions were strongly intercorrelated, as they must be if they are designed to measure the same underlying attitude: attitudes towards the police service (ranging from positive to negative evaluations). However, this is not enough to demonstrate that a single attitude construct is being measured. Using the statistical technique of factor analysis (which is discussed in Units 16 and 19/20), the researchers showed that two dimensions underlie the patterns of responses: the ability of the police to fight crime and policing style. This analysis allowed the researchers to develop two distinct scales, one for each of the dimensions.

This example shows the strengths of highly structured methods, provided they are carefully piloted. A large sample can be used (admittedly, the use of a telephone survey in the McIver study helped here but the point is generally true for structured questionnaires) and sophisticated forms of analysis can be brought to bear on the problem revealing an interesting duality in the public's perceptions of the police. It is the ways in which structured methods lend themselves to a wide range of numerical and statistical analysis which have proved an enduring attraction to investigators. Only structured methods such as the standardized questionnaire allow a reasonably large number of respondents to be interviewed within a practicable timespan and within feasible limits of cost. It is also the case, of course, that standardized questionnaire surveys (and experiments even more so) seem to be more 'scientific', more like the proven methods of the natural sciences (with all the prestige which science has), and capable of impressing consumers of social research — particularly those who influence or determine political and social policy. In other words, by placing methods in the positivistic traditions of enquiry, this style of social research makes implicit claims to be regarded as a legitimate branch of the exact sciences.

ACTIVITY 5

Now look again at the illustrative sequence in the Video-cassette entitled 'A relatively structured interview'. It illustrates a data-collection task which students carried out on the predecessor of this course using a questionnaire called 'People in society'. This was a national quota sample directed at investigating people's images of social class.

As you view the extract, take notes on the following:

1. How does the interviewer introduce herself and her purposes? What sort of 'research bargain' is offered? How does she indicate how the respondent *should* answer?

2. How does the interviewer deal with the respondent's uncodeable response to the question 'What sort of people are working class'?

3   How well (i.e. how non-directively) does the interviewer reply to the respondent's query 'I've got to choose one of these?' when offered two statements on a show card?

4   Note down *one* example each of good interviewer practice and of bad interviewer practice.

5   Finally, how well do you think this structured interview represents the respondent's images of social class?

Compare your notes with mine at the end of this unit.

4 UNSTRUCTURED METHODS OF ASKING QUESTIONS

Many social scientists have long held doubts about the validity of highly structured methods of social investigation and data collection. The attempt to study the attitudes, beliefs, and perceptions of respondents using artificial, unnaturalistic, procedures is held to entail an unacceptably high degree of reactivity, no matter how well it is done. And to reduce what the respondent says in reply to a question to one of a set of pre-determined answer categories is unnecessarily constraining of the respondent who may well not feel that his or her 'real' opinions have been correctly represented. Clearly, office coding of responses to open-ended questions goes some way to meet these criticisms, but there still remains the artificiality of structured methods of data collection and the *procedural reactivity* which such methods entail. Procedural reactivity means that the very artificiality of highly structured methods leads to the respondents withdrawing from the situations in which they normally act. As Hammersley (1979) puts it: 'This [highly structured method] results in the suspension of the relevances and constraints embedded in those situations, which may be important in structuring people's everyday activities, and in their replacement by rather unusual relevances and constraints.' And he goes on to say, 'We must ask, therefore, what the relationship is between what people do and say in these "artificial" situations and what they do and say in everyday life... .' That is, the procedures used to question respondents — to elicit data — may distort or bias what the respondent believes, or how he or she might act in a natural situation. This is procedural reactivity.

Responses in highly structured methods are elicited in social interactions which are very artificial; this is obviously so in the case of questionnaire investigations, but it is none the less true in interviewer-led methods of data collection. A conversation, as Garfinkel (1967) points out, has a highly normative structure in which there are expectations of 'turn-taking' and of 'equality' between conversationalists. That is, topics are expected to be initiated by both parties rather than just by one, dominant, interviewer. Thus, in naturalistic methods of data collection, social scientists seek as far as possible to conduct their research in natural settings, in places where social activities are already in progress or where 'interviewers' fit into the 'scenery' and where social science investigators play a role in which they disturb the processes of social interaction as little as possible. This is *naturalism*, which seeks to minimize the procedural reactivity of more highly structured methods of asking questions.

> In order to minimize procedural reactivity, ethnographers [i.e. non-positivistic social scientists using unstructured methods of investigation] seek as far as possible to conduct their research in natural settings, in places where social activities are already in progress. Only in this way,

they argue, can we hope to avoid unwittingly studying artificial responses, or at least behaviour which is not representative of people's everyday lives. In doing research on such settings, the ethnographer tries to play a marginal role, so as to disturb the processes of social interaction occurring there as little as possible.

(Hammersley, 1979)

4.1 LESS STRUCTURED METHODS

There are a number of ways in which the ethnographer plays a role in which he or she disturbs the processes of social interaction as little as possible. Perhaps the most distinctive of these roles is that of *participant observer*, considered in Unit 12, and the research role in which 'marginality' is most vital. The participant observer may ask no questions in any formal sense; he or she participates in a social group, and questions that are asked are often incidental and arise from the normal social interaction of the group in which the participant observer finds a role. More artificial, because more contrived, is the *unstructured interview* in which a naturalistic conversation is recorded in full (or nearly so) for later analysis. The interviewer cannot hope, in this method of asking questions, to merge with the scenery and to be as unobtrusive as the naturalistic form of asking questions demands. Some explanation of the interviewer's purposes and needs is required and a degree of procedural reactivity is necessarily introduced because people, in everyday life, do not submit to an interview at length, except on well-defined occasions such as job interviews.

However, the unstructured interview typically involves far less procedural reactivity than the standardized format of the interview schedule or the questionnaire; it appears to be more naturalistic, and it is so because the questions asked and the order in which they are asked flow from the respondent's replies rather than being entirely imposed by the interviewer's pre-determined list of questions. It must be said, however, that interviews in the ethnographic style are diverse and a single prescription for the ideal unstructured interview would give the false impression of a single interviewing method in ethnographic research; however, very directive forms of interviewing in which the interviewer openly controls the interview and uses standardized questions, are rarely used and then only to probe the 'fronts' which members of the group may have put up.

4.2 UNSTRUCTURED METHODS OF INTERVIEWING: A RESEARCH EXAMPLE

The example is taken from some research which I am currently undertaking. It is a study of a sample of 40 people who were in long-term residential care in the 1940s and 1950s. I was particularly concerned to understand the informants' own interpretations of their experience, including the transition which they made from the Home to the world of work and of independent living.

I used three waves of interviews for each informant: firstly, one which presented myself and my research aims and sought to gain their co-operation in a data-collection process which demanded a considerable period of their time. Because the topics to be covered were sensitive and likely to touch on difficult periods in their lives, it was important to establish a climate of trust, particularly concerning whether their current partner was to know of their background. This preliminary interview was not tape recorded (which would, I judged, have seemed excessively formal to my informants) but I took brief contemporaneous notes and wrote up more detailed notes immediately after each interview had finished (when I was alone). These notes were used in conjunction with my theoretical objectives for the research to prepare a list of relevant topics (or interview guide) which could be tailored to the specific experiences of each informant. This formed the structure for the second interview (which was tape recorded) and which the informant believed to be the actual beginning of the research. The third interview was, again, unstructured but designed to elaborate topics and interpretations which were gained in the second interview. All interviews took place in the respondent's home and were naturalistic in style. The first interviews were ones in which I presented myself and explained my purpose; they also allowed me to gain a knowledge of the respondents' current position in respect of work, family relationships, and evaluations of their experience in the Home. The notes which I took from the first interview gave me a list of topics for the second interview, but tailored in language to the lived experience of the respondent.

Some of the topics I listed for Interview 2 (before tailoring to each individual in the light of Interview 1) were as follows, in the order which I would have preferred, although the order had to be modified according to the respondent.

> What are you doing for a living now? (Subsidiary topics/questions, to trace work and post-compulsory school histories.)
>
> How many children do you have, their ages/genders? (Subsidiary topics/questions, to explore aspirations for their own children *and* begin to probe indirectly into marital histories and stability of family relationships.)
>
> Do you still keep in touch with Sister L. or Sister F. — the staff who had been responsible for the group, both still alive? (Subsidiary topics/questions, exploring the nature of their relationship with the mother-substitutes and inviting comparison with their natural parents.)
>
> Where did you go when you first left the Home? Were you apprenticed? Where were you living? (Subsidiary topics/questions, to explore the transition from institution to independence *and* begin to probe early coping strategies and continuing dependence on the Home.)

Very sensitive topics were left towards the end of the interview, if I could do so, particularly questions on the circumstances in which the informant came to be taken into residential care, including child-abuse (sexual or violent or both), illegitimacy, family break-down, etc.

Note that I have listed topics rather than actual questions. Specific questions to each informant were phrased naturally, taking into account what they had already told me in Interview 1 and the flow of information during Interview 2. Nothing sounds more stilted or artificial than asking a set question regardless of what has gone before. The naturalism of unstructured interviewing requires the illusion that the interview is a 'conversation' rather than a formal interview between researcher and subject: one in which the informant can initiate questions and elaborate answers (without prompting) just as much as the interviewer.

Note also that my structure was a list of topics which I wanted to cover, not a list of questions in a set order. During the interviews, the informant, who is encouraged to speak as freely as possible, is never obviously redirected if she or he veers off onto another topic than the one which the interviewer has succeeded in introducing. The connections between events which the informant makes have to be *understood* by the researcher in their natural context. Apparently disconnected recollections in interviews can be especially revealing of what the informant holds to be significant to them.

Let me illustrate most of these general points with an extract from one of my Interview 2 transcripts from the Experience of Residential Care Study. Some background information is necessary to understand the exchanges between the informant, P., and the researcher (me — M.W.).

This is a study of children (now adults) who experienced a long period of residential care in the 1940s and 1950s. They were a group in the care of a large voluntary children's home, founded in the 1860s, which, in the 1940s and 1950s, believed in long-stay residential care (the situation has now changed). The group which I studied were members of two 'family groups' each in the care of a Sister

(Sister L. and Sister F.) both of whom are still alive, but retired. All of the group left the Home between 1954 and 1959. I was one of them.

Follow-up studies of children who have been in care suffer from an extremely poor response rate. Social workers who select a random sample from Local Authority lists typically get a response rate of 5 per cent, with all the unrepresentativeness that such a low figure implies. In addition, the fact that former inmates of residential homes are approached by a social worker risks a personal reactivity which my study avoids. My informants trusted me as one of them; even so there was personal reactivity, but of a different kind.

The following extract is from an interview (second wave) with P., now aged 54. He works as an engineer in the computer industry, has two grown-up children, and has been married for 25 years to a former Sister (i.e. an ex-staff member) of the Home. This is an extract from a sensitive part of the interview:

M.W.: What happened to D. [his brother, 2 years younger]?

P.: He's a bloody alcoholic, hides a bottle of rum under a bush whenever we go and see him. Christ, he's been in and out of work for ages and lives in a ... room in London which is a complete tip and his woman left him I'm not ... surprised how did she put up with him for so long? My Dad's to blame ... drank like a ... fish, never saw anybody in the Navy do it like that and they could ... drink all that ... free rum, and all that.

M.W.: Yeah, never knew anything about your Father tell me about him and your Mum.

P.: Yeah, didn't know anything about yours either we never talked about it did we? (M.W.: Right.) Mine split up when I was seven, that's when we were at Doddington remember that you was a right little ... ? You were great mates with D. though, you two were always together until we smashed the place up Christ you couldn't half throw a brick (M.W.: an old saucepan and so could you, and eggs as well! — [laughter]) and when they sent us to [another branch of the Home] you two got split up didn't you? After ... [the Governor] caned us in front of everyone else, when we got there, bastard! Remember the baths we had to take afterwards, bloody glass in them too?

M.W.: Yeah never forgot it, but [Governor] is dead now did you know? (P.: Yeah, good job.) They put us in [different houses] but we still saw a lot of each other. He didn't like [an area of north London] where they put him in digs did he?

P.: He ... hated it! The job [in a bakery] and the ... landlady who was a right cow and wouldn't let him have any visitors we had to meet in the caff. My Dad went to see him once only time he did and she turned him away wouldn't even tell D. he'd been there.

M.W.: Did your Mum keep in touch?

P.: No never saw her after we went to Doddington, she took up with another man but I never saw him didn't want to know about us I suppose, starting again with another man — had more kids too but I've never seen them.

M.W.: Where is she now, do you know?

P.: Don't know and I don't want to know after all this time.

M.W.: Why do you think D. turned into an alkie, you didn't?

P.: Family I think what with my Dad I don't know about my Mother and D. had a bad time when he first left [the Home] and never got sorted out ... different women and he spent a lot of time then with H. [later convicted of murder and sentenced to life imprisonment] you remember him you three were always together he drank a lot and D. caught it from him I think but I don't really know. He's weak he always was you led him around by the nose and H. too so I suppose he got into the wrong lot and drank too much.

(Wilson, work in progress)

The shared references to mutual experiences between P. and me need to be taken into account when assessing the impact that I had on the information collected. There are frequent references to people and events which we had both known and this gave the interview a more natural feel. It is similar in some ways to the sorts of interviews which might arise in a study using overt participant observation following a period in the field studying the group — that is, where there is a sense of the observer belonging to the group and being accepted as a member. In this case, my role is perhaps less marginal than it is for most participant observers. On the other hand there is reaction, by P., to me as an individual with his memories of me as a boy, what I had been like, and my part in his brother's alcoholism. This is personal reactivity, which is an issue in any method of interviewing. One must ask how such reactivity may have biased the responses obtained.

4.3 INTERVIEWER CONTROL IN UNSTRUCTURED INTERVIEWS

ACTIVITY 6

Look back over the last section. What elements of structure — of control by the interviewer of the flow and direction of the conversation — do you detect?

Notice how, in the extract above, I replied (naturally) to the specific yet partly rhetorical questions which P. asked (e.g. 'Remember the baths ... ?') but turned the interview back to the issues which I wanted to explore. Thus I remained in control of the interview, appeared to be non-directive, and preserved the naturalism of this method of interviewing.

However, a full transcript would show that I had not fully followed the rules of 'turn-taking' and of conversation between equals that real conversations have (see, e.g. Garfinkel, 1967). Although I spoke less than P., I nearly always moved the interview on towards topics and issues which were on my agenda rather than P.'s. In other words, I took control and imposed my structure or agenda on to P. and still maintained an essential rapport with him.

This research example is, perhaps, unusual in that, even though a research interviewer, I had a natural role in the conversation — as one of the original group. If the aim of finding an acceptable role without a background of shared participation is to succeed, some role for the interviewer must be found which is accepted by the informant. Yet, at the same time, the interviewer must remain detached in order to structure the interview according to his or her research interests. The need to engage with the informant yet remain detached is a difficulty of naturalistic methods of investigation. It is most obvious in participant observation studies where finding a role to play is the first concern of researchers. Lacey (1979) was a teacher at a northern grammar school when he undertook his study of the underachievement of working-class boys in grammar schools, and although his role seemed natural and blended into the scenery of the school he reports the strains between being perceived as a teacher, who was interested in matters not normally discussed by either teachers or pupils, and the need to remain detached, even though the headmaster knew he was a researcher.

So it is with one-to-one interviews where the interviewer always has a role in the eyes of the informant, yet it must be a role which allows the informant to think that he or she has been listened to carefully and understood. Nevertheless, it is the interviewer who structures the interview even though he or she may do less talking than the informant. It is the interviewer who changes the subject, asks clarifying questions, who refers back to something said earlier, and who finally, ends the interview. Thus, although the unstructured interview may appear just that, it still contains a structure largely dictated by the researcher rather than by the informant. The opposition between structured and unstructured methods of data collection is in many ways a false one; all are structured, but in different ways. The best one can say is that there are degrees of structure in all methods of asking questions.

ACTIVITY 7

Now look again at the extract in the Video-cassette entitled 'A relatively unstructured interview'. Make notes on the following points and compare your answers to mine.

1. What examples can you find of the interviewer's 'direction' of the interview, i.e. how does she impose her agenda of interest on the respondent?

2. How does the interviewer maintain rapport? What examples can you find of non-judgemental prompting?

3. What examples of poor interviewing practice are there in this extract?

4. What are the main contrasts between this extract and the 'Relatively structured interview' from Activity 5?

My answers are at the end of this unit.

5 CONCLUSION: VALIDITY AND DEGREES OF STRUCTURING

It is important to define at the outset what the ideal researcher's objectives should be when assessing and evaluating published research. I shall follow Martyn Hammersley (in Block 1) in adopting a *realist* position on the nature of validity. That is, there exist phenomena (such as beliefs, opinions, facts) independent of the observer, which the researcher is endeavouring to collect, and which may be distorted or *biased* by poor techniques; the phenomena may be misrepresented and the accounts given of the respondents' beliefs, attitudes, opinions or factual data may be untrue or invalid. However, it would be naïve to think that there exists a 'true' response to any given question, because every reply is an artefact produced by the particular interviewer's interaction with a specific respondent in a context. What can be said is that there is a body of methodological knowledge, built on researchers' experiences, which shows how certain biases may be introduced by poor techniques. There exists in social research a set of good practices in data collection which aims at minimizing bias in the process of collecting data by interview methods. The ideal in using interview methods is to show that the methods used would produce similar results from the same sample of respondents if repeated by another interviewer using the same methods. This is *reliability* and is an important criterion in assessing and evaluating research products.

The central problem in data collection in the human sciences is that it usually involves personal, social, interaction between the observer and the observed or between the interviewer and the respondent. Even when postal questionnaires are used there is still social interaction. The respondent is asked to give time and application, usually for little reward except, perhaps, a feeling of satisfaction. Willingness to assist the investigator depends on the *context* in which the respondent is asked to take part. A request to complete a four-page questionnaire which comes from the respondent's family doctor and which is concerned with patients' experiences at local hospitals when referred as out-patients is likely to get a better response rate than a market research questionnaire posted to a sample of new car buyers. The patient survey is being conducted in the context of a satisfactory provision of medical services to the very respondents who are asked to take part — there is the satisfaction of being asked for your opinion in a matter which is of great personal concern. The market research questionnaire carries little or no sense of reward; it is simply a chore for most respondents, and response rates in this sort of research are notoriously low, as I have already mentioned. The context in which respondents are asked to answer questions does not just affect their willingness to respond; it also can alter the responses, and so it is an aspect of the *validity* of the data-collection method. This is so not just in naturalistic face-to-face interviews, in which the way the interview was set up (e.g. what is said about the nature of the research, the characteristics of the interviewer, etc.) matters greatly because the respondent will *react* to his or her perceptions of the nature of the questions and to the characteristics of the interviewer. It applies equally to standardized questionnaires. These are conducted in a context too and although, apparently, more objective there is still social interaction between the researcher and the respondent. The latter applies whether or not the questionnaire is self-administered or conducted by an interviewer.

Context in data collection is one of the dimensions on which I compared data-collection methods in the Introduction to the unit. One other analytical dimension on which I distinguished different methods of data collection was that of the procedures which are used. At one end of a dimension of differences in procedures of collecting data lies the standardized, impersonal (apparently) methods of the laboratory experiment. The experimenter uses a fixed set of instructions for each subject and is rarely allowed to vary the wording or to give further information even when subjects ask for it. Frequently, the experimenter will not know the hypothesis which is under investigation. All this is to prevent the experimenter unwittingly biasing the results by indicating, however subtly, what is the preferred response or behaviour (i.e. the one which will confirm the investigator's hypothesis). On the face of it, this sort of procedure appears objective and scientific — in fact it is clearly derived from the experimental procedures of the natural sciences, hence it belongs to the *positivistic* school of the philosophy of science and is open to the same objections. There is known (through experiments about experiments in the social sciences, see Crowle, 1976) to be less objectivity in experimentation on human subjects than some of its proponents as 'the scientific method' have thought. In particular, the subjects may lie to the experimenter. The problem is, as Crowle puts it, that ' ... the human subjects are of the same order of complexity as the experimenters', and may detect what the experiment is really about and alter their behaviour accordingly or give false responses. Subjects may react in undesired ways to the rigid procedures of the experiment and the data which is gathered may be biased in unknown ways, thus making interpretation of the results ambiguous. And by needing to work out in advance the entire procedures of the experiment and not being able to change them, this method of data collection is inflexible and forecloses the possibility of exploring connections and potential analyses which may emerge during the course of the investigation.

It was in reaction to positivistic methods of conducting social research that some researchers long ago adopted methods of data collection which are naturalistic in their procedures, such as the unstructured interview. In Section 4, I showed that such methods were not unstructured despite superficial appearances to the contrary. This means that we cannot say that research based on ways of asking questions which are relatively unstructured is more valid than research using highly structured methods. Less structured methods minimize procedural reactivity and allow the freer exploration of respondents' meanings and beliefs. They do this at the possible expense of reliability — the ability of another researcher to obtain the same results using the same methods, something which is stronger in highly structured methods. However, less structured methods do sometimes have a reflexive account of the research in which the investigator *reflects* on the context and on the procedures which were adopted and tries to assess the impact which these might have had on the responses obtained and on the interpretations which are placed upon them. There is a partial, and implicit, reflexive account in my research example in Section 4.2.

However, procedural reactivity is only one source of bias; there remains *personal reactivity*, i.e. the effect which a particular researcher's interactions with the respondents might have had on the research. Personal reactivity is maximal in less structured methods and minimal in highly structured ones. In the experiment, the behaviour of the experimenter is closely controlled with a view to minimizing the impact of her or his persona on the experimental result; the same is attempted in highly structured interview studies, through standardization of questions and procedures and the standardized training of interviewers.

Validity, then, is a matter of trade-offs: between procedural and personal reactivity, and between reliable and less reliable methods. Whichever method of data collection is chosen attention must be paid to the objectives of the research and the methods adopted must be evaluated in this light. I had, for example, considered using highly structured methods of research for my study of the 40 respondents who had been in residential care, but I rejected this because it would be impossible to have avoided the personal reactivity which would have followed from my knowing them since childhood. More importantly, I wanted *their* understanding of what it was like to be in care, and this would have been impossible without employing a method which allowed me to explore their memories using *their* meanings rather than to impose mine from the outset.

ANSWERS TO ACTIVITIES

ACTIVITY 5

1 'I'm a student at the Open University ... ' says the interviewer, asking for help on altruistic grounds (i.e. please help me I am studying for a qualification and need your co-operation). She promises confidentiality very effectively. There is no research bargain apart from this. The interviewer says 'say what you really think ... ', that is there are no right or wrong answers.

2 By using the prompt 'anything else', which is non-directive (good practice), when the respondent's first reply is 'people who work for a living'.

3 By saying 'you can say you don't know'. Bad practice would have been to insist on the respondent's choosing one of the two statements, whatever their reluctance to do so. As it was, a substantive reply was obtained without pressure.

4 Examples of good interviewer practice in this extract include the ways in which the interviewer dealt with the prompts in answers 2 and 3 above. Other examples could include 'four to five social classes ... OK' which does not make the respondent feel that her reply is inadequate, even though it is difficult to code in the questionnaire used and might have proved irksome to some interviewers. Further, the promise of confidentiality was given with sufficient detail to be convincing, and in so doing the interviewer gave the impression of being very 'ordinary', so lessening any social distance between the respondent and the interviewer. This tends to encourage the expression of true opinions, rather than trying to impress the interviewer or what the respondent *ascribes* as opinions to the interviewer on the basis of her perceptions.

Two examples of poor interviewer practice were noticeable to me. At the beginning, there are vague references to the physical length of the questionnaire and it is shown to the respondent. It is much better to say something like 'This will only take about half-an-hour of your time'. The other example is when the interviewer says 'I haven't got a category for it!' The respondent should not be told that, no matter how extended their answer, it is to be reduced summarily to a pre-determined category. This can alienate many respondents and jeopardise the interview and the responses made.

5 There is a reluctance on the part of the respondent to use the conventional language of social classes. Notice how she temporized in her answer to 'What sort of people are working class?' And when shown two statements on a show card defining different images of the social structure (the 'football team' image on the one hand and the 'opposite sides' image on the other) she is reluctant to choose either one; when she finally does so, she adds 'this is the idealistic way'. In her answer to the first question 'Do you see yourself as belonging to a particular group in society?' she identifies herself as a woman rather than as a member of any other sort of group, including a social class. Social class does not seem very salient to this respondent as a way of classifying people or behaviours, but when her responses have been coded and added to the many others in this survey this point will have disappeared from view.

ACTIVITY 7

1 The interview starts with a specific question to the respondent, thus starting the data-collection process. The frequency of questions is much greater at the beginning of the interview as the interviewer tries to focus on the issues relevant to her research — all this directs the interview process. Later, there is a clear example of moving the agenda along when the interviewer asks, 'Did you stay in secretarial work?'

2   The extract shows a great deal of smiling and nodding by the interviewer, all of it useful for encouraging rapport and a sense of sympathetic understanding for the respondent. At the point when it is revealed that Michele has been married three times, widowed once with young children, and divorced once, the interviewer (wishing to probe these events further) says, 'Lot of events compressed in a short time … ?' which is ideally non-directive. The eliciting of Michele's educational aspirations (and their frustration) is completed with a number of good non-directive prompts.

3   The start of the interview, where the interviewer is explaining the purpose of the meeting and putting the respondent at her ease, is not well handled. The request to tape record is clumsy; the phrases 'as much as you need to know' and 'what do you think you're doing here?' could have been resented by some respondents. One question is put in a very directive way: 'Did you have any money problems — expect you would?' This is partly understandable, although still bad practice, because the catalogue of woe which the respondent narrates would normally call for expressions of sympathy from a listener, and as the unit argues, an unstructured interview does follow the rules of natural conversation.

4   The main contrast for me between the two interviews is the differences in Michele's view of social class which emerge. In the structured interview she is reluctant to use the conventional language of social class differences or to see significant class structuring of society. In the unstructured interview she explains her father's professional background, the milieu in which she was brought up, and the fact that her first two husbands were professional men (notice how she insists on 'professional' engineer for her second husband). Her early world was clearly divided between professional people and others. Her third marriage to a carpenter is probed by the interviewer and Michele emphasizes how he is self-employed (i.e. of a higher class status than as an employed manual worker) under the interviewer's encouragement. The respondent also recounts her educational and career ambitions both in the past (frustrated) and in the future. Thus from the unstructured interview I get a clear impression of someone to whom professional status is very important. This did not emerge at all clearly in the structured interview.

REFERENCES

Coxon, A.P.M. (1989) 'Something sensational: the sexual diary as a tool for mapping detailed sexual behaviour', *Sociological Review*, vol. 36, no. 2.

Crowle, A.J. (1976) 'The deceptive language of the laboratory', in Harre, R. (ed.) *Life Sentences: Aspects of the Social Role of Language*, Chichester, Wiley.

Department of Employment (annual) *New Earnings Survey*, London, HMSO.

Eysenck, H.J. (1970) *Crime and Personality*, Harmondsworth, Penguin.

Garfinkel, H. (1967) *Studies in Ethnomethodology*, Englewood Cliffs, N.J., Prentice-Hall.

Hammersley, M. (1979) 'Data collection in ethnographic research', in *Research Methods in Education and the Social Sciences*, DE304, Block 4, Part 3, The Open University, Milton Keynes.

Lacey, C. (1979) 'Problems of sociological fieldwork: a review of the methodology of Hightown Grammar', in Wilson, M.J. (ed.).

Mack, J. and Lansley, A. (1985) *Poor Britain*, Harmondsworth, Penguin.

McIver, J., Carmines, E. and Zeller, R. (1980) 'Multiple indicators', in Zeller, R. and Carmines, E. (eds).

Miller, P. and Wilson, M.J. (1983) *A Dictionary of Social Science Methods*, Chichester, Wiley.

Morton Williams, J. (1990) 'Response rates', *Newsletter*, vol. 10, no. 1, Joint Centre for Survey Methods, SCPR/LSE.

Oppenheim, A. (1979) 'Methods and strategies of survey research', in *Research Methods in Education and the Social Sciences*, DE304, Block 4, Part 2, The Open University, Milton Keynes.

Pahl, R. (1984) *Divisions of Labour*, Oxford, Blackwell.

Shepherd, M., Cooper, B., Brown, A. and Kalton, G. (1966) *Psychiatric Illness in General Practice*, London, Oxford University Press.

Simkin, C. (1992) *The Psychological Effects of Unemployment*, unpublished M.Sc. dissertation, The Open University, Milton Keynes.

Sissons, M. (1970) 'The psychology of social class', in *Making Sense of Society*, D101, Units 14–18, The Open University, Milton Keynes.

Slack, C. (1992) *Long Term Unemployment and Health Status*, unpublished M.Sc. dissertation, The Open University, Milton Keynes.

Van Dijk, J., Mayhew, P. and Killias, M. (1990) *Experiences of Crime Across the World*, Deventer, Kluwer.

Wilson, M.J. (ed.) (1979) *Social and Educational Research in Action*, London, Longman.

Zeller, R. and Carmines, E. (eds) (1980) *Measurement in the Social Sciences*, Cambridge, Cambridge University Press.

UNIT 12 OBSERVATIONAL RESEARCH

Prepared for the Course Team by Peter Foster

CONTENTS

Associated study materials		**38**
1	**Introduction**	**39**
	1.1 The advantages and limitations of observational research	40
	1.2 Approaches to observational research: more- and less-structured observation	41
2	**Relationships and roles in observational research**	**45**
	2.1 Negotiating access	45
	2.2 Developing relationships	50
	2.3 The researcher's role	52
	2.4 Managing marginality	56
	2.5 Ethical issues	57
3	**What to observe**	**59**
	3.1 Focusing research	59
	3.2 Representative sampling	60
4	**Recording observations**	**61**
	4.1 More-structured observation	61
	4.2 Less-structured observation	65
	4.3 Using technology	67
5	**Assessing the validity of observations**	**69**
	5.1 Threats to validity	69
	5.2 Ways of assessing validity	70
6	**Conclusion**	**72**
Answers to activities		**74**
References		**82**
Acknowledgements		**86**

ASSOCIATED STUDY MATERIALS

Offprints Booklet 3, 'Inside the primary classroom', by M. Galton, B. Simon and P. Croll.

Reader, Chapter 15, 'Observation and the police: the research experience', by M. Punch.

1 INTRODUCTION

Within everyday life we are all observers. We constantly observe the physical organization of the environment around us, and we observe the behaviour of the human beings who inhabit that environment. Observation involves watching, of course, but information from sight is supported by that received through our other senses — through hearing, smelling, touching and tasting (these are even more important for blind or partially sighted people). The information from these various senses is usually combined, processed and interpreted in complex ways to form our observations — our mental images of the world and what is going on in it.

In everyday life we use observation to gain information or knowledge so that we can act in the world. In this way, my observation of traffic enables me to drive in such a way that I avoid colliding with other vehicles (if it is successful!), my observation of the behaviour of my three-year-old son enables me to decide when he is tired and I should put him to bed, and my observation of the behaviour of strangers I meet enables me to decide whether they are friendly or threatening (amongst other things) and how I should behave towards them. In fact, my observation, and of course interpretation, of the behaviour of others is a major influence on my interaction with them. Without observation, participation in the world would be impossible — and when our senses are impaired that participation becomes more difficult.

Observation also informs, and enables us to test, our common-sense theories about the social world. We all interact with others on the basis of, often taken-for-granted, ideas about how particular types of people are likely to behave in particular circumstances. These theories are built up, and continually refined, by observation of the behaviour of others and of ourselves.

Observation fulfils similar purposes in research, but there is an important difference. Again, the aim is the collection of information about the world with the intention of guiding behaviour. However, observation is not usually done simply to enable the researcher to decide how to act in the world or to inform his or her common-sense theories. Its aim is the production of public knowledge (empirical and theoretical) about specific issues, which can be used by others in a variety of ways. This knowledge may influence the behaviour of those who access it, but its influence will be less direct than is the case with everyday observation.

Do you think there are any other differences between observation in everyday life and observation in research?

I think there are two further distinctive features of observation in research — first, the way it is organized and second, the way observations are recorded, interpreted and used. In research, observation is planned and conducted in a systematic way, rather than happening spontaneously and haphazardly as it usually does in everyday life. Appropriate techniques are carefully selected for the purposes at hand. Observations are systematically recorded rather than stored only in personal memory, and are carefully interpreted and analysed, again employing systematic and planned procedures. Moreover, the data produced by observational research are subjected to checks on validity so that we can be more confident about their accuracy than is usually the case with observational data produced routinely in everyday life.

As part of research, observation can be used for a variety of purposes. It may be employed in the preliminary stages of a research project, to explore an area which can then be studied more fully utilizing other methods, or it can be used towards the end of a project to supplement or provide a check on data collected in interviews or surveys (see, for example, Stacey, 1960; Bennett, 1976; Rex and Tomlinson, 1979). Where observation is the main research method employed, it may be used to obtain descriptive quantitative data on the incidence of particular sorts of behaviour or events (see, for example, Galton et al., 1980; Sissons, 1981), or to enable qualitative description of the behaviour or culture of a particular group, institution or community (see, for example, Malinowski, 1922; Whyte, 1981). In the latter case, observation is used as part of a broad approach to research, usually referred to as ethnography, which uses a combination of data-gathering techniques (I discuss this further in Section 1.2). Observation may also be used to develop and test particular theories, and situations or cases may be deliberately selected for observation in order to facilitate this (see, for example, Glaser and Strauss, 1967, 1968; Brophy and Good, 1974).

The range of topics which have been studied by means of observational research is vast. Almost every aspect of human behaviour has been investigated. To pick just a few examples, in recent years there have been studies of particular sorts of behaviour such as children's play (Pellegrini, 1989), political oratory (Atkinson, 1984), homosexuality (Humphreys, 1970) and petty crime (Ditton, 1977); studies of categories or groups of people such as football hooligans (Williams et al., 1984), street gangs (Patrick, 1973), police officers (Brewer, 1991); studies of particular events or changes in people's lives such as children's transition from primary to secondary school (Measor and Woods, 1984) or the socialization of medical students (Becker et al., 1961); studies of particular places and institutions such as courts (Atkinson and Drew, 1979), schools (King, 1978; Ball, 1981) or psychiatric hospitals (Rosenhan, 1982); and there have been studies of residential (Hannerz, 1970), religious (Barker, 1984) and minority ethnic communities (Pryce, 1979).

1.1 THE ADVANTAGES AND LIMITATIONS OF OBSERVATIONAL RESEARCH

Observation as a research method has a number of clear advantages over interviews and questionnaires. First, information about the physical environment and about human behaviour can be recorded directly by the researcher without having to rely on the retrospective or anticipatory accounts of others. For a number of reasons such accounts may be inaccurate. For example, they may be shaped by the particular role the person plays in ways that make the account misleading, the information may not have been systematically recorded and may therefore contain errors, or the account may be distorted by the person's concern to present a desirable image of him- or herself. Since observation enables the researcher to note down what he or she sees as it occurs, observational data are often more accurate.

Second, the observer may be able to 'see' what participants cannot. Many important features of environment and behaviour are taken for granted by participants and may therefore be difficult for them to describe. It may require the trained eye of the observer to 'see the familiar as strange' and provide the detailed description required. Moreover, important patterns and regularities in environment and behaviour may only be revealed by careful, planned observation by a researcher over a period of time.

Third, observation can provide information on the environment and behaviour of those who cannot speak for themselves and therefore cannot take part in interviews or complete questionnaires — babies, very young children and animals are obvious examples. It can also give data on the environment and behaviour of those who will not take part in interviews or complete questionnaires because they have not the time, or because they object, or because they fear the consequences. In fact, some form of observation (perhaps covert) may be the only way of collecting information on the behaviour of people who are extremely busy, are deviant, or are hostile to the research process for some reason (see Taylor, 1984, for example).[1]

---

[1] I discuss the ethical issues raised by certain forms of observational research in Section 2.5.

A final advantage, which I mentioned earlier, is that data from observation can be a useful check on, and supplement to, information obtained from other sources. So, for example, the information given by people about their own behaviour in interviews can be compared with observation of samples of their actual behaviour.

However, there are also limitations to observation as a research method. The environment, event or behaviour of interest may be inaccessible and observation may simply be impossible (or at least very difficult). This may be because the social norms surrounding the event or behaviour do not usually permit observation (as with human sexual behaviour, for example), because the behaviour deliberately avoids observation (as with many forms of deviance), because the event or behaviour occurs rarely or irregularly (as with disasters), because the observer is barred from access to the event or behaviour (as is frequently the case in studying powerful élite groups), or because the event or behaviour happened in the past. Sometimes events and behaviour are just not open to observation.

A second limitation is that people may, consciously or unconsciously, change the way they behave because they are being observed, and therefore observational accounts of their behaviour may be inaccurate representations of how they behave 'naturally'. This is the problem of reactivity which we will discuss later in the unit, in particular in Sections 2.2, 2.3 and 5.1.

A third limitation is that observations are inevitably filtered through the interpretive lens of the observer. It must therefore be emphasized that observations can never provide us with a direct representation of reality. Whatever observational method is used, what the observer obtains from observational research are constructed representations of the world. Moreover, observers inevitably have to select what they observe and what observations they record. Sometimes the basis of these selections is made explicit, but at other times it is not, and clearly there is a danger that the researcher's preconceptions and existing knowledge will bias his or her observation.

Finally, it is worth emphasizing that observational research is very time consuming, and therefore costly, when compared with other methods of data collection. This means that the researcher may only be able to observe a restricted range of subjects or a small sample of the behaviour that is of interest. As a result, the representativeness of observations may often be in doubt. In some cases interviews or questionnaires may be a more economical way of collecting detailed data which are more broadly representative.

1.2 APPROACHES TO OBSERVATIONAL RESEARCH: MORE- AND LESS-STRUCTURED OBSERVATION

There are a number of different approaches to observational research. One important distinction is between more-structured (sometimes referred to as 'systematic') observation and less-structured (sometimes referred to as 'ethnographic' or 'unstructured') observation. These two approaches originate in different academic traditions, and have different aims, purposes and procedures.

More-structured observation

The roots of more-structured observation are in the positivist tradition in social science where the aim has been to emulate, to one degree or another, the approaches and procedures of the natural sciences. The emphasis in this tradition has been on the accurate and objective measurement of observable human behaviour, on the precise definition and operationalization of concepts, on the production of quantitative data, on the examination of relationships between variables using experimental and statistical techniques, and on the systematic testing of theories using what has been termed the 'hypothetico-deductive' method.

The aim of more-structured observation, then, is to produce accurate quantitative data on particular pre-specified observable behaviours or patterns of interaction.

These data concern the frequency, duration or, in some cases, quality of particular behaviours, and may also record the types of people involved, or the physical, social or temporal context in which the behaviour occurs. It may be used to describe patterns of behaviour amongst a particular population or in a particular setting, or, especially where the data are produced in controlled experiments, to test pre-existing theories and hypotheses concerning the nature and causes of behaviour.

The essential characteristic of more-structured observation is that the purposes of the observation, the categories of behaviour to be observed and the methods by which instances of behaviour are to be allocated to categories, are worked out, and clearly defined, before the data collection begins. So, in this sense, there is maximum prestructuring. A variety of different techniques is used to record behaviour (I will elaborate in Section 4), but all involve some sort of pre-set, standardized observation schedule on which a record (often ticks or numbers) of the type of behaviour of interest can be made. The role of the observer is to follow carefully the instructions laid down in the observation schedule, thereby minimizing observer subjectivity.

An example of a structured observation system used to record aspects of teacher–pupil interaction in classrooms can be found in the Flanders interaction analysis categories, as illustrated in Table 1. The behaviour, observed at three-second intervals, is coded into one of ten categories. The schedule can give useful data on the proportion of class time taken up by different types of activity.

It is possible to use more-structured observation to collect data on a large scale by employing a team of observers all using the same observation schedule in the same way. As observational procedures are standardized, the data collected by each observer can be collated, and quantitative comparisons can be made on a number of dimensions — for example, different situations, times and subject types. Using the Flanders schedule, for example, we could compare the proportion of school class time taken up by different activities between teachers, schools, curriculum areas, time periods, etc. The results of such research are cumulative, which means we can build up our knowledge of the particular behaviour in question over a period of time. It is also possible to establish the reliability of more-structured techniques by, for example, comparing the data from two researchers observing the same behaviour and using the same schedule.

READING AND ACTIVITY I

You should now read 'Inside the primary classroom', by M. Galton *et al.*, which is reproduced in Offprints Booklet 3. This describes the observation methods used in the Observational Research and Classroom Learning Evaluation (ORACLE) project. In part, the project originated in debates concerning the relative merits of 'traditional' and 'progressive' teaching in primary schools. Its aims were to collect accurate and objective data, which were (and are!) rather lacking in the debate about the nature of teacher and pupil behaviour in primary schools, and to search for factors which might explain any differences in teacher behaviour. Fifty-eight teachers in nineteen schools were studied by nine observers. When you have read the extract, check your understanding by answering the following questions:

1 On what aspects of (a) pupils' behaviour and (b) teachers' behaviour did the observers focus?

2 How did the observers sample (a) pupils and pupils' behaviour and (b) teachers and teachers' behaviour?

3 How did the researchers check the reliability of the observational techniques?

4 What sorts of contextual information did they collect?

5 Finally, try to make a brief assessment of the research methods used. What advantages and disadvantages can you identify?

You will find my answers at the end of the unit.

Table 1 Flanders' interaction analysis categories* (FIAC)

Teacher Talk	Response	1 *Accepts feeling.* Accepts and clarifies an attitude or the feeling tone of a pupil in a non-threatening manner. Feelings may be positive or negative. Predicting and recalling feelings are included.
		2 *Praises or encourages.* Praises or encourages pupil action or behaviour. Jokes that release tension, but not at the expense of another individual; nodding head, or saying 'Um hm?' or 'go on' are included.
		3 *Accepts or uses ideas of pupils.* Clarifying, building, or developing ideas suggested by a pupil. Teacher extensions of pupil ideas are included but as the teacher brings more of his own ideas into play, shift to category five.
	Initiation	4 *Asks questions.* Asking a question about content or procedure, based on teacher ideas, with the intent that a pupil will answer.
		5 *Lecturing.* Giving facts or opinions about content or procedures; expressing *his own* ideas, giving *his own* explanation, or citing an authority other than a pupil.
		6 *Giving directions.* Directions, commands, or orders to which a pupil is expected to comply.
		7 *Criticizing or justifying authority.* Statements intended to change pupil behaviour from non-acceptable to acceptable pattern; bawling someone out; stating why the teacher is doing what he is doing; extreme self-reference.
Pupil Talk	Response	8 *Pupil-talk — response.* Talk by pupils in response to teacher. Teacher initiates the contact or solicits pupil statement or structures the situation. Freedom to express own ideas is limited.
	Initiation	9 *Pupil-talk — initiation.* Talk by pupils which they initiate. Expressing own ideas; initiating a new topic; freedom to develop opinions and a line of thought, like asking thoughtful questions; going beyond the existing structure.
Silence		10 *Silence or confusion.* Pauses, short periods of silence and periods of confusion in which communication cannot be understood by the observer.

* There is *no* scale implied by these numbers. Each number is classificatory; it designates a particular kind of communication event. To write these numbers down during observation is to enumerate, not to judge a position on a scale.

(Source: Flanders, 1970, p.34)

Less-structured observation

The origins of less-structured observation lie in anthropology and in the application of its ethnographic approach to the study of communities and groups in industrialized societies, pioneered, for example, by the Chicago School of Sociology (a brief history of this can be found in Burgess, 1982). Research in this tradition has generally rejected the positivist approach to social science and has stressed that to understand human behaviour we need to explore the social meanings that underpin it. It has emphasized studying the perspectives of social actors — their ideas, attitudes, motives and intentions, and the way they interpret the social world — as well as observation of behaviour in natural situations and in its cultural context.

Less-structured observation therefore aims to produce detailed, qualitative descriptions of human behaviour which illuminate social meanings and shared culture. These data are combined with information from conversations, interviews and, where appropriate, documentary sources to produce an in-depth and rounded picture of the culture of the group, which places the perspectives of group members at its heart and reflects the richness and complexity of their social world. Less-structured observation is characterized by flexibility and a minimum of pre-structuring. This does not mean that the observer begins data collection with no aims and no idea of what to observe, but there is a commitment to approach observation with a relatively open mind, to minimize the influence of the observer's preconceptions and to avoid imposing existing preconceived categories. It is not unusual, therefore, for the focus of the research to change quite dramatically during the course of data collection as ideas develop and particular issues become important. The aim of less-structured observation is also often to develop theory, but here theory tends to emerge from, or be grounded in, the data (Glaser and Strauss, 1967). Rather than developing a theory and then collecting data specifically to test that theory, data collection, theory construction and testing are interwoven. So theoretical ideas develop from initial data collection and then influence future data collection — there is a cumulative spiral of theory development and data collection.

As one of the key aims of this type of observation is to see the social world as far as possible from the actor's point of view, the main technique used is participant observation. Here the observer participates in some way with the group under study and learns its culture, whilst at the same time observing the behaviour of group members. Observations are combined with interviews, conversations and so on, and are generally recorded using field notes and, where possible, audio or video recordings.

Obviously, less-structured observation cannot provide the large-scale comparative data on particular behaviours that is possible with more-structured methods, but it can produce far more detailed data on the behaviour of particular individuals or groups in particular settings. It gives qualitative data which, in combination with data of other kinds, can explicate the social and cultural basis of human interaction. Less-structured observation frequently involves the researcher spending long periods of time in the field, building relationships and participating in social interaction with subjects. The aim is that subjects come to trust the researcher and become accustomed to his or her presence. Consequently, the data produced may be less influenced by reactivity — by the researcher and the research process. Less-structured observation provides data which enable us, as outsiders, to see the social world more from the point of view of those we are studying — it gives us some sense of an insider's perspective. Because we are more able to appreciate the cultural context of behaviour and examine the motives and meanings given to behaviour by subjects, we may be better able to understand their social action. Less-structured observation also gives us the opportunity to examine the way interactions and social meanings change and develop over time, and the way in which social order is actively constructed by social actors through interaction. Finally, the method is particularly suited to the development, rather than the rigorous testing, of theory.

READING AND ACTIVITY 2

You should now read Chapter 15 in the Reader, 'Observation and the police: the research experience', by M. Punch. This is a discussion of the methodology adopted in a study of the occupational culture of uniformed police officers and of policing methods in an inner-city area of Amsterdam.

When you have read the chapter, check your understanding by answering the following questions:

1 Why and how did Punch select this particular group of police officers to study?
2 How did he gain access to the group?
3 What strategies did he use to develop positive relationships with the police officers?
4 How did his role in the group change over the course of the fieldwork?
5 What ethical issues do you think are raised by Punch's research?
6 Why did Punch use participant observation as his main research method?
7 What other sources of data, apart from observation, did he utilize?
8 Do you think he succeeded in reaching 'the inner reality of police work' (p.184)?

You will find my ideas at the end of the unit.

Which observational approach is adopted in a particular research project depends on the nature of the problem or the issue being investigated, the theoretical and methodological sympathies of the researcher, various practical considerations, and sometimes the stage which the research has reached.

To some extent, my division of the two approaches is rather artificial. In practice, researchers often use a combination of approaches. Sometimes research which adopts more-structured observation as its main method may begin with a period of less-structured observation. This may form part of the pilot work, and can help the researchers identify the type of behaviour on which they wish to focus and enable them to become accustomed to the research setting. It is also quite common for research which employs an ethnographic approach to utilize more-structured observational methods at some stage. This may happen when the researcher requires quantitative data on particular forms of behaviour. In my own research (Foster, 1990), for example, I was interested, among other things, in teacher–pupil interaction in multi-ethnic classes. I was concerned with whether teachers gave more of their time and attention to children from certain ethnic groups. My overall approach to the research was ethnographic and my observations were generally less-structured, but in this case I felt the need for more quantitative data on specific aspects of teacher behaviour and so I used a structured observation system developed by Brophy and Good (1970). This enabled me to count the number of different types of interaction that teachers had with students of different ethnic groups (the details of this part of my research are contained in Foster, 1989).

2 RELATIONSHIPS AND ROLES IN OBSERVATIONAL RESEARCH

2.1 NEGOTIATING ACCESS

Gaining access to settings in order to conduct observational research is a problem for both more-structured and less-structured observation. Whichever observational technique is used, the researcher has to get to a physical position from which he or she can observe the behaviour of subjects, and this usually involves negotiating entry to a group, institution, community or social setting of some sort. However, there are some differences between the two observational approaches. More-structured observation is more likely to involve access, sometimes by multiple and paid observers, for short periods to a relatively large number of settings. For example, in the ORACLE research (Galton *et al.*,1980) there were nine researchers who observed 58 classes in nineteen different schools for three days each term. In contrast, in ethnographic studies, where less-structured observation is the main method, often a lone researcher is concerned to gain access to a single or a small number of settings for a relatively long period of fieldwork. Lacey (1970), for example, conducted fieldwork in one school, to which he gave the pseudonym 'Hightown Grammar', over a three-year period. These differences mean that sometimes different strategies for gaining access need to be adopted.

The problem of access is of greatest significance early in research when the researcher is negotiating entry to the overall setting under consideration — a particular school, factory, village, community, etc. — in order to begin observation. But, for ethnographic research in particular, it remains an issue throughout data collection as entry to sub-settings within the overall setting has to be continually negotiated, and sometimes renegotiated, as the research progresses.

A number of different strategies are used to gain access. Which one is adopted depends, in the main, on the nature of the setting (or sub-setting) and what behaviour is to be observed. Settings (and sub-settings) vary in their openness to observation. Public places and events such as streets, shopping centres, parks, football matches, some religious services or public meetings are relatively open and may pose few problems of access. Here usually no-one's permission is required to observe, an observer role can be taken relatively easily since it is common for people in such situations to watch the behaviour of others, and the researcher can remain relatively unobtrusive. The research of Marsh *et al.* (1978), for example, on the behaviour of football crowds, was conducted in part by standing on the terraces of Oxford United and observing crowd behaviour (whilst also watching the match!); and research by Lofland (1973), on 'waiting styles' in public places, was conducted by observing in bus depots and airports.

However, this does not mean that observation in public settings is always unproblematic. Sometimes observation, or at least very close or obvious observation, can be inappropriate. This may be particularly the case in public settings where evasion of social interaction is the norm or where a person's presence in the setting is normally brief or transient. Here the observer may have to adopt techniques to conceal his or her observation or justify 'hanging around', such as observing from behind a newspaper or pretending to be legitimately waiting. It may also be difficult to observe behaviour of a private nature even though it takes place in a public setting. Humphreys (1970), for example, observed male homosexual activity in public lavatories. He had to justify his observation by adopting the role of 'watch queen' which meant he posed as a voyeur and acted as a look out for the men.

Access to what are considered more private settings will generally prove more difficult than access to public ones. One strategy here is to observe covertly. Access to the setting is obtained by the researcher secretly taking on an established role in the group under study or using his or her existing role to conduct research secretly. No formal permission to do the research is requested. The researcher simply becomes, or already is, a participant member of the group, and he or she uses this position to observe the behaviour of other participants. One example of this type of research is a famous study by Festinger *et al.* (1956) of an apocalyptic religious sect in which observers secretly joined the sect as new members. Another is a study by Holdaway (1983) who took advantage of his position as a serving police sergeant to observe the occupational culture of fellow officers.

Covert research is most likely to be used when there is a strong possibility that access is unlikely to be gained using open methods. This may be because groups fear the consequences of research, perhaps because they are involved in behaviour which could be considered deviant, or because they are hostile towards the idea of research itself (see, for example, Homan, 1980). In such cases it may be the only option if the research is to go ahead. Sometimes, as Chambliss (1975) discovered in his study of organized crime in an American city, covert study may only be necessary for the initial period of the research. Once relationships have been established it may be possible for the researcher to become more open and honest about him- or herself and his or her purposes.

Covert observation is also used when reactivity is likely to be a problem if research is conducted openly. For example, the Glasgow gang observed by Patrick (1973) would almost certainly have behaved very differently if they had known they were being researched. However, covert research in certain circumstances is potentially dangerous. When researching criminal groups, for example, if the researcher's 'cover is blown' there could be violent consequences. If the researcher's real identity and purposes are discovered, at the very least it is likely that the research will be forced to end. Doubts have also been widely expressed about the ethics of covert research.

Access in covert research is dependent on the researcher's ability to play an established role convincingly or at least to convince existing members that he or she is a genuine new entrant to the group. This obviously depends in part on the researcher's physical characteristics, but also on his or her ability to use a variety of impression management techniques and to display cultural competence in the setting. For example, in his study of Pentecostal church groups, Homan took an active part in worship and Bible study and used Pentecostal language and forms of greeting in order to present himself as a new member (Homan, 1980; see also Homan and Bulmer, 1982). However, he did not undergo baptism, as Pryce (1979) did as part of his research on Pentecostal groups in the Afro-Caribbean community of Bristol.

Where observational research is conducted openly the researcher generally has to seek formal permission from subjects and/or those responsible for them in order to observe in the setting. In the case of laboratory experiments, which generally involve more-structured observation, the researcher deliberately creates the setting; subjects, in agreeing to take part in the study, give their consent to observation of their behaviour in that setting. Subjects are recruited by a variety of methods — by advertising, word of mouth, offering inducements, etc. — and researchers will usually explain the purposes of the research and the possible consequences of taking part. Having said this, however, subjects have sometimes been deceived about the true nature of experiments and their potential effect. For example, in experiments on obedience to authority conducted by Milgram (1974), subjects were told that they were taking part in a scientific study of memory and learning. During the study they were duped into thinking that they were administering increasingly severe electric shocks to learners. What was in fact being studied was the extent to which they would obey authority figures instructing them to administer the shocks.

In the case of research in more natural settings — groups, institutions, organizations, etc. — the researcher has to negotiate access with a number of 'gatekeepers', perhaps at different levels of an institutional hierarchy (although, sometimes it is not always clear who the key gatekeepers are). Gatekeepers usually have positions of authority within the group or institution and can grant or withhold permission to conduct research in their particular sphere of authority. They may also be the subjects of the research. For example, if I wanted to gain access to a school in order to study teaching methods I would probably have first to seek the permission of local education authority (LEA) officers (if the school was LEA maintained), school governors and the headteacher, and then, in order to gain access to sub-settings within the school, I would have to approach heads of department, teachers and perhaps students as well. This would probably involve lengthy discussion and negotiation, a process which can be a useful source of data on the political structure of the group and on the perspectives of key group members.

Gatekeepers will be concerned to protect their own interests and the interests of group members from any threat posed by the research. Consequently, they may refuse access altogether, place limitations on the type of research which can be done, or try to manage the impression of individuals and the group that the researcher receives and documents (for discussion of this in the context of studying military élites see Spencer, 1973). The last of these strategies may involve presenting individuals, or the group, to the researcher in a particular way, restricting or influencing access to particular areas, times or events, and/or placing constraints on what the researcher can publish. Gatekeepers may also try to use the research for their own purposes. They may, for example, try to use research data to monitor the behaviour of particular individuals or sub-groups, or use published accounts to enhance the interests of the group. Interestingly, the Royal Ulster Constabulary (RUC) police officers studied by Brewer (1991) used the research as an opportunity to air their grievances to senior staff.

ACTIVITY 3

Imagine that you are a gatekeeper in a group or institution with which you are familiar. You are approached by a researcher wishing to spend a number of weeks observing in your group or institution:

- What sort of questions would you ask the researcher?

- How would you respond to his or her request and why would you respond in this way?

Make a note of your answers before you continue.

One of the factors which influences the response of gatekeepers to access requests is their preconceptions of research and researchers. These derive from any previous experience of research they have had, or from the way research is presented to them by others or by the media. Sometimes conceptions of research and researchers are negative and access may be denied. This was Homan's (1980) perception of the Pentecostal church members he studied and was a key influence on his decision to conduct covert research. On other occasions conceptions may be more positive and the researcher may be welcomed and given considerable assistance. More commonly, the conceptions of gatekeepers consist of a mixture of positive attitudes and scepticism, trust and suspicion.

In negotiating access, researchers try to influence the conceptions gatekeepers have of the research. They adopt a number of techniques. Sometimes they simply explain fully the purposes and nature of the research and the methods to be employed in the hope that the gatekeepers will be sufficiently interested and willing to allow the research to go ahead. This was the approach adopted by Stenhouse and his team who conducted research on library use in school sixth forms (Stenhouse, 1984). They wrote to headteachers explaining the aims of the project and the research methods to be adopted, and offered to visit the school to discuss the research at greater length. Most of the schools approached agreed to take part in the research.

On occasions, however, the account of the research given may be selective or involve an element of deception. As I explained earlier, part of my own research was concerned with whether teachers gave more attention in the classroom to students from certain ethnic groups (Foster, 1990). When negotiating access to classrooms for this part of the research, I did not tell the teachers that this was specifically what I was interested in because I thought that, if I did, they would make a conscious effort to distribute their attention equally. I kept my explanation deliberately vague and said that I wanted to observe teaching methods and student behaviour.

Researchers are also concerned to influence how gatekeepers see them as people. As a result, they use, consciously or unconsciously, many self-presentational techniques to convey an impression of themselves which will maximize their chances of gaining access. They dress and conduct themselves in ways which give the impression that they will 'fit in' and that their presence is unlikely to cause offence, disruption or harm to subjects and that they can be trusted. Delamont, for example, reflecting on her research in a Scottish girls' public school in the 1960s, describes how she 'always wore a conservative outfit and real leather gloves' when meeting headteachers. On the other hand, she wished to give a slightly different impression to the pupils and so wore a dress of 'mini-length to show the pupils I knew what the fashion was' (Delamont, 1984, p.25).

Another technique used when negotiating access is to offer inducements to gatekeepers. Researchers may, for example, emphasize the potential knowledge gains to the community as a whole or to the subjects themselves in comparison with the small amount of time or disruption that the research will require. They may offer services in return for access and enter into bargains with gatekeepers. For example, a number of researchers who have conducted ethnographic case studies in schools have taken on a part-time teaching load in part to facilitate access (see, for example, Burgess, 1983); and in my research (Foster, 1990) I offered to act as a 'consultant' to the school, which involved encouraging teachers to reflect on and improve aspects of their practice.

Researchers may also offer to protect the interests of subjects by guaranteeing the confidentiality of data, using pseudonyms, and/or stressing their commitment to established ethical principles (see, for example, British Sociological Association, 1992). Sometimes gatekeepers are offered some control over the research — perhaps the opportunity to scrutinize, and maybe veto, plans and research techniques, or to control the use of data or the publication of a final report. Walford and Miller (1991), who studied Kinghurst, a new City Technology College, offered the headteacher the opportunity to write an unedited 15,000-word section of the planned book to encourage her to give them access (see Walford, 1991, for a discussion of this). Collaboration with subjects is seen as highly desirable by some researchers (see, for example, Day, 1981). It is suggested that this not only facilitates access, but also respects more fully the rights of subjects to be consulted and involved and means that the research is more likely to address their concerns and produce knowledge which they will find useful.

Another common strategy used in gaining access, especially in ethnographic research, is to use the assistance of a sponsor. This is generally an established and trusted figure within the group or institution who can vouch for the researcher and reassure subjects about the purposes of the research and intentions of the researcher. Sponsors can be very helpful in gaining access to groups or settings which might otherwise remain closed. Taylor (1984), for example, used the assistance of John McVicar (an ex-professional criminal), whom he got to know while conducting research in Durham prison, to gain access to the world of professional criminals. Sponsors can also be useful guides to the structure, organization and norms of the group and can provide invaluable advice on the most appropriate ways of collecting data. They can usefully act as informants, too, providing another valuable source of observational data. Indeed, they may have access to areas which are closed to the researcher, and they may have useful background knowledge which can enable a better understanding of behaviour. The most well-known researcher's sponsor, Doc in Whyte's study of Cornerville, performed all these roles (Whyte, 1981). Without Doc to show him around, introduce him, vouch for him, supply him with information and answer his questions, Whyte's research would probably have been impossible.

On the other hand, there are disadvantages in relying too heavily on a sponsor. Access to certain individuals, sub-groups or sub-settings can be restricted by too close a relationship with a sponsor who is perceived by other subjects to be hostile to their interests. Also, the research may be channelled in particular directions by the sponsor's contacts.

Researchers frequently rely upon personal contacts to find sponsors. Indeed, research settings are often selected, and access facilitated, because researchers have some prior experience of, or contact with, the group or institution. In such cases the researcher has already established some form of identity in the eyes of subjects and can capitalize on this when negotiating access. Gillborn (1990), for example, researched the school he had attended as a pupil, and Cohen and Taylor's research in Durham prison came about because they were already involved in adult education work with long-term prisoners (Cohen and Taylor, 1972).

ACTIVITY 4

Suppose you were interested in conducting research in the group or institution for which in Activity 3 you were a gatekeeper:

- What methods would you use to gain access?
- What problems would you anticipate in gaining access and how would you overcome them?

Briefly note down your answers before you continue.

2.2 DEVELOPING RELATIONSHIPS

Researchers are not only interested in gaining physical access to particular settings, they are also concerned with observing behaviour which naturally occurs in those settings. In other words, they desire access to behaviour which has been influenced as little as possible by the researcher's presence or the research process. The latter form of reactivity is, of course, eliminated in covert research because subjects are not aware that they are being studied. The former is not eliminated, however, because the researcher in his or her participant role may have an influence on behaviour. For example, Festinger *et al.* (1956), in joining the apocalyptic religious sect, telling the members fictitious stories about their 'psychic experiences', and joining in group activities, inevitably reinforced the beliefs of the group they were studying.

Researchers who are conducting their work openly adopt a number of techniques to become unobtrusive in the setting and minimize reactivity. They often pay attention to their own physical position in the setting and to the positioning of any recording equipment they are using. They also take care to dress and behave in ways which will allow them to blend into the setting — the aim being to reduce the extent to which subjects are conscious of their presence and of their observation. King (1984), for example, during his research in infant school classrooms, tried to avoid eye contact with the children and at one stage used the Wendy House as a 'convenient "hide"'.

Ethnographers often spend considerable periods of time in the field so that subjects become accustomed to their presence. They also make great efforts to build relationships of trust with subjects in order to facilitate access and reduce reactivity. As with negotiation with gatekeepers, what is involved here is the negotiation of the researcher's identity with subjects. The researcher wishes to be seen as a certain type of person and will try to influence (sometimes consciously, but often unconsciously) the way he or she is perceived by controlling or manipulating the information that the subject receives. Subjects (like gatekeepers) will have certain preconceptions and developing perceptions of the researcher, both as a person and as a researcher.

ACTIVITY 5

Consider a group or institution of which you are a member. A stranger — a smartly dressed, middle-aged woman carrying a brief case — enters the setting:

- What identity(ies) would you attribute to her?
- If the stranger declares herself to be doing research, what other interpretations of her identity spring to mind?

Make a note of your responses.

Obviously, how you answer this will depend on your conceptions of the possible roles such a person could have in this particular setting and of the characteristics you attribute to a middle-aged woman (smartly dressed and carrying a brief case) in such roles. It will also depend on your conceptions of researchers generally.

This, in a sense, is the researcher's starting point. She (or he) tries to build on, adjust or change these initial conceptions using types of impression management techniques similar to those I discussed earlier in connection with gatekeepers.

What impression the researcher tries to give depends, of course, on the role he or she takes in the group. If the research is covert then the researcher seeks to give subjects the impression that he or she is indeed a real participant (perhaps initially a novice one) with the characteristics of such a person. If the research is conducted more openly then the researcher may wish to give the impression that he or she is what Hammersley and Atkinson (1983) term an 'acceptable marginal member'.

This may involve dressing in acceptable ways. This does not necessarily mean that clothes need to be identical to those worn by subjects. Parker (1974), for example, in his research with 'down town' adolescent boys in Liverpool, adopted a style of dress — 'black shirt, black jeans, burgundy leather (jacket)' — which enabled him to blend in, but which did not copy exactly the boys' style.

It may also require behaving in ways which enable the researcher to fit into the group. In *Street Corner Society*, for example, Whyte (1981) describes how he 'learned to take part in the street corner discussions on baseball and sex'. He also recounts a mistake he made when, after listening to a man's account of his illegal gambling activities, he suggested in discussion that the police had been 'paid off'. The reaction of his subjects suggested that such a statement was unacceptable in public talk and Whyte felt 'very uncomfortable' for the rest of the evening.

The researcher may trade on existing experience, skills and knowledge in developing subjects' conceptions of his or her identity. Pryce (1979), for example, utilized his identity as a Jamaican and his knowledge of Jamaican religious affairs to establish a rapport with his subjects. And in my own research (Foster, 1990) I frequently made use of my experience of teaching in a nearby school to convey the impression that I was knowledgeable about, and sympathetic to, the teachers' concerns — in a sense that I was one of them, rather than some sort of expert or critic.

On reflection I also, generally unconsciously, presented myself as, for want of a better phrase, an ordinary, decent type of person — someone who was honest, approachable, friendly, sensitive and understanding. I did this by engaging in everyday, sociable conversations, openly discussing aspects of my past and present life and exchanging day-to-day information. This type of self-presentation is crucial in gaining acceptance. Also important is how the researcher actually behaves. One has to demonstrate one's trustworthiness, openness, reliability and so on since behaviour provides subjects with direct evidence of one's attributes. Indeed, subjects may sometimes actually test the researcher out in these respects.

On occasions, the researcher may be more consciously selective in the self presented to subjects. For example, he or she may play down or conceal certain aspects by disguising or failing to reveal personal views or political commitments. This was the case in Fielding's (1982) research on the National Front. He suppressed his disagreement with the ideology of the organization and presented himself as an 'unconverted sympathiser'. The researcher may also deliberately emphasize other aspects of self. Hobbs (1988), for example, in his study of deviant entrepreneurship and police detective work in East London, cultivated a view of himself as 'entrepreneurial and sharp' and 'sexist and chauvinistic' in order to blend in and become an insider (although, interestingly, he drew the line at racism). What aspect of self the researcher chooses to reveal or emphasize may change during the course of the research, as his or her role changes and as relationships with subjects develop.

Offering services is another means by which researchers negotiate their identity. Anthropologists have often provided simple medical and technical advice in the pre-industrial communities they have studied. In this way they have been able to demonstrate their commitment to the group and avoid being seen as exploitative outsiders. Similarly, ethnographers of institutions and groups in modern, industrial societies have given a whole range of services, such as assisting with teaching and extra-curricular activities in schools, giving legal advice to subjects in trouble with the law, serving as secretaries on committees, or merely lending a sympathetic ear. In fact, the participant role taken by many ethnographers involves working with and therefore helping subjects in the course of their everyday activities (see, for example, the study by Punch, 1979, about which you read in Activity 2). This help is often crucial in building up relationships of trust and openness.

There are, of course, limits to the identities the researcher can negotiate with subjects. Ascribed characteristics such as age, gender, 'race' and ethnicity limit the sort of person the researcher can become and also the sort of relationship that can be developed with subjects. They may therefore restrict access to settings and to data. But ascribed characteristics can also facilitate identities, relationships and access. As a 40-year-old white male I would find it difficult to present myself as a young 'rap' music enthusiast, or develop close peer-type relationships with school pupils, or directly access the world of radical feminists. On the other hand, I might find it easier to present myself as a mature, professional person, to develop relationships with school teachers, or to access the world of white, male-dominated clubs. In saying this, I do not mean to imply that the researcher must be of the same age, gender or 'race' as his or her subjects. It is simply that sometimes age, gender, or 'racial' characteristics can aid in the construction of certain types of identity and relationship. And, as Hunt (1984) pointed out in her research on the police, it is possible to renegotiate identities attributed on the basis of ascribed characteristics. In her research, she was initially perceived by male officers as an 'untrustworthy feminine spy', but, by utilizing a variety of impression management strategies such as spending time on the pistol range, displaying a skill in judo, and 'acting crazy' (in other words taking unusual risks), she was able to negotiate a more acceptable and productive identity as 'street-woman-researcher'. (See Warren, 1988, for a more general discussion of the influence of gender on relationships in the field.)

ACTIVITY 6

Think about your own ascribed characteristics. In what ways would they limit and facilitate the identities, relationships and access you could negotiate in particular research settings?

Note down your response before you continue.

2.3 THE RESEARCHER'S ROLE

The role taken by the researcher in the group or setting under study varies according to the purposes of the research, the nature of the setting, the means of gaining access and the observational method employed. His or her role is more likely to be that of detached, non-participant observer when the purpose of the research is to collect data on specific observable behaviours using more-structured techniques, and it is more likely to be that of an involved participant when the purpose is the collection of ethnographic data using less-structured techniques. This highlights one key dimension of the researcher's role — the extent of participation in the group or setting.

Junker (1960) and Gold (1958) suggest four types of role along this dimension. These are illustrated in Figure 1.

1 *The complete observer* has no interaction with the subjects during data collection. In some psychological research, for example, subjects are observed through a one-way mirror and so do not come into direct contact with the observer. This was the case in the early stages of a study by Corsaro (1981) which examined children's behaviour in a nursery school. Corsaro utilized a pre-existing observation area in the school. (He later moved out into the main body of the school

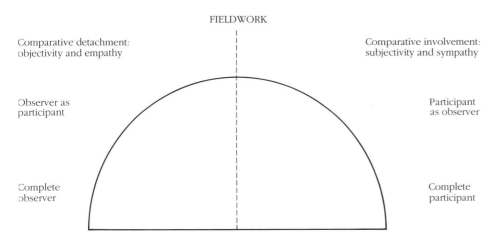

Figure 1 *Theoretical social roles for fieldwork*
(Source: derived from Junker, 1960, p.36)

and observed whilst participating with the children in their activities.) The behaviour of subjects is sometimes recorded with hidden cameras and/or microphones. This method was used in research by Haney *et al.* (1973) which simulated a prison environment in a laboratory setting. Volunteer subjects played the roles of warders or prisoners and their behaviour was recorded on video and audio tape as well as being directly observed from behind an observational screen. On some occasions video tapes of behaviour made for non-research purposes can be utilized. Such tapes were used by Marsh *et al.* (1978) in their research on football crowd behaviour, and by Atkinson (1984) in his study of political oratory. Sometimes observation may be conducted from vantage points which conceal the observer, or at least result in minimum contact. For example, in a study of children's playground aggression and playfighting, Serbin observed children's behaviour with binoculars from an adjacent building (reported in Pellegrini, 1991).

The benefit of the complete observer role is that it should eliminate the reactivity which stems from the immediate physical presence of the observer.

But do you think it eliminates reactivity altogether?

It only eliminates reactivity completely if the subjects are unaware that they are being observed, as is the case with covert research. But sometimes subjects are aware, or at least suspect, that they are being observed. This is often the case in laboratory experiments. Even though subjects cannot see the observer they know that they are being observed. As a result, they may behave differently from how they would have behaved if unobserved.

Another advantage of this role is that the observer can remain detached from the subjects and therefore uninfluenced by their views and ideas. He or she is also free to concentrate on data recording, and possibly even to discuss data with another observer during data collection.

However, the role of complete observer places limitations on the behaviour and settings that can be observed, especially in natural situations. Also, the researcher may not be able to collect supporting data by asking the subjects questions. As a result, he or she may fail to appreciate the perspectives of the subjects and to understand the social meanings which underpin their interaction. This is one reason why this role is most often used in more-structured observation where the researcher is interested only in categorizing instances of observable behaviour.

2 *The observer as participant* — here the observer interacts with subjects, but does not take on an established role in the group. His or her role is that of researcher conducting research. He or she may develop more participant roles with some subjects, but the key role is that of researcher. Typically, the researcher is 'the person writing a book about ...' or 'the person investigating ...'. This type

of role is often used in more-structured observation in natural situations where the researcher(s) spends short periods of time observing behaviour in a relatively large number of settings. For example, the team of researchers led by Rutter, who investigated the relative effectiveness of twelve comprehensive schools in London, conducted observations of all the lessons taken by one class in each school for one week (Rutter et al., 1979). The researchers made it clear that their role was to observe and tried to keep their interaction with pupils and teachers to a minimum.

This role is also sometimes used in ethnographic work. In such cases the nature of the researcher's identity may be more fully developed and negotiated, and the researcher may be more likely to construct roles which involve greater participation, but the essential role is that of researcher. Woods (1979), for example, in his study of a secondary school, thought of himself as an 'involved' rather than a participant observer. He deliberately did not take an existing role in the school, although he did occasionally help out with lesson supervision and extra-curricular activities.

As with the complete observer role, one advantage of this strategy is that the researcher is more able to maintain his or her detachment from the subjects and take an outsider's view. Participation in a researcher role also enables him or her to move about within the group to observe behaviour in different sub-settings. Consequently, the researcher is able to get a fuller, more rounded picture of the group or institution. It is also much easier to sample sub-settings, events, times, subjects, etc. systematically and to develop and test theoretical propositions.

The danger is that the researcher is viewed with suspicion by subjects. He or she may be viewed as an inspector or critic, an intruder or snoop. As a result, subjects may change their behaviour in order to present themselves in a particular way to the researcher, and even react to him or her with hostility. This is particularly likely if the researcher remains with the group for a period of time and fails to negotiate an acceptable identity, or if he or she does not conform to subjects' expectations.

ACTIVITY 7

Think again about a group or institution of which you are a member. How would people respond to the presence of an observer? Briefly note down your answer.

3 *The participant as observer* — this involves the researcher taking an established, or certainly a more participant, role in the group for the bulk of the research. In a number of school case studies, for example, researchers have worked as part-time teachers. As mentioned earlier, this was the case in Lacey's (1970) research in a grammar school. He taught alongside the teachers in the schools whilst also acting as a researcher.

Often, taking a participant role facilitates access to the group or institution and to sub-settings within it. Offering to assist subjects with their work in return for access may be part of the bargain that the researcher negotiates with them. And working or living alongside people may help in building rapport and relationships of trust and openness which will help to reduce reactivity. Indeed, it may be that, because the researcher is a participant, subjects forget that he or she is doing research and behave more 'naturally' as a result. At times like this it might be said that the research becomes covert, although it is difficult to tell when this happens.

ACTIVITY 8

Following on from Activity 7, do you think your response to an observer would be any different if the researcher was a participant observer? Note down what this response might be before you continue.

The other main advantage of this role is that the researcher is better able to see the social world from the point of view of his or her subjects. He or she has to learn the culture in order to operate as far as possible as an insider, and gains access to information not available to outsiders. In this way, the researcher is more likely to appreciate and understand the subjects' perspectives and the meanings which underpin their interaction. In short, the researcher can put him- or herself in their shoes. For this reason this type of role is usually taken by researchers conducting ethnographic or less-structured observation.

However, a major problem with taking a participant role is that it places restrictions on the data that the researcher can collect. Access to sub-settings within the group or institution may be prevented by rules and norms which apply to the participant role. As a participant, the researcher may be expected to behave in certain ways and may be seen by subjects as having particular loyalties. Pryce (1979), for example, found it difficult to move between different Afro-Caribbean religious congregations in Bristol once he had established ties with one of them.

Developing and playing a significant role may also be very time consuming and mean that little time is available for recording and processing data. It can sometimes be stressful, too, when the expectations of the participant role are in conflict with those of the research role. Lacey (1970), for example, describes the tension he felt between the role of teacher and that of researcher. There is also the possibility that the more the researcher participates the greater is his or her influence on the group.

An associated problem is what is sometimes termed 'going native'. In its extreme forms the researcher actually gives up the research and becomes a real member of the group. This is rare. A greater danger is of over-rapport with subjects or identifying too closely with them. The researcher loses his or her sense of detachment and adopts an over-sympathetic view of subjects. This may lead researchers to be selective in their observations and interpretations of behaviour so that they present a one-sided, and therefore inaccurate, account. This problem is not confined to the participant observer role. Hammersley and Atkinson (1983, pp.98–9) argue that Willis (1977), who adopted more of an observer-as-participant role, erred in this way; but it becomes more likely the more involved the researcher is with subjects.

4 *The complete participant* — here the researcher plays an established role in the group and is fully immersed in that participant role, but uses his or her position to conduct research. Sometimes the research may be covert. There are two possibilities here. The researcher may secretly join the group or institution as a new member — for example, the observers in the study by Festinger *et al.* (1956) secretly joined a religious sect, and those in Rosenhan's (1982) study posed as psychiatric hospital patients. Alternatively, the researcher may already be a member and thus uses his or her established position to conduct covert research — Holdaway (1983), for example, used his position as a serving police officer to research the occupational culture of fellow officers, and Davis (1959) took advantage of his job as a Chicago taxi driver to study the interaction between drivers and their customers.

The complete participant may also conduct research openly, however. This is the case in much practitioner research in education where teachers research aspects of their own practice or institution. They work primarily as teachers, but engage in research with the aim of improving professional practice (see, for example, the case studies contained in Hustler *et al.*, 1986, and Hopkins, 1985; for a more theoretical discussion see Elliott, 1991). Another example is research by Rubinstein (1973) on the police in Philadelphia. After working as a police reporter, Rubinstein trained for a year as a police officer and then worked alongside a number of police units. The officers he directly worked with knew he was a researcher, although he concedes that this was not the case with those from other units or with members of the public.

Again, the advantage of the complete participant role is that it facilitates access. As I have already pointed out, covert research in a participant role may be the only way of gaining access to certain groups. And where research is conducted openly the researcher's established role and identity may ease access to sub-settings and individuals. The approach also has the advantages of the insider role explained above, and, in the case of covert research, the particular advantage of reducing that reactivity which occurs as a result of the subjects knowing that they are being observed.

There are, however, limitations similar to those with the participant observer role. The restrictions on data collection are, if anything, more severe as the researcher has to maintain his or her participant role. Sometimes the attention that has to be paid to playing the participant role means that the time and opportunities for data collection are limited. The danger of 'going native' may also be more serious, as will the potential for role conflict and strain on the researcher's sense of identity. There is also a greater possibility that the researcher, as a full participant, will influence the people he or she is studying, or find his or her research is controlled by a superior.

Having outlined these types of role, it should be emphasized that, in ethnographic work in particular, research roles usually change during the course of the research. Sometimes, for example, the researcher takes on a participant role at some stage during the research. He or she may move from a rather naïve, detached observer role in the early stages of the research to a fuller, more participant role in the later stages (see the example of Punch, 1979, mentioned earlier); or, as in Corsaro's (1981) research in a nursery school, from a complete observer behind a one-way screen to a participant observer; or, as in Lacey's (1970) research, from a participant role in the early stages to a research role later.

Barker (1984), in her study of the Moonies, distinguishes between different types of activity in her research role. In the initial stages she was a 'passive' observer, spending her time watching and listening. She then became more 'interactive' and joined in conversations and discussions. Although she was conducting research openly, she was sometimes taken by unacquainted Moonies to be a member of the sect during this phase. In the final stage of the research she adopted a more 'active' role in which she argued with sect members, asked awkward questions and played 'devil's advocate'. Barker's work draws attention to the way different roles can be used to generate different types of data.

It is also the case that researchers take on multiple sub-roles which differ according to the sub-setting and the particular individuals with whom they interact. Woods, for example, in his secondary school study, claims that he played at least five different roles. He was a 'relief agency or counsellor' to pupils and sometimes staff, a 'secret agent' to the headteacher (a role he avoided playing), a person to be 'appealed to' or 'consulted' during 'power struggles', a 'substitute member of staff', and 'fellow-human' (Woods, 1979, pp.261–2).

2.4 MANAGING MARGINALITY

A major problem faced by researchers adopting a more ethnographic approach is that of balancing the insider and outsider aspects of their role — what has been termed 'managing marginality'. There are clear dangers of the researcher identifying too closely with subjects, allowing this to bias observations and interpretations, and thereby presenting a distorted picture. Over-rapport may also lead the researcher to concentrate on one particular sub-group or setting which may influence his or her relationship with, and access to, other sub-groups or settings. There are also advantages in adopting an outsider position. It enables the researcher to see subjects' behaviour in a relatively detached way with the freshness of a stranger. He or she may be able to see things which participants take for granted and will also be able to take a broader, more rounded view of the group which includes its various sub-groups or settings.

At the same time there are, of course, dangers in remaining too detached, too much an outsider. If relationships of trust do not develop, subjects will remain hostile or suspicious and are therefore likely to behave differently. It is unlikely that they will talk openly about their experiences and views, or that the researcher will develop a knowledge and understanding of the social meanings that underpin group interaction and the perspectives of subjects. As a result, the picture of the group they present may be based in large part on their own preconceptions.

The researcher's aim must be to balance the insider and outsider roles and combine the advantages of both — in other words, to manage a marginal position *vis-à-vis* subjects. Being at one with the group and yet remaining apart, being a 'friend' yet remaining a 'stranger', can be a difficult and sometimes stressful experience. But, as Hammersley and Atkinson (1983) emphasize, it is essential for good ethnographic work.

2.5 ETHICAL ISSUES

A number of ethical issues are raised by the relationships and roles developed in observational research. One of the most significant of these concerns deception (see Bulmer, 1982). As I have pointed out, deception is a strategy sometimes used by researchers to gain access and develop relationships with subjects.

There are varying degrees of deception and the extent differs between and within studies. At one extreme there is covert research where the researcher takes on a role in the group, or uses his or her existing role, to conduct research secretly. His or her real identity and purpose are concealed from all subjects (see, for example, Humphreys, 1970; Homan, 1980; Holdaway, 1983). Then there are studies where subjects (or some of them) are deceived about the researcher's identity and purpose for some of the time. Fielding's (1982) research on the National Front was of this type. He conducted interviews openly as a researcher, but observed secretly as a potential new member at party meetings. Pryce (1979) adopted a similar mix of overt and covert research in his study of the Afro-Caribbean community in Bristol. There are also studies in which the subjects know they are being researched, but are deceived about the real nature of the research. Many laboratory experiments, such as those by Milgram (1974) which I described earlier, are of this kind. And, as I also mentioned, my account to subjects of part of my own research (Foster, 1990) was, shall we say, less than the whole truth.

At the other extreme, even in completely 'open' research there is often some deception. The researcher may conceal certain aspects of his or her identity, or exaggerate (perhaps even fabricate) others, in order to influence favourably subjects' perceptions (see, for example, Hobbs, 1988). Selective self-presentation like this is characteristic of everyday life as we present ourselves and our purposes to others in what we consider are favourable ways (Goffman, 1959). The researcher may also deliberately cultivate what might be termed 'fake' relationships in order to obtain data. Friendships, for example, may be developed primarily because they facilitate data collection and not because there is genuine feeling for the befriended person. As Bulmer (1982) points out, there is also the deception which occurs unintentionally or unavoidably when the researcher fails to tell everyone involved in the research that he or she is doing research. It is often simply impractical to inform everyone, and many people with whom the researcher comes into contact assume that he or she is an ordinary group member (see, for example, Punch, 1979). It is also often the case with ethnographic work that the researcher him- or herself is unsure about the focus of the research until well into the fieldwork and therefore cannot make clear to subjects exactly what the research is about.

Many researchers have grave concerns about the ethical acceptability of deception, particularly when it involves covert research or gross misrepresentation of the purposes of the research. Their concern, of course, derives from the value of honesty and the view that subjects should be fully informed about the nature of any research in which they are involved. It also derives from a fear that subjects may be harmed by any deception — by, for example, feeling misled or taken advantage of — and that the prospects of future research may be damaged if people's perceptions of research are adversely affected.

It is worth looking at what the British Sociological Association *Statement of Ethical Practice* has to say about covert research. It recommends that 'as far as possible sociological research should be based on the freely given informed consent of those studied', and that researchers have a responsibility to 'explain as fully as possible, and in terms meaningful to participants, what the research is about, who is undertaking and financing it, why it is being undertaken, and how it is to be disseminated' (British Sociological Association, 1992, p.1). However, it does not rule out the possibility of covert research:

> There are serious ethical dangers in the use of covert research but covert methods may avoid certain problems. For instance, difficulties arise when research participants change their behaviour because they know they are being studied. Researchers may also face problems when access to spheres of social life is closed to social scientists by powerful or secretive interests. However, covert methods violate the principles of informed consent and may invade the privacy of those being studied. Participant or non-participant observation in non-public spaces or experimental manipulation of research participants without their knowledge should be resorted to only where it is impossible to use other methods to obtain essential data. In such studies it is important to safeguard the anonymity of research participants. Ideally, where informed consent has not been obtained prior to the research it should be obtained post hoc.
>
> (British Sociological Association, 1992, p.2)

ACTIVITY 9

Before you read on, think about whether you agree with what has just been said about covert research. Do you think covert research is ever justified? If so, to what extent and under what circumstances? And what about 'milder' forms of deception — such as selective self-presentation, or 'fake' relationships?

Make a note of your responses.

My view is that there are no cut-and-dried, easy answers to these questions. I think we have to try to balance in each case the potential value of the research findings against the value of honesty and the ideal of informed consent. As Hammersley (1991) points out, we must recognize that in everyday life we are often not totally truthful all of the time. There are circumstances in which we deceive others either by failing to give them information, by giving partial information, or even by giving false information. We do this sometimes to enhance our own interests, and sometimes to protect the interests of others. It may be that there are occasions when it is appropriate to apply the value of honesty selectively both in everyday life and in research.

Another important ethical issue raised by observational research concerns privacy. People may feel that research intrudes into their 'private' lives, and makes public what is considered to be private. This was a criticism made of the research by Humphreys (1970) on homosexual behaviour in a men's public lavatory (see Bulmer, 1982). This research not only involved observing behaviour, but also tracking down the men by using their car number plates and conducting follow-up interviews under the auspices of a wider survey on health. Here, again, concern derives from the value of privacy in relation to certain sorts of behaviour, and also from the possibility that subjects, and the prospects of future research, may be harmed by such intrusion. One of the problems, of course, is that there are no clear dividing lines, and there is no clear consensus about what is 'private' and what is 'public'. And, indeed, conceptions of public and private vary according to which individuals are involved. Again, there are no easy answers and we have to weigh up our commitment to the value of privacy, and to the rights of subjects, with the importance of the research findings.

Ethical questions also arise when subjects are involved in deviant behaviour. These questions are most difficult when the researcher adopts a participant role and may therefore be required to become involved in deviant activity in order to develop relationships with group members. Hobbs, for example, in his study of East End entrepreneurship, appears to have flirted with organized crime: 'I was willing to skirt the boundaries of criminality on several occasions', he explains, 'and I considered it crucial to be willingly involved in "normal" business transactions, legal or otherwise' (Hobbs, 1988, p.7). But even when researchers are not active group members they may witness serious deviant behaviour and must decide where their loyalties lie. Should they remain observers and protect the interests of their subjects, or should they try to prevent the deviant behaviour and the harm it may do to others, or should they perhaps even abandon their research and report offenders to the authorities on the grounds that their wider commitment is to society or to particular values? Again, complex judgements must be made in individual cases.

3 WHAT TO OBSERVE

3.1 FOCUSING RESEARCH

The behaviour the researcher chooses to observe and record will depend on the overall topic and research questions which are being investigated. These will be determined by the researcher's theoretical and substantive interests. In more-structured observation these ideas will produce categories of behaviour which will be specified in advance of fieldwork in the observation schedule, although sometimes more-structured observation is preceded by a period of less-structured exploratory observation. These pre-specified behavioural categories become the primary focus of observations.

In less-structured ethnographic observation the initial focus of the research is often less clear. Researchers will probably begin fieldwork with certain theoretical and substantive questions in mind — what are sometimes termed 'foreshadowed problems'. They will also bring with them certain sensitizing concepts drawn from previous research. Beynon (1985), for example, was interested in initial encounters between teachers and pupils in secondary schools and so his observations concentrated on the beginning of the school year for a newly arrived pupil intake. He also brought to the research certain concepts, such as teacher and pupil coping strategies, which had emerged from earlier work on teacher–pupil interactions. But in less-structured observation ideas are frequently undeveloped and general, and researchers usually try to avoid a commitment to pre-existing theoretical categories. The focus of initial observations is therefore wide, and the researcher is concerned like any new member to obtain a broad overview of, and basic information about, the group or institution under study. In addition, he or she will probably record, in a relatively unselective way, any data which appear to be relevant or interesting. As research progresses, theoretical ideas develop in conjunction with data collection. More specific research questions, propositions and hypotheses emerge from an examination and analysis of initial data. These then form the basis of, and provide the focus for, future data collection. This gradual refinement of research questions and the concentration of observations on specific issues and areas is often referred to as 'progressive focusing'.

Research may focus on particular subjects or sub-settings within the overall setting, or it may focus on particular times, events, behaviours or social processes. One strategy sometimes used in this process is theoretical sampling which you met in Unit 7. Here different cases — or subjects, sub-settings, times or events within a case — are selected for observation specifically to test and develop hypotheses. Observational instances are often chosen in such a way as to minimize or maximize differences which are thought to be theoretically important.

By minimizing the differences it is possible to clarify the detailed characteristics of a theoretical category. And by maximizing the differences the researcher will be able to establish the range of a particular set of categories. So, for example, if I were interested in how teaching style was affected by the number of pupils with behavioural problems in a class, I could look at teaching in classes with a large and small number of such pupils and at teaching in classes with similar numbers of such pupils. In this way I could attempt to identify the differences in teaching style which seemed to be the result of differences in the numbers of behavioural problems.

Theoretical sampling also influences how many observations the researcher should make. Glaser and Strauss (1967) suggest that data are collected on a particular theoretical category until it is 'saturated' — that is, until nothing new is being learned about that category.

3.2 REPRESENTATIVE SAMPLING

Observational research also often involves representative sampling of different types within the case that is being studied. It is rarely possible for the researcher to observe every subject, sub-setting, event or instance of behaviour in which he or she is interested, and even if it were possible it would not be necessary or desirable to do so. What observational researchers generally do (like researchers using survey/interview methods) is select samples and base their analysis and conclusions on data from these samples. Observing a sample is obviously much less time consuming and, as a result, it is possible to collect more detailed and accurate data. But, as with surveys, there is a danger of error arising from unrepresentative sampling. If the subjects, settings, events, or behaviour sampled and observed are unrepresentative of the general population of subjects, settings, events, or behaviour with which the researcher is concerned, then it will not be legitimate to generalize from the sample.

In more-structured observation, and sometimes in the early stages of an ethnographic study, researchers are concerned to select representative samples of people, places, times, behaviours or events within a case so that they can make generalizations to the relevant population or establish general patterns in the setting they are studying. Some form of random or systematic sampling is often used. This may involve selecting a random or systematic sample of subjects to observe. So if I were interested in studying middle-managers in an industrial organization I might select a random sample from this population to observe. It may also involve observing behaviour at a random or systematic sample of times. For example, if I were studying a hospital or hospital ward I might select a random sample of days or times of the day (including the night shift) to observe. I would at least ensure that I did not conduct all my observations on the same days and at the same times. Where an institution is organized around a periodic cycle of time — as are schools and colleges with their academic years — it would also be important to spread my observations across the organizational cycle. There are obvious dangers of unrepresentativeness if observations are concentrated at particular times of the cycle, unless, of course, it is these particular times in which the researcher is most interested, as in Beynon's (1985) research which focused on initial encounters between teachers and pupils. In such cases these events or times become the population from which samples are selected.

Time (or point) sampling is frequently used in more-structured observation. Here the researcher records and categorizes the behaviour which is observed at regular timed intervals. In the ORACLE project (Galton *et al.*, 1980), for example, teacher and pupil behaviour were each observed and coded at 25-second intervals. The behaviour occurring at such times was then held to be representative of behaviour in general in the classrooms studied (although, as I indicated in my response to Activity 1, I have my doubts about the validity of this).

Where the researcher has pre-existing knowledge about the heterogeneity of an organization, he or she may also select random or systematic samples of places or sub-settings within the overall setting. In a study of a school, for instance, a researcher might select a sample of departments or corridors to observe. He or she might also select samples of particular events or behaviours. In a school the researcher might try to observe, say, a random sample of assemblies, department meetings, lesson openings, or demonstrations in science lessons. However, it may be difficult to specify and identify events or behaviours in advance so that they can be sampled. In this case ethnographic researchers sometimes sample from the descriptions of behaviour contained in their field notes. There are, of course, dangers with such a strategy because the behaviours recorded in field notes may be an unrepresentative sample of all such behaviours.

Having said all this, in ethnographic research in particular the selection of what to observe is often not done on a random or systematic basis. Accurate sampling frames may not be available in advance and access to particular subjects, sub-settings, times and events may be difficult or impossible to obtain. Pragmatic considerations in the selection of observations often loom large. What the researcher actually selects to observe may very much depend on the opportunities that arise, the role he or she takes within the group and the relationships which have been developed with subjects. Often observation depends on the co-operation of subjects or gatekeepers and the researcher has to concentrate on those who are willing to co-operate. One strategy that is sometimes used is 'snowball sampling'. Here one observed subject passes the researcher on to another, vouching for him or her and acting as a sponsor. The advantage of this strategy is that sponsorship encourages co-operation and therefore facilitates access, but, of course, the limitation is that the snowball sample may be unrepresentative.

4 RECORDING OBSERVATIONS

One of the greatest differences between more-structured and less-structured observation is the way observations are recorded.

4.1 MORE-STRUCTURED OBSERVATION

As the aim of more-structured observation is to produce quantitative data on specific categories of observable behaviour, the nature of the categories and the procedures for allocating instances of behaviour to them must be clearly specified before data collection. These form the basis of an observation schedule in terms of which the researcher can code his or her observations.

The nature of categories and procedures obviously varies according to the aims of the research and the particular behaviour to be observed. At a very simple level, a researcher may be interested in a dichotomous variable such as whether a person is or is not talking. However, it is more usual for researchers to be concerned with several, more complex, multiple-category variables — as was the case in the ORACLE research you looked at earlier.

Paul Croll (1986) provides an interesting discussion of the process of defining variables, observational categories and procedures for allocating behaviour to categories in research on teachers' questions:

> [This] example arises from a research interest in the use of questioning by teachers. Initially, this interest could be operationalized into a dichotomous variable of the simple form:
>
> TEACHER IS ASKING A QUESTION
>
> TEACHER IS NOT ASKING A QUESTION

In principle, all classroom occurrences can be accurately categorized in this fashion although certain problems of definition will still occur. Rules will have to be constructed to decide, for example, how rhetorical questions ('Why can't I get any peace and quiet?') are to be coded. This might involve a coding rule (for example, all utterances with the formal structure of questions are to be coded as such) or a new category (for example, 'quasi-questions' or 'rhetorical questions').

However, the researcher will almost certainly want to make more sensitive distinctions than between 'question' and 'not-question'. He or she may want to distinguish between questions such as 'Who succeeded Queen Victoria?' and 'Who has got the glue?' and may want to further distinguish questions such as 'Who succeeded Queen Victoria?' and 'How different do you think it would have been to be at school in Victorian times?'

A concern to make such distinctions might lead to a more complex series of categories making up the variable. For instance:

QUESTIONS — CLASSROOM MANAGEMENT

QUESTIONS — FACTUAL RECALL

QUESTIONS — OPEN ENDED IDEAS

OTHER QUESTIONS

NOT QUESTION

This might serve the purposes of a particular piece of research but it is more likely that the researcher will want to further break down the category of 'other questions' and may also want to incorporate other aspects of the teacher's use of questions. To go back to the first example, there may be an interest in whether questions are asked of the whole class or of groups, or of individuals (or of individuals in the context of a class lesson). This can be accomplished by devising a longer set of categories to take all these possibilities into account:

QUESTION — CLASSROOM MANAGEMENT	WHOLE CLASS
QUESTION — CLASSROOM MANAGEMENT	GROUP
QUESTION — CLASSROOM MANAGEMENT	INDIVIDUAL
QUESTION — FACTUAL RECALL	WHOLE CLASS
QUESTION — FACTUAL RECALL	GROUP
QUESTION — FACTUAL RECALL	INDIVIDUAL
QUESTION — OPEN ENDED IDEAS	WHOLE CLASS
QUESTION — OPEN ENDED IDEAS	GROUP
QUESTION — OPEN ENDED IDEAS	INDIVIDUAL
OTHER QUESTION	WHOLE CLASS
OTHER QUESTION	GROUP
OTHER QUESTION	INDIVIDUAL
NOT QUESTION	

This, as it stands, is fairly manageable; a variable with thirteen categories into which any instant of classroom life can be coded (most instants presumably falling into 'not question'). However, if it is decided to make the category 'other question' more meaningful by turning it into a number of separate categories then the list of categories may begin to get long enough to present a problem for the observer trying to use it. If additional aspects of the questions asked are also to be included (such as the area of the curriculum the question refers to) the list of categories will almost certainly become unmanageable.

In this sort of instance, where a long list of categories of variables result[s] from an interest in different aspects of questioning, then the information required is best organised into a number of separate variables. Rather than use a single category to indicate that a question was concerned with classroom management and was asked of an individual, three separate variables can be coded to indicate whether a question is being asked, whether it is managerial or concerned with curriculum content and whether it is asked of the class, group or individual. The single variable above would be replaced by:

QUESTION — FACTUAL	MANAGERIAL	INDIVIDUAL
QUESTION — OPEN ENDED	CURRICULUM CONTENT	INDIVIDUAL/CLASS
OTHER QUESTION	OTHER	INDIVIDUAL/GROUP
NOT QUESTION		GROUP
		CLASS

All instances to be coded will be assigned to a category of each of the three variables and in the analysis it will be straightforward to reconstruct any of the detailed categories of the original single variable. Categories of any of the three new variables can be further divided or new categories added without complicating the other variables and if an additional aspect of questioning is to be investigated a fourth variable can be included. The only constraint on the number of variables is that of the number which can be accurately coded by an observer within the observation procedure being used.

(Croll, 1986, pp.57–9)

The researcher may also be interested in distinguishing between the frequency and the duration of observed behaviours. How often a person does something may clearly be a different matter from how much time they spend doing it. *When* a behaviour occurs in time and *where* it occurs in a particular sequence of behaviours may also be important. Thus some means of recording the temporal location of behaviour is sometimes needed. As Croll (1986) points out, there are three main possibilities.

The first possibility is some sort of continuous recording. In this, a time chart is used and the type of behaviour which occurs is coded continuously on the chart. When the behaviour changes, a new code is used from the time of the change. This type of recording allows the observer to locate the behaviours in time and to record their frequency and duration, and also where they occur in a particular sequence of behaviours. A simple example of continuous recording has been used in research on eye contact in interpersonal interaction. Here researchers have been interested in the frequency and duration of eye contact between two interacting individuals. Often utilizing video recordings, observers note on a time sheet the period over which one, or both, or neither subject is engaging in eye contact. Other more complex variables may also be recorded (see Scherer and Ekman, 1982, for a discussion).

A more complex example was used in research by Vietze *et al.* (1978) which looked at the interaction between mothers and their developmentally delayed infants. Observations of the behaviour of both mother and infant were recorded continuously by two observers — one focusing on the mother, the other on the young child. The infant's behaviour was coded into five categories — visual attention to the mother, non-distress vocalization, smile, distress vocalization, and no signalling behaviour. Likewise, the mother's behaviour was coded into five categories — visual attention to the infant, vocalization directed to the infant, smile, tactile play stimulation, and no behaviour directed to the infant. From their observations the researchers could discover the frequency and duration of particular mother and child behaviours, and also of the combinations of different types in interaction. They also had information about the sequences of behaviour.

However, continuous recording may be difficult where behaviour changes frequently and rapidly, as, for example, with question and answer sequences in a school classroom. It is also difficult to record more than one variable or category of a variable at a time unless more than one observer is used, as in the case above. Moreover, if the nature of behaviour is ambiguous and the coding decision cannot be made until some time after the behaviour has begun, continuous recording will not be possible.

A second possibility is time (or point) sampling. As I noted in Section 3.2, this often involves the coding of behaviour which is occurring at regular times — for example, every 25 seconds in the ORACLE research (Galton *et al.*, 1980). The observer can record the behaviour occurring at what is hoped is a representative sample of times, and can therefore estimate the proportion of time taken up by particular behaviours. The ORACLE researchers were able to say, for example, what proportion of class time teachers spent asking questions, or pupils spent 'fully involved and working on ... task work' (Galton *et al.*, 1980, pp.62–3). Again, as we saw in the ORACLE research, the observer can also code a relatively large number of variables. It is also possible to establish the sort of times at which particular behaviours occur. However, this method does not usually allow researchers to establish the frequency of behaviours since the sample is of times rather than events; nor does it permit the recording of the sequence of events within which behaviour occurs.

Time sampling can also involve coding the behaviour which occurred in regular timed periods. At a time signal the observer notes down whether particular behaviours occurred during the preceding period. A study of science teaching by Eggleston *et al.* (1975) utilized such a system. Observers noted whether any of 23 different types of behaviour occurred (categories included types of teacher–pupil interaction and pupil use of resources) during each three-minute period. The advantages of this method are that a large number of behaviours or events can be recorded and some indication is gained of their minimum frequency. The problem is that the method will underestimate the frequency of behaviours which are clustered in time, and will tell us little about the duration of behaviours.

A third method of recording involves focusing on events. Here, whenever the behaviour of interest occurs, its nature, and sometimes the time at which it occurs (and less commonly its duration), is recorded. A good example of such a system is the Brophy and Good Dyadic Interaction System used for studying teacher–pupil interaction (Brophy and Good, 1970). In this complex system the observer records the nature of teachers' communications to pupils, students' responses to these communications, and teachers' responses to students' responses, every time such events happen. So, for example, the observer would record the type of question asked of a pupil, then the nature of the student's response to the question, followed by the teacher's response to the student's answer. A similar strategy was utilized in research by Black (1980) on police–citizen encounters (see also Reiss, 1971) in several American cities. Here the nature of each incident the police were requested to deal with was coded, as was the nature of police response, the behaviour of the police on arrival, and several other aspects of the encounter. In this research an overall event — police–citizen encounter — was broken down into a series of sub-events, the details of which were recorded.

The advantage of event recording like this is that it gives data on the frequency of events or behaviours, and possibly where they occur in time and in a sequence of behaviours. However, the method does not usually give information on the duration of behaviours and may prove difficult to operate when events of interest occur frequently in rapid succession.

ACTIVITY 10

Think of an example of behaviour which is fairly easy for you to observe and on which it might be interesting to collect quantitative data. When I thought about this I came up with the following ideas:

- Children's play — what types of activity do my young children engage in and how long do these last? Are boys' play activities different from girls'? Do boys dominate collective play space?

- Family roles — who does what in the home? How often? How much time is spent on different activities?

- Shopping — do shop assistants give more time and help to customers of their own ethnic group or gender?

- My work — how do I break up my time? What sorts of things do I do? How long do I spend on different activities?

- Meetings at work — who contributes and what is the nature of their contributions? Do some contribute more than others?

Devise a simple observation schedule that you can try out during a brief period of observation. You will need to think about the sorts of categories into which the behaviour could be divided, and rules for allocating observed instances of behaviour to them. Think too about how you will select behaviours to observe and how you will record your observations. When you have devised your schedule and tried it out, make a note of the difficulties you encountered. You will find my efforts at the end of this unit.

4.2 LESS-STRUCTURED OBSERVATION

In contrast, the aim of less-structured observation is to produce detailed qualitative data on behaviour as part of a rounded description of the culture of a particular group of people. The emphasis is on flexibility and on recording behaviour and events in their wholeness — that is, taking full account of the social and cultural context in which they occur, and examining the perspectives and interpretations of participants. As such, fieldwork data will include records of conversations, discussions and interviews as well as the observed behaviour of subjects. The usual method of recording data is in the form of field notes. These are notes taken either during the observation itself, when this is possible, or shortly afterwards, and they form a running record of the researcher's observations.

It is obviously impossible to record everything that happens in a particular situation. Selection is inevitable and necessary. As I pointed out in Section 3.1, what is written down depends on the initial research questions and the stage the research has reached. During the early stages, an initial relatively wide focus is adopted and the researcher generally tries to note down a broad, general outline of what is happening, perhaps making a more detailed record of incidents which seem particularly interesting or revealing. At this stage the researcher may find some behaviour difficult to understand, but will often keep a record of it, as the data may be understandable and useful at a later stage. As the research progresses, and theoretical ideas begin to develop, the researcher focuses more carefully and makes more detailed records of particular aspects of behaviour or situations.

At such times it is very important to record as much detail as possible about what was said, both verbally and non-verbally. The actual language used may provide key information about subjects' perspectives which can be followed up in interviews and conversations. It is also important to record as much as possible about the physical, social and temporal context in which the behaviour occurred. Detail of such contexts may be essential for later analysis, and also for an assessment of any reactivity. But, of course, the more detail which is collected on particular behaviours the narrower the range of events which can be recorded. As Hammersley and Atkinson (1983) note, there is an inevitable trade-off here between detail and scope.

Generally, the more detailed the description the more likely it is to be accurate, and the less likely to be subject to distortion. But we should always remember that even detailed accounts are the product of selection and interpretation. It is important therefore that the researcher reflects carefully on the degree to which his or her own ideas and perspectives, and, of course, behaviour, have influenced the account produced. Indeed, it is useful if what is often referred to as a reflexive account, which discusses these influences, runs alongside the researcher's field notes.

A major influence on the accuracy of field notes is *when* they are made. Notes should preferably be made as soon as possible after the observation. The longer this is left the more is forgotten and the greater is the chance of inaccuracies and biases creeping in. Sometimes it is possible to make notes during the observation. I did this in my research, for example, when I was observing lessons in the classroom (Foster, 1990). The teachers, on the whole, if they were prepared to allow me to observe their lessons, did not seem to mind me taking notes. Sometimes, particularly in the early stages of the research, they were curious about what I was writing and what I would do with the data, and I had to reassure them about confidentiality. On occasions, I gave them my notes to read, partly to reassure them, and partly to provide a check on the validity of my accounts (I discuss the assessment of validity in Section 5). Taking notes in the classroom seemed to be a legitimate activity, perhaps because the teachers felt that in this context they were more publicly accountable or because others engage in the same activity, most notably inspectors and tutors of trainee teachers. But the act of note taking inevitably affected the teachers' perceptions of me. My conversations with them revealed that they saw me as more threatening, more as an evaluator and less as a colleague because of this.

However, often social norms in the setting do not permit note taking. For example, I thought it was inappropriate to take notes in the social area of the school staff room. In this case I had to write up my observations in the evening, or move into the work area adjoining the main staff room and 'make out' that I was working! When the research is covert, note taking during observation is usually impossible. In most situations note taking is not a usual or acceptable activity. The exception is when writing is an integral part of the participant role, as it might be if one were observing student behaviour in lectures, for example. Here covert note taking is feasible. Interestingly, the researchers in Rosenhan's (1982) study of psychiatric hospitals, who posed as patients, found that they could make notes fairly openly on the wards. Their 'continual writing' was interpreted by staff as further evidence of their insanity!

On occasions it may be possible for the researcher to play a role in which note taking is expected. Whyte (1981), for example, during his fieldwork, acted for some time as secretary to the Italian Community Club and therefore kept records of meetings. Sometimes researchers can take notes covertly, without the cover of a 'writing role'. Hammersley (1980), for example, jotted brief notes down on his newspaper when observing in the staff room of the school he studied.

Where note taking during observation is not possible, the researcher will have to retreat to some private area of the field — an office, a tent, even the lavatory — or leave the field altogether for a period, to write up his or her notes. Where the field is officially constituted for only part of a day, as with schools and many other contemporary institutions, it may be possible to do this when the field has 'closed down' — the evenings or weekends, for example. At these times memories and hurried jottings taken in the field can be elaborated, written down, recorded and filed. But it will also probably be necessary to have more substantial breaks from the field, not only to catch up on note taking, but to organize, examine and analyse data and to reflect on the research itself. These breaks from data collection are essential to plan future data collection effectively and also to recuperate from the stresses and strains of fieldwork.

It is perhaps impossible to overstress the dangers of spending too much time in the field and too little time recording and analysing data. As Lacey (1976) pointed out, there is a tendency to fall into the 'it's happening elsewhere' or 'it's happening when I'm not there' syndrome. Researchers often feel that they have to be in the field all the time and preferably in several places in the field at once. If they succumb to this temptation, often the result is forgotten, and therefore wasted, observations, and/or an overwhelming mass of unanalysed data.

Field notes vary in form, and individual researchers usually develop their own particular style and organization. Some use note books and divide pages into sections for descriptive accounts and analytical or methodological reflection. My own preference is for files from which I can take out pages easily for copying or reorganization. Some researchers type out their notes in full, others write notes in their own idiosyncratic shorthand. Some make extensive use of diagrams, especially to record the organization of physical space in the field, others prefer the narrative form.

Whatever the style or format, it is essential that notes contain basic information — date, time, place, etc. — and any other information about the context of an event or behaviour which may be relevant. It is also important to distinguish clearly between verbatim records of speech, summaries of events, and interpretations, and to note any uncertainties in one's account. Some space should also be given in field notes to an assessment of reactivity and to methodological reflection in general.

Once notes have been made they must be organized in such a way that information can be located and retrieved fairly easily. This will require some sort of cataloguing and indexing system, perhaps using a computer system. In fact, the organization of data into sections, categories and themes for this purpose forms part of the analysis of the data which proceeds alongside data collection.

ACTIVITY 11

In this activity I would like you to try a short piece of less-structured observation. Again, choose a setting in which it would be relatively easy to observe. Think briefly beforehand about the sort of things you want to focus on, and then spend a short period (say, about 10 minutes) observing. Try to make notes during the observation. If you are unable to do this, then write down your observations as soon as possible afterwards.

When you have completed your account, go over it carefully:

- Do any fruitful lines of enquiry or analysis suggest themselves?
- What do the data tell you about the perspectives or culture of your subjects?
- Finally, what difficulties did you encounter in collecting observational data in this way?

At the end of the unit you will find Martyn Hammersley's notes on an attempt at this activity, which were written for a previous Open University research methods course (Hammersley, 1979, pp.170–2).

4.3 USING TECHNOLOGY

Paper and pencil are the basic tools of the trade, but in our increasingly 'high tech' world electronic recording devices are frequently used. Whether to use such devices — the most common being audio or video recording — as aids to observation is a question common to both main approaches to observational research. Their advantage is that they provide a more complete and accurate record of behaviour and can be used to supplement or check data records produced by the researcher, such as field notes or tallies produced by systematic observation. They may therefore be useful in assessing the validity of data recorded live. Using audio or video recordings it is also possible to conduct a more careful and sometimes more complex analysis of data, since we can stop and replay the recording in order to consider the coding or categorization of the data. Audio or video recording may actually be essential in some studies where information is needed on the details of interaction and/or on the specific language that is used, as in conversation analysis. This was the case, for example, in a study by Tizard and Hughes which compared young children's language development in the home and in nursery schools (Tizard and Hughes, 1984; see also 1991 for a discussion of methodology). The researchers designed tunics for the girls to wear (the study observed girls only) which contained small, unobtrusive microphones. These microphones recorded the actual conversations between parent and child, and teacher and child. These data were supplemented by direct observation to record the context of the conversations.

On the other hand, electronic recording is not cheap and permission to record may not always be easy to obtain. Observation may therefore be limited to certain settings or sub-settings. Where permission is obtained it is likely, particularly with video recording, that reactivity will increase. This problem may reduce as subjects become accustomed to the presence of recording equipment, and it may be less significant than in the past as modern equipment is more compact and unobtrusive. Nevertheless, reactivity is a serious drawback.

There is also the danger that the researcher may be swamped with a large amount of data far beyond what it is necessary or possible to analyse. When electronic recording is possible, there is a great temptation to avoid selection decisions and to try to record almost everything. For the purposes of data analysis it is usually necessary to have a written record of verbal interaction. Audio and video tapes therefore have to be transcribed, a process which is extremely time consuming and sometimes difficult if the recording quality is poor.

This last point draws attention to the technical problems that can occur. Recording devices can fail and important data can be lost. Furthermore, it is important to realize that recording equipment cannot provide a complete record of behaviour. Audio recording obviously misses non-verbal communication and video has a restricted visual range. Neither method can adequately record complex verbal interaction between a large number of subjects such as that which occurs in a school classroom where pupils are working on a variety of assignments simultaneously. Nor can they provide an adequate record of the wider social context in which behaviour occurs.

Audio and video recordings are by no means the only example of technological aids used in observational research. Stopwatches are often used to time the duration of behaviour precisely. Sometimes still photography has been used to provide a record of behaviour at particular instants or, where repeated photographs are taken, of changing spatial patterns (see, for example, Bell, 1990). Electronic devices are sometimes used to record observations directly into computer data bases. For example, in the study I mentioned earlier on mother–infant interaction by Vietze *et al.* (1978), observers utilized a twelve-button keyboard connected to a cassette recorder to record their observations. The data were then transferred automatically to computer disc. I have no doubt that more sophisticated equipment is available now.

Another interesting example of a technological aid to observation was used by Bechtel (1970) to study standing and movement patterns amongst museum visitors. He called the device a 'Lodemeter'. It consisted of many pressure-sensitive pads covering the floor of a large room, and every time a person walked on a pad a counter increased by one. In this way, Bechtel was able to build up an accurate picture of which areas of the room were most used.

Of course, technology is not only used as an aid to recording. Sometimes devices are used to ensure that observation is unobtrusive. Serbin (reported in Pellegrini, 1991), for example, used binoculars to observe children's play from a distance.

Another, rather amusing, example was the use of a periscope by Middlemist *et al.* (1976) to help study the effects of the invasion of personal space on stress levels. The setting was a three-urinal men's toilet and the subjects were toilet users whose personal space was 'invaded' by a confederate to the study. Subjects' stress levels were measured by delays in the onset of urination and a shortening of its duration. Urination was observed by a researcher in a nearby toilet stall with the assistance of the periscope! One wonders whether anything is considered private by some researchers!

5 ASSESSING THE VALIDITY OF OBSERVATIONS

As with other research data, we must always be concerned about the validity and reliability of observations. Validity refers to the extent to which observations accurately record the behaviour in which the researcher is interested. One aspect of validity is reliability. This refers to the consistency of observations, usually whether two (or more) observers, or the same observer on separate occasions, studying the same behaviour come(s) away with the same data. Of course, if observational techniques are unreliable they are highly likely to produce invalid data.

5.1 THREATS TO VALIDITY

The validity of observational data can be threatened in a number of ways. First, there is the possibility of reactivity — both personal and procedural. In this case, actual observations of behaviour may be accurate, but subjects do not behave in the way they normally behave. Personal reactivity occurs when subjects behave differently because of the personal characteristics or behaviour of the observer. They may behave in particular ways because the observer is male or female or belongs to a certain 'racial' or ethnic group, or because he or she dresses or conducts him- or herself in a particular way. What is important here is how the subjects perceive the observer, how they interpret his or her behaviour, and how they behave as a result. Where two or more observers are involved, as in many more-structured observations, and subjects react differently with different observers, then problems of reliability emerge too.

Procedural reactivity occurs when subjects behave differently because they know they are being studied or observed. They change their behaviour in response to the procedures involved in the process of observation itself. This form of reactivity is most marked in experiments where subjects are often placed in 'artificial' situations and what goes on is deliberately manipulated. However, it is eliminated altogether in covert research where the subjects are unaware that they are being observed. Where procedural reactivity is high the ecological validity of the observations — the extent to which they can be generalized to other settings — will be in doubt.

A second possible threat to validity comes from the inadequacies of the measuring instruments used in the observation. The preconceived categories of an observation schedule may be unsuitable or inadequate for describing the actual nature of the behaviour which occurs. They may ignore aspects of behaviour which are important given the aims of the research (see my answer to Activity 10, for instance), or may force the observer to code behaviour which is significantly different under the same category. As a result, the descriptions produced by the observation system may be invalid. A number of observers of school classrooms, for example, have been concerned to estimate the extent of unequal treatments by teachers of children from different social groups (see, for example, Green, 1983; French and French, 1984). One research technique has been to count the number of interactions teachers have with different pupils. Unfortunately, though, this may give an invalid measure of the extent of unequal treatment because it ignores qualitative differences between individual interactions. These are obviously important to any assessment of inequality.

Techniques used in ethnographic research may also be inadequate. Selectivity in note taking and the distortion which can occur when the researcher relies upon memory when writing field notes can be significant sources of error.

A third potential threat to validity comes from observer bias. All observers have particular cultural knowledge, and approach observation from particular theoretical and sometimes political standpoints. These subjectivities can affect what behaviour is selected for observation, and how this behaviour is interpreted and recorded. They may therefore result in invalid data.

In more-structured observation, precisely what is to be observed is set out in advance and is clearly a product of the researcher's theoretical ideas. But in this type of observation the aim is to minimize the effects of observer subjectivity by ensuring that all observers observe behaviour in the same way and follow the same coding rules. Unfortunately, there is sometimes inconsistency in the way rules are applied by different observers (and sometimes by the same observer on different occasions). This happens particularly when there are ambiguities in the coding system or where coding requires inferences about observed behaviour. As I mentioned in my answer to Activity 1, Scarth and Hammersley (1986) criticize aspects of the ORACLE research (Galton *et al.*, 1980) on these grounds. They argue that the coding rules for categorizing teachers' questions are ambiguous and require the observer to infer teachers' intentions. They suggest that the variations in the questioning styles between the teachers discovered by the research could have been artificially produced by differences between observers. The data produced may therefore have been invalid (see also Croll and Galton, 1986, and Scarth and Hammersley, 1987).

Ethnographers have more often been accused of allowing their theoretical and political preconceptions to bias their observations. Perhaps the potential for this type of bias is greater with ethnography because what is to be observed, and how, is not systematically set out before the observation begins. The work of the anthropologist Margaret Mead (1943), on the island of Samoa, has been criticized on these grounds. Freeman (1984) has suggested that the conclusions she came to about the stress-free nature of adolescence there were to a considerable extent the product of her own preconceptions. His observations revealed rather different experiences and behaviour amongst young people. One of the weaknesses of ethnographic research is that it is largely the product of the ideas, choices and negotiative strategies of an individual researcher. As a result, the picture produced by one researcher of a group or institution may be very different from that produced by another.

A related threat to validity arises from misperception or misinterpretation of behaviour. The observer may simply misunderstand the 'real' nature of the behaviour he or she observes. This is more likely when behaviour is complex or when the observer is unfamiliar with the social situation and the meanings which are in play. For example, in my own research in a multi-ethnic school I observed a situation in which a white adolescent boy called an Afro-Caribbean boy a 'nigger'. I initially interpreted this as a clear instance of racial abuse. However, I discovered later that the two boys were the best of friends and regularly swapped racial insults as a way of reinforcing a sense of camaraderie. My initial observation was clearly invalid (if we define 'racial abuse' as implying negative evaluation of the person to whom it is directed).

5.2 WAYS OF ASSESSING VALIDITY

How, then, do observational researchers assess the validity of their observations? One method is to check the reliability of research techniques. The main way of doing this is replication. Sometimes whole studies are repeated using the same procedures, with different observers. At other times, parts of a study may be repeated (as in the ORACLE research — see Croll, 1980). Replication is more feasible in experiments and studies involving more-structured observation where procedures are clearly specified and therefore can be fairly easily repeated.

One form of replication involves examining the extent of agreement between two observers of the same behaviour. This technique is more often used in more-structured observation. Here it usually involves comparing the individual coding decisions of two observers to see to what extent they agree. This is termed absolute agreement. Alternatively, it may involve comparing their overall coding results to see whether the total number of behaviours allocated to the categories of the schedule tally. This is called marginal agreement. Obviously, absolute agreement is a much stronger test of the reliability of observations, but it is not always possible to conduct such a test with all observation systems.

Inter-observer agreement is usually worked out for each variable in the observation system and can be expressed as the proportion of instances when the two observers agree on appropriate coding. So if they code 80 out of 100 instances of behaviour in the same way, we have 80 per cent agreement. This was the technique used in the ORACLE research you read about earlier, although, as I pointed out in my answer to Activity 1, the researchers do not give reliability figures for the separate categories.

Replication is not usually feasible in ethnographic research. Procedures are not prestructured, and the course of the research is very much a product of the ideas and personal idiosyncrasies of the researcher and the way he or she interacts with subjects. Moreover, procedures are not usually recorded in sufficient detail to allow another researcher to reproduce them in the same way. The nearest ethnographers come to replication is the re-study. The same group or institution is studied again some time after the original study (see, for example, Burgess, 1987). Re-studies provide limited information on reliability because, although the research setting may be the same, the research questions and procedures, the sub-settings, sub-groups and individuals studied are often very different. Moreover, in the period of time since the original study, the group or institution will probably have changed considerably and differences in data and conclusions may be the product of these changes.

Techniques such as reflexivity, triangulation and respondent validation are more often used in ethnographic research to assess validity. Reflexivity involves the continual monitoring of, and reflection on, the research process. During and after the fieldwork the researcher tries to assess the extent of his or her own role in the process of data production and how the data were affected by the social context in which they were collected. Reflection during data collection may influence the process of future data collection because it may throw up methodological hypotheses and suggest alternative ways of collecting data. When the fieldwork is complete it forms the basis of the researcher's own methodological assessment of the data.

Sometimes researchers provide readers with a reflexive account of their work in the form of a natural history. These are sometimes contained in methodological appendices to the main work (see, for example, Whyte, 1981) or are sometimes published separately (see, for example, Burgess, 1984). These accounts can be useful to the reader in assessing the researcher's role in the production of data and the conclusions of the study.

Triangulation is more a direct check on the validity of observations by cross-checking them with other sources of data. If a researcher's conclusion is supported by data from other sources then we can be more confident of its validity. Triangulation can involve comparing data on the same behaviour from different researchers (as in reliability checks in more-structured observation) who possibly adopt different roles in the field. Alternatively, it can involve comparing data produced by different methods — for example, observational data can be compared with interview data — or it can involve comparing data from different times, sub-settings, or subjects.

Comparing data from the researcher's observations of behaviour with data from the various subjects involved is one form of respondent validation. Here the aim is to check the validity of the researcher's observations by reference to the subjects' perceptions. This may take a number of forms. The researcher may discuss his or her observations with subjects, asking them whether they feel the observations are accurate and what their perceptions of a particular incident were. Alternatively, the researcher may ask participants to supply written accounts of a particular instance or period of behaviour. These can then be compared with the researcher's own observations. Ball (1981), for example, in his study of mixed-ability teaching in a comprehensive school, sometimes compared his account of lessons with those provided by teachers. And, finally, the researcher may feed back his or her observations to subjects and ask for their comments (again a technique used by Ball — see Ball, 1984).

The advantage of such techniques is that the researcher may be able to access important additional knowledge about the behaviour under consideration — for example, about the thoughts and motives of subjects, their perceptions of the behaviour of others, and about the social context in which the behaviour occurred — which is not available from observation. They may also provide a valuable alternative perspective on the behaviour which occurred, as well as useful information on subjects' perspectives. As Fielding (1982) found in his study of the National Front, they may also be a useful way of encouraging the involvement of subjects in the research.

However, respondent validation does not automatically ensure the accuracy of data. Subjects may be more concerned to manipulate the impression of behaviour which is contained in the data as a way of enhancing or protecting their own interests. Their accounts may therefore present behaviour in certain ways or may give particular interpretations of that behaviour. These accounts will, of course, be influenced by the social context in which they are delivered, and by their perception of the researcher and of the use to which the data will be put. Moreover, it is important to recognize that subjects' accounts of their actions and perceptions are reconstructions from memory which may not necessarily correspond to their thoughts or perceptions at the time the behaviour occurred. We must recognize and try to assess, too, the potential threats to validity in respondent accounts.

6 CONCLUSION

In this unit I have tried to introduce you to the different styles and techniques used in observational research. I identified two basic styles — more-structured observation, and less-structured or ethnographic observation. Although there are clear differences between the two styles, I do not want to leave you with the impression that they are opposed and mutually exclusive. I must emphasize that observational research often involves both styles and that, at times, both raise similar issues and problems.

All observers have to gain access to subjects. In a narrow sense this means getting to a physical position from which subjects can be observed. But it also often means developing relationships with subjects so that, as far as possible, the way they behave 'naturally' can be observed. Similar ethical problems — concerning deception, invasion of privacy and harm to subjects, for example — are involved in both styles; and in both styles decisions have to be made about what to observe. In more-structured observation those decisions are more likely to be made prior to the actual fieldwork, whereas in less-structured observation decisions are made during the course of fieldwork itself. Nevertheless, researchers must choose what to focus on and select appropriate samples. The major difference between the two styles is that more-structured observation requires observers to allocate behaviours to preconceived categories of an observation schedule, whereas less-structured observation involves written accounts in field notes describing the nature of behaviour in more detail.

In the final part of the unit I have considered various threats to the validity of observational data, and the main ways in which researchers check validity. Producers of observational research should always be concerned with the validity of their data. Observational research will only make a useful contribution to the bank of public knowledge that I mentioned in my introduction if we can be reasonably confident of its validity. Readers of observational research should also keep matters of validity in the forefront of their minds. A consideration of such matters is essential to any assessment of research. As producers and consumers of observational research we can never, of course, be absolutely sure of the validity of observations, but we must decide and make clear to what extent confidence in that validity is justified.

UNIT 12 OBSERVATIONAL RESEARCH

ANSWERS TO ACTIVITIES

ACTIVITY 1

1(a) The observers focused on one pupil at a time (the target pupil) and recorded a number of aspects of behaviour — whether the pupil was waiting for the teacher, or paying attention to others, or engaging in disruptive behaviour; the extent of the pupil's involvement in work tasks; and the pupil's location. They also recorded the nature of the pupil's interaction with other pupils, and with the teacher or other adults.

1(b) When observing the teachers, the researchers concentrated on the different types of interactions teachers had with pupils. They distinguished between oral and silent interactions, and, in the former, between questions and statements (of different types).

2(a,b) The researchers selected three local education authorities (LEAs). It is not clear how these were chosen, but in part this reflected a wider concern of the study with pupil transfer to a later stage of education: each LEA had a different transfer age. In each LEA two receiving schools, contrasting in their internal organization but similar in their catchment areas, were chosen with the help of LEA advisers. Once these schools agreed to take part in the wider study, their feeder schools became the sample of primary schools. One school decided not to take part and in one LEA an unspecified number of other schools were added. The teachers studied were those who taught pupils in the year (or two years) prior to their transfer.

The observers spent three days each term with each class over a one-year period. We are given no information on how the days were selected. They observed for six 55-minute sessions during their stays. In each session the teacher was observed for a continuous period of nineteen minutes — sometimes at the beginning, sometimes at the end, and sometimes in the middle of the session; and eight target pupils were selected by dividing each class into four ability groups — one high ability, one low ability, two of middle ability — and by choosing a boy and a girl at random from each group. Observations were conducted of both the teacher and the target pupils at 25-second intervals.

3 The observers underwent two weeks' 'intensive training' and refresher training during the study. This may help to improve reliability, but it does not, of course, ensure it. In order to check reliability, towards the end of the second year of the study four classrooms were observed by pairs of observers using the teacher and pupil records at synchronized times. The researchers checked the extent of agreement between the observers by comparing their coding of behaviour at each time unit. The observers' coding was the same on the pupil record in about 90 per cent of cases, and on the teacher record in 76 per cent of cases. The researchers maintain that these levels of reliability were acceptable for the study. Part of the ORACLE study was also replicated in the second and third year of the research and the consistency of certain data was checked (a discussion of this can be found in Croll, 1980).

4 When observing pupils the observers recorded the teacher's activity and location, and also the behaviour of any adult or pupil with whom the target pupil interacted. When observing the teachers they noted the type and composition of their pupil audience and also the curricular activity of pupil(s) with whom the teacher interacted. The observers also recorded more general information about the classes such as seating arrangements, classroom management, organization and grouping, curricular activities, and the use of materials, books and apparatus. They also seem to have noted basic information about the schools and their catchment areas.

5 I have identified the following advantages in the research methods used. The very fact that the ORACLE research used observation was an advance on other

studies of classrooms such as the one by Bennett (1976) which relied in the main on teacher-completed questionnaires for data on classroom organization and behaviour. The research also involved a relatively large amount of classroom observation compared to other observation studies of classrooms. More-structured observation allowed the researchers to provide a more rigorous, quantitative description of variations in teacher and pupil behaviour than is possible using a less-structured approach. It was also possible for the observations of several different researchers to be compared and combined to provide a broader picture. The researchers could assess the reliability of the observational techniques employed, and replicate aspects of the study. (In the second year of the research some of the children were observed again with different teachers and the same observation instruments were used.)

However, I can also see a number of problems. The sample of LEAs, schools and teachers was not selected in a way that made it likely to be representative of any wider population of LEAs, schools or teachers. Moreover, the size of the time samples of classroom behaviour (three days each term) was very small in comparison with the total amount of class time in a year and the samples do not appear to have been random. Their representativeness must also therefore be in doubt. It is difficult to know whether we can generalize on the basis of these samples about behaviour in these particular classrooms, or about classroom behaviour in a wider population of classrooms.

One thing that is not clear (at least from this extract) is why the ORACLE researchers were interested in the particular categories of behaviour that appear in their observation schedules. Presumably these were taken to be indicators of particular teaching styles or types of classroom behaviour. However, it is difficult to judge the validity of the categories as measures without some discussion of this.

Some of the categories in the observation schedules give me cause for concern. I think it must have been difficult to code behaviour unambiguously into certain categories. Although the researchers produced and utilized a coding manual (Boydell and Jasman, 1983), which provided detailed rules for coding behaviour, Scarth and Hammersley (1986) argue that this did not eliminate all potential problems. They consider the categories of 'teacher questions' and point out that coding sometimes required assessments by the observer of the teachers' expectations of pupils' answers and therefore inferences about teachers' thinking. This raises doubts in their minds about the validity of the observational findings.

Scarth and Hammersley (1986) also note that the reliability scores are aggregates for all the categories on the teacher and pupil records. They therefore may conceal large variations. It is possible, for example, that reliability was 100 per cent for some categories of behaviour, but much lower than the average for others. Thus on certain crucial variables reliability may have been poor. Furthermore, the reliability scores were calculated on observations conducted in the second year of the study when the observers presumably had become fairly familiar with the observation schedules. Reliability might have been more of a problem in the earlier stages of the study.

Another issue raised by Scarth and Hammersley (1986) is that of reactivity. Given that observer visits were relatively short and infrequent, and that teachers (and maybe pupils) knew they were going to be observed by a relative stranger, it is likely that reactivity would have been high.

A final point worth bearing in mind, should you examine the results of the study, is that time sampling — at 25-second intervals — conflates frequency and duration. So, for example, we cannot say from the data produced whether the teacher asked a large number of short questions or a small number of long ones.

ACTIVITY 2

1 Punch initially tried to study police forces in Britain, but his proposals were rejected by the Home Office (he does not explain why). He decided to study the

Dutch police because he felt there was a better chance of his proposal being accepted, as individual forces in Holland can make their own decisions about research. He had also lived for a short period in Holland and had a Dutch wife. Punch is not very clear why he wanted to study an inner-city force in Amsterdam. He seems to have been attracted by the potential excitement and controversy which sometimes surrounds police work in inner-city areas, and he implies that Amsterdam was more typical of other large 'cosmopolitan' cities than were other Dutch cities. His contact and sponsor, Dr Rom Fris, seems to have chosen the specific station and the police officers with whom Punch spent his first period of fieldwork. It is difficult to judge to what extent the officers Punch studied were representative of any wider population.

2 Punch's informal contacts with the International Police Association enabled him to spend two weeks with two 'community relations officers' (p.183) in Rotterdam. Here he got to know Dr Fris, a psychologist working for the Amsterdam police. Fris seems to have acted as a sponsor and arranged Punch's access to a specific station and officers. Punch tells us little about how he developed these contacts and how Fris acted on his behalf. He does say that being a foreigner was an advantage in gaining access because he was perceived as less 'threatening. He also explains that after his first spell in the field (one month) he sent copies of his report to 'strategically placed people' (p.189) and was given permission to do a further three months' fieldwork.

3 Punch tells us more about how he built up relationships with the officers he studied. The fact that he could speak Dutch (or was learning) obviously helped. He concentrated on one 'shift' of officers and demonstrated that he was willing to be with them during their work at all times (including the night shift) and in all weathers. Perhaps more importantly, he helped the officers with their work in a number of ways. He assisted on routine tasks such as making coffee and clearing up in the canteen or sweeping the road after an accident, but also on more important work such as translating during the interrogation of English suspects, and even the discovery and arrest of drug traffickers. The officers themselves sometimes found it useful for Punch to pose as a detective. In these ways Punch demonstrated that he was willing to get involved in police work, that he had an empathetic approach to the officers, and that he was someone who could be trusted. He also mentions that he deliberately presented himself as anti-intellectual.

4 Punch seemed to take part in police work increasingly over the course of the fieldwork. His role changed from a relatively uninvolved observer/researcher to a more actively involved officer-assistant/observer/researcher.

5 Punch's research was not covert as regards the police officers. They knew he was doing research, although how much they knew, or were told, about the aims and focus of the research is difficult to tell. But the ordinary citizens, with whom Punch observed officers dealing, did not know he was a researcher. Indeed, it is clear that many thought he was a police officer. These subjects, if we accept they were subjects, were deceived, or at least not informed, about the research. However, it is difficult to see how in many situations Punch could have consulted them about the research.

Punch's active role as an assistant officer clearly had an adverse effect on some of these 'subjects'. In the case of the drug traffickers, Punch's actions led to their arrest. Some of these subjects were clearly harmed (in the sense that they were more likely to be arrested and convicted) by the research. Punch had to weigh up a number of competing commitments here — his commitment as a citizen to particular values and laws, a researcher's commitment to protect his or her subjects' interests, and a commitment to the importance of his research which benefited from an enhanced relationship with his police officer subjects. When considering his criminal subjects, Punch seemed to side with the first and third of these commitments. Indeed, he makes his position *vis-à-vis* the interests of many of the criminals with whom he came into contact pretty clear on pages 196–7. He is more ambivalent about what his position would have been had he discovered police malpractice or crime. 'Fortunately', he says, 'this problem did not arise' (p.196) in his research, although earlier in the extract (p.192) he describes being given considerable information, at a party, about police corruption.

6 Punch argues that participant observation enabled him to 'penetrate' (pp.184–5) the occupational culture of police officers. He claims that the police often erect barriers which prevent public scrutiny and utilize strategies to present a favourable image of their work. Participant observation enabled him to see 'the inner reality of police work' (p.184), to get beneath public representations and see policing, both on the street and behind the scenes, as it really is. He argues that much police work consists of unique face-to-face encounters involving considerable discretion on the part of individual officers, and that observation is required to get at this complexity. He implies that 'more-structured techniques' (p.185), by which I think he means interviews and questionnaires, would not have given accurate information on what officers actually do.

7 During the fieldwork he obviously made use of informal conversations and discussions with officers. He also had access to documentary and statistical evidence, although he does not say much about what types. Following the fieldwork, he conducted interviews with an unspecified number of officers of different ranks.

8 I think the data he collected give us a more detailed and accurate account of police work (or the work of these particular officers) than we would obtain from other methods. To some extent Punch did gain an insider's view of the occupational culture of this group of officers. But we must remember that Punch's account is a constructed representation of police work. It is a representation based upon lengthy observation and close study and is therefore more likely to be valid than others which are not based on such extensive research. But nevertheless it is a representation coloured by Punch's ideas and viewpoints, and therefore does not exhaust the 'reality of police work'.

Punch's account is also, of course, a product of what he was able to observe and of what the officers were prepared to tell him. Aspects of the 'reality of police work' may have been concealed from him. Indeed, in the section of the extract where he discusses police corruption, Punch concedes that 'a subterranean police culture ... had largely escaped me' (p.192). The account is also a product of what Punch selected to observe and record. My impression is that Punch focused on particular events which were exciting and exotic rather than routine.

ACTIVITY 10

Just after I wrote this activity I had a conversation with a female colleague who claimed that departmental meetings (I work in the education department in a 'new' university) were almost always dominated by men. I decided to observe the next departmental meeting to put her claim to the test. Of course, the meeting I observed may not have been typical and, as her claim was of a probabilistic nature, observing one meeting was not a real test. Nevertheless it provided the basis for a useful exercise. I have tried here to reproduce briefly my thoughts as I prepared this exercise.

I had to think first about behavioural indicators of 'dominance'. One possibility I thought of was a simple count of the number of contributions made to the meeting by men and women. In this case I would simply have two categories of behaviour — contribution or no-contribution to the meeting — and all I would have to do would be to record whether a contribution was being made and if so whether it was made by a man or a woman.

There were two problems — I had to decide what series of behaviour made up 'the meeting', and what behaviour constituted 'a contribution'. The former was relatively easy to resolve. I decided that the meeting began when the chairperson (a man) called it to order and raised the first item on the agenda, and that it ended when he formally closed it. I therefore *excluded* informal talk before and after the meeting, which actually in part concerned the business of the meeting, and included certain informal/social talk, not relevant to the agenda, which occurred during the meeting. This did raise doubts in my mind about my definition of the meeting. The second problem was more difficult. How should I define 'contribution' and what rules would I have for deciding whether a particular instance could be coded as a contribution? I decided to exclude non-verbal behaviour, and single word utterances — such as 'yes', 'no', 'what', 'how', etc. — and formulated the following definition: 'a contribution consists of a verbal utterance of a phrase or more, addressed to the general body of the meeting'. I decided that a phrase consisted of two or more words, but pondered over how I would decide whether or not utterances were 'addressed to the general body of the meeting'. I wanted to exclude comments which were made as asides to immediate neighbours or to sub-groups and concentrate on the formal talk which made up the meeting. (Was my definition of 'the meeting' changing?) I decided to see how things went during my observation.

Something else that occurred to me was that just counting contributions took no account of the length of those contributions. It was clearly possible for a person to make only a small number of contributions and yet take up a large proportion of the meeting time. I decided therefore to use a system of continuous recording which would enable me to time the length of individual contributions. I would have to indicate on a time schedule when a contribution started and finished and whether it was made by a man or a woman. I would then have data on the frequency and the duration of contributions made by men and women.

My preparations thus made, I set out to observe the meeting. I decided to focus on the first 30 minutes of the meeting, partly because I thought this would be long enough to try out the technique, and partly because I knew there were subjects in the second half of the agenda on which I wanted to contribute. This obviously further restricted the representativeness of my observations, but it also highlights the difficulty — in fact I think the impossibility — of conducting live more-structured observation in situations in which one is actively involved. I must confess that I did not seek the consent of the members of the meeting to my observation. I placed myself on the periphery of the meeting and observed covertly. I felt this was acceptable because this was just an exercise rather than a 'real' piece of research, and because seeking informed consent would have involved time-consuming negotiation which I could not afford. I also felt that no-one would be harmed, and that people might have behaved differently had they known I was observing them. You may disagree with my ethical judgements here.

The schedule, taken from the middle of the observation period, and shown in Figure 2, illustrates the type of data I collected.

You may be interested to know that men made 43 per cent and women 57 per cent of the contributions to the meeting. However, men's contributions tended to be longer — they took up 62 per cent of the total contribution time, compared to 38 per cent for women's. In considering the questions of dominance and equity, we would perhaps have to adjust these figures to take account of the different number of men and women present in the meeting. On this occasion there were fourteen men and eleven women present. (Thus we would expect men's total contribution to be a little higher, whether or not they were dominant.)

I had a number of problems collecting these data and I also have reservations about the data I produced. For the sake of brevity let me list these:

1 I found it difficult to record precisely the beginning and end of a contribution. This was mainly because I was using the second hand of my watch. I really needed a stop-watch.

2 I found concentrating on the recording quite hard work (especially as I was trying to listen to the subject matter of the meeting) and when the half hour was up I was quite relieved.

3 On several occasions there were overlaps when two (or more) people were talking at once which made accurate recording difficult.

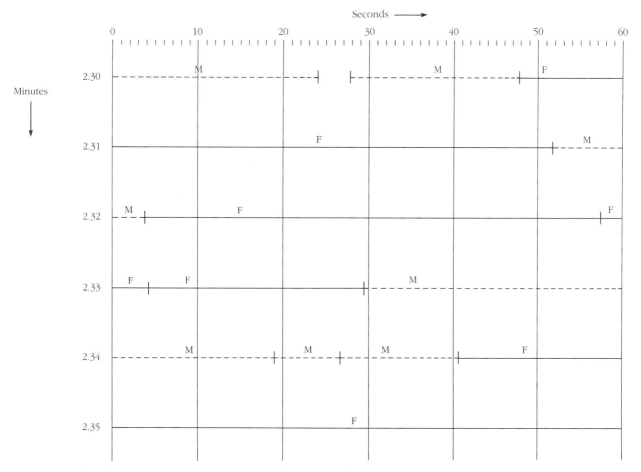

Figure 2 Extract from departmental observation schedule

4 There were also a number of ambiguous 'contributions', as I expected — for example, comments made which were not directed to 'the general body of the meeting'. I am not sure that I recorded these consistently. All these problems raise questions about the reliability of the method I used.

5 Perhaps more serious is the question of whether number and length of contributions are valid indicators of dominance. If men (or women) speak more often and for longer in meetings (given their numbers in the meeting), does this mean they have 'dominated' the meeting? If contributions are proportionate does this constitute parity? On reflection, I think these are fairly weak indicators of dominance. Dominance surely also involves *what* people say. It is possible for a person to say very little and yet control the conduct and content of a meeting by the nature of what they say or the way in which they say it. Dominance may also involve having a key influence over certain phases of a meeting — for example, when decisions are made. Again, a person may say very little during a meeting but when it comes to the key function of a meeting — to make a decision on some matter — theirs is the dominant voice. Dominance in this sense may be better indicated by who gets their way in terms of decisions. Moreover, dominance can also be a matter of setting and controlling the agenda of a meeting. Key decisions may be taken before the meeting even begins.

So perhaps I needed data on other indicators of dominance. For instance, I could have divided the nature of people's contributions into different categories and then coded each category — such categories might have included, for example, questions, information giving, expression of opinion, procedural comments, etc. However, I suspect you can imagine some of the problems this would raise. I perhaps also needed data on who made important decisions, and who set the agenda, amongst other things. (See Hargreaves, 1981, for a discussion of dominance in meetings based on a more ethnographic approach.)

ACTIVITY 11

In my first attempt to do this activity I decided on a Chinese take-away shop as the location. I chose this setting because on previous visits I had been fascinated by some of the patterns of interaction occurring there. Thinking about possible lines of analysis before I went, I came up with three ideas: the meeting of different ethnic cultures (i.e. Chinese and English); the dramatic analogy between the front and the back of the shop, as frontstage and backstage (see below); and some idea of leisure cultures — patterns of association, interest and values associated with leisure activities.

When I arrived at the shop there was only one person there: a man sitting down reading *The Sun* who collected his food and left almost immediately after I had arrived. No-one else came into the shop while I was there. The man serving in the shop spent all the time in the back part of the shop until he brought out the food I had been waiting for. There was a Liberal Party Political Broadcast on the colour television.

My response to this situation was that nothing was happening. The only possibility was to use the stage–backstage idea, but I could not develop it any further than it had already been developed by Erving Goffman (1959) from whom I had borrowed it in the first place. He had observed that service establishments are frequently divided into two areas: a front area where those working in the establishment present a front to clients, and a back area to which clients are not admitted.

Given the failure of my first shot at the activity to produce anything, I decided to have another go, using the same setting. As you will see, not much more seemed to be happening on my second visit, but I made a little more of it.

I shall present my jotted notes first, then my written-up version of the field notes and then the outline of a possible analysis.

Jotted notes

Middle-aged couple, well-dressed, woman in fur coat, man in a coat with a fur collar.

Man standing reading paper.

Woman (of the couple), reading extracts from paper. American accent. 'That's ours'. Collects Chinese food.

TV faces just one side of room. Man who serves is in back of shop.

Man standing glances at violence on TV, puts paper down and watches. (Filling in time)

He is standing, arms folded.

(When I first arrived there was a couple just collecting Chinese and leaving. Man: 'It's ready, come on, let's get home that film's on').

(Goffman)

(Activities which occur at standard times/those slotted in.)

Written-up field notes (written up on return from the take-away)

I enter and sit down on the left hand side of the room (R).

A man and woman (A and B) sitting on the left of the room, in their twenties, casually dressed, jeans etc. The server comes through the curtain from the kitchen, holds a packet of food towards the young couple.

A to B: 'It's ready come on let's get home that film's on.'

The server goes back into the kitchen.

Middle-aged couple (D and E), well-dressed, woman wearing fur coat, man in a car coat with fur collar. The woman is reading out excerpts from the newspaper to the man in a 'have you seen this?' kind of way.

The server reappears.

D: 'That's ours?'

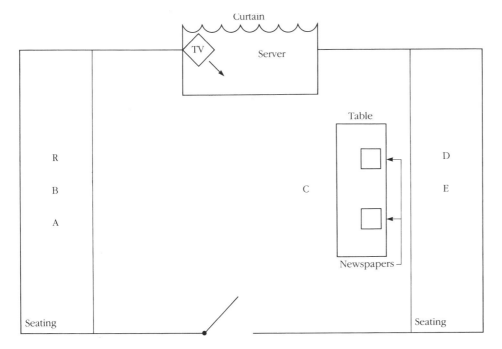

Figure 3
(Source: Hammersley, 1979, p.171)

They leave.

Man (C) standing in the middle of the room reading a newspaper. TV programme relates to the everyday lives of two American policemen and at this point a particularly violent scene seems to occur (by the sound of it, I can't see the picture). C glances at the TV screen a couple of times, then puts down the paper and stands watching it, arms folded.

Outline of a possible analysis

A fairly obvious idea which struck me during the course of the observation was that what these people were doing was filling in time (whereas on *this* occasion I was not). In other words, they had not come to this place specifically to perform these activities — chatting, reading, watching TV etc. Furthermore, these activities would be curtailed as soon as the food arrived — they are in that sense low status or low priority activities. (I can imagine that this is not always the case. For example, if by chance one meets a friend in this setting, the conversation may be continued after the food arrives, though there is a cost to this — cold food!)

I then began to wonder if we could categorize activities in terms of those which are time- and place-bound and those which are 'portable' and can be fitted in anywhere, and between those which are high and low priority/status, a distinction which may or may not coincide with the first. However, even from the little bit of data collected here we can see that this is not the case: while watching TV can be a 'fill in', it can also be a high priority activity which people go to particular places at particular times to do — witness A's comment to B as he collects the food. Nevertheless, while the same activity can vary in its priority and portability, there do seem to be certain kinds of activity — smoking and chatting, for example — which are standard time fillers.

However, I wonder whether the notion of filling or killing time is really satisfactory. These people are in fact doing something: they are waiting. The point is better formulated in terms of the level of involvement associated with an activity on a particular occasion and thus the degree to which other activities can be performed simultaneously. Waiting requires a minimal level of involvement, presumably one must simply watch out for the food to arrive, and thus it can be combined or 'filled' with other activities.

This is as far as my analysis got in the time available.

REFERENCES

Atkinson, M. (1984) *Our Masters' Voices: The Language and Body Language of Politics*, London, Routledge.

Atkinson, M. and Drew, P. (1979) *Order in Court*, London, Macmillan.

Ball, S.J. (1981) *Beachside Comprehensive*, Cambridge, Cambridge University Press.

Ball, S.J. (1984) 'Beachside reconsidered: reflections on a methodological apprenticeship', in Burgess, R.G. (ed.) (1984).

Barker, E. (1984) *The Making of a Moonie*, Oxford, Basil Blackwell.

Bechtel, R.B. (1970) 'Human movement and architecture', in Proshansky, H.M., Ittelson, W.H. and Rivlin, L.G. (eds) *Environmental Psychology: Man and His Physical Setting*, New York, Holt, Rinehart and Winston.

Becker, H.S., Geer, B., Hughes, E.C. and Strauss, A.L. (1961) *Boys in White: Student Culture in Medical School*, Chicago, IL, University of Chicago Press.

Bell, P.A. (1990) *Environmental Psychology*, 3rd edn, Fort Worth, TX, Holt, Rinehart and Winston.

Bennett, N. (1976) *Teaching Styles and Pupil Progress*, London, Open Books.

Beynon, J. (1985) *Initial Encounters in the Secondary School*, Lewes, Falmer Press.

Black, D. (1980) *The Manners and Customs of the Police*, New York, Academic Press.

Boydell, D. and Jasman, A. (1983) *The Pupil and Teacher Record: A Manual for Observers*, Leicester, University of Leicester.

Brewer, J.D. (with Magee, K.) (1991) *Inside the RUC: Routine Policing in a Divided Society*, Oxford, Clarendon Press.

British Sociological Association (1992) *Statement of Ethical Practice*, London, British Sociological Association.

Brophy, J.E. and Good T.L. (1970) 'Teacher–child dyadic interactions: a new method of classroom observation', *Journal of School Psychology*, vol. 8, no. 2, pp.131–8.

Brophy, J.E. and Good, T.L. (1974) *Teacher–Student Relationships: Causes and Consequences*, New York, Holt, Rinehart and Winston.

Bulmer, M. (ed.) (1982) *Social Research Ethics: An Examination of the Merits of Covert Participant Observation*, London, Macmillan.

Burgess, R.G. (ed.) (1982) *Field Research: A Sourcebook and Field Manual*, London, George Allen and Unwin.

Burgess, R.G. (1983) *Experiencing Comprehensive Education*, London, Methuen.

Burgess, R.G. (ed.) (1984) *The Research Process in Educational Settings: Ten Case Studies*, Lewes, Falmer Press.

Burgess, R.G. (1987) 'Studying and restudying Bishop McGregor School', in Walford, G. (ed.) *Doing Sociology of Education*, Lewes, Falmer Press.

Chambliss, W. (1975) 'On the paucity of original research on organized crime', *American Sociologist*, vol. 10, pp.36–9.

Cohen, S. and Taylor, L. (1972) *Psychological Survival: The Experience of Long-Term Imprisonment*, Harmondsworth, Penguin.

Corsaro, W.A. (1981) 'Entering the child's world: research strategies for field entry and data collection in a pre-school setting', in Green, J.L. and Wallat, C. (eds) *Ethnography and Language in Educational Settings*, Norwood, NJ, Ablex.

Croll, P. (1980) 'Replicating the observational data', in Galton, M. and Simon, B. (eds) *Progress and Performance in the Primary Classroom*, London, Routledge and Kegan Paul.

Croll, P. (1986) *Systematic Classroom Observation*, Lewes, Falmer Press.

Croll, P. and Galton, M. (1986) 'A comment on "Questioning ORACLE" by John Scarth and Martyn Hammersley', *Educational Research*, vol. 28, no. 3, pp. 185–9.

Davis, F. (1959) 'The cab-driver and his fare: facets of a fleeting relationship', *American Journal of Sociology*, vol. 65, no. 2, pp. 158–65.

Day, C. (1981) *Classroom-Based In-Service Teacher Education: The Development and Evaluation of a Client-Centred Model*, University of Sussex Education Area, Occasional Paper 9.

Delamont, S. (1984) 'The old girl network: reflections on the fieldwork at St. Luke's', in Burgess, R.G. (ed.) (1984).

Ditton, J. (1977) *Part-Time Crime: An Ethnography of Fiddling and Pilferage*, London, Macmillan.

Eggleston, J., Galton, M. and Jones, M. (1975) *A Science Teaching Observation Schedule*, London, Macmillan.

Elliott, J. (1991) *Action Research for Educational Change*, Milton Keynes, Open University Press.

Festinger, L., Riecken, H. and Schachter, S. (1956) *When Prophecy Fails*, Minnesota, MN, University of Minnesota Press.

Fielding, N. (1982) 'Observational research on the National Front', in Bulmer, M. (ed.) (1982).

Flanders, N. (1970) *Analysing Teaching Behavior*, Reading, MA, Addison Wesley.

Foster, P. (1989) *Policy and Practice in Multicultural and Anti-Racist Education: A Case Study of a Multi-Ethnic Comprehensive School*, PhD thesis, Open University.

Foster, P. (1990) *Policy and Practice in Multicultural and Anti-Racist Education: A Case Study of a Multi-Ethnic Comprehensive School*, London, Routledge.

Freeman, D. (1984) *Margaret Mead and Samoa: The Making and Unmaking of an Anthropological Myth*, Harmondsworth, Penguin.

French, J. and French, P. (1984) 'Gender imbalances in the primary classoom: an interactional account', *Educational Research*, vol. 26, no. 2, pp.127–36.

Galton, M., Simon, B. and Croll, P. (1980) *Inside the Primary Classroom*, London, Routledge and Kegan Paul (extract reproduced in Offprints Booklet 3).

Gillborn, D. (1990) *'Race', Ethnicity and Education*, London, Unwin Hyman.

Glaser, B. and Strauss, A. (1967) *The Discovery of Grounded Theory*, Chicago, IL, Aldine.

Glaser, B. and Strauss, A. (1968) *Time for Dying*, Chicago, IL, Aldine.

Goffman, E. (1959) *The Presentation of Self in Everyday Life*, New York, Doubleday.

Gold, R.L. (1958) 'Roles in sociological fieldwork', *Social Forces*, vol. 36, pp.217–23.

Green, P.A. (1983) *Teachers' Influence on the Self-Concept of Pupils of Different Ethnic Origins*, unpublished PhD thesis, University of Durham.

Hammersley, M. (1979) 'Data collection in ethnographic research', Part 3 in Block 4 of *DE304 Research Methods in Education and the Social Sciences*, Milton Keynes, Open University Press.

Hammersley, M. (1980) *A Peculiar World? Teaching and Learning in an Inner City School*, unpublished PhD thesis, University of Manchester.

Hammersley, M. (1990) *Reading Ethnographic Research: A Critical Guide*, London, Longman.

Hammersley, M. (ed.) (1993) *Social Research: Philosophy, Politics and Practice*, London, Sage (DEH313 Reader).

Hammersley, M. and Atkinson, P. (1983) *Ethnography: Principles in Practice*, London, Tavistock.

Haney, C., Banks, C. and Zimbardo, P. (1973) 'A study of prisoners and guards in a simulated prison', *Naval Research Reviews*, vol. 30, no. 9, pp. 4–17.

Hannerz, U. (1970) *Soulside: Inquiries into Ghetto Culture and Community*, New York, Columbia University Press.

Hargreaves, A. (1981) 'Contrastive rhetoric and extremist talk: teachers, hegemony and the educationist context', in Barton, L. and Walker, S. (eds) *Schools, Teachers and Teaching*, Lewes, Falmer Press.

Hobbs, D. (1988) *Doing the Business: Entrepreneurship, the Working Class, and Detectives in East London*, Oxford, Clarendon Press.

Holdaway, S. (1983) *Inside the British Police: A Force at Work*, Oxford, Basil Blackwell.

Homan, R. (1980) 'The ethics of covert methods', *British Journal of Sociology*, vol. 31, no. 1, pp.46–59.

Homan, R. and Bulmer, M. (1982) 'On the merits of covert methods: a dialogue', in Bulmer, M. (ed.) (1982).

Hopkins, D. (1985) *A Teacher's Guide to Classroom Research*, Milton Keynes, Open University Press.

Humphreys, L. (1970) *Tearoom Trade*, Chicago, IL, Aldine.

Hunt, J. (1984) 'The development of rapport through the negotiation of gender in fieldwork amongst the police', *Human Organization*, vol. 43, pp.283–96.

Hustler, D., Cassidy, T. and Cuff, I. (eds) (1986) *Action Research in Classrooms and Schools*, London, Allen and Unwin.

Junker, B. (1960) *Field Work*, Chicago, IL, University of Chicago Press.

King, R. (1978) *All Things Bright and Beautiful? A Sociological Study of Infant Classrooms*, Chichester, Wiley.

King, R. (1984) 'The man in the Wendy House: researching infants' schools', in Burgess, R.G. (ed.) (1984).

Lacey, C. (1970) *Hightown Grammar: The School as a Social System*, Manchester, Manchester University Press.

Lacey, C. (1976) 'Problems of sociological fieldwork: a review of the methodology of "Hightown Grammar"', in Shipman, M. (ed.) *The Organization and Impact of Social Research*, London, Routledge and Kegan Paul.

Lofland, L.H. (1973) *A World of Strangers: Order and Action in Urban Public Space*, New York, Basic Books.

Malinowski, B. (1922) *Argonauts of the Western Pacific*, London, Routledge and Kegan Paul.

Marsh, P., Rosser, E. and Harré, R. (1978) *The Rules of Disorder*, London, Routledge and Kegan Paul.

Mead, M. (1943) *Coming of Age in Samoa*, Harmondsworth, Penguin.

Measor, L. and Woods, P. (1984) *Changing Schools*, Milton Keynes, Open University Press.

Middlemist, R.D., Knowles, E.S. and Matter, C.F. (1976) 'Personal space invasions in the lavatory: suggestive evidence for arousal', *Journal of Personality and Social Psychology*, vol. 33, pp.541–6.

Milgram, S. (1974) *Obedience to Authority: An Experimental View*, London, Tavistock.

Parker, H.J. (1974) *View From the Boys: A Sociology of Downtown Adolescents*, London, David and Charles.

Patrick, J. (1973) *A Glasgow Gang Observed*, London, Eyre Methuen.

Pellegrini, A.D. (1989) 'Elementary school children's rough and tumble play', *Early Childhood Research Quarterly*, vol. 4, pp.245–60.

Pellegrini, A.D. (1991) *Applied Child Study: A Developmental Approach*, Hillsdale, NJ, Lawrence Erlbaum.

Pryce, K. (1979) *Endless Pressure*, Harmondsworth, Penguin.

Punch, M. (1979) *Policing the Inner City: A Study of Amsterdam's Warmoesstraat*, London, Macmillan.

Punch, M. (1979) 'Observation and the police: the research experience', in Hammersley, M. (ed.) (1993) (DEH313 Reader).

Reiss, A.J. (1971) *The Police and the Public*, New Haven, CT, Yale University Press.

Rex, J. and Tomlinson, S. (1979) *Colonial Immigrants in a British City*, London, Routledge and Kegan Paul.

Rosenhan, D.L. (1982) 'On being sane in insane places', in Bulmer, M. (ed.) (1982).

Rubinstein, J. (1973) *City Police*, New York, Ballantine.

Rutter, M., Maughan, B., Mortimore, P. and Ouston, J. (1979) *Fifteen Thousand Hours: Secondary Schools and Their Effects on Children*, London, Open Books.

Scarth, J. and Hammersley, M. (1986) 'Questioning ORACLE', *Educational Research*, vol. 28, no. 3, pp. 174–84.

Scarth, J. and Hammersley, M. (1987) 'More questioning of ORACLE', *Educational Research*, vol. 29, no. 1, pp.37–46.

Scherer, K.R. and Ekman, P. (eds) (1982) *Handbook of Methods in Nonverbal Behaviour Research*, Cambridge, Cambridge University Press.

Sissons, M. (1981) 'Race, sex and helping behaviour', *British Journal of Social Psychology*, vol. 20, no. 4, pp.285–92.

Spencer, G. (1973) 'Methodological issues in the study of bureaucratic elites: a case study of West Point', *Social Problems*, vol. 21, no. 1, pp.90–103.

Stacey, M. (1960) *Tradition and Change: A Study of Banbury*, Oxford, Oxford University Press.

Stenhouse, L. (1984) 'Library access, library use and user education in academic sixth forms: an autobiographical account', in Burgess, R.G. (ed.) (1984).

Taylor, L. (1984) *In the Underworld*, Oxford, Basil Blackwell.

Tizard, B. and Hughes, M. (1984) *Young Children Learning: Talking and Thinking at Home and School*, London, Fontana.

Tizard, B. and Hughes, M. (1991) 'Reflections on young children learning', in Walford, G. (ed.) *Doing Educational Research*, London, Routledge.

Vietze, P.M., Abernathy, S.R., Ashe, M.L. and Faulstich, G. (1978) 'Contingency interactions between mothers and their developmentally delayed infants', in Sackett, G.P. (ed.) *Observing Behaviour, Vol. 1 Theory and Applications in Mental Retardation*, Baltimore, MA, University Park Press.

Walford, G. (1991) 'Researching the City Technology College, Kinghurst', in Walford, G. (ed.) *Doing Educational Research*, London, Routledge.

Walford, G. and Miller, H. (1991) *City Technology College*, Milton Keynes, Open University Press.

Warren, C. (1988) *Gender Issues in Field Research*, Beverly Hills, CA, Sage.

Whyte, W. (1981) *Street Corner Society: The Social Structure of an Italian Slum*, 3rd edn, Chicago, IL, University of Chicago Press.

Williams, J., Dunning, E. and Murphy, P. (1984) *Hooligans Abroad*, London, Routledge and Kegan Paul.

Willis, P. (1977) *Learning to Labour: How Working Class Kids Get Working Class Jobs*, Aldershot, Gower.

Woods, P. (1979) *The Divided School*, London, Routledge and Kegan Paul.

ACKNOWLEDGEMENTS

Grateful acknowledgement is made to the following sources for permission to reproduce material in this unit:

TEXT

Croll, P. (1986) *Systematic Classroom Observation*, Falmer Press.

FIGURE

Figure 1: adapted from Junker, B.H. (1960) *Field Work*, University of Chicago Press. © 1960 by the University of Chicago. All rights reserved.

TABLE

Table 1: Flanders, N. (1970) *Analysing Teaching Behavior*, Addison-Wesley, © Ned A. Flanders.

UNIT 13 DOCUMENTARY SOURCES, STATISTICAL RECORDS AND DATA BASES

Prepared for the Course Team by Ruth Finnegan and Ray Thomas[1]

CONTENTS

Associated study materials		88
1	**Introduction and preview**	89
2	**The importance of existing information**	90
3	**Statistics as facts about society**	91
4	**Problems in usage**	94
	4.1 Unemployment	95
	4.2 Homelessness	96
	4.3 Poverty	97
	4.4 Limited but indispensable	98
5	**Documentary sources**	98
	5.1 The nature of documentary sources: some initial distinctions	102
	Primary versus secondary sources	102
	'Direct' and 'indirect' uses of documentary sources	103
	5.2 How do documentary sources come into being?	103
	5.3 Summary of some further questions to ask	106
	5.4 Some final points	111
6	**The impact of new technology**	112
	6.1 Access to online data bases	112
	6.2 Secondary analysis and microdata	113
	6.3 Local availability of administrative data	114
	6.4 Geographical information systems	115
	6.5 Optical storage	115
	6.6 Implications of technological developments for social research	116
7	**Conclusion**	118
Answers to activities		119
References		120

---

[1] Ruth Finnegan, Sections 1 and 5; Ray Thomas, Sections 2–4, 6 and 7.

UNIT 13 SOURCES, RECORDS AND DATA BASES

ASSOCIATED STUDY MATERIALS

Reader, Chapter 12, 'Research analysis of administrative records', by Catherine Hakim.

Offprints Booklet 3, 'Measures of unemployment: the claimant count and the Labour Force Survey', by John Lawlor and Chris Kennedy.

1 INTRODUCTION AND PREVIEW

Interviews, questionnaires, observation and experiments — the forms discussed so far — are all important sources of data in social and educational research, and widely drawn on by researchers. But they do *not* comprise all the forms of information gathering, despite what is sometimes implied in 'methods' textbooks. Existing sources, whether in writing, figures, or electronic form, are also important bases for research. They can function both to supplement information from other sources and to be themselves the main source for the researcher's conclusions.

Some understanding of the use of such sources is highly relevant for the aims of this course in three main ways:

- First, documentary and related sources form a major source of data in social research. This type of source is often played down, perhaps because, since it is shared with a number of other disciplines, it may not seem quite so distinctive of the social sciences as data generated through questionnaires, surveys, or experiments. However, social researchers have in fact built extensively on the existence of such sources as government reports, official and unofficial records, private papers, and statistical collections. As with the other forms of information gathering discussed in this block, these sources have both advantages and limitations, and they can be used well or badly.

- Secondly, the use of existing sources comes in at various stages of the research process (in so far, that is, as these stages are separable). One phase is that of the preliminary 'literature search'. This usually comes near the start of any research endeavour and so is not highlighted in this unit which is concerned primarily with the 'data collection and construction' phase. However, there is frequently some overlap between these phases if only because existing sources are not only a source of data for producing research findings in the first place, but are also commonly used for their criticism, or for further development later. Thus, they are doubly important in assessing research.

- The third point recalls a theme that will by now be familiar in the course: that is, these sources are not neutral asocial data whose import is necessarily self-evident. Their selection and interpretation are affected not only by practical constraints like access or timing but also by the researcher's aims and viewpoint. As you will see, this theme needs to be further extended into the question of how the sources themselves come into being. Since there can be selection and interpretation here too, a piece of research building on documentary sources needs to be judged (among other things) by how carefully the researcher considers and explains these aspects of the sources.

This unit is designed to amplify these points. That is, it will: give examples of the use of existing sources in research; explain and analyse the nature of documentary sources and their usage by researchers; comment on the implications for assessing research and for further appreciating the nature of research processes and their assessment. It will thus contribute to and reinforce the *general* objectives of Block 3 (including awareness of the 'constructed' nature of data, and of the practicalities and politics of the research process more generally), and fill what would otherwise be a gap in coverage by complementing the stress on observation and interviews in earlier units by attention to existing sources as data.

It is worth noting at the outset that although the phrase 'documentary sources' obviously was first used to refer to sources in the form of written documents (still one prime meaning of the term and a leading form of existing source material), it is nowadays sometimes widened to include other existing sources, such as radio or film material which are neither primarily in writing nor in 'documents' in the traditional sense. Both in this unit and elsewhere you will encounter both senses.

Indeed the ambiguity is not without its uses, in reminding us that existing sources comprise materials of many different kinds. Most consist of words or numbers, and these sources figure largely in this unit (the latter particularly elaborated in Sections 3 and 4). But there are also such forms as maps, charts and photographs; and audio or video sources are now increasingly exploited as well. The medium for their storage, transmission and consultation also varies. Some are in manuscript, others published in print. Some are on paper, others on microfilm or microfiche, in audio-visual media or (increasingly important and discussed directly in this unit) in electronic form.

The aims of the unit could, therefore, be summarized as follows:

1 To complement the discussion of the use of other kinds of data earlier in the block by describing the nature and use of existing sources of data and their relevance for the evaluation of research.

2 To highlight the relevance for the assessment of research of enquiring into the nature of the existing sources being relied on.

3 To draw attention to the importance of an informed and critical awareness of the constructed nature of documentary and related sources for understanding and evaluating research.

4 To provide an opportunity for applying the above to the aims of the course (and in particular to the critical evaluation of research using these types of sources) and for reflecting on the principles involved.

2 THE IMPORTANCE OF EXISTING INFORMATION

> The first rule for understanding the human condition is that men live in second-hand worlds; they are aware of much more than they have personally experienced; and their own experience is always indirect. No man stands alone confronting a world of solid facts ... In their everyday lives the experience of men is itself selected by stereotyped meanings, and shaped by ready-made interpretations. Their images of the world ... are given to them by crowds of witnesses they have never met and never will meet. Yet for every man these images — provided by strangers and dead men — are the very basis of his life as a human being. For most of what men call solid fact, sound interpretation, suitable presentation, every man is increasingly dependent on the observation posts, the interpretation centres, presentation depots, which in contemporary society are established by means of what I am going to call the cultural apparatus.
>
> (C. Wright Mills, *The Cultural Apparatus,* a radio talk given on the BBC Third programme, March 1959)

Knowledge derived from existing sources of information influences the conduct of research in various specific ways. A search for relevant literature, for example, will often be made and the research hypothesis and the design may be modified in the light of the results of that search. Existing sources may also be used directly. A research study will often, for example, use a sampling frame in aiming to be representative of a particular population. That frame is usually derived from preexisting administrative records.

The specific influences which existing information have on research may not be as important as the general influences. Existing sources of information are important in that research is conducted within a particular social context. Research is itself created, shaped, and evaluated in the light of existing sources of information, mediated by what Wright Mills described as the cultural apparatus. The focus of any research is largely determined by the perceptions of those conducting the research. These perceptions do not derive from any truly 'independent' position. They may reflect support for the prevailing cultural patterns, or they may reflect dissatisfaction with some aspects of the prevailing cultural patterns. But these perceptions cannot escape from the prevailing cultural patterns which are themselves the product of existing sources of information.

The *findings* of research may step outside prevailing cultural patterns. But the report of the research can be expected to relate the findings to the stock of knowledge represented by existing information. This process usually puts the new findings in context, and helps make the findings intelligible to a wider audience than would otherwise understand or appreciate their significance. The work of the 'observation post', to use Wright Mills' phrases, is supplemented by that of the 'interpretation centres' and 'presentation depots'.

In a similar way existing sources of information are important from the point of view of the user of research reports and so are specially important from the point of view of this course. Consistency with the evidence available from existing sources of information is also one of the criteria used in assessing the value of research reports.

3 STATISTICS AS FACTS ABOUT SOCIETY

The variety of sources of information on human activity is almost unlimited. Any artefact, or evidence of artefact, can be used as evidence about human behaviour and is a potential source of information. The science of archaeology, which focuses on the remains of past cultures, provides evidence which can also be used by the social scientist. The invention of writing enabled the creation of descriptive records of human activity. The invention of printing multiplied the copies available and hence the possibilities of obtaining evidence from such accounts. The mass media, including printing, radio, and TV, multiplied beyond what could previously have been imagined the volume of evidence which can be used to inform, misinform and, by selection of evidence, influence social research. The growth of organizations has been associated with the creation of a wide variety of written records and statistical records pertaining to human activity — as is emphasized by Hakim's article associated with this unit (which you will be asked to read in Section 5).

All these sources of data are part of the 'second-hand world' identified by Wright Mills in the quotation above. Of these sources statistics, as facts about society, are most commonly used by social researchers.

In other parts of this course and elsewhere the term 'statistics' is commonly used to refer to statistical method. You should note that in this unit the term 'statistics' *as facts about society* is used in contradistinction to the term 'statistical method'.

Statistics as facts about society are commonly referred to as official statistics. Most statistics are collected by government agencies. But the degree to which they are 'official' varies. Some, like vital statistics, are the by-product of administrative processes, in this case the statutory registration process for births, marriages, and deaths. Others, like many of the surveys conducted by the Office of Population Censuses and Surveys, are based on the collection of data by voluntary interview, on much the same lines (and sometimes using the same interviewers) as market research or public opinion surveys.

Many other agencies produce statistics as facts about society (see Keynote, 1989; Mort and Siddall, 1985, for details). The mass media, for example, produce their own statistics. Statistics on the size of audiences for TV programmes — the ratings

— are just the best known example. There are half-a-dozen organizations devoted to the conduct of market research and social surveys through home interviews, which include the opinion pollsters ('If there were an election tomorrow how would you vote?', etc.), and worthy of special mention (see Table 1 below) is Social and Community Planning Research (SCPR) — a non-profit making organization which has been conducting attitude surveys on a wide range of topics every year since 1983.

The collection processes involved in gathering most of these statistics follow systematic procedures which give the statistics reliability. Many of them are collected on a regular monthly, quarterly, or annual basis. The resulting time series provide a check of reliability. Statistics are also accessible. Details of the range of governmental statistics are published in a boring but indispensable work of reference called the *Guide to Official Statistics* (Central Statistical Office). The results of the collection process are published in aggregate form in a wide range of publications — mostly, but not exclusively — published by Her Majesty's Stationery Office.

The biggest single collection of facts about British society, or about any advanced industrial society, constitute what are generally called economic statistics or national income statistics. These statistics cover such topics as consumer expenditure, industrial output and investment, international trade and the balance of payments, prices, and employment, etc. These statistics can be regarded as administrative tools for managing the economy and for co-ordinating levels of government spending with revenue from taxation. When, and usually only when, these economic statistics relate directly to human activities, such as the statistics for employment and unemployment, do they become of special and direct interest to the social researcher.

Another major category of facts about British society is obtained from social surveys of various kinds. An indication of the richness of data available is illustrated in Table 1 which lists nine major surveys (based mainly on household interviews) most of which are carried out annually and which cover nearly all important areas of human activity in the UK. These nine surveys represent only a fraction of the total range of available statistical facts about society obtained through the conduct of surveys. But each of these nine surveys is of sufficient importance to be of interest to most social researchers.

These surveys cover where people live and where they used to live, their nationality and ethnic group, how people live in terms of household composition, people's sources of income, their patterns of expenditure (especially on food), their health, their education and qualifications, employment and occupational status and how these may have changed, their ownership of cars and other consumer durables, their travel patterns, the crimes they have suffered from, their voting intentions at the next election, and their attitudes on almost every subject under the sun. The only major area of human activity missed out in this catalogue is that of sexual activity. This defect will be remedied before this unit is printed, in part as a consequence of increased public concern about the dangers of AIDS (as anticipated by Wadsworth and Johnson, 1991).

The summary results of the surveys listed in Table 1 are available in published volumes, but researchers can also get access to the microdata on which they are based through the ESRC (Economic and Social Research Council) Data Archive at the University of Essex and through other agencies (see Section 6 for further discussion).

It is difficult to generalize about the myriad other kinds of administrative and survey statistics. Administrative statistics include population and vital statistics which could be considered as the basis for most social research, and a host of other administrative statistics collected by governmental and non-governmental organizations. The number of applications made to an organization, the number of cases notified, incidents reported, individuals employed, interviews conducted, licences issued, tickets sold, etc., are commonly recorded as part of the day-to-day activities of an organization. These figures are often collated and processed to create statistical series which can become valuable evidence to the social researcher.

Table 1 Selected major surveys in the UK

Survey and frequency	Sample size	Main topics covered
Census of population: decennially since 1801	20 million households. Self-completed	Usual residence/visitors. Household composition, housing, occupation, work place, car ownership
National Food Survey: annually since 1940	8,000 households	Quantities and value of food purchased
Family Expenditure Survey: annually since 1953–4	12,000 households	Expenditure patterns. Household composition. Income: from all sources
National Travel Survey: 1965, 1972/3, 1975/6, 1978/9 and 1985/6	26,000 individuals	Travel by all means of transport including walking and cycling
General Household Survey: annually since 1971	20,000 individuals in 10,000 households	Topics have included education, employment, fertility, health, housing, income, and migration
Labour Force Survey: started 1973, biennially until 1983, annually since; quarterly from 1992 (standard EEC survey)	60,000 households	Employment, unemployment, housing, nationality, ethnic groups
British Crime Survey: 1981, 1985 and 1988	16,000 individuals	Crimes whether reported or not. Attitudes to crime and the police
The Longitudinal Study: started on sample of 1971 Census	'1%' of total population	Changes in marital status, employment, housing tenure, qualification, etc.
British Social Attitudes Survey: annually since 1983. Conducted by SCPR, funded by Sainsbury, etc.	3,000 individuals	Attitudes on enterprise, the family, health, unions, welfare, etc. International comparisons
Opinion polls: irregular, but frequent when possibility of an election. Conducted by Gallup, Mori, NOP, etc., financed by newspapers	Typically 700 to 1,500	Voting intentions. Attitudes on any topic

Survey based statistics include a host of *ad hoc* as well as regularly conducted surveys. A significant but unknown proportion of these are conducted by central government. The government's Survey Control Unit reports about a hundred different surveys each quarter. A recent list illustrates the range and variety. It includes titles such as The Nature of the Demand for Housing in Rural Areas, Discipline in Scottish Schools, Consumer Views of the Attendance Allowance Medical Examination, Survey of Undergraduate Attitudes to Careers, and Pedestrian Reaction to New Signals at Traffic Lights.

Surveys are also conducted by many larger organizations in the public and private sectors. Social research conducted by academics commonly involves the conduct of surveys which produce facts about society. Most of these surveys are published. The results of many of them are also deposited in the ESRC Data Archive.

ACTIVITY 1

What are the main factors which distinguish the surveys listed in Table 1 from other social surveys?

What are the main differences between survey statistics and administrative statistics?

4 PROBLEMS IN USAGE

The major problem in using many of these statistics is that they have been produced in order to serve governmental and other organizational purposes — or that the way they are produced echoes the character of statistics produced for governmental and other organizational purposes (see Thomas, 1984, for further discussion of the function of statistics). The concepts, definitions and data-collection processes used in the production of these statistics are commonly determined by the purpose the statistics serve and the functions of the organizations which are their primary users. These concepts, definitions, purposes and functions are part of a world created by the needs of the machinery of government and the management of organizations.

Where the researcher is concerned with the activities of government and other organizations, as many researchers are, the world created by statistics has to be taken into account in the conduct and reporting of research. However, existing statistics, even where they are related to social rather than organizational matters, are likely to be most closely related to the problems of the past. They are unlikely to focus squarely on current social concerns or current social research.

Sociologists use the term 'social construction' to describe the ways in which language, knowledge, and evidence of all kinds is seen as created by society (Berger and Luckman, 1966). The process of social construction commonly involves interaction between different parties. Such interaction is less common in the production of statistics. It is more appropriate to view statistics as being *organizationally* rather than socially constructed (Hindess, 1973; Irvine *et al.*, 1979). A view from some of those who actually produce the statistics is that:

> It is extremely difficult, if not impossible, to make a really radical criticism of society using available statistical sources, which imprison us in the concepts and concerns which dominate official and political and economic life.
>
> (Government Statisticians' Collective, 1979, also reproduced in the Reader)

The collectors and many users of these organizational statistics have no problem in defending them in terms of the correspondence theory of the truth (as outlined in Unit 1/2). The sceptics' criticism that the definitions used in the statistics have no real-world justification is met with the reply that, in the collection of statistics, decisions have to be taken as to where the boundary line is drawn, and that line is often somewhat arbitrary. The criticism could well be countered with an offer to produce the statistics using a different definition if that definition is considered less arbitrary. The sceptics' criticism that the statistics do not fully correspond with reality would be acknowledged. The reality out there, the producers of the statistics might say, is highly complex — involving thousands of individuals each of whom is unique. But the organizational reality is limited to the responsibilities and power of the organization. The statistics aim to capture that slice of reality which is relevant to the responsibilities and power of the organization. More than that would be to attempt, unnecessarily, to take into account aspects of the life of individuals which are not the proper concern of government or any other organization.

A widespread influence on many statistics as facts about society derives from governmental responsibilities for the management of the economy. These responsibilities favour the collection of statistics on what is usually called the formal sector of the economy (see, for example, the annual publication from the CSO, *National Income and Expenditure* — the 'Blue book'). In the context of national income statistics words and terms acquire meanings which are significantly different from their meaning in day-to-day speech and in non-economics literature (see, CSO, 1985, *UK National Accounts — Sources and Methods*). Thus economic activity is defined in terms which requires a financial transaction. Employment means only paid employment. Value means money value. Investment refers only to physical or paper assets.

4.1 UNEMPLOYMENT

The ways in which governmental functions are expressed in statistical form are exceptionally well documented in the case of statistics of unemployment (as was indicated in Unit 5). Governments need statistics for the number of unemployed for two sets of purposes. Unemployment statistics are used as an economic indicator of short-term changes in the state of the labour market for monitoring of the economy on a month to month basis. Unemployment statistics are also useful as an input to longer term planning — such as the provision of training facilities, identifying unused labour supply, and forecasting future levels of unemployment.

For the former purpose the definition used is a count of claimants — number of individuals applying to draw unemployment pay. This statistic is compiled from computerized administrative records and is available monthly within a few weeks of collection. For the latter purposes the definition used is that of the International Labour Office (ILO) which is designed to identify individuals who would like to be in paid employment, who have taken some step within the past month to get employment, and who would be available to take up employment within two weeks. These definitions often give a measure for the total number of unemployed which is similar in size. But this similarity disguises the extent of differences in definition. A lot of individuals who are counted as unemployed according to the count of claimants are not included in the ILO definition of unemployed, and a lot of individuals who are included in the ILO definition are not counted as claimants.

READING AND ACTIVITY 2

Study the article reproduced in Offprints Booklet 3 on 'Measures of unemployment' which compares the statistics of the count of claimants and those produced by the Labour Force Survey (LFS) based on the ILO definitions.

Make a list of the major categories included in one set of the statistics and not in the other. Write a few words on each category describing the relevant characteristics of those included.

The count of claimants and the ILO definition of being unemployed both serve the UK government's responsibilities for management of the economy and belong to the discourse of national income statistics. They are both organizationally constructed definitions of unemployment which are dependent upon a definition of employment which is narrower than the historic and everyday use which would commonly be given to the term (or its synonyms such as 'work' or 'occupation'). It would not be valid to use these statistics for investigation related to forms of employment which are not classified as in the formal economy. It is not valid to use these statistics in ways which attach meanings to paid employment and unpaid employment of kinds other than the fact that one is paid and the other is not.

A student, a mother with young children, any individual who 'keeps house' for others, a son or daughter whose full-time job is as a carer for an elderly parent all have employment in the traditional sense of the word. But activities of these kinds are not counted as employment in the statistics. Even where, for example, an individual is paid an attendance allowance for caring for a relative with a disability, that individual does not count as employed because the payment is not part of a contract between employer and employee.

Statistics of unemployment (and employment) are of limited validity for investigation of related areas such as the numbers engaged in child rearing. In the discourse of national income statistics child rearing is usually classified as in the informal economy. Statistics showing the growth in recent decades of working mothers, and statistics showing the growth of individuals employed in child caring activities, cannot be regarded as indicating an increase in employment in the everyday sense of the word. Such statistics show growth in the numbers who are employed formally on a contractual basis. But that growth is to some degree at the expense of those who would otherwise be employed informally in child rearing. The statistics indicate extension of the formal economy into the informal economy.

Broadly parallel considerations apply to statistics relating to employment of older workers. Walker (1991) points out that the proportion of men aged 65 or over who were classified as retired increased from under 0.5 per cent in 1931 to 78 per cent in 1971. The numbers in paid employment, it can be assumed, declined equally dramatically in the same period. But it is difficult to believe that such a statistic accurately reflects changes in the 'employment' of older men where 'employment' is defined in a less tight and restrictive way.

It is worth noting that the use of statistics in this context of older workers has played a part in creating a culture of dependence. The increase in the dependent retired population has been engineered in the interests of the formal economy. A desire to reduce unemployment as measured by the official statistics, and a desire to increase productivity by removal from the labour force of those with traditional skills and relatively low marginal productivity, have combined to encourage the growth of retirement.

The official statistics of unemployment, to summarize, give a rich picture of an individual's relationship to economic activity as defined by national income statistics. But they are misleading or irrelevant in what they say of the significance of the work or other kinds of activity that people do or might wish to do. Broadly speaking the official statistics are valid only for investigation of areas relevant to economic growth as conventionally defined.

4.2 HOMELESSNESS

The management of the economy is an organizational purpose which determines or influences the nature of many kinds of statistics. A variety of other kinds of organizational purposes also determine the nature of many statistics. Statistics of homelessness, for example, provide a parallel example to those of unemployment in that there are two series which serve different organizational purposes.

The official statistics for homelessness are those produced by local authorities. In order to be counted as homeless for inclusion in these statistics an individual or family must have some claim to living in the area, they must be within a social group for which the authority accepts housing responsibility, and they must not be 'intentionally' homeless. The other main set of statistics available is those collected by voluntary agencies which count the number of individuals and families in hostels for the homeless and people sleeping rough.

Each of these sets of statistics measures the number of homeless in accordance with the functions of the statistical collection agency. The official statistics enable central government to monitor the performance of local authorities in dealing with homelessness, and enable local authorities to monitor their own performance in dealing with the problems of homelessness. The statistics collected by voluntary agencies enable these organizations to estimate the extent and nature of manifestations of homelessness in their area and to make best use of the resources available to the different agencies involved (see, for example, Gardner and Stanyer, 1991).

Neither the official statistics nor the voluntary agencies attend to, or try to attend to, the host of different family and personal experiences which lead to homelessness. Both sets of statistics exclude living in overcrowded conditions, and people in bed and breakfast accommodation wanting to be rehoused. Conflicts which teenagers have with their parents, mental illness, marital breakdown, loss of job, release from prison, cuts in the local authority housing programme, house repossession, etc., are all among the factors which contribute to homelessness. Knowledge of crucial factors of these kinds is necessary to deal with individual cases and to describe the real extent of homelessness as a social problem. But these factors are not measured by the statistics.

4.3 POVERTY

Statistics of the numbers living in poverty can also be used to illustrate the limitations of statistical evidence. Two types of measures are commonly used nowadays for the numbers considered as living in poverty. One measure is derived from official criteria in that it is based on current levels of welfare payments made by central government. This measure counts the number of people living at or below a poverty line which is defined by levels of welfare payments. The second type measures poverty in relative terms. This measure counts the number of households and people living at or below, say, half of the average level of income. (See, for example, Oppenheim, 1990, for a summary of recent trends.)

There are difficulties with both of these types of measure (see Johnson and Webb, 1989). They are, for example, based on the family unit (in the case of measures based on welfare payments levels) or the household (in the case of UK statistics of relative poverty). They are not based on the individual, and the figures in effect assume a degree of equality or equity of incomes within the household which may not exist. There are also objections which are specific to each type of measure.

Government itself sometimes objects to the first type of measure because the numbers living in poverty is positively related to the level of welfare payments. If welfare payments are increased then the numbers in poverty increase as well. The objections to the second type of measure are similar. Relative measures are susceptible to changes which are independent of the levels of income of those classified as suffering from poverty. If the level of incomes of those with high income increases, this will increase the average level of incomes and hence the numbers living at or below half the average income will increase. The measure will show an increase in poverty even though the level of incomes in the lower half of the distribution may not have changed.

Neither of these objections can be seriously sustained. The level of welfare payments can be presumed to be the result of proper governmental processes, and in a democratic society the legitimate result of community decision making. As such the level of welfare payments constitutes an authorized criterion for deciding where to draw the line. It is equally easy to defend the use of a relative standard of poverty. When goods such as cars, television sets and telephones are available to the majority of households they establish what is regarded as normal, and they lessen the availability of alternative means of transport, entertainment and communication. Those who do not have access to goods and services which are regarded as the norm suffer from deprivation.

Peter Townsend's seminal work *Poverty in the United Kingdom* (1972), largely based on statistics produced from specially designed surveys, demonstrates the multidimensional character of poverty. Like unemployment and homelessness, poverty is not a condition which can adequately be summarized by any single measure or criterion. Exactly where to draw the line between households in poverty and other households is unavoidably arbitrary. But any estimate of the numbers in poverty which is useful for making comparisons between different areas, for different groups, or over time, has to be based on a limited number of criteria. The level of welfare payments and the level of half-average income constitute defendable criteria to use. The objections to these criteria, and the answers to these objections, illustrate the limitations which are unavoidable with any statistics for the numbers living in poverty.

4.4 LIMITED BUT INDISPENSABLE

The weaknesses of statistics as facts about society discussed in this section and illustrated by reference to unemployment, homelessness and poverty should be seen as indicating significant limitations in the use of statistics for social research. However, these limitations should not be regarded as a dismissal of the value to social research of statistics as facts about society. The value of statistics to the social researcher can be as great as the value to an organization. Statistics can give reliable evidence of the world which is outside the direct experience of the researcher as well as that which is outside the direct experience of members of the government or the managers of organizations. That evidence contributes to the effective functioning of governmental and other organizations. The statistics help to define the goals of government and the purpose of organizations, and they enable government and other organizations to monitor their own performance.

In similar ways statistics can provide an indispensable background for research designed to obtain new information. They provide a check on the reality of assumptions in the mind of the social researcher. They provide a framework within which the findings of new research can be presented in a research report. And they can provide yardsticks which can contribute to the evaluation of research reports.

5 DOCUMENTARY SOURCES

So far the focus has been on the use of documentary sources mainly in numerical form — statistics as sources of facts about society which, as Bulmer (1980) points out, have been neglected by many sociologists. This section moves on to consider some further principles for evaluating existing sources as data, this time with the main focus on documentary sources in the traditional sense of textual documents which are written (or otherwise reproduced typographically) largely in the form of *words*. (As you will see, this needs some qualification as we go along, but for the moment we will let it stand.)

There is a reason for taking mainly *written* texts as the primary focus here. Written documents exist in huge numbers in our society, both of a private or personal kind and in the form of what Hakim refers to as 'administrative records':

> Vast quantities of information are collated and recorded by organizations and individuals for their own purposes, well beyond the data collected by social scientists purely for research purposes.
> (Hakim, 1987, also reproduced in the Reader, p.131)

Indeed, both the proliferation of written records and communicating through writing more generally are widely seen as major features of modern society. Some scholars would go so far as to regard them as *the* defining attributes of Western industrial cultures, whether because of the (arguably) central role of print in our modern consciousness or through the development of modern bureaucracy with its reliance on written rules and administrative records (for some of the arguments on this see Goody, 1986 and Finnegan, 1988). However you react to these theories, it is certainly a fact that writing is one dominant medium in our culture for the storage, dissemination and retrieval of information. There may indeed be problems in using written sources — as with any method — but they can and do provide a wealth of information for social researchers.

Something of their variety can be judged in the paper by Catherine Hakim on research in the sphere of administrative records alone, i.e. only one category among many others.

READING AND ACTIVITY 3

Read the paper by Catherine Hakim, 'Research analysis of administrative records', reproduced as Chapter 12 in the Reader. As you do so, you will find it useful to bear the following questions in mind and make brief notes for your answers. For my comments see the end of this unit and also the discussion that follows.

1. How does Hakim define 'administrative records' and what examples does she give?

2. How does she consider that data collection based on administrative records differs from survey or experimental research in (a) its design and (b) its issues.

3. What practical issues does Hakim raise in relation to the case of administrative records as sources?

4. Hakim concentrates on administrative records. Are there other forms of existing documentary sources that researchers might wish to use as sources?

5. The main focus in Hakim's paper is on records that are reproduced and consulted in basically written/typographic form — as texts in the traditional sense of the term. Are there other possible forms?

6. Why should someone interested in the critical assessment of social research need to interest themselves in existing documentary sources?

Hakim's account concentrates only on 'administrative records' in the sense of collections of documents of (mainly) factual information, largely compiled and used by organizations. These are, it is true, extremely important and commonly used sources in social research to which anyone evaluating social research is likely to need to give some attention. However, there are other forms of a less 'official' and organizational nature, such as diaries, newspapers, memoirs, letters or works of reference. Indeed some sources to be found even within organizations are of a more discursive, qualitative and personal nature than emerges in Hakim's paper. All these sources too can be — and are — at times exploited by social researchers.

Such sources can be classified in a number of different ways. Table 2 gives one possible summary which, even if the details are open to contention (you can see a different classification in Unit 22, for example), can still serve to illustrate something of their variety.

It will be clear from this what a vast resource is provided by sources (most of them written) and the role they can play in the data-collection process within social research: and hence the need to consider them, among other sources, in the evaluation of research.

Table 2 Summary of types of sources for the contemporary and recent UK

Standard and official sources

- Works of reference, e.g. *Whitaker's Almanack, Statesman's Year Book, Annual Abstract of Statistics, The Times Index, Keesing's Contemporary Archives, Who's Who, Annual Register of World Events*
- Government reports including (a) Parliamentary papers (i.e. all papers ordered by or laid before either House of Parliament and papers printed by command of the government, including Reports of Royal Commissions); and (b) non-command papers (e.g. reports of departmental committees)
- Statistical records, including the Census and the Registrar-General Reports (the decennial Census, and the annual Registrar-General's Statistical Review of England and Wales and Annual Report of the Registrar-General for Scotland). For further examples see Table 1
- Annual and special reports, local and unofficial, including reports by local Medical Officers of Health, and reports of companies, societies, schools, universities, political parties, trade unions, etc.
- Parliamentary debates (*Hansard*)
- Documents on foreign policy issued by, or with the co-operation of, the Foreign Office

Cabinet and other papers

- Cabinet records. Because of the '30 year rule' these cannot be consulted for the most recent period
- Other government documents. The same difficulty applies
- Private papers, e.g. private papers of politicians (many deposited in libraries throughout the country), trade unions or political parties

Memoirs, diaries and biographies

(These may be particularly useful for the period for which government records are closed by the '30 year rule')

- Biographies and autobiographies
- Diaries (not very many available)
- Memoirs (available in abundance: a sometimes informative but hazardous source to use)

Letters, contemporary writing

- Current affairs including works by journalists as well as by social scientists
- Social surveys, including public opinion polls, etc.
- Novels, poetry, plays (imaginative writing provides source material of a particular kind, more useful for answering some kinds of questions than others)
- Newspapers and other periodicals

Images, sounds and objects

- Film
- Photographs, maps and pictures
- Sound and video recordings (including audio- and video-cassettes; also programmes currently going out via radio and television and the records of these — if preserved — in the archives)
- Interviews, tape-recorded and other
- Museums and their contents
- History on the ground: townscapes, landscapes, aerial photographs, etc.

Computerized records

- Any one or more of the above stored or distributed electronically (e.g. the BBC 'Domesday' interactive video-disc; statistical records stored as computer data bases)

(Source: derived from Mowatt, 1971)

Not all existing sources follow the traditional model of written documents either. For one thing, paper with typographically set-out text is not the only medium for reproducing words. For another, modern technologies have made possible the storage and dissemination of sights and sounds other than traditional verbal texts: in radio for example, film, or photographs, and other categories listed under 'Images, sounds and objects' in Table 2. Varieties of documentary sources include:

- *Medium.* For example papyrus, parchment, stone, tape, cassette, microfilm/fiche, electronic.
- *Form.* Usually words/text and figures, but also other related forms: graphic, pictorial, audio, video and material; and all of these forms expressed in digital technology (as discussed in Section 6 below).

These other (non-written) forms and media are now common enough to be given the label of 'documentary' — as explained above, this is now an expanded sense of the originally more limited application to documents in writing. Whatever your reaction to this broad use of the term (which remains a little controversial, even though now quite widely used), it is certainly true that sources such as photographs, audio recordings of various kinds, film, or broadcasts are increasingly used as sources in social research. They also quite often appear in its final presentation.

As such it is not just written documents that need attention in our consideration of the use of sources in social research. In fact each of these examples really calls for a unit in its own right and in an ideal world would have had it. Unfortunately the structure of this course and the constraints it has to work within do not allow this. All is not lost however. It is true that each source has certain specific features of its own (some of which can be followed in, for example, Becker, 1974, 1981, which deal with photographs). However, many of the underlying principles used to assess these sources are the same as those for written sources. The following discussion therefore, though couched in terms of the traditional 'written-texts-in-documents' model has much of relevance for the critical analysis of audio-visual forms as well.

A final point that emerges from the Hakim reading is of particular relevance for our discussion here. This is her comment that where researchers rely on documentary sources for their data their methods have to be evaluated in rather a different way from that applied to research based on interviews, observation or experiment. As she puts it, researchers using documentary sources

> ... have to compile their own *post hoc* account of the procedures and methods used to compile ... the records on which a study is based. This account replaces the usual methodological report on how data were specially collected in other types of study ...
>
> (Hakim, 1987, also reproduced in the Reader, p.136)

Therefore to understand — and so be able to produce a critique of — the methodological procedures in document-based research we need to explore further something of the nature of documents and how they are compiled: how they come into being. Some of the basic principles at work here are considered in the rest of this section (further treatment of more specialist and advanced techniques for textual analysis is given in Unit 21).

5.1 THE NATURE OF DOCUMENTARY SOURCES: SOME INITIAL DISTINCTIONS

Let us start by looking at some distinctions both between different types of documentary sources and between different ways of using them. Both distinctions have their uses. They also, as we will see, have their limitations — and limitations which, in their turn, can be illuminating.

Primary versus secondary sources

When considering how researchers use documentary sources to collect and analyse evidence, one of the most commonly invoked distinctions is between 'primary' and 'secondary' sources. Historians and others conventionally regard as primary sources those that were written (or otherwise came into being) by the people directly involved and at a time contemporary or near contemporary with the period being investigated. Primary sources, in other words, form the basic and original material for providing the researcher's raw evidence. Secondary sources, by contrast, are those which discuss the period studied but are brought into being at some time after it, or otherwise somewhat removed from the actual events. Secondary sources copy, interpret or judge material to be found in primary sources. Thus the Magna Charta would be a primary source for the history of thirteenth-century England, while an account of thirteenth-century politics by a twentieth-century historian would be a secondary source. Both can be useful — but they are different. There are many possible controversies over detailed definition here, but by and large the distinction between primary and secondary material is widely accepted as a fundamental one, defined in terms of the 'contemporaneity' of the source and closeness to the origin of the data. True research, it is often implied, should ideally involve acquaintance with all the relevant primary and secondary sources for the topic being studied, but with particular emphasis on the primary sources — the basic and original data for study.

It is true that this distinction can be pressed too far, and ultimately (as will become clear in the later sub-sections) breaks down. But at one level it can be very helpful for assessing others' usage of documentary sources in their research. A report which purports to be based on the detailed evidence about some complex question, but in fact depends only on consulting secondary accounts without ever getting to grips with the detailed primary sources, could certainly be open to criticism. Examples might be drawing conclusions about a company's financial standing from a speculative newspaper comment (secondary) rather than its detailed balance sheets, or generalizing about the family structure of a particular town in say, 1881, not by studying such sources as the 1881 Census Enumerators' books (primary) but by generalizing from twentieth-century secondary accounts. General matters outside the researcher's main topic of interest are, reasonably enough, not usually followed up in primary sources. Time and cost constraints play a part here, as so often, in limiting the researcher's scope. Similarly, primary sources would not need to be researched for matters of common and agreed knowledge (like, say, the date of the establishment of the European Common Market). They would not need to be researched, that is, unless that topic itself became a matter of controversy turning on some fine point of interpretation, or the researcher wanted to counter conventional wisdom. In such cases it is not uncommon to 'go back to the original sources' precisely so as to issue a well-founded challenge.

Each case, then, must be taken according to its specific circumstances. But in general asking about the *nature* of the sources used to obtain the information for the research is one key question to pursue in assessing a piece of research. And one of the central aspects of this is whether the researcher made use of primary or of secondary sources and how far such a choice can be judged the appropriate one.

'Direct' and 'indirect' uses of documentary sources

One way of approaching a given source is to seek information directly from the factual content contained in it. Thus a university's published annual report will give information about numbers of students, staff, departments or courses, its library resources, its future plans and so on — useful information for someone researching on such topics. Similarly a newspaper report, a biography, or a column in *Hansard* will provide direct information about certain events or situations which could be essential for answering questions to which a researcher needs the answers. The same could be applied to just about any other documentary source you could think of: Parliamentary papers, the Census, diaries, letters, broadcasts, advertisements, organizational records, etc. All of these could, on appropriate occasions, be the source of direct information.

Does the statement above raise any problems?

You will probably have identified the fundamental problem here even before I asked you — the problem, that is, of whether you can trust the overt message in the source. The *Hansard*-recorded speech, the newspaper account, the advertisement, even the 'authoritative' biography might all have their own hidden agendas, and twist or select the evidence to fit their own purposes.

So if we cannot trust this overt content, does that then mean the source is useless? This is where the *indirect* use of sources comes in. The glossy public relations leaflet for a firm or a university might not — to put it baldly — state 'the truth, the whole truth, and nothing but the truth'. But the *gloss* put on the message can itself convey indirect information about, say, the ideals aimed at, the standard terminology used in a particular place or period, the kinds of subterfuges engaged in, or the sort of images thought likely to appeal to the intended market. Similarly even the most self-indulgent and flagrantly non-factual autobiography might tell you something unintentionally about, say, the author's perspective, motivations, personality or imagined audience, or about the social context in which she or he was writing. In other words, a great deal of information can often be gained from a source *indirectly* even when a *direct* approach employing a (perhaps simplified) model of information-transfer in terms of literal truth is likely to be less successful.

As with the primary/secondary distinction, the direct/indirect distinction becomes more complex and muddy the more closely you look at actual source usage, and ultimately it too breaks down. It is a useful one to start out from however, and the 'indirect' use of sources is particularly worth bearing in mind in the following subsection.

5.2 HOW DO DOCUMENTARY SOURCES COME INTO BEING?

Faced with written or numerical records, it is easy to forget that these sources do not just arise automatically through some asocial natural process. They may look authoritative, as if they could not have been produced in any other way. But in effect, all these sources are the results of human activity. As came out well in the comment by Wright Mills quoted earlier (Section 2), they are produced by human beings acting in particular circumstances and within the constraints of particular social, historical or administrative conditions.

Often these sources rest on a series of human decisions. An individual decides to write a diary or memoir, a committee agrees to issue a report, a sociologist decides to work on a book about drug addicts, a political party decides to publish an election manifesto or a business organization to issue an annual report (this may be as much a result of a taken-for-granted routine as of a single once-and-for-all decision — but a decision in some sense is involved). This may be followed by further decisions: that the diary (or memoir) will be, for example, indiscreet or hard-hitting, that the report will stress one aspect of the situation more than another, that the sociological study will concentrate on one particular locality, that the manifesto or the annual statement will play up certain issues and factors and play down or even suppress others. All these decisions will obviously affect the nature of the source as it comes into existence. It can equally be affected by what could be called 'unconscious decisions'. The diarists may (not admitted even to themselves) be really writing with an eye to later publication and so be representing events, personalities and even inner feelings in the light of this; the committee may, without members themselves fully realizing it, form part of a general reaction within the organization against the increasing influence of some special group and be directed as much to countering that influence as to stating isolated recommendations; the sociologist may turn the research direction to fit the interests of those who control research funds or the accepted wisdom of the moment among established academic colleagues; the details in the party manifesto may result from a compromise between several opposing factions; and so on.

In all these cases a series of choices has been made — at least in the sense that the result *might* have been otherwise. The resultant source can thus often be better assessed if one can discover the kind of process by which it came into being. We can in this way learn more about the author's circumstances, and (perhaps) about the influences on him or her by other individuals or groups, who may sometimes bear more responsibility than at first appears. A particular statement by a party leader may, for example, be made under duress (physical duress is one possibility, but more often political pressure like a threat to his/her leadership or the need to avert a backbench revolt which might bring the government down) — if so, knowing the background helps us to assess the statement as a source. Again, if some account has come into existence through rumour rather than concrete evidence, this too is relevant. Or some particular source might be a forgery — if so, it is essential for someone using the source to know this. The cautions about statistical sources made earlier could equally well have been brought in here: to assess them effectively we need to know how they were collected and by whom. So, too, we can bring in the whole process of exactly how material on a particular subject has been gathered. Daryll Huff makes this point vividly in his amusing but useful little book *How to Lie with Statistics,* when he quotes an experienced judge's advice to an eager young British civil servant in India:

> When you are a bit older you will not quote Indian statistics with that assurance. The government are very keen on amassing statistics — they collect them, add them, raise them to the nth power, take the cube root and prepare wonderful diagrams. But what you must never forget is that every one of those figures comes in the first instance from the *chowty dar* [village watchman] who just puts down what he damn pleases.
>
> (Huff, 1973, p.72)

This may be an amusing exaggeration, but the basic point is worth bearing firmly in mind. Knowing how a source came into being may be directly relevant both for understanding *who* was responsible for it (and thus the kind of interpretation likely to be involved) and for assessing its reliability.

There is a further aspect too. This is a matter of the audience or purpose towards which a particular source is directed. A political speech may be prepared and delivered to stir up the party faithful and have more comments about what *ought* to be so than descriptions of actual situations; reports in particular newspapers may be directed to a readership which demands, or is thought to demand, personalized and dramatic stories rather than dispassionate analysis in depth; scholarly books and articles are often directed to a readership consisting of academic colleagues and competitors. Who this supposed audience is and the extent to which the creator of the account/speech/report shares the audience's preconceptions is likely to affect both what is said and what is left unsaid — once again, essential background information for an assessment of that source.

How material is presented is also likely to be affected by the audience the author has in mind. Certain styles of presentation have become accepted as the appropriate ones for particular types of publication — in other words the style gives yet another clue to the nature of the source, and hence what you can expect from it. Academic articles, for example, can adopt a number of different formats, but one common pattern is for them to be expressed in relatively dispassionate language ('is' rather than 'ought' statements predominate, with critical discussion of the central concepts), to relate explicitly the content of the article to work by other scholars, and to pursue a coherent argument ending up with a conclusion referring to some general or theoretical point. Political memoirs, on the other hand, generally are in a more chatty and personal style, giving a vivid picture of events and of the author's contributions to them rather than reaching any general conclusion. Newspaper styles vary considerably according to readership and editorial policy, but once again — as, too, in television — there tends to be an emphasis on personalization and the glamour of unusual or striking events. Statistical tables, by contrast, especially in official publications, have their own appropriate style of presentation: impersonal, starkly quantitative and unlikely to be chatty.

Without really thinking about it you can no doubt recognize these different styles, but may not have realized how far they depend on current conventions and (implicit) decisions about appropriate ways of presenting information to different audiences. This is yet another form of human interpretation and construction which will affect the form in which 'the facts' are formulated in documentary sources.

The same point also applies to those apparently neutral reports: transcriptions from taped interviews (see Unit 11, Section 4.2). These *seem* to rest on a mechanical process of merely transferring the taped words into a handy written form, resulting in 'text' which can be analysed like any other. But — quite apart from any problems in the spoken interview itself — it is now increasingly realized that transferring from the spoken to the written word raises many problems akin to those of translation. A great deal is lost in moving from the multi-channel medium of words to the single-channel medium of writing. And what is lost may be essential to the meanings the researcher is trying to discover. So the decisions to transcribe in one particular way rather than another are seldom unchallengeable and often highly political (see Ochs, 1979; Finnegan, 1992, pp.190ff., 230ff., and references given there).

So although the distinction between primary and secondary sources is indeed a useful one, *no* source is really primary in the literal and ultimate sense of giving the plain unvarnished facts. There is always some element of production and shaping, some process by which the source came into being.

Further, we can now go back again to the 'direct' and 'indirect' uses of sources. When we grasp the many complexities behind the creation of sources, it seems too simple just to contrast the 'surface' message of a document with all the indirect or implicit meanings that could be drawn from it. For, as will become even clearer in a later discussion, most, perhaps all, texts contain a series of meanings and functions. These depend on both the viewpoint of the creator (or creators — for sometimes there are multiple strands even at the most simple level) and that of anyone reading or hearing it. Texts are typically multi-functional and multi-vocal, and which elements one picks out of these is seldom a simple direct/indirect alternative, but a matter of judgement and interpretation.

There is also the simple but extremely important point that what counts as primary (or secondary) or as direct (or indirect) depends crucially on the *purpose* of the reader — or the researcher. Once again, the role of documentary sources (like so many others) turns out to be relative, rather than absolute.

The implication of all this for assessing researchers' use of written sources as data must by now be obvious. Sources have to be *interpreted* not just consulted. And one fundamental criterion for how sensibly the sources are thus interpreted in the research you are assessing is precisely what the researcher has used them for, and how far he or she *has* taken account of how they came into being: by whom, under what circumstances and constraints, with what motives and assumptions, and how selected. To ignore all these aspects and merely take the sources at face value is, admittedly, more disastrous in some cases than others. But it is *always* a question to be asked about any use of written sources as data. So one of the most illuminating yardsticks to use in assessing the use of documentary sources as data is how far the researchers are explicit about their purposes, and how far they seem to take account of these features of the sources they use — indeed how far they discuss such problems explicitly at all.

It has to be admitted, however, that using this yardstick is not necessarily a simple or easy task. For the corollary is that you can apply it most effectively only if you know something about these — or similar — sources for yourself and you are able to engage in informed and reasonable interpretations.

5.3 SUMMARY OF SOME FURTHER QUESTIONS TO ASK

Thinking about how the sources have come into being will lead to other related questions to ask when assessing the use of documentary sources as data. Among these are the following, all useful touchstones to decide whether the researcher has used his or her sources knowledgeably and critically. Some of these questions overlap with the more overarching point made in the last section, but it can still be useful to list them if only as a handy *aide-mémoire*.

One further point needs highlighting, before moving on to the list. As in all the discussions of the critical evaluation of research in this course or elsewhere, the precise relevance of such critical questions will, of course, depend on *who* is doing this evaluating, and for what purpose (see, for example, the discussion in Unit 10, Section 5). So the questions are merely listed as some possible general principles. Their exact application to particular evaluations will have to remain a matter for your own judgement.

1 *Has the researcher made use of the existing sources relevant and appropriate for his or her research topic?*

Given the wealth of existing sources indicated above — verbal, numerical, audio-visual, electronic — this is a sensible prior question to ask in assessing any piece of research. Sometimes of course there are *no* relevant sources, or problems about access, quality or specific nature make their use less appropriate than data gathered more directly by the researcher. But often they *are* available and their use would save time, money and trouble — and in some cases (arguably) lead to more accurate or insightful results.

This is partly a matter of the overall design of the research and of the initial 'literature search' (see Unit 10). But it also affects the data-collection phase (in so far as this can be separated as a specific stage): collecting and analysing the information needed for the researcher's final conclusions. 'Not knowing, or not consulting, the relevant sources' is an effective and not uncommon criticism of someone's research.

Even more than with the other questions in this section, using this criterion to assess someone else's research necessarily depends on knowing something of the extent of these sources yourself. Sometimes no doubt you will — and in that case will be in a strong position to make a knowledgeable assessment (that, of course, is why it is often experts in the specific area covered who are asked to write book reviews or to assess research proposals). But even if you do not it can be at least of some help in assessment if you know something of the *range* of sources that do exist and might have been tapped.

2 *How far has the researcher taken account of any 'twisting' or selection of the facts in the sources used?*

This is a simple question in one way — it is an *obvious* consideration to raise, after all. But in another way it can prove an elusive question, one extremely hard to elucidate. Deliberate falsification, forgery, or explicit propaganda are perhaps relatively straightforward, even if sometimes in practice missed by naïve or uninformed researchers. More difficult to assess is the less conscious shaping of what is represented in written reports. Whatever form these take there is bound to be some social filtering, possibly because they are produced by interested parties to suit their own views and preconceptions, dictated by particular administrative needs and arrangements, influenced by currently dominant models, theories or interpretations among scholars — and so on. It is worth remembering that a source purporting to represent generally held views or an 'objective assessment' of the situation sometimes expresses only the views of a minority or of a particular interest group. Indeed it is not uncommon for people to speak rhetorically of the common good rather than of their own specific interests. They rightly consider they will in this way get a better hearing for their case, as well as sometimes being sincerely convinced that their own and the general interest coincide.

Besides such cases, there is always the possibility that what are assumed to be the views of 'the public' are in fact no more than those of the rich, educated or powerful. Marx put this point with particular clarity and force when he wrote:

> The ideas of the ruling class are, in every age, the ruling ideas: i.e. the class which is the dominant *material* force in society is at the same time its dominant *intellectual* force. The class which has the means of material production at its disposal, has control at the same time over the means of mental production, so that in consequence the ideas of those who lack the means of mental production are, in general, subject to it.
>
> (Marx, *German Ideology*, translated in Bottomore and Rubel, 1963, p.63)

One need not agree with the details of Marx's analysis (or even with his use of the concept of 'class') to appreciate the point being made here.

It could be argued that the problem is less for someone studying the present than for historians of the past where the smaller amount of source material sometimes meant a concentration on the views of certain groups (in practice usually of the educated and powerful groups). Nowadays, there is perhaps more source material that goes right across the board, applying to all groups of society, or at least arguably more so than in the past. This may be so, but it is still important *to ask this question* about a researcher's use of any source. It is often particularly pertinent for statements by articulate and well-organized interest groups.

However, bias or selectivity need not be deliberate or ill-motivated to be pervasive in the sources. Indeed 'bias' may not even be the correct term here, suggesting as it does a concept of some absolute and asocial correspondence with the 'bare facts' which could be reached if we could only get through the misleading veil of the 'bias'. As you will remember from Unit 1/2, there are many philosophical controversies over the nature of 'truth', but one common position among many social scientists would now certainly be that *all* human formulations are inevitably shaped by the social and cultural contexts in which they are created, and by the individuals or collectivities who create them. It does not follow that they are necessarily 'false' in some simplified sense, nor that they are valueless. But it does mean that interpretation rather than just some automatic 'reading off' of the results is needed in analysing any human-constructed formulation, written, spoken or gestured.

Examples might be: an interpretation of the facts and figures relating to people of Afro-Caribbean origin now settled in the UK according to (a) a supporter of the National Front or (b) a member of the Commission for Racial Equality; an explanation of the events in Northern Ireland over the last 25 years by (a) a member of the Orange Order or (b) a member of the provisional IRA; an academic study of educational opportunity in the UK in which data were collected and analysed on the assumption (nowhere proved) that (a) there is a clear-cut and homogeneous 'working class' in the UK or (b) opportunity is fully open to merit.

Kitson Clark sums this up well in his older — but still extremely pertinent — study, *The Critical Historian*, in words which apply equally well to social and educational research based on documents.

> Into the consideration of anything which lies beyond the framework of fact the human element will intrude. This is obvious in relation to any question of interpretation, but it is also true of any question of disputed fact. It will be necessary to take into account the extent and limitations of the powers of human beings to observe, to form inferences from what they observe, to remember, to record, to present what they have recorded in a newspaper or history book. But not only will the powers of human beings to observe, infer and record be in question, but also the ways in which they do these things will be controlled by their wills, by their passions, by their interests and by the very fact that they are human beings.
>
> (Kitson Clark, 1967, pp.125–6)

This question is therefore always worth pursuing even in the most impartial-seeming source (an academic textbook, for instance) which appears to have considered the evidence fully and dispassionately. It is often the most elusive question of all to get an exact answer to — but equally it is perhaps the single most important question to ask. Of course, if you accept the same model, etc. as the writer, you may not consider what is said as 'twisting' the facts. Even then, however, it is still worth asking the question for it may make you more aware that both what is said in the source and the researcher's interpretation of it could be *controversial* even if you happen to believe it is true.

3 *What kind of selection has the researcher made in her or his usage of the sources and on what principles?*

Sometimes the amount of source material potentially relevant to a particular issue is huge and *some* selectivity is necessary; it will also of course depend on the aims and parameters of the research. But with documentary, as with any other sources, *how* the selection is made is crucial. Written sources sometimes come in relatively measurable units. If so, similar sampling techniques to those discussed in earlier units might well — depending on the nature of the enquiry — be appropriate. Many do not, in which case has the researcher adopted some other principles to ensure a fair and representative coverage of the questions to be investigated? Either way there are still problems. How can you test whether or not the treatment has been representative without knowing the full list of possible sources from which the selection has been made? And what counts as 'fair' or 'representative' may depend on one's viewpoint.

However, even if the answers are not always in practice easy, the questions remain important. Certainly in assessing research it would be at least a *prima facie* ground for criticism if only one or two cases were taken as evidence for more general trends (although it might be judged acceptable to use them on a more 'case study' basis to highlight possible issues or complexities for further research, or to take a 'life history' or 'biographical' approach).

A similar question could be asked, not just of the researcher's conscious or unconscious selection among the sources, but also of the picture conveyed by those sources themselves.

The above assumes that the sources *are* in existence and that the researcher's usage can be judged by how far he or she takes advantage of their availability. But there is also the further problem — and a common one — that sources do not just 'exist' in some natural state, for the researcher to 'sample'. They are preserved selectively, and, once again, in a social context. Quite apart from the accidents of time, some written sources are more likely to be lost than others — depending among other things on their content, medium or location — and further selectivity in their preservation is imposed by, for example, changing academic or political fortunes. There are also the possibilities of direct censorship, secrecy and confidentiality, particularly if there is something in the sources perceived as to someone's discredit, and prevention of access by those controlling the sources. It can never just be assumed without checking that to consult just the existing and available documentary sources provides a fair coverage.

4   *How far does a source which describes a particular incident or case reflect the general situation?*

This is a relatively straightforward question, though it can also lead into some more detailed points like the usefulness or otherwise of 'case studies' (see also the issues of case selection raised in Block 2). Often one has to go to other sources besides the original one studied to answer the question. Can the account also be taken as true of other kinds of people and situations? It may be that there is no explicit claim in the account that what is described there also applies to other cases, but there may be an *implication* that it does — and this is sometimes all the more effective from *not* being explicitly stated.

It is often worth bearing in mind here the common tendency for the news media to highlight the flamboyant and the unusual rather than the humdrum and usual, and to personalize events rather than fill in the overall social background.

So when a researcher is using documentary sources to gather information, how far does he or she appear to be alive to these possible distorting effects, and to have taken account of them?

5   *Is the source concerned with recommendations, ideals or what ought to be done?*

If so it does not necessarily provide any evidence about what *is* done or is so in practice — but it is often tempting for researchers using such sources to leap to this mistaken conclusion.

Explicitly normative statements (i.e. those which clearly state that something *ought* to be done) are relatively easy to recognize and criticize. But, in other cases, this can be a tricky question to answer, since what are really normative statements about what *ought* to be are often expressed in language more suited to describing what *is*. When it is a question of policy statements it is often hard to sort out just how far the statement is merely an empty ideal or for propaganda purposes and how far a guiding principle for practice (with perhaps certain unavoidable exceptions). However, difficult to answer as it is, this is often a question worth asking, and a researcher who seems not to have considered such issues could certainly be criticized as naïve.

6   *How relevant is the context of the source?*

The particular points described or emphasized in the source may need to be interpreted in the light of the historical context in which the source came into being: the particular crisis in which the author was involved, the political state of play, the nature of public opinion at the time — in fact, all the background factors which influence how both the author and the intended audience would understand the words in the context in which they were originally said or written (see Section 5.2 above). Taken out of context, this original meaning may be misunderstood. Similarly the context in which particular administrative records were compiled or the constraints under which the compilers acted are all part of the background which a critical researcher has to consider.

7   *With statistical sources: what were the assumptions according to which the statistics were collected and presented?*

Statistical records too are not just self-evident facts of nature. They have to be collected, interpreted and presented. In so doing a number of assumptions must inevitably be made about, for instance, what is a suitable sample, what categories are to be counted, how they are to be defined, the questions used to get at data, and so on.

One particularly important set of assumptions are those which shape the basic categories employed — what are the statistics in effect *about*. In statistics referring to 'the crime rate', for example, what is the category 'crime' assumed to mean? If it is 'crimes known to the police', that will result in one figure; if 'people prosecuted', in another (lesser) figure; if 'persons found guilty', yet another (lesser still). For this reason, always look carefully at the *title* of any table or other figures being cited by researchers.

Here too some considerable background knowledge of the subject is often near-essential for evaluating a researcher's use of the figures. This enables one to look at the assumptions behind statistical sources on the subject more critically and knowledgeably. Knowing how they were collected, by whom and in what circumstances is one unavoidable precondition for interpreting statistics. So too may be some grasp of the ways new categories or definitions can be introduced such as those in the definitions of 'employment' or of 'poverty' in the UK in the 1980s.

8 *And finally having taken all the previous factors into account, do you consider that the researcher has reached a reasonable interpretation of the meaning of the sources?*

This central question is seldom a simple one to answer. But it has to be faced. For irrespective of all the care we can take in considering the background, counting the units, analysing the contents: in the end few or no humanly created sources are just transparent purveyors of clear-cut and objective 'truth'. Interpretation is always needed, not only by those constructing the documents, but also by those intended and unintended audiences who consult them.

This is more complex because of the multi-layered nature of meaning, something of which we are nowadays becoming increasingly aware. A document — whether the transcript of a speech, a government paper, a personal diary or a set of business records — may be perceived in one way by one reader, in another by others. The interpretations may vary as between different interested parties, historical periods and geographical cultures — and this without any of these interpretations necessarily being 'wrong' (some may well be, of course). And it is always a possibility that a source which it would be misleading to interpret as evidence for one purpose (interpreting a firm's publicity handout as providing the facts about its actual financial standing) may well be an excellent source if interpreted as evidence for, say, the current conventions in the public relations industry and the sorts of values thought likely to appeal to its targeted readership. This recalls the difference which Arthur Marwick (1977, p.63) neatly makes between the 'witting' and 'unwitting' evidence provided by sources. *Which* of these is considered, for what purposes, and in what mix, is also a matter of interpretation.

In the end there is no easy way to measure this, and you will have to exercise your own judgement in the light of all the evidence you have as to how reasonably the researcher has reached his or her own interpretation.

It will be clear from the above discussion that a full assessment of how well a researcher has made use of the appropriate sources can really only be made by people themselves knowledgeable about those very sources and their background — and, furthermore, knowledgeable about the researcher's own preconceptions in using those sources. This ideal situation may not be open to you. But as a second best it is always worth at least *asking* the kinds of questions above, and considering whether the research report provides any information to suggest how far the researcher has considered the issues.

ACTIVITY 4

1 Take (a) one specific example of research in the course and/or (b) any example known to you where research conclusions have been reached based on existing written sources — whether within an organization, of an individual nature, in the mass media or wherever — and list the kind of probing questions you would find illuminating in assessing its validity and reliability. Do you consider some more useful than others?

2 You may wish to rephrase the eight questions detailed above to make them more adaptable to your own use. How might you try to do this and/or are there any more *general* headings under which you would prefer to group them?

3 What common features can you see between the research use of documentary sources as data and that of other information-gathering methods discussed in this block which might be relevant for evaluating the research derived from them?

My responses to these questions are at the end of this unit.

5.4 SOME FINAL POINTS

Three additional points need to be made here: two which are relatively detailed, and one of more general significance.

First, the questions in Section 5.3 have mostly been expressed in terms of *written* sources. However, it is worth returning to the point made earlier, that most of them can also be applied to existing sources in other media, including those in audio or video form. Such sources are now attracting greater interest from researchers, whether broadcast over the air, shown in the cinema, taken over from other researchers, or stored in a variety of archives. (Audio sources, for example, have now become important enough for the British Library to have published a special directory to recorded sound resources in the UK: Weerasinghe, 1989.) It is sometimes tempting to suspend the usual sceptical approach to sources when considering audio and video because of the impression they can somehow purvey of representing direct and unvarnished 'reality'. But like any other source, they are humanly constructed and need to be approached with the same range of probing questions as written sources — as does the work of any researcher depending on them as data.

Secondly, researchers using existing sources sometimes speak of 'content analysis'. This applies particularly (though not only) to research in a mass communication framework and on the mass media: analysis of television programmes for example, radio broadcasts or the popular press. This is not the place for a detailed exploration of this approach, except to say that it usually depends on a high degree of quantification and claims to have developed scientific procedures for measuring the occurrence and recurrence of specific items in the 'documentary records' being analysed (for further discussion see Unit 21). The procedures are controversial ones — or at least their theoretical rationale is, often resting on arguments about measureable 'objective' content as against subjective 'meaning'. But irrespective of such arguments the relevant point here is that exactly the same kinds of questions can be asked of this approach as of other uses of documentary and existing sources: for example, how was the original source constructed in the first place, and how critically and knowledgeably did the researcher interpret it?

The final and most important point is that any researcher's use of sources — selection, interpretation, evaluation — will be influenced by her or his own theoretical, political and perhaps moral assumptions. What counts as the 'appropriate' sources, a fair selection, or a 'valid' interpretation is certainly not just subjective or relative — but often it cannot be a purely objective or agreed matter either. The same applies to your own assessment of that researcher's use of the documentary sources. Ultimately what is involved at every level is not just a technical procedure, but a matter of informed and critical personal judgement.

6 THE IMPACT OF NEW TECHNOLOGY

The predecessor of this course, DE304 *Research Methods in Education and the Social Sciences*, was presented with only minor modification, and with the approval of independent academic referees, for a fourteen-year period from 1979 to 1992 — the longest running course ever produced by the Faculty of Social Sciences. Social science research methods have not greatly changed in recent decades. One of the justifications of the remake of DE304 as DEH313 is development in the technology supporting social research. The most obvious manifestation of this development is the widespread use of the general purpose microcomputer as a tool of social research. When used as a word processor the micro enables you to write, edit, and print your notes and assignments. When used as a spreadsheet or calculator the micro supports statistical calculations of a size and complexity which would have required a mainframe computer a generation ago. The microcomputer also has the potential to support social research in a variety of other ways, particularly when used with a modem for data communication through the telephone network, and when equipped with a drive capable of reading data stored in optical form, as a means of access to sources of optically stored information such as a CD-ROM (compact disc read-only memory).

The development of the microcomputer is the most obvious information technology development of the past decade. But there have been contemporaneous advances in communications and data storage which also influence the ways in which social science research can be conducted.

This section aims to identify ways in which these developments seem most likely to affect the conduct of social research. The section discusses the use of remote data bases, the secondary use of survey data, the availability of administrative statistics, possibilities in the development of geographical information systems, and the development of optical storage methods.

6.1 ACCESS TO ONLINE DATA BASES

A notable starting point for this advance was the United States' space programme. Mistakes in space technology can cost hundreds of millions of dollars. Therefore to minimize the risk of failures the supporting research aimed to be comprehensive. This led to the establishment of the world's largest data base of relevant literature, which covered the social sciences as well as the natural sciences and technology. The data base created was, of course, computerized to facilitate rapid searching.

Telecommunications developments allowed access to the data base through the telephone network. Since the early 1970s it has been common for social scientists in the UK, and in other countries, to conduct searches of the literature held on the Dialogue data base (formerly owned by the Lockheed Corporation) in Palo Alto, California. There have been parallel developments in Europe with the establishment of the European Space Agency (ESA) data base at Frascati in Italy. In more recent years many new data bases have been created. At the time of writing it is estimated that there are more than 3,000 data bases world-wide which are accessible online through the telephone network. Dialogue Information Service and the ESA have become hosts for giving access to hundreds of these data bases.

Data bases cover two kinds of material of special importance for social research. One category comprises the abstracts of articles in academic journals and PhD dissertations. The data bases cover most of the leading academic journals back to the 1970s or earlier. The other category comprises the full text of non-academic journals such as the 'heavy' newspapers, *The Economist*, and many specialist journals of interest to social scientists — such as those concerned with management.

For both categories the search technique is similar. The researcher identifies key words or phrases covering the area of interest. The computer program identifies abstracts or articles which include those key words. The researcher would use a combination of key words of the form 'gender' OR 'sex' AND 'pay' OR 'earnings' OR 'salaries' AND 'teaching'. Such a search query might be expected to identify articles which covered differences between mens' and womens' earnings in teaching. The AND and OR in this context are called Boolean operators. The Boolean operator NOT is also sometimes used (Humphrey and Melloni, 1986).

What are the weaknesses of the search query given above for identifying articles which covered differences between mens' and womens' earnings in teaching? What alternative search queries might be more effective?

The major problem in using these online data bases for most researchers is cost (Turpie, 1987). Typically the cost is about £80 per hour. This is a small cost in relation to the time which might be saved. But it is a large cost to pay for learning to use a query language. Therefore such searches are commonly conducted by a specialist librarian working with the researcher.

The computer has also influenced the work of librarians in other ways. The catalogue of nearly all major libraries is nowadays computerized. Just as the modem gives access from the library to data bases in California and Italy, so can it give access from home or office to the library catalogue. Members of polytechnics and universities can, through JANET (the Joint Academic NETwork), examine the catalogue of almost any other polytechnic or university library and get access to a range of other services. You can consult the catalogue of your nearest university library if you equip your computer workstation with a modem and telephone connection.

6.2 SECONDARY ANALYSIS AND MICRODATA

The typical statistical survey involves centralizing a mass of information into a single data set. For many decades these data sets comprised a mass of forms and punched cards. Restriction on access was inevitable because duplication of the data set would have been costly. Central control was necessary in order to make checks on accuracy and to enable unanticipated enquiries of the data set to be answered. The results of these surveys could only be made available as aggregate data, i.e. as statistical tables.

The advent of the modern computer has changed the situation. When the data set is expressed in electronic form it becomes more tractable in every way. The technology makes it easier to exercise central control. It can easily be made anonymous so that individual records cannot be identified. Computer programs can facilitate checks on accuracy. Programs can usually deal with unanticipated queries.

The technology can also be used to duplicate and communicate. The data set can be made available to anyone, anywhere, who has suitable computing and communications equipment. If you have suitable programs you can make your own extractions and analysis of the data. Provided that the microdata are anonymous so that it is not possible for individuals to be identified, there is little necessity for central control. Centralization in terms of the collection of statistical information can be part of a system which is quite decentralized in terms of the distribution of the results (see Thomas, 1990 for further discussion).

In the late 1960s the Survey Archive (now the ESRC Data Archive) was established at Essex University to exploit the new possibilities. Any organization which has conducted a survey is encouraged to deposit a copy with the archive so that it can be made available in the form of microdata to researchers for what is usually called secondary analysis. Microdata can be defined as data sets giving information on individual records. Microdata can be contrasted to aggregate data as given in statistical tables. Access to the microdata means that, with the help of suitable programs, any kind of table can be constructed.

Secondary analysis has been defined as 'any further analysis of an existing data set which presents interpretations, conclusions, or knowledge additional to, or different from those presented in the first report on the enquiry as a whole' (Hakim, 1982). However, the term 'secondary analysis' has become problematized and largely out-dated by information technology developments.

It is important to note that the use of the term 'secondary' in 'secondary analysis' is different from that in the term 'secondary source', as discussed earlier in this unit. Secondary sources are those which are brought into being some time after the events they describe or are otherwise removed from the actual events. The term 'secondary analysis' is used of work done using the same primary sources, but made after a first analysis has been conducted.

Information technology developments make this distinction between first and secondary tenuous. In many major surveys (such as those listed in Table 1) all users of the microdata are equally removed from the actual events (e.g. the interviews conducted by interviewers with respondents). In recent years there have been a number of surveys which are designed primarily for secondary analysis. One such is the annual General Household Survey (GHS) — first conducted in the early 1970s — the main report of which is usually published two years after it has been conducted. Another example is the British Social Attitudes Survey conducted annually by Social and Community Planning Research, the main report of which is usually published in the year following the conduct of the survey.

The term 'secondary analysis' assumes that there is a 'first report on the enquiry as a whole'. But it would be surprising if reports were not made by client departments within central government on the basis of the General Household Survey microdata before the main GHS report is published. The book published annually on the British Social Attitudes Survey is comprised of chapters written by individual authors on particular aspects of the survey, each of which might be considered as secondary analysis. The ease with which data sets can be copied and disseminated appears to make the distinction between first and secondary analysis otiose.

6.3 LOCAL AVAILABILITY OF ADMINISTRATIVE DATA

Survey data are characteristically multi-dimensional in the sense that they include many different attributes of the population surveyed. There is scope for analysis of many different kinds. Administrative data characteristically, by contrast, have few dimensions, but are typically collected on a 100 per cent basis rather than as a sample. Administrative data often include the address of the subject. Because the data are collected on a 100 per cent basis, they can be used to produce reliable information for local areas. It seems likely that the main way in which information technology developments will enhance the value of administrative data for social research will be through using address data.

The influence of information technology in this case is mostly indirect. The use of automatic sorting devices and optical readers by the Post Office has been associated with the use of postcodes for small areas. Nowadays virtually every address in the UK is postcoded and lists are available which make it possible to attach postcodes to an address which is otherwise complete. This means that, for the first time, it becomes possible to code all addresses according to geographical location.

Central government holds many records which include addresses: income tax, national insurance details, child allowances, welfare payments, etc. Gas, electricity and mortgage companies, likewise hold records which include the addresses of their customers. In principle these data could now be made available on the basis of postcode areas (or aggregates of postcode areas if there was a danger of revealing information on individuals). The value of statistics of these kinds to local government could be substantial. For the first time it would be possible for local government social services departments, for example, to monitor the level of central government welfare payments in their area.

Will this happen? Will these administrative data become available for local areas? At the time of writing in 1992, all that can be said is that precedent has been set with statistics for the number of registered unemployed. Local authorities have been able to obtain monthly figures for the number of registered unemployed on a postcode basis through the Data Archive at Essex University since 1982.

6.4 GEOGRAPHICAL INFORMATION SYSTEMS

An important aspect of social research is the synergy of bringing together information of different kinds to increase understanding. This synergy can be graphically illustrated by the use of what has become known as a Geographical Information System, or GIS for short. GIS can be defined, in understated form, as the use of computers to produce maps. Maps have always been tools of the social scientist — not just the geographer. But usually maps are seen as part of the background to social research; a component which says in an illustration what would otherwise require many words to be written, and to be read. The potential of GIS is to become a major tool of the social scientist in its own right. Where data from different sources can be displayed in many different ways at the press of a few keys, then it is possible to gain insights, learn things and detect patterns which could not easily be achieved by other means.

A classic example is the use of GIS to relate the incidence of leukaemia to the distribution of atomic energy power stations (see Economic and Social Research Council, 1991). The location of cases of leukaemia by itself did not yield clear evidence. The calculation of incidence rates for local areas would produce only a slightly less clear picture. But using GIS to bring together information of this kind with the location of power stations revealed a much clearer pattern. There were concentrations of leukaemia associated with power stations. But there were also concentrations associated with other locations which had nothing to do with power stations.

An impression of the state of development of GIS can be obtained from the monthly journal *Mapping Awareness and GIS in Europe*. Up to the time of writing the major developments in GIS have been utilized for research into matters belonging to the physical world where existing information is used such as that from maps, and information which can be collected automatically is used such as that from an aerial photographic survey. The only major data set relating to human populations which has the 100 per cent coverage necessary for local area analysis has been that of the decennial Census of population.

This situation may change substantially if, as suggested above, administrative data become increasingly available for local areas. The ready availability of maps bringing together information such as income levels, unemployment, crime rates, educational achievements, etc., and the facility to automatically compute and display descriptive statistics of any kind on the basis of these data, could have a major impact on the way much social research is conducted.

6.5 OPTICAL STORAGE

The developments described so far have depended upon advances in communications technology, and upon computer technology based on magnetic storage of data. Access to large remote data bases, for example, is supported by a microcomputer equipped with a modem to enable direct interrogation of the data base. The microdata for quite a large social survey could also be made available on what, at the time of writing, is the standard floppy disk with a capacity to store 1.4 Megabytes of information. A byte is typically one character. A disk of 1.4 Megabytes can carry about 200,000 words — the equivalent of a couple of books of average length. Such disks which use magnetic storage are relatively inefficient in terms of disk space compared with optical storage. The compact disc used in entertainment carries 55 Megabytes of information. When that same technology is used to store data of interest to the social researcher the disk is called a CD-ROM and stores the equivalent of a bookshelf with about 20 feet of shelf space.

Storage at this density competes effectively with obtaining information online from large data bases. The data bases can be delivered to the user on disk instead. Bibliographical data bases, full-text data bases, microdata for large surveys, and a variety of administrative data can all be delivered to the user, and once the cost of acquisition is met, the CD-ROM can be used without further cost or the distraction of the 'running taxi-meter' of online charges.

A wide ranging discussion of the prospects for CD-ROM was published by Microsoft (a dominant microcomputer software firm) in the mid-1980s (Lambert and Ropiequet, 1985; Ropiequet, 1987). There have been many developments since that time, but the principles discussed in these volumes have not changed. A list of the CD-ROMs available at the time of writing which are of special interest to social researchers is given in Table 3. Their cost, at the time of writing, varies from a few pounds to over £4,000.

6.6 IMPLICATIONS OF TECHNOLOGICAL DEVELOPMENTS FOR SOCIAL RESEARCH

People often write about the information explosion or the information revolution. However, there is little explosive or revolutionary about the growth, described in this section, of information usable for social research. It may well be that the word revolution can be applied, with justification, to developments in the supporting technology. But the growth of useful information has been steady and incremental. The technology itself does not create new information.

The value of most of the new information services described in this section is not that they provide new information. The value of these services is that they make information which was already available, typically in the form of print, available in digital form. Expression in digital form is a very significant step. It allows systematic search and analysis, and contributes greatly to ease of communication and storage. The processing of digital information makes it possible to conduct some kinds of research which would not otherwise be possible.

The most obvious consequence of the growth in information services is the growing number of research reports that can be produced based wholly or in part upon existing sources of information. Another consequence is a growth in the extent to which information from existing sources can be used to help evaluate research reports. But the technologies which support the use of existing sources also support research involving the use of new data. There seems no reason to expect that research reports based on existing sources of information will grow at the expense of research involving the collection of new information.

What can be said is that the technology is not neutral with regard to the type of information which can be processed. A limitation on the information made available by the new technology is the cost of inputting data — in other words the cost of converting the information from, say, print into digital form. Typically, information has become available in digital form because the producing organization has been computerized. Newspapers, for example, have taken up computerized printing. It is relatively easy then for the information to be supplied to a full-text data base because it is already in digital form. One consequence is that the information available in digital form is very selective. Typically data bases may cover a journal back as far as some time in the 1980s when that journal became computerized. The lack of comparability with earlier periods is a significant limitation on the value of the information relating to current periods.

Table 3 Selected CD-ROM data bases relevant to social research

Title	Contents
'Academic' bibliographic data bases:	
Econlit	Corresponds to the *Journal of Economic Literature* and Index of Economic Articles. Covers journal articles, dissertations, books, chapters in books, and conference proceedings
ERIC	Comprises Current Index to Journals in Education covering 775 periodicals, and Resources in Education covering fugitive document literature
Psyclit	Covers 1,300 journals. From the PsychINFO department of the American Psychological Association
Sociofile	Journal articles published in Sociological Abstracts since 1974, dissertations since 1986, Social Policy and Development Abstracts (SOPODA) since 1986
'Professional' bibliographic data bases:	
CINAHL	Cumulative Index to Nursing and Allied Health Literature. Covers English language nursing journals and 3,200 biomedical journals
Healthplan-CD	350,000 citations from 1981 covering non-clinical aspects of health care delivery. Supplied by US National Library of Medicine and the American Hospital Association
LegalTrac	Bibliographical coverage of 800 legal publications and law-related articles from 1,000 other periodicals from English-speaking world since 1980
POPLINE	150,000 citations on population, family planning and related health care, law and policy issues. Reaches back to 1827
Other relevant data bases:	
British Social Attitudes Survey	Microdata for the British Social Attitudes Survey, from 1983 to 1989
Cross-cultural CD	Full-text files with extracts from more than 500 anthropological, sociological, and psychological monographs on life in 60 different societies. Vol. 1, Human Sexuality/Marriage; vol. 2, Family Crime and Social Problems; vol. 3, Old Age; vol. 4, Childhood and Adolescence; vol. 5, Religious Beliefs and Practices
Electromap World Atlas	Uses maps as a way of accessing information on a country's economy, communications, travel, politics or people
Postcode Address File	Postcodes and matching addresses within the UK with name for businesses, property number/name, street, district, post town, Ordnance Survey grid reference
World Factbook	Covers political, geographical, and economic make-up, including maps, of all countries together with information on their population and communications

Contemporary or near-contemporary sources are generally more likely to be available in digital form than historic sources and so are more likely to be available to the social researcher. Journals of all kinds, because they are published regularly by a relatively small number of publishers, are more likely to become available in full-text and bibliographical data bases than sources such as books — which are published irregularly by an almost countless number of publishers. This systematic bias in the accessibility of sources may lead to relative neglect of sources such as books and historical sources of many kinds which are not favourably supported by information technology developments.

7 CONCLUSION

The sources of evidence discussed in this unit are inevitably historical in nature. But that is not the crucial characteristic from the point of view of the social researcher. The evidence on which the social sciences is based always relates to past human behaviour. The crucial distinction is between the evidence which social researchers have arranged to be collected with a particular purpose in mind, and the evidence from other sources which has not usually been brought into existence with the social scientist's research purpose in mind.

A most useful distinction to make in approaching the use of existing sources of information is that mentioned in Section 5.3 between wittingly and unwittingly gathered evidence. Where the social scientist arranges for evidence to be collected, that evidence is wittingly gathered with the purpose of the study in mind. But where other sources are used the first question which the researcher must ask is whether that evidence came into existence in order to serve the same or similar purposes to the study being made.

In many cases the answer will be positive. Where a study replicates an earlier study or one made of a different population, for example, the purposes may be similar or identical. An important aspect of many of the regularly conducted surveys described in Table 1 is to maintain comparability with earlier surveys. The researchers who conduct these surveys can usually add value to their findings by reference to earlier surveys which have wittingly been gathered for more or less the same purposes.

Much of the evidence of value to the social scientist will have come into existence for quite different purposes. In other words it provides unwitting evidence. The second question the researcher must ask is about the nature of the purpose which led to the evidence being created. Why was the letter written? What was the purpose of collecting the statistic? Who took the photograph, and why did he or she take it?

A difference in purpose may not reduce the value of the evidence. But it is important to know the collection purpose in order to be able to interpret the evidence properly and to assess its value. Nearly all the points made in this unit stem from asking such questions about the ways in which the evidence which may be useful for social research was created.

ANSWERS TO ACTIVITIES

ACTIVITY 3

1 See the second paragraph of Hakim's paper.

2 (a) See Hakim's first paragraph of the section 'Varieties of records-based studies'.

  (b) See the second paragraph of the section 'The nature and quality of data from administrative records'. Hakim's comments here and in the following paragraphs are extremely important for the critical evaluation of a piece of record-based research (see also further comments in this unit's text).

3 Issues of access (including negotiations when records are not public, inaccessible records, censorship, questions of confidentiality); enough time and resources for the necessary familiarization; processing or collating of records; problems peculiar to specific sets of records; potential misunderstandings of the records or of their scope and content (the classifications used may be incompatible with the researcher's purpose); legal and ethical issues (not discussed in detail).

4, 5 For discussion of these points read on in this unit's text.

6 See 2(b) above, also a discussion follows in this unit's text.

ACTIVITY 4

1 The answers here are left to your own judgement.

2 One set of categories now relatively often used in social research (see Platt, 1981; Scott, 1990; Barrat and Cole, 1991) groups the questions to be used in assessing documentary sources under the following.

  (a) Authenticity: soundness and authorship.

  (b) Representativeness: survival and availability.

  (c) Meaning: literal and interpretative understanding (see especially Scott, 1990).

In so far as the aim is to assess someone else's use of documentary sources as data, the point here is not so much the detailed terminology, as the questions of how far the researcher was critically aware of these kinds of questions in the research and was able to inspire you with a confidence in his or her analytic, critical, and knowledgeable use of the sources.

3 Again there is no one answer, but recurrent issues you may wish to invoke might include notions of reliability, validity, data construction, interpretation, the research population, the relativity of the concept of 'truth', practical problems like access, and perhaps ethics.

REFERENCES

Barrat, D. and Cole, A (1991) *Sociology Projects: a Students' Guide*, London, Routledge.

Becker, H.S. (1974) 'Photography and sociology', *Studies in the Anthropology of Visual Communication*, vol. 5, pp.3–26.

Becker, H.S. (ed.) (1981) *Exploring Society Photographically*, Chicago, Northwestern University Press.

Berger, P. and Luckman, T. (1966) *The Social Construction of Reality*, Harmondsworth, Penguin.

Bottomore, T.B. and Rubel, M. (eds) (1963) *Karl Marx: Selected Writings in Sociology and Social Philosophy*, Harmondsworth, Penguin.

Bulmer, M. (1980) 'Why don't sociologists make more use of official statistics?', *Sociology*, vol. 14, pp.505–23.

Central Statistical Office (1985) *United Kingdom National Accounts — Sources and Methods*, London, HMSO.

Central Statistical Office (annual) *Guide to Official Statistics*, London, HMSO.

Central Statistical Office (annual) *National Income and Expenditure*, London, HMSO.

Central Statistical Office (annual) *Social Trends*, London, HMSO.

Central Statistical Office (quarterly) *Statistical News*, London, HMSO.

Department of Employment (monthly) *Employment Gazette*, London, HMSO.

Economic and Social Research Council (1991) *Mapping the Future*, Slough, ESRC (video).

Economic and Social Research Council (quarterly) *Data Archive Bulletin*, University of Essex, ESRC Data Archive.

Finnegan, R. (1988) *Literacy and Orality. Studies in the Technology of Communication*, Oxford, Blackwell.

Finnegan, R. (1992) *Oral Traditions and the Verbal Arts: a Guide to Research Practices*, London, Routledge.

Gardner, S. and Stanyer, A. (1991) *The Single Homeless in Coventry*, Coventry Polytechnic, Department of Social Science and Policy Studies.

Goody, J. (1986) *The Logic of Writing and the Organization of Society*, Cambridge, Cambridge University Press.

Government Statisticians' Collective (1979) 'How official statistics are produced: views from the inside', in Hammersley, M. (ed.) (1993) (DEH313 Reader).

Hakim, C. (1982) *Secondary Analysis in Social Research: a Guide to Data Sources and Methods with Examples*, London, George Allen & Unwin.

Hakim, C. (1987) *Research Design: Strategies and Choices in the Design of Social Research*, London, Unwin Hyman [Chap. 4, 'Research analysis of administrative records', is reproduced in Hammersley, M. (ed.) (1993) (DEH313 Reader)].

Hammersley, M. (ed.) (1993) *Social Research: Philosophy, Politics and Practice*, London, Sage (DEH313 Reader).

Hindess, B. (1973) *The Use of Official Statistics in Sociology*, London, Macmillan.

Huff, D. (1973) *How to Lie with Statistics*, Harmondsworth, Penguin.

Humphrey, S.M. and Melloni, B.J. (1986) *Databases — a Primer for Retrieving Information by Computer*, New Jersey, Prentice-Hall.

Irvine, J., Miles, I. and Evans, J. (1979) *Demystifying Social Statistics*, London, Pluto Press.

Johnson, P. and Webb, S. (1989) 'Counting people with low incomes: the impact of recent changes in official statistics', *Fiscal Studies*, November, pp.66–82.

Keynote (1989) *The Source Book*, London, Keynote Publications Ltd.

Kitson Clark, G. (1967) *The Critical Historian: Guide for Research Students Working on Historical Subjects*, New York, Garland.

Lambert, S. and Ropiequet, S. (eds) (1985) *CD-ROM — The New Papyrus*, Redmond, Microsoft Press/Penguin.

Lawlor, J. and Kennedy, C. (1992) 'Measures of unemployment: the claimant count and the Labour Force Survey', *Employment Gazette*, July, pp.347–55 (reproduced in Offprints Booklet 3).

Marwick, A. (1977) 'Introduction to history', in *An Arts Foundation Course*, A101, Units 3–5, The Open University, Milton Keynes.

Mort, D. and Siddall, L. (1985) *Sources of Unofficial UK Statistics*, London, Gower.

Mowatt, C.L. (1971) *Great Britain Since 1914*, London, Hodder & Stoughton.

Ochs, E. (ed.) (1979) 'Transcription as theory', in *Studies in Developing Pragmatics*, New York, Academic Press.

Oppenheim, C. (1990) *Poverty: The Facts*, London, Child Poverty Action Group.

Platt, J. (1981) 'Evidence and proof in documentary research: 1, Some specific problems of documentary research; 2, Some shared problems of documentary research', *Sociological Review*, vol. 29, pp.31–52, 53–66.

Ropiequet, S. (ed.) (1987) *Optical Publishing Vol. II*, Redmond, Microsoft Press/Penguin.

Scott, J. (1990) *A Matter of Record: Documentary Sources in Social Research*, Cambridge, Polity Press.

Social and Community Planning Research and The London School of Economics and Political Science (quarterly) *Joint Centre for Survey Methods Newsletter*, London, SCPR.

Thomas, R. (1984) 'Why have government statistics? (and how to cut their cost)', *Journal of Public Policy*, vol. 4, no. 2, pp.85–102.

Thomas, R. (1990) 'The case for the abolition of the government statistical service', *Radical Statistics*, vol. 46, pp.7–12.

Townsend, P. (1972) *Poverty in the United Kingdom — a Survey of Household Resources and Standards of Living*, Harmondsworth, Pelican.

Turpie, G. (1987) *Going Online 1987*, London, Aslib.

Wadsworth, J. and Johnson, A.M. (1991) 'Measuring sexual behaviour', *Journal of the Royal Statistical Society*, Series A, vol. 154, pp.367–70.

Walker, A. (1991) 'The social construction of dependency in old age', in Loney, M. et al. (eds) *The State or the Market: Politics and Welfare in Contemporary Britain*, London, Sage, pp.41–57.

Weerasinghe, L. (1989) *Directory of Recorded Sound Resources in the United Kingdom*, London, British Library.

UNIT 14 WHAT IS DONE WITH DATA

Prepared for the Course Team by Betty Swift

CONTENTS

Associated study materials		124
1	**Introduction**	125
2	**Establishing the nature of the problem**	127
3	**Prior structure, method of recording and sample size**	131
	3.1 Prior structure	131
	3.2 Method of recording	135
	3.3 Sample size	136
4	**Getting the data into shape for analysis**	137
	4.1 Getting the pre-coding right	140
	4.2 Coding open-ended questions	143
	4.3 Coding data from unstructured interviews	146
	4.4 Representation versus 'anchored' and 'hypothesis-guided' approaches to coding	148
	4.5 Correcting errors	152
5	**Data manipulation during analysis**	153
	5.1 Coping with missing values	153
	5.2 Recoding variables	154
	5.3 Constructing new variables	155
	5.4 Weighting	156
Answers to activities		159
References		163
Acknowledgements		164
Appendix		165

ASSOCIATED STUDY MATERIALS

There is no set reading associated with this unit, but you will need to use data files DOC1 to DOC4 from your data disk 'DATASET'. Data files DOC5 to DOC8 (data set, documentation and suggested activities) provide a further resource.

1 INTRODUCTION

This unit is about a process which receives scant attention in many research reports: namely, the process of transforming 'raw' data into variables that can be analysed to produce the information found in the results sections of such reports. In other words, we shall be looking at the extent to which the data on which research arguments are based are not 'found in the world', but are *constructed* by the researcher(s). This is not to say that data are false or fictional — all our knowledge of the world is constructed because it all depends crucially, not just on perception, but on *interpretation* of what we experience. As readers of research, however, we need to remind ourselves of the extent to which interpretation and manipulation take place even before data are analysed. In this unit we shall be considering mainly quantitative data — data expressed in numbers and counts — because numbers give the strongest impression of factual accuracy and do not appear to bear the marks of interpretation. The degree of interpretation involved in qualitative research is more obvious to the reader and is discussed elsewhere in the course.

In some cases, the procedures for processing and analysing quantitative data are well established and routine, based on previous experience, experimentation and research. Examples are public opinion surveys of voting intentions carried out by organizations such as Social Surveys (Gallup Poll) Ltd and National Opinion Poll (NOP), and repeated surveys such as the General Household Survey (OPCS, annual). In such projects the data are pre-coded and collected in a form that can easily be checked for accuracy. They are then keyed into a computer and aggregated, counted and analysed according to a predetermined plan to produce the tables and graphs that will be familiar to you from newspaper reports. The process progresses smoothly and quickly with a minimum of intervention by the researcher. Except when something goes wrong, the researcher's input will typically be (1) design of the study and the measurement instruments; (2) specification of tables and other analyses; and (3) report writing. The rest will be taken care of by procedures which ensure that the data are collected and processed in a routinized way that keeps error to a minimum. (That the procedures are routinized does not, of course, mean that the data are not constructs. The procedures now used were devised by researchers over time and involved decisions about what to do and what was important. Further, even routinized procedures on major repeated surveys such as the Census are not static but develop with new ideas and new technology.)

At the other end of the continuum, the researcher is personally and actively involved in the process of transforming the raw data into a form suitable for analysis. For example, if the data are unstructured (open-ended), they will have to be explored and specifications drawn up for categorizing them. If they are very detailed, summary measures may be needed — for example, age groups constructed from a raw variable 'age'. If there is incomplete information, the extent of it and the best strategy for coping with missing data will need to be worked out, and so on. The activities that comprise the process of preparing data for the 'data analysis' stage are inextricably bound up with the way in which the data have been obtained. The less the data have been subjected to researcher control and prestructuring — or if they have not been amenable to this — the more decisions there are to be taken at the data handling stage (which is the concern of this unit).

With the exception of highly structured data which are to be analysed in a prespecified way, the process always involves exploration of the characteristics and the structure of the data. This is the stage at which the researcher 'tunes into' the meaning and messages in his or her data and builds up an appreciation of the nuances and structure and the possibilities for analysis. The appreciation includes recognition of errors and omissions as well as the building up of a deepening understanding of the comparisons and other possibilities for analysis that are likely to be productive. It can be carried out according to formulae and procedures set out in textbooks, but it is an art form as much as a science. Even for an experienced researcher, every occasion of 'taking a first look at the data' is one in which there are novel things to be appreciated and new possibilities for developing his or her methodologies and ideas.

The exploration ranges from browsing for orientation purposes through a sample of the records that have been collected — for example, individual questionnaires and audio-tapes — through to some preliminary data analysis. The latter is important because it may identify the need for further transformation over and above any coding and error correction carried out during the process of preparing the raw data (as recorded on questionnaires and records of interviews, etc.) for data analysis. For example, inspection of initial frequencies (counts of the frequency of given answers/occurrences) may indicate the need for any or all of the following:

1 Recoding the data to more appropriate scale points.

2 Collapsing together of some of the categories because the numbers are small.

3 Merging groups of informants, etc. so as to secure adequate numbers for between-group comparisons.

4 Reweighting the data to take account of stratified sampling and, for certain kinds of studies (e.g. studies of populations), weighting the data so that they better reflect the nature of the population which the respondents represent.

5 Creation of new variables from the initial set of variables.

In summary, the major objectives of the process are:

1 Quality assurance: minimizing error in the data, in so far as this can be checked and remedied.

2 Appropriate categorization and grouping of the data in a form suitable for counting, comparison and any other analysis that is planned.

3 Transformation of the data into the numerical or other formats that are appropriate for the particular methods and techniques which are to be used in the data analysis proper.

4 Further reduction of the raw data, if needed, to summary categories and scores which adequately reflect the variety in the data.

5 Weighting of cases, if needed, so that statistics derived from the sample represent the best estimates possible for the population from which they were drawn.

6 Preliminary data analysis to check the size and nature of sub-groups which are to be used in tables reporting statistics or for purposes of hypothesis testing.

Most of this course has been aimed at the reader of research, the person faced with a research report to understand and evaluate, rather than the actual practitioner of research. What is under discussion here, however, is that part of the analysis which is largely invisible in the final report — the tidying-up and recategorization which precedes the main data analysis. You will seldom be able to examine what goes on at this stage in any detail when you read research reports, but you need a strong awareness of it in order not to be seduced by the 'facts' with which you are presented; many, if not all, of the findings follow this stage of the research process and are therefore at least in part a construction of the coding and manipulation process. For this reason I have written this unit as if you were going to be required to *do* the manipulation; it is only by doing this, or sitting beside someone who is doing it, that you will come to realize *what* is done. The unit is concerned mostly with quantitative analysis — analysis of data which come in numerical form or have been converted into numbers during this stage of pre-analysis. Some of the processes are parallel to ones which occur in qualitative analysis, however, as you will see in Unit 17/18.

2 ESTABLISHING THE NATURE OF THE PROBLEM

The rest of this unit is, in effect, a large-scale role-play in which I am inviting you to participate. In my job in the Institute of Educational Technology, the Open University's 'in-house' research unit, I am continually being approached by all kinds of people — 'management', course teams, fellow lecturers who have been doing research, research students, administrators, outside agencies. What they have is data, which they have collected, acquired or inherited from a predecessor. What they want to know is what to do with these data — how to get them into the best shape for analysis in order to answer their research questions. From this point in the unit, I want you to put yourself in my sandals and see what you would do if you were in my job, or sitting next to me, when such questions arise.

A consultation begins, of course, with a request. Figure 1 shows some possible beginnings to the consultation, which we can call 'presenting problems'.

I've got ...

    some questionnaires

    some interviews

    maths scores and some other data

    some videos

    some tapes

and I want to ...

    analyse them

    put them in on the computer

    code the answers

    produce the tables

    talk about the kinds of statistical analysis I can do

    analyse gender differences

    do an analysis of variance [or some correlations, or a factor analysis]

    construct some scales about ...

    construct a typology

    see if there are any patterns in the data

    construct a model explaining ...

    test my hypotheses about ...

    identify the ...

    prepare a report for ...

    make some recommendations about ...

Figure 1   *Examples of presenting problems*

The 'presenting problem' may be at any level of generality and address any stage of the process of preparing the data for analysis. It may be a contained problem, involving just one small part of the process of dealing with data. For example, the researcher might just want to discuss the problem of categorizing answers to a particular open-ended question — for instance, 'What have you found particularly excellent about studying with the OU?'. In this case, all that may be needed is a session with the researcher, involving inspection of a sample of the data together with discussion of possible options for categorizing and coding the data in the light of his or her objectives. This might be followed up, perhaps, by later discussions of problems arising in the client's initial attempts to categorize the answers to the question. In many cases, however, problems which appear to be quite contained nonetheless require that we build up knowledge about the data and the project as a whole. Without the requisite knowledge, we might make suggestions which are all right in principle but inappropriate or not possible given the resources and time available:

1. Decisions about what to do with data require an understanding of the particular characteristics of the data, based on information about how they have been collected as well as their content and the nature of the sample.

2. They also require an understanding of the desired 'outcomes' of the research. Information on outcomes is needed because, in making what we hope will be optimum decisions, we shall be continually (a) checking back to see in what ways we are constrained by the design decisions (including compromises that had to be made), and (b) looking ahead to the data analysis to optimize on the possibilities for achieving the research objectives.

3. Beyond this, it is useful to have in mind the kind of report that is required. For example, for an academic paper it might be appropriate to work towards transformation of the raw data into scales that summarize the data prior to hypothesis testing. For many audiences, it is more appropriate to keep quite close to the original data so that readers can see the relationship between the original questions and the results.

Even in the most apparently clear-cut cases it is useful to check a few basic details. Thus, as consultants, we would probably want a briefing interview and to look at a sample of the data. This would be supplemented, if needed, by study of any documents which (1) described the research design and objectives; and (2) set out any subsequent decisions or problems at the data collection stage that affected the nature of the data collected.

The process of learning about the data goes on throughout the consultancy, but it is only when we have got our first bearings that we can be sure that the presenting problem is the real problem and give any advice. All that our client may need is a little help and encouragement. The odds are, though, that the presenting problem does not indicate all the help needed. It may not even point to the real problems in handling the data in a way that will achieve the research objectives.

ACTIVITY 1

Think back to what you have learnt so far in DEH313 about research design and data collection.

What information might we need to understand before we can begin to discuss what to do with the data produced by any enquiry?

Spend five minutes or so drawing up a list of the broad areas in which we might need information. Write your answers down in the form of questions to which we would want answers.

The four basic questions I would ask in response to this are given below — but note that each one is a beginning question only, in that it leads on to further questions like the ones listed beneath the first question. I would continue with these and similar subsidiary questions until I had obtained the information needed to confirm with the client the nature of the problem. Only at that point could we discuss issues and procedures related to doing something appropriate with the data.

1. What is the nature of the data that have been collected?
   — What was the method of data collection?
   — Are the data basically structured, or will they require structuring, e.g. categorizing, prior to data analysis?
   — How many cases are there; who or what are they; and how were they selected?
   — How were the data recorded and in what form are they at present?

2. What kind of analysis of the data is planned?

3. What are the research objectives; and what kind of report is planned?

4. What is the time-scale and what resources are available for data handling and analysis?

Let us ask the first question and see what kind of answers we get.

Question 1: What is the nature of the data that have been collected?

Here are some replies from various hypothetical clients — most of these replies are from real situations, but the details have been changed to preserve anonymity:

A 'It's information to help with the development of DEH313. I've got 250 questionnaires from a random sample of students who've taken DE304[1] in its last two years. The data relate to reactions to DE304 and to features the students would like in the new course. I need to put the data on computer and talk through the appropriate data analysis.'

B 'I've got some tapes of interviews with patients, doctors and nursing staff in two local hospitals. They ask about views on the existing facilities and needs. I want to build up a picture of the facilities and the main gaps in provision in the two hospitals.'

C 'I've got some data from a data bank and I want to do some secondary analysis. They come from interviews with staff and clients in various voluntary organizations. I want to see how client satisfaction relates to the type and size of organization. I also want to test some hypotheses about gender. I think client satisfactions will be different according to whether the voluntary sector worker and the client are the same gender or different genders. Most of the information I need is there, but I need a bit of help in checking it out and constructing the scales I need.'

D 'Other members of a working party and I have collected a lot of information in order to look at equal opportunities in our town. We've got some national and local statistics, records of what has been said in the Council, interviews with ten local employers and also a small survey on attitudes collected from people living on one of the estates. We think some new initiatives would help a lot — and there are grants going. The information we have collected might be used to support an application. What is the next step in analysing the information?'

E 'They are data collected from students attending a residential weekend at Reading and I have been asked to analyse them. I got the questionnaires and put the info in a database on my PC. Now I've had a look at the first results I'm not very happy. For example, the figures for the number of hours spent

---

[1] *DE304 Research Methods in Education and the Social Sciences:* the predecessor to this course.

on the first TMA look a bit odd — the average number of hours is far too high. And there are lots of other oddities; there are only 60 women in the sample yet I've got about 85 answers to the questions that only the women were supposed to answer. How should I go about sorting it all out?'

F   'I'm interested in developmental education and I've got some interview data from two year-groups in my school. I've also got their exam grades in various subjects. The aim is to look at children's knowledge of various countries and attitudes to people in those countries by age group and stage of cognitive development. I'm interested at this stage in getting a picture of how the attitudinal information hangs together. If possible I would like to make up some scales that would be stronger measures of the concepts I'm interested in than the individual questions.'

G   'I've been interested for quite some time in trade unions and I've collected quite a lot of information about six unions. I've got some data from the archives on how they developed, membership, decision-making structure, the policies they've voted for at TUC conferences, and strikes. I've also got access to some interview data from members of the six unions. I want to look at factors related to "militancy".'

The answers to Question 1 (or Q1) from our hypothetical clients A to G give us 'hooks' into the essential information that we need in order to establish the nature of the data that have been collected. However, as is the case with all broad open-ended questions, the information we need about the formal characteristics of the data as collected is mixed up with other pieces of information about different aspects of the research — for example, the research objectives. These latter details supply us with important information about goals, but the options for what can be done with data all relate to the formal characteristics of the data, not to the research objectives.

ACTIVITY 2

1   Spend a minute thinking about what you have learnt in the earlier units about the major differences in types of data. What would be the major thing that we would want to establish about the data? Write down your response in a phrase or sentence.

2   Spend ten minutes doing the following: look at the basic questions (listed in my response to Activity 1) that we are going to ask our clients and also at the hypothetical answers to the first question. These are listed in file DOC1 on your data disk and you can print them out using FRAMEWORK on your wordprocessor. Pick out the elements in each answer that you think relate to the various questions and record your answers.

Note: You might like to adopt one or other of the following strategies for carrying out the task:

1   Circle groups of words that embody the various pieces of information in the answers and write the number of the question for which you think they have most relevance beside the various groups. (Bear in mind that Q1 has four parts.)

Or:

2   Set up a list of headings Q1(a), Q1(b), Q1(c), Q1(d), Q2, Q3 and Q4. Under these headings list all the phrases in the answers that you think relate to the various questions indicated by the headings.

Or:

3   Use the cut and paste facilities offered by your word processor. Make a copy of DOC1 (which contains the list of hypothetical answers) from the data disk to a new document, then cut and paste the appropriate phrases until you have all the statements appropriate for Q1 listed under the heading Q1, and similarly for the other questions.

If it went well, then you have already completed your first piece of analysis in this unit! The answers are data, and you have just reduced them to a classification.

How did the activity work out? Were you able to identify elements in the answers that referred to each of the questions? And were ideas forming in your mind about further questions that you would like to ask each of our clients next in order to establish more details about the kind of data they have collected?

As the client gave his or her first answer to Question 1, I would normally be jotting down a list of keywords, such as 'structured questionnaire' and 'postal survey', from the answer. I would be particularly keen at this stage to form a clear picture of:

1 The method(s) of data collection.

2 The type of questions that had been asked of informants or that had guided the data collection.

Also, I would be keen to know:

3 Details of the cases, who or what they comprised and the number of cases.

4 The method of recording the data and the current form of these data: for example, raw data recorded on a questionnaire, edited data on a computer file, etc.

All these pieces of information would guide the next steps in handling the data. Other information, such as details of how the sampling of cases had been done and the sub-groups, would be important pieces of information but would only become essential later. For example, in the case of raw data we would make sure, at the data preparation stage, that we recorded membership of particular sub-groups that were needed for analysis purposes. At the analysis stage it might be very important to know just how the cases had been sampled and how many cases there were in each sub-group, but the information would not be essential for the first steps in doing something with the data.

3 PRIOR STRUCTURE, METHOD OF RECORDING AND SAMPLE SIZE

Let us take a closer look at methods of data collection and their implications for the extent to which data are already structured at the point when we try to do something with them. How they were recorded and how many cases we have will also shape our decisions.

3.1 PRIOR STRUCTURE

Table 1 indicates various methods of data collection which produce different types of data that require different handling strategies. It contains two main groups of data: data collected from informants (items 1 and 2) and data secured from other sources (items 3 and 4). The first group is amenable to researcher control during data collection, but for the second the data are limited by what is available.

Table 1 Methods of data collection

1	Tests
2	Questionnaires and interviews
3	Direct observation — of individuals, groups, communities or events, for example
4(a)	Trace records — that is, indicators of some variable that have been left behind (e.g. contents of household, amount of pavement wear, proportion of 'gentrified' houses in the street)
4(b)	Archive documents — running records (e.g. Census data, hospital admission statistics, court reports); episodic records from private and institutional sources (e.g. sales catalogues, published accounts, committee papers, correspondence, diaries, speeches, newspaper reports)

(Source: based on a classification in Runkel and McGrath, 1972)

The information about the method of data collection gives clues as to the likelihood of the data being already highly structured — a very important feature as this indicates the operations needed to handle the data. In a highly structured data set a great deal will already have been determined. In contrast, with highly unstructured data the major task of the data handling is to determine both the variables that are to be abstracted from the raw data and the appropriate answer categories. It may even be that the research problem and any hypotheses are to be decided in the light of the content and the clues to underlying variables that are suggested by the data.

The method of data collection also points to the likelihood of the data being complete in terms of there being the same information for all the cases (at least, in principle). Where the data have been specially collected — for example, using tests, questionnaires and interview schedules — the likelihood is that we will have information for most cases on most variables. Where the data represent observations of naturally occurring events, or are the product of searches for traces of past events or archive searches, the likelihood of incomplete data increases.

The implication of the latter is that handling the data may involve bridging gaps in the evidence when we attempt to categorize, scale or structure the data. For example, we might have to decide that quite disparate 'events' and possessions were indicators of the relative wealth of households; that is, there might be no *single* indicator of wealth for all cases in the data set, so we might have to assess it on a *range* of evidence. Occasionally, it may not be possible to establish 'common ground' for comparing cases — the responses are very different from each other, or there is a great deal of missing information, and not the same missing information for each case. If you are in this situation, probably all you can recommend is that the cases be presented individually, as illustrating possible cases, rather than shaping them up for comparison. Mostly, however, it is possible to 'work over' the data so that some kind of valid comparison can be made.

Tests usually imply data which are highly structured. The stimuli or the questions are presented in a given order and with specific instructions which set the framework for measuring 'performance'. The data are scores which are either produced directly by some calibrated instrument or derived from the 'raw data' according to given rules. Usually norms are available which indicate the meaning of given scores in terms of the performance of a general population and sub-groups of the population. (It can be a problem at the data interpretation stage to decide the extent to which the norms for the populations on which the scores were standardized are appropriate to one's own sample.)

Test data clearly include scores on variables such as height and weight, and scores in exams, etc. They arguably also include scores on standard personality inventories. The latter are based on questions to which there is no right answer, but the sum of answers to particular questions is used as a measure of standard dimensions of personality: for example, introversion/extraversion. *Tests* can even include scores on such tests as the 'Draw a Man' test, in which a child draws a person and a trained interpreter then analyses various elements in the drawing, and the relationship between elements, according to a set of rules and gives a numerical score to the child's stage of cognitive development.

Data from tests will generally be expressed as numbers on an interval or ratio scale — 'real numbers' with which you can do arithmetic and calculate means. You will remember from earlier units that there are four distinct scales of measurement, each with its own properties:

1. *Ratio scales*, where the intervals between adjacent numbers mean the same up and down the scale, and multiplication can be carried out (e.g. an increase of one mile per hour means the same whether it is an increase from 30 mph or from 60 mph, and 60 mph is twice 30 mph).

2. *Interval scales*, where the intervals mean the same up and down the scale but multiplication is not meaningful (e.g. an increase of 1 degree means the same additional heat up and down the scale, but 80 degrees Celsius is not twice 40 degrees Celsius in terms of heat delivered).

3. *Ordinal scales* are ordered, but the intervals are not constant (an example would be educational qualifications: GCSE, 'O' level, 'A' level, diploma, degree).

4. In *nominal scales* the numbers are just labels for discrete items, and not even an ordering is implied.

Sometimes it will be necessary to degrade the numbers by recoding to a less powerful type of scale (ordinal or even nominal); this will be discussed later in the unit. It is worth noting, however, that in principle *anything* can be measured at least at the nominal level (e.g. as 'present' or 'absent', coded 1 or 0).

Tests such as we have been discussing are one special case of the general class of structured *questionnaires*. The distinguishing feature that separates questionnaires from other types of data collection method is that they ask exactly the same questions of all informants, and in the same order. Thus they produce data that can be treated in the same way for all cases — converted into scores or categorized according to rules set out in a coding frame. The result is a score or value for each informant on each of the variables that are under investigation — at least in principle, though there can be missing data. In other words, questionnaires produce data that are amenable to easy quantification.

The questions asked can be divided into two types: 'closed' questions and 'open-ended' questions:

1. *Closed questions* specify a task and also the range of possible responses to it. The respondent is forced to choose from one of a set of numbered options (although one of these might be 'don't know' or 'cannot decide'). Numbers (codes) may be assigned to the possible answers on the questionnaire itself, or they may be written in 'in the office' when the questionnaire is returned, but the range and meaning of the numbers is decided in advance. These questions are relatively unproblematic at the pre-analysis stage: the numbers can be entered directly into the database.

2. *Open-ended questions* pose a question or specify a 'task' just as closed questions do, but the informant has the freedom to answer in his or her own way rather than in terms of the researcher's predefined answer categories. Open-ended questions can, in principle, be reduced to numerical scores in the same way as any other questionnaire item. (In Unit 17/18 you will be introduced to an alternative way of looking at open-ended questions, but for the purposes of this unit we will refer only to this specific form of measurement.)

Figure 2 gives examples of both an open-ended and a closed question.

> **Open-ended question:**
>
> Please identify anything particularly useful in the course you have just read.   *Write in.*
>
>
>
> **Closed question:**
>
> (a) Which of the following did you find particularly useful in the course you have just read? *Ring all those that apply.*
>
> (b) Which feature of the course did you find most useful?   *Ring one answer only.*
>
> | | (a) Particularly useful [1] | (b) The most useful [2] |
> |---|---|---|
> | The explanation of concepts | 1 | 1 |
> | The explanation of techniques | 1 | 2 |
> | The statistics teaching | 1 | 3 |
> | The computer teaching | 1 | 4 |
> | The video | 1 | 5 |
> | The audio | 1 | 6 |
> | Other *(specify below)* | 1 | 7 |
> | .... | | |
> | .... | | |
> | Nothing at all | 1 | 0 |
>
> *Note:* 1 Part (a) of the question generates eight variables with values '1' and '0', with '0' representing 'not particularly useful'.
> 2 Part (b) of the question comprises one variable with eight answer codes.

Figure 2   *Examples of open-ended and closed questions*

Some points to note:

- In the case of closed questions, the data reflect the researcher's prior structuring of the 'universe'. In contrast, open-ended questions identify a topic and task but the respondent has freedom to select what is relevant.

- When open-ended questions are asked of all informants — for example, through a questionnaire or during an interview — the answers can be transformed into variables for which there are values for all cases. These values can be treated quantitatively to produce statistics, just as with the closed questions.

- Pre-coding of the data is possible with closed questions, but the information from open-ended questions has to be structured and transformed into a form suitable for statistical and other analyses. This is probably carried out after all the data have been collected.

- Some apparently open-ended questions in interviews may be treated just like closed questions in self-completion questionnaires. The interviewer may have a list of previously determined codes for those answers that are of interest.

Instead of writing down the informant's words, the interviewer rings a numerical code to indicate which one of a predetermined set of answers has been given.

As you are aware, not all research proceeds by asking people questions. For example, data may also be gathered by *direct observation*. Sometimes observation is carried out purely to form an understanding of what is going on, with no intention of analysing frequencies of occurrence (though even here a few relevant numbers can improve a report). It is also possible, however, to carry out an *observational survey*, using a structured form of data collection to count and/or measure relevant aspects of what is being observed — the number of cars passing a given point, the extent of aggressive behaviour in a school playground, the number of references to women as 'girls' in a given kind of text, for instance. In this case most of what we have said about questionnaires applies also to observation. 'Structured observation' generally proceeds by recording data in predetermined categories, but there could, in principle, be the equivalent of open-ended questions as well — descriptive notes, written in the field, to be coded into categories in the office.

The extent of structuring in the data produced through direct observation of people and events tends to reflect the extent to which what is recorded is itself contained and structured. For example, there will be a relatively large number of points of comparison between videos of children performing a computer-aided learning task — and hence quite a lot of scope for classification of the children's behaviour. There would probably be relatively little in common between videos of different children recorded at 3 o'clock in the afternoon on the first day of their school holiday. Typically, the less structured the situation the more likelihood there is of one or both of the following being characteristic of the data: (1) a high proportion of the behaviour occurring is irrelevant to the researcher's interests and has to be discarded; and (2) a low incidence, or even absence, of behaviours that are of special interest to the researcher, except where the researcher's specialist interest is the individual case rather than comparison across cases.

Finally, we measure the past by inference from *traces* in the physical environment — for example, assessing the flow of traffic through a doorway by measuring the degree to which the step has been worn away — or from *archive* data, by using numbers collected at the time or making our own counts of relevant features from records. The degree of structure in the data collected by these methods will vary a great deal according to component subsets of data and how they were collected. Some sets of data may be highly structured and, indeed, preprocessed — for example, data from a survey archive which have been processed for other analysis purposes, or data which largely comprise published statistics (sets of company accounts and sales records, etc.). Sometimes, however, the data will show very little structure in that the records will have been drawn from many sources and there may be a lot of missing data or other gaps. Archive source materials and trace records are also likely to contain material that is irrelevant for the purposes of the study. A major task at the data-processing stage is, therefore, often that of bringing some order to the assembled materials. It could involve: sorting the materials that are pertinent to the enquiry from those that are not; organizing the former in some order; abstracting and summarizing relevant data; and, in general, preparing the materials in such a way that the process of investigating relevant data can be carried out efficiently.

3.2 METHOD OF RECORDING

In the case of questionnaires and similar pre-coded documents, typically all the information is recorded on the questionnaire itself, either by the informant or an interviewer or (later) by a coder. The coder codes the open-ended questions and enters the appropriate code in the relevant place on the questionnaire. The numbers representing the data are then keyed into a computer.

Sometimes the process is even more automated. In the case of some telephone interviews everything is computer controlled—for example, the dialling; the presentation of the appropriate question on a screen for the interviewer to read out; and, at the end of the process, there is 'real-time' recording of the interviewers' codes for answers so that up-to-date results are always available. In Activity 1 in Unit 9 you read about a survey of television viewing which used a machine plugged into the television to record when the television was on and what channel was showing: this would be another example.

As the open-endedness of the questions and the data-gathering situation increases, the complexity and diversity of material to be recorded increases also. One way of recording the data is to do 'real time' recording using appropriate machines such as audio-cassette recorders and video cameras. The advantages and disadvantages of using such recording devices were discussed in Section 4.3 of Unit 12, and for the purposes of this unit it only needs to be said that their use means that questions and the verbatim answers and events can be captured as they unfold. It also means that the data available for processing have not had to be abstracted from the on-going situation and that the recordings are available in full for replay and analysis as many times as the researcher wishes. However, quite a lot of effort is needed at the data-handling and analysis stages to abstract data from the tapes unless the latter are transcribed (itself a time-consuming and sometimes problematic task, as indicated in Unit 12).

In some cases, this type of recording is not possible — the equipment may not be available, the interviewee may object, or the recording equipment would intrude and perhaps influence what was said or done. In such cases, the only record may be notes made during interviews and observations, or recollections written up subsequently. The information available for processing from each record has already been partially degraded and some potential data have been lost because they have gone unrecorded. Further, the information recorded has been filtered through the preconceptions and theories of the person who has made the notes.

Where topics are researched by identification and retrieval of existing records, researchers have no control over the medium in which the information has been recorded: they must take the data as they come. Typically, they will photocopy documents when they can and, when this is not possible, abstract information in the form of précis, quotations, tables, graphs and whatever seems most suitable for making a personal record of these data. Inevitably, there will be diversity in the format of the information that they assemble and, as I noted in Section 3.1, it is quite likely there will be a high proportion of missing information. The first task at the data-processing stage will be to bring order to the raw data by, perhaps, working out an appropriate filing system for the various records that will allow ready access when needed.

3.3 SAMPLE SIZE

When we considered the information we needed in order to be able to advise on data handling, the number of cases, and their nature, came quite high on the list of priorities. This most basic information alerts us to the kind of comparisons that will be possible, and hence whether any initial data handling should be geared towards transformation of the data into a form suitable for case history-type analysis or for statistical analysis. Let us take a brief look at the surface implications of the following sources of information:

- The 20 students attending the DEH313 Induction Meeting at Reading.
- 600 secondary school students.
- 250 companies participating in a CBI survey.
- Six trade unions.
- Our village.

'Our village' is probably a case history. What we are likely to have is detailed information about one location over time, and this lends itself most readily to 'telling the story' rather than to 'presenting the figures'. However, if appropriate data have been collected, it might be possible to locate the village in some greater space through relating its features to national statistics and comparative information secured in studies of other villages.

In the case of the six trade unions and the 20 DEH313 students, some primitive counting and some comparisons of the data for given variables might be possible, but testing for statistical significance[2] would be inappropriate because the number of cases is too small. It would therefore not be worth the trouble of coding the open-ended questions, as we do in the case of questionnaire data for large numbers of cases.

The data sets comprising information for 250 companies, and information from or relating to the 600 students, open up the possibilities for treating the data quantitatively, undertaking sub-group analysis and, if appropriate, doing tests of statistical significance. But we would be alerted to possible trouble ahead if we had been told that the company data had been collected through open-ended questions. This would point to the possibility that huge resources might need to be committed if all the data had to be coded into variables suitable for statistical analysis.

4 GETTING THE DATA INTO SHAPE FOR ANALYSIS

Looking back to the Introduction, six objectives were identified as being important in respect of what we do with data. Key phrases which arise from these objectives are: 'error reduction/minimization', 'data representation', 'data transformation' and 'data reduction'. In this section we will be considering these phrases or 'concepts' in the context of handling the data that have been collected. In this case, 'handling' means shaping the raw data so that they are transformed into variables to enable us to inspect or analyse them more readily.

Think of the situation that might apply at the end of the data collection process. There could be bundles of questionnaires, notes or tapes of interviews, perhaps videos and, in the case of archive materials, folders containing copies of original documents, sets of notes containing abstracts, and possibly more. What are we aiming to do and how do we begin? In many kinds of social research, the objective is to structure the records in such a way that the data become elements in a data matrix. This might sound alien and off-putting, but in fact it is quite simple. People have been constructing data matrices from the time of the earliest records, and you have probably been doing it yourself for years.

Basically, a data matrix comprises a grid of rows and columns. Traditionally, the rows represent cases, the columns represent variables and the entries are the data. If you were planning a holiday and wanted to put the information from the brochures, and the various comments from travel agents and friends, in some order, you might construct a data matrix like the one shown in Table 2.

---

[2] You will learn how to test for statistical significance of differences in Block 4.

Table 2 A matrix of holiday information

Destination	Number of nights	Accommodation	Food	Price
Brest	7	Single	Half	High
Quimper	7	Single	Full	High
Huelgoat	7	Single	Self-catering	Medium
St Brieuc	5	Single	Self-catering	Medium
Rennes	7	Single	Half	Medium
Val-Andre	7	Single	Half	Low
Le Rochell	6	Shared	Half	Medium
Perpignon	12	Shared	Self-catering	Low

By organizing the data on holidays in this way, we can analyse them relatively easily. Clearly, however, there are likely to be more items of data collected in research projects than in the case of our holiday example. Where there are many cases and fairly complete records for each case, it is usual to code all the data that come in so that they can be held in a parsimonious format with numbers and letters (called 'alphanumerics') representing them. In this instance, the data matrix might look like that shown in Figure 3.

There is one major difference between the data matrix in Figure 3 and that representing data about holiday destinations in Table 2. Given the information that it is a data matrix, we are pretty confident that the rows represent cases and the columns variables, but we lack the information to interpret it. Secondly, we cannot draw up the instructions for processing it even though it is obvious that the values can be counted and the cases divided up into groups. In the case of the variables, individual columns (digits) might represent discrete variables, but they could equally well be a representation of data such as age which might require two columns to represent the full data collected. It is clear that, unless the data matrix records the raw data in a way that we can recognize (e.g. 'male', 'female'), a set of instructions must have been drawn up for transforming the data into codes and for identifying the location of all the variables. This set of instructions is called the *coding frame*. A coding frame always includes three pieces of information for each variable. These are (1) a reference back to the source data (e.g. Q12(b) or 'age of informant'); (2) a list which comprises the codes and their associated symbols; and (3) an identification of the column location of the variable within the matrix. Figure 4 is an example of a coding frame.

Given this coding frame, we could read off the data for individual cases, just as we could read the data in the matrix for holidays. Secondly, we could give all the instructions needed for (1) naming the variables and the categories so that they can be recognized by a computer and also printed out on the tables; and (2) writing a specification for analysing the variables — counting the data, dividing the cases into groups and analysing according to group membership, relating variables to each other, and so on.

```
A10156M1197012253722B51195741188221     ...3
A10478F311205432126328 263141322510     ...3
                       .
                       .
Z10530F4132331413261195A734118    270   ...2
```

Figure 3 *A research data matrix*

Column	Variables/codes
1	Location of sample: 1 Hospital 2 Rest home 3 Own home
2–4	Case number (3 digits)
5–6	Age (2 digits)
7	Gender (M or F)
8	Are you able to move around your house without help? 0 No answer 1 Yes 2 With some difficulty 3 With great difficulty 4 No
9	What help do you receive to move around your house? 0 No information 1 None 2 Aids (e.g. stick) **Note: If 2 and 3 are indicated, code as 3** 3 Personal help
10	Are you able to move around outside the house without personal help? 0 No answer 1 Yes 2 Garden, but not beyond 3 Garden, but with great difficulty 4 No 9 'Don't want to go out' and other refusals to answer

Figure 4 *An example of a coding frame*

Data matrices like the one described above are clearly best suited to machine analysis, in that much of the meaning of the data is not obvious. But the same concepts apply to matrices held on paper, with 'hand counting' of the frequency of particular codes.

As I pointed out at the beginning of the unit, however, data are constructed by the researcher, not just 'found', and the coding frame is one of the major means by which this construction takes place. Whether the codes are established beforehand (i.e. the questions pre-coded), or whether the coding frame is 'derived from the data' (in the case of open-ended questions or unstructured interviews coded after data collection), the outcome is the result of a series of decisions taken by the researcher. The researcher may try to minimize error and to represent the views and characteristics of the sample faithfully, but in practice this means that it is the researcher who determines what shall count as error and what is acceptable as a faithful representation. In the next section we look at some of these decisions and how they are taken.

4.1 GETTING THE PRE-CODING RIGHT

This topic seems on the surface to be quite a trivial one compared with the important decisions that researchers have to make about the coverage and structure of their questionnaires and the questions asked of informants. Naturally, researchers focus on these decisions and sometimes pay scant attention to the technicalities of getting the pre-coding right. As consultants to researchers who come to ask about what to do with their data, we would see the consternation of clients who had got it wrong. Instead of proceeding smoothly to the interesting task of analysing the data, scarce resources of time or money might be needed to put things right — and time would be lost.

The particular advantages of pre-coding are that it cuts the time and costs of data handling and also one source of error: that is, error introduced at the coding stage. Especially in the case of large-scale surveys, the ideal is to have a questionnaire which requires little more than clerical checking for respondent errors (e.g. an answer circled instead of its code, or too many codes circled) and, if required, coding of open-ended questions before the questionnaires are passed on to the people who will key the data into a computer file. The task of these operators is to key for each case (respondent) a sequence of letters and numbers (the codes) in the given column locations, so pre-coding involves the allocation of column numbers as well as answer codes for each variable.

Clearly, problems arise when insufficient columns have been allocated to hold the data for each question. An example is age: only one column might have been allocated for this variable, but the data require two columns. Worse, a badly worded question might result in many informants circling several answers between which we cannot discriminate and therefore want to record in full — and a deceptively simple open-ended question can generate replies that require an unexpectedly large number of columns to record. All of this is supposed to be ironed out by pilot studies of the design and coding of the questionnaire, but mistakes still slip through.

Sometimes there may be a more basic problem: the pre-coding may not reflect the logical structure of the data and hence have implications for data analysis. In pre-coding a questionnaire for data analysis the requirement is to identify variables correctly as variables, to allocate appropriate codes for given answers and to give each variable a unique location. If you look back to Figure 2, you will see that part (a) of the closed question generated eight variables with two possible codes (zero and one), whereas part (b) produced one variable with values of 0 to 7 to reflect the single answer that informants were asked to give.

ACTIVITY 3

Figure 5 shows some real examples of attempts at pre-coding. There are errors of various kinds that would require quite a lot of work to remedy before the data could be keyed into a data matrix.

Test out your skills in pre-coding structured questionnaires by doing some error spotting:

1 Spot some of the problems, list them and, for each error that you have identified, make brief notes on what is wrong. Note: the errors might relate to failure to follow conventions for identifying columns and categories. They may, however, be more radical in that what constitutes a variable has not been correctly identified.

2 Have a go at providing solutions to the problems. Identify the variables and assign them 'column' numbers and also assign a number (or other symbol) to the various categories or scale points within each variable. In the case of column numbers, follow the convention adopted in Figure 5; that is, (21) = column 21.

The column number with which you start is arbitrary — the questions are abstracted from questionnaires — but your column numbers should be in sequence, so start with (21) as in the figure.

1   Educational and professional qualifications held: *Please ring and write in, as appropriate*

Bachelor's degree	1	(21)
Class: 1st	1	(22)
2.1	1	(23)
2.2	1	(24)
3rd	1	(25)
Pass	1	(26)
No post 'A' level qualification	1	(27)
HNC/HND	1	(28)
Other undergraduate diploma/certificate	1	(29)
Postgraduate diploma/certificate	1	(30)
Master's degree	1	(32)
PhD	1	(33)
Professional qualification *Please specify*	1	(34)

....

Other post 'A' level qualification   *Please specify*   1   (35)

....

2   Please identify the subject fields in which you obtained:

    (a) your HNC/HND or undergraduate diploma/certificate
    (b) your bachelor's degree
    (c) your postgraduate diploma/master's degree/PhD

Indicate your answers by entering ticks where appropriate

	HNC/HND; undergrad. dip.	Bachelor's degree	Postgrad. dip.; master's; PhD	
Arts, *including languages and law*	☐	☐	☐	(36)
Social studies	☐	☐	☐	(37)
Business studies	☐	☐	☐	(38)
Science/maths	☐	☐	☐	(39)
Engineering	☐	☐	☐	(40)
Other: please specify				(41)

....

3   Please write in your raw score on the BS test *(e.g. 097)*   Your score: ☐ (42)

[Continued overleaf]

4   Please indicate the strength of your agreement with the following statements by ringing the letters in each row:

	Low				High	
The main benefit of a degree is to develop good all round generalist skills	a	b	c	d	e	(43)
The main benefit of a degree is to develop in depth knowledge of a particular subject area	a	b	c	d	e	(44)

5   Please rank the subjects listed below on a scale 1 to 5 (**Rank 1** = least valuable and **Rank 5** = most valuable) according to the value for employment purposes placed on them by (a) yourself and (b) employers, and (c) tick to indicate your personal interest in the subjects (H = high, M = medium, or L = low)

| | Yourself | Employers | Personal interest |
			H M L
Arts, *including languages and law*	☐ (45)	☐ (50)	☐ ☐ ☐
Social studies	☐ (46)	☐ (51)	☐ ☐ ☐
Business studies	☐ (47)	☐ (52)	☐ ☐ ☐
Science/maths	☐ (48)	☐ (53)	☐ ☐ ☐
Engineering	☐ (49)	☐ (54)	☐ ☐ ☐

Figure 5   *An example of pre-coding with errors*

The symbols for the answer categories are also arbitrary, but it is easier to deal with numbers rather than alphanumerics (letters) at the data analysis stage, so use numbers unless there are good reasons for using alphanumerics.

I suggest that you write in your solutions in red or another colour in the appropriate places on the examples.

You will find my answers at the end of the unit.

When you have finished this activity go to your data disk on which you will find a document, DOC2. DOC2 gives a questionnaire format that is one solution to the problem on which you have just been engaged. You might be interested in comparing it with yours. An alternative format is also given for the questions. Some of the questions have been modified so that the task of answering is clearer and easier to do. Others secure the basic information that was of interest to the client. All have appropriate codes indicated so that the job of checking and coding the data produced by the Figure 5 format could be reduced from many days to a few days.

4.2 CODING OPEN-ENDED QUESTIONS

Many questionnaires and other documents contain open-ended questions. To transform the raw data from these questions into a form in which we can analyse them efficiently requires a lot of effort and thought in the initial stages of handling the data. In the case of open-ended questions in pre-coded questionnaires, provision will have been made in the pre-coding for codes derived from the written-in answers, but we shall need to prepare a code list for these later. If we decide to go ahead and code the written-in information, the checking and coding phase which precedes any data keying is the obvious time to do this — coding at a later stage and inserting the codes into a data matrix is tedious, and sometimes substantial computer skills are needed to merge the new data with an existing data matrix on the computer. Thus we face an important decision: to code the open-ended information or to analyse it by hand — listing the data for inspection, then quoting comments that are typical or of special interest in the report.

If it is essential for the project that we code given open-ended questions (e.g. if we need to report the frequencies of the answers or to relate the answers to the open-ended questions to other variables), then there is no option. We have to find the time and person resource to draw up a coding frame and code the answers on the questionnaires prior to data keying. If time presses — for example, a report has been promised in the near future in which the major interest will be in the closed questions — we might decide that the best course is not to have the open-ended data coded and keyed in, but to treat them by other means as best we can.

If there is any doubt about whether to code, then we must get more information. In this case, 'getting more information' means selecting a stack of questionnaires — possibly 50 or so — and taking a look at the raw data. We would be interested in the *kind* of answers written in and the *numbers* of informants who had written something in the space on the questionnaire. The cases (questionnaires) may be picked out for inspection in a variety of ways. They could be (1) picked at random from the various batches as they came into the office; (2) sampled more systematically on the basis of the groups represented in the survey; or (3) chosen in a way that might ensure that the diversity in the answers was as great as possible. For example, we might want to represent both men and women and both younger and older people.

The initial inspection might just involve opening up the questionnaires at the relevant page, reading the answers for the sample and forming an impression about whether the answers were of sufficient interest and diversity to warrant coding. A better variant of this quick inspection might be to stack the questionnaires in piles according to our impressions of which answers to a given question were of the same kind. We might then go through each pile a second and perhaps a third time, re-sorting as necessary with the aim of ending up with as small a number of piles as possible, with a reasonable set of questionnaires in each pile, and with the answers in each pile representing a particular category of response. It would be important that the piles differed from each other in some significant way, not in some trivial respect. They should represent answer categories that were of interest in relation to the research objectives. Finally, there should be only a small number of answers that we could not classify. At this stage, we would have the basis for our initial coding frame for the particular open-ended question. In the light of this initial coding, either we might decide to go ahead with coding the questions, or we might make a decision not to go ahead on the grounds that the categories were not sufficiently interesting to warrant investing the resource and time needed to do the coding.

A different approach is to invest in typing out the responses or keying them into a document on a computer. This involves a greater initial investment of time, but the record is permanent and allows sorting and re-sorting (e.g. through 'cutting' and 'pasting') until we feel we have got it right. It also allows the various concepts that the respondents may have given in the answer to a question to be split up and allocated to different categories. Even if a decision is made not to code, we have a useful set of keyed-in answers that can be used for illustrative purposes and extended, if need be, by adding further answers from a larger sample of the questionnaires.

Given that the decision is to code, we would then draw up a coding frame using the same principles that guided the assignment of codes to the closed questions; that is, a unique value for each category. Typically, we would set this out in the format illustrated in Figure 6. Note that this format contains all the information needed for someone else to carry out the task of coding the data. It also contains all the labelling information needed to identify the question to which the data refer and the location of the variable in a data matrix.

You might note that, if space had been allowed on the questionnaire for coding two variables, there would be the possibility of coding two or more referents in a respondent's answer. For example, if the answer was 'better job prospects and personal development', we could code 'better job' (the first element of the answer) in the first of the allocated columns, and 'personal development' (the second element) in the second column. If the numbers of cases were very large and the categories very diverse, we would have the option of using the two columns to record categories '01' to '99'.

The next stage might be trial coding on a larger sample, or we could go straight on to the task of coding all the questionnaires. In either case, we might find answers that could not be coded. If relatively few, they might be coded as 'other'. If substantial in number and representing new themes, we might well want to modify the coding frame. This might be done through the addition of further categories or it might require abandoning the existing frame and starting again. Whenever the modifications were other than trivial, it would be good practice to go back over all the coded questionnaires and check that the code that had been assigned still applied.

Col. 20	Q3 'Why did you decide to study with the OU?' 1st reason	
0	No answer	
1	Job/career reasons	(get better job; start a new career; re-enter paid employment)
2	Personal development	(develop wider perspectives; become more confident as a person; develop new interests)
3	Subject-related reasons	(interested in maths; wanted to gain skills in computing; learn more about the social sciences)
4	To get a degree or other qualification	(to get a degree; gain the credits needed for BPS recognition; HSW diploma; Advanced Diploma in Education, etc.)
9	Other answers	
Col. 21	Q3 'Why did you decide to study with the OU?' 2nd reason	
	As above (Col. 20)	

Figure 6 A coding frame with examples of typical answers

ACTIVITY 4

The Appendix to this unit gives two sections (Sections 3 and 4) from a report I wrote on the reactions of teachers to a pack of learning materials that they had used (Swift, 1991a). The materials had been devised to help teachers like themselves make full use of their teacher placement in business and industry. The sections selected relate to:

1   The teachers' written-in comments on their objectives in undertaking a placement (Section 3); and

2   The additional comments that they made at the end of the questionnaire (Section 4).

The open-ended answers in the two sections represent responses to different types of question. Those in Section 3 relate to a question asking for specific information: that is, the teachers' objectives. In contrast, the answers in Section 4 are responses to a very general invitation — 'If you would like to say anything about teacher placements in general or your own placement, please feel free to write in'.

The objective in the report was to give a flavour of the verbatim comments. There was minimal organization of the raw data. In Section 3, I summarized some common themes and then listed alphabetically all the comments typed for a sample of the cases. Even this primitive ordering helped partially to group comments with the similar themes. In the case of Section 4, the comments comprise a smaller selection of the replies, but they are individually more complex and varied than the data on teacher motivations. I arranged the Section 4 comments roughly to indicate positive reactions and negative/critical comments.

You should now:

1   Take a quick glance at both sections in the Appendix, including the text as well as a few of the comments.

2   Decide which set you would rather work with. (If you decide to work on the motivations data in Section 3 of the Appendix, you might start off by sampling these rather than looking at all the comments.)

3   The task is to draw up a coding frame — or to get as far into this task as possible in the time you have available.

I suggest that you set aside about 20 minutes for the activity.

Note

You might like to work with a pencil, working through the list several times to identify the comments that seem similar. As you work, write a code against those you have identified as belonging together. Keep a list of the codes: this list is your trial coding frame. An alternative strategy is to use a highlighter, but that is not as easy to change as pencil. If you prefer to work on your computer, copies of the documents are available in data disk files DOC3 and DOC4. Using your word processor, you can cut and paste the items, or appropriate parts of them, as you wish in order to develop your coding frame. One great advantage will be that, at the end of the task, you will have done quite a lot of the coding as well as having a (hopefully small) group of items which are the ones that do not fit your coding frame for the question.

Having tried out your skills and experienced some of the problems of coding data, we can now go on to consider data collected in a situation where the questions are not as standardized as the ones you have been considering. But first we might note that not all coding operations require the drawing up of a new coding frame. An example is coding information on occupations. In this case, the initial task of identifying categories has been done by a variety of organizations that have devised coding frames to suit their particular requirements. Thus there are coding frames such as those used in coding Census data which try to reflect the ways in which occupations group together, and there are coding schemes that are more concerned to measure social status. (The coding of social class and occupation is discussed in Unit 16.) Researchers generally choose the coding scheme that best fits their purposes and then proceed to code their own data in terms of the published coding frame. Where this strategy is used, the research data can, of course, be compared with any published data.

4.3 CODING DATA FROM UNSTRUCTURED INTERVIEWS

In instances where the questions are asked of all informants and/or the answers are relatively short and simple (like the motivations data in Activity 4), the process for interview data is much the same as that in the activity you have just done. However, when there is deviation from this type of question and answer, the nature of the problem, and thus of the coding process, changes.

ACTIVITY 5

Think briefly about what you now know about:

1 Unstructured data collected in interviews in which standard questions were not presented in a predetermined order.

2 The way data are influenced by the manner in which they have been recorded.

Can you specify at least two things that would make the task of coding unstructured interview data more complex than the coding you tried out in Activity 4? Make a note of your answer before reading on.

My answers to this question included:

1 Differently phrased questions are asked.

2 Informants are allowed, even encouraged, to develop their answers, so that a considerable amount of material may be secured on a given topic for certain informants, but not others.

3 Topics and variables cannot be defined by the answers to particular questions. For example:

   (a) given questions (or topics) may provide material which is relevant for *several* of the variables in the final coding frame;

   (b) conversely, the same codes on given variables might be based on answers to different questions in the case of different informants. In other words, all the interview data have to be taken into account. We cannot, for best results, treat individual parts of the data as if they were separate and unrelated to the rest.

4 What we can do with the data is in part defined by the type of record that has been made.

If the record comprises notes on an interview, the data, however substantial and detailed, will have been influenced by the process of abstracting what appeared relevant at the time of making the notes. It will be a partial or even a biased record. In analysis of his or her notes, a researcher may try to reconstruct the situation and remember exactly what had been said rather than just dealing with the notes at their face value. Thus he or she may write further notes on the things recollected and annotate the record to indicate possible meanings. In the case of group discussions, and also of direct observation of interactions and events, the problem is even more acute if the only record comprises notes made at the time or soon afterwards. A verbatim record in the form of an audio-tape or a video gives greatly improved access to what was said or what happened; however, a skilled interviewer's, or observer's, own notes can usefully supplement these recordings.

The first step in appreciating the potentialities in the information that has been collected is to become thoroughly acquainted with it. Let us imagine we are engaged in this task. If the information was recorded in the form of notes, we would read through these, perhaps several times, and make further notes identifying things that seemed of particular importance, or add annotations to particular passages. If audio- or video-tapes are available, the first step would be to listen to or view them, replaying sections as needed. As we listen or view, we might jot down brief notes on ideas that form in the mind about themes and meanings, perhaps identifying variables that might be derived from the data.

The second step with audio-tapes might be to transcribe the interview data: listening and note-taking is not always enough. We might need to have the raw data in a 'hard copy' form that we can manipulate according to the system that suits us best. My method involves making copies of the transcribed data so as not to lose them in their original format. I then split up the records into what seem to me the basic elements or concepts that have been expressed, or I use a highlighter to mark what I see as variables and as categories within variables. (It is more difficult to transcribe video-recording; systems do exist for transcribing the action on videos, but they tend either to simplify what is going on very grossly indeed, into a very few theory-derived categories, or to require a great deal of work to transcribe a very short sequence of video.)

What the variables are is not always clear, especially when there have been no interview agenda or issues which had to be covered and the interviews have elicited diverse information. In such cases, I might split up the verbatim records into elements that I could group and sort rather than try to treat individual interviews one by one. (I would take care, though, to label each of the elements with a number or mnemonic for the person who made the comment and with the question number, if applicable, so that I had the information to hand.) I would then, as my first strategy, sort the elements according to a theme or topic that had to be looked at because it was central to the objectives of the research or the research hypotheses, setting aside those that seemed to have no bearing on the topic. This process would continue until I felt fairly confident that I had identified the set of variables that I needed and could measure, and had also identified some of the main categories of each variable. This step completed, I would then proceed to construct a coding frame following the steps indicated for coding information on discrete questions.

There are at least three ways of thinking about data that are much more common in this kind of data analysis than in the coding of responses to a single open-ended question. These are:

1. Thinking about what the variables comprise and the boundaries between variables.

2. Thinking about the meaning of any new and unexpected categories that have emerged from the data and the extent to which they could help understanding of the topic. Stimulated by the data in front of us, we might identify variables and categories that *potentially* exist, that are hinted at by the data but cannot be explored properly because we do not have much information. This might lead to a new project in which we would explore the issues in a different way with an appropriate sample of people, to test this new insight and to see whether the potential new variables or categories emerge. In my case, I might represent the idea in a list of statements in a survey I would carry out later. I could then see whether the respondents recognized the idea and 'owned it' in the sense that their responses were meaningful and informative when related to other variables.

3. Thinking about meanings and, possibly, about causal relations.

For example, suppose we carried out some interviews with employers who sponsored Open University (OU) students with the aim finding out the employers' views on the quality and relevance of OU courses and their views on the OU system. Our first focus would probably be on what they said about the OU. We might start by looking at the data for the following overall groups of employers who are:

- Happy with OU courses/provision and experiencing no problems in relating to the OU as an institution.

- Happy with OU courses/provision but experiencing problems in relating to the OU as an institution.

- Critical of OU courses/provision but experiencing no problems in relating to the OU as an institution.

- Critical of OU courses/provision and experiencing problems in relating to the OU as an institution.

At a more detailed level, we would be able to identify a variety of aspects of happiness and unhappiness in relation to the OU's offerings and the OU as an organization, and these data might provide a basis for variables and categories. But suppose we had a sense of unease. For example, the categories with which we had ended up might not give us much insight into the research question, or the statements within each category might be an uneasy mix of generalities and very precise appreciations and criticisms. Also, interviews with some employers might have become focused on issues which scarcely emerged in other interviews.

Possibly we should start again, this time focusing on an employer's own organization rather than on the OU. It might be that the positive and negative reactions to the OU, and specific criticisms, made more sense when viewed in terms of the constraints and systems within the employer's organization. For example, criticisms of the OU's courses might relate not to the inadequacies in OU provision but to an employer's inability to make use of relevant courses, and the same might be true at the level of the OU as an institution. From this new perspective, even if the data were partial because the focus of the interview had been on the OU rather than on the employer's organization, the beginnings of a model might emerge that made sense and was informative about the research problem.

In summary, a systematic approach helps the task of drawing up a coding frame for the diverse data from unstructured interviews. Normally, this starts with getting acquainted with the data from each interview and proceeds to a search for similarities across interviews in terms of the variables under investigation. Given openness on the part of the researcher to the less obvious messages in the data, perhaps clearly expressed in only one or two comments, new perspectives on the research problem may be formed and become a basis for further codes or new research. (The same applies in respect of good open-ended questions in questionnaire-based studies.)

As Erickson and Nosanchuk (1977) remarked in the context of exploring data, 'You never look for *the* interpretation of a complex data set, or *the* way of analyzing it, because there are always lots of interpretations and lots of approaches depending on what you are interested in. There are many good answers to different questions, not just one right answer as in the detective story' (p.5).

4.4 REPRESENTATION VERSUS 'ANCHORED' AND 'HYPOTHESIS-GUIDED' APPROACHES TO CODING

So far I have talked about the process of drawing up a coding frame as if a good solution will naturally emerge if we have the right raw material. This is seldom the case: variables and categories are constructs and are not just 'out there' with their own independent existence. This applies as much to closed questions, and lists of items within closed questions, as to the coding of less structured interview material. In the case of some closed questions, however, a topic may have been so thoroughly explored that the categories seem self-evident to the researcher and informant.

Drawing up a coding frame is governed by the approach the researcher takes in respect of data in general in terms of what the data signify and useful ways of understanding them. I find it helpful to group the approaches in three ways. A researcher may:

1   View the data (e.g. the words that have been said) as expressing in their surface content what is 'out there'. In this case, the researcher's main concern will be to produce a set of codes which reduce the data to their essentials, with the codes reflecting the surface meaning of the raw data as faithfully as possible, independently of any views that the researcher may have about underlying variables and meanings.

2   View the data as having additional and implicit meanings which come from the fact that they are anchored in, and are dependent on, the data-gathering context. Thus what is relevant will have been communicated to informants through information about the enquiry and, indirectly, through the questions or the interview agenda. According to this perspective, in order to maximize on the usefulness for the particular project, the pre-codes and also the categories derived from the open-ended data should be aligned with the research context, or anchored in the appropriate external 'reality', as well as in the words said. For example, in investigating employers' happiness or unhappiness in respect of the OU, we might want to do this within a framework comprising types of formal and informal OU–employer interactions to which the OU commits resources. So our variables might include brochures, other mailings, enquiry services, 'roadshows', visits to employers, transactions about fees, and so on. The words given by the informants could also be 'interpreted' to produce codes on more than one dimension relating to the context. For instance, (a) *nature of contact*: informal versus formal contacts, initial contact versus continuing contacts, etc.; (b) *initiator of contact*: OU versus employer. When this approach is taken, the coding frame takes into account 'facts' in the situation, rather than treating the data individually as though they are context free. This creates a bridge to the 'world outside the research'. In cases in which the research involves recommendations, it may open up the path to action.

3   View the data as having a variety of meanings according to the theoretical perspective from which one is approaching them. This view has some similarities with Approach 2, but both are distinctive from the 'representational' perspective of Approach 1. In this case, the data do not have just one meaning which refers to some 'reality' approachable by analysis of the surface meaning of the words. For example, a data set might contain data on illnesses and minor upsets that the informants had experienced during the year. A researcher taking the 'representational' approach (Approach 1) might classify them according to the various types of illness. In contrast, a researcher taking the 'hypothesis-guided' approach (Approach 3) might use the raw data and other apparently quite disparate material to create and/or investigate variables that were defined in terms of his or her theoretical perspectives and research purposes. The illness data might be used as an indicator of a particular kind of stress or of ageing or of a reaction to a traumatic event. The coding frame would specify how mentions of particular illnesses, or ill health versus good health, were to be coded. However, the coding frame would be one based on the researcher's views and hypotheses rather than on the surface meanings of the set of written-in answers.

ACTIVITY 6

A survey that I carried out (Swift, 1991b) for the Open University School of Management during the first presentation of the B886 MBA dissertation included the following question:

'What experience of research/investigation had you had before doing your MBA dissertation?'

There were seven pre-coded categories, listed below, plus an 'other' category. (The percentages refer to frequencies of response in the survey.)

UNIT 14 WHAT IS DONE WITH DATA

		Percentage
1	Little or no previous experience of research	28
2	Evaluated research projects/proposals in my capacity as a manager	32
3	Commissioned one or more substantial pieces of research	16
4	Carried out desk (literature-based) research	35
5	Carried out database and similar research work	19
6	Carried out one or more substantial research project(s) at work	24
7	Completed a dissertation/thesis as part of a degree/qualification	52
8	Other research experience *Please specify below*	8

Here is a sample of the responses in the 'other' category:

1 'Consultancy work.'

2 'Clinical trials.'

3 'Biochemistry PhD 20 years; scientific research.'

4 'Research paper for Dip. NEBSS.'

5 'Technical research and development not management research.'

6 'Taught research at university — supervised and examined postgraduate research students.'

7(a) 'Scientific research.'

7(b) 'Experience with short research problems relating to the use of drugs in patients, i.e. practice research.'

8 'My job as an investigator involves examining documents and interviewing people to establish the cause of some failure, therefore there is an element of fact finding on research.'

Now try your hand at constructing three different coding frames:

1 A frame which reflects the essentials of the surface content of the 'other' answers.

2 A frame which also takes account of and is 'anchored in' the nature of the research project.

3 A more 'theoretical' or 'hypothesis-guided' coding frame.

You will find my answers at the end of the unit.

Notes and hints

1 The number of codes in each of your coding frames may be quite small, if that is all that is required.

2 In the case of your 'anchored' and 'hypothesis-guided' coding frames, there may well be categories that are not represented by this small sample of data. Indeed, this is very likely for the 'hypothesis-guided' coding frame; that is, you will want the frame to be able to reflect important concepts, if only by showing that they did not occur among the responses.

3 For the 'anchored' frame, you may wish to consider the concept of relevance to the task which the student faces.

4 For the 'hypothesis-guided' frame you may want to think about what kinds of previous experience are most likely to be useful for the task of preparing an MBA dissertation.

In conclusion to this section on coding, I would like to reiterate that data are not just something that exist, there to be collected and reported on. Rather, they are constructs. They are created through the questions asked of informants, the questions that guide record searches, and so on — and also through the processes of data collection, recording, coding or other representation. This does not mean, however, that all data are false. One of the things that researchers take most seriously is that they should not build bias into their data by imposing on them structures (codes) that are not applicable. At the stage of coding open-ended questions (and in drawing up the categories that will be pre-coded), this means being involved actively in thinking about how the topic might best be mapped in terms of variables and categories.

Finally, as an antidote to all the discussion about numbers and representations of data, you might be interested to note an approach taken by a colleague of mine, Nick Farnes, in analysing life history data that he had collected. He chose to analyse his data through 'coding' the information, for each of the people he had interviewed, in terms of a series of charts. In these he plotted careers (education, family life, health, etc.) in which he was interested against the age of the informant. Some of the charts plotted presence or absence of events against the informant's 'lifeline'. Others explored aspects of single events and yet others identified the linkages that the informant made between different events. An example of a chart summarizing the careers of one informant is given here as Figure 7.

The juxtaposition of the lifelines in Figure 7 enables actual or possible interactions between the careers of this student to be identified. On the basis of detailed information relating to the timing of the student's Open University courses, the researcher noted that:

1   She began her first OU course in 1984 after she finished her first part-time employment, after her miscarriage, when her first child was nearly three and when she was involved in the Mother and Toddler club (employment — health — childcare — community — education careers).

2   Between the second and third OU course (1985–87) she had another child, her husband became unemployed, she took on a community responsibility and began a computer studies course (education — childcare — husband's employment — community — further education).

3   Around the time she started the third course (1987), she began part-time employment as a playleader (education — employment).

This particular way of coding is an unusual one, but it has links with the other strategies we have discussed in that it facilitated theory-oriented exploration of the data set.

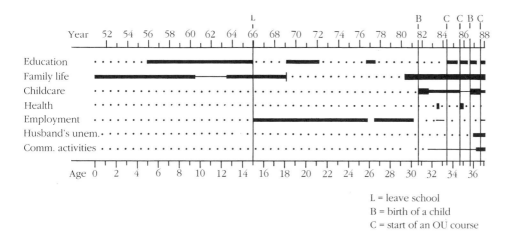

L = leave school
B = birth of a child
C = start of an OU course

Figure 7 *Summary of life history data for one informant*
(Source: Farnes, 1992, p.9)

4.5 CORRECTING ERRORS

Thinking back to the beginning of this unit, you will remember that, as consultants, we were concerned to find out about the nature of the data, and how they had been collected and recorded, for two reasons:

1. To guide the decisions we made about handling the information collected so that it was transformed into data that we could analyse.

2. To ensure quality through the reduction of error and bias. This has two aspects:

    (a) correction, if possible, of errors and biases in the data; and

    (b) minimization of the error and bias that could be introduced during handling of the data.

Let us look at the first phase of handling questionnaires and similar structured records before keying into the computer. Can you think of two sources of error in the replies to questionnaires that might be identified and possibly corrected before data keying? The major sources of error that can be identified in the questionnaire-checking process are:

1. Those introduced by the researcher through the wording of the questions and erroneous pre-coding and coding.

2. Those introduced by the respondent in completing the questionnaire. These might involve 'errors' in interpreting the question, and (in the case of self-administered questionnaires) failure to record the answer according to instructions. Where the questionnaire is interviewer-administered, the recording and coding errors of the interviewer would also fall into this category.

Where appropriate — in other words, where the changes can be made without changing the informant's clear intentions — the errors are corrected at the data checking stage. If an error has been made that cannot be corrected and would lead to erroneous statistics if left in, the answer is either crossed out or a note made that it is to be corrected during data analysis by either recoding or collapsing of categories.

Many respondent/interviewer errors are obvious and can be corrected immediately by the coder: such errors might include ticks by codes rather than circling of the numerical code and entry of a single digit where two are required (e.g. forgetting to insert a leading zero for the numbers of hours spent on a TMA — writing '9', for instance, instead of '09' — even though asked to do so). Omitted answers are also fairly obvious — where a respondent has simply failed to answer part of the questionnaire, or has failed to follow the 'routeing' (e.g. instructions to answer certain questions if the answer to a previous one was 'yes', or to move on to another part of the questionnaire) — and are generally dealt with by insertion of a 'missing value' code or by leaving the column(s) blank and treating blanks as missing values at the analysis stage. Sometimes missing information can be filled in at this stage, if the answer to a question is present somewhere else in a questionnaire. For example, if the 'head of household' occupation is not filled in, but we have the respondent's occupation and know that the respondent is 'head of household', then the information can simply be transferred.

More difficult to correct are errors which involve the provision by the respondent (or interviewer) of inappropriate information. Where the respondent is recorded as having no children, for example, but children's ages have been filled in, we might have to exercise judgement as to whether we code the respondent as having children, or delete the answers about children's ages, or code this whole sequence of values as 'missing information' because we do not feel confident enough to make a decision. Multiple answers (several choices circled) on a question where only one answer was required are also a problem — as in Figure 2 in Section 3.1, for example, if several course components were coded as 'the most useful'. Here it may be possible to make a decision on behalf of the respondent if the purpose of the survey is limited: for example, if we were only really interested in how useful students found the statistics teaching, and students have listed both this and something else as the most useful components, then we might ignore that other component. In other cases, it would probably be necessary, again, to code the question as 'missing information', because the answers that have been given cannot be interpreted within the structure of the question or the questionnaire as a whole.

Errors which originate with the researcher and the design of the questionnaire are often the most difficult to correct. Occasionally, the solution will be easy: for example, where the coding frame does not allow the correct number of columns for the data, it is not difficult to change the coding frame after data collection has taken place by making use of spare columns. Less can be done when questions have been asked wrongly, however — important items omitted from lists of pre-coded categories, for example, or inadequate instructions given on how to answer a question, or ambiguities in a question, or poor routeing instructions so that respondents are not directed to the questions that they ought to be answering. Sometimes something can be salvaged. Where there is an open-ended component to the question (e.g. an 'others' category in a list, or a 'why is that?' question, where respondents are invited to write in their responses), it may be possible to deduce what the answer ought to be. Sometimes the information obtained from badly designed questions is still usable, but the researcher has to keep in mind that the question was ambiguous or the instructions unclear and that interpretation of the results therefore needs to be cautious. Sometimes, however, questions have simply to be omitted from the analysis as uninterpretable.

I have talked mainly about pre-coded questionnaires in this sub-section, but some of the same processes are at work when less-structured interview material is coded for statistical analysis. In instances where a given topic was not covered in an unstructured interview or no answer is given to an open-ended question, sometimes the missing information can be inferred from other parts of an interview or from the answers to other open-ended questions. Where an informant was not asked for his or her attitudes to hostels for people with learning difficulties, for example, but we know that he or she is a member of the 'Friends of the Hostel', we may reasonably infer that the attitudes are positive. Where an informant has not answered a question about, say, the quality of the video component of a course, but has listed video as one of the less useful components elsewhere, then we may reasonably infer that he or she rates the quality as poor.

5 DATA MANIPULATION DURING ANALYSIS

5.1 COPING WITH MISSING VALUES

I have noted above that, where data are missing or uninterpretable, we can often do no better than to record the item as 'missing' for the case. Missing values are, of course, no problem when we have planned that they shall be missing — in instances where a question is answered only by those in paid employment, for example, and therefore is not answered by anyone who is *not* in paid employment. Where values are missing for other reasons, however, they can be a problem. It is important, when reporting on the analysis of data, to state in any tables the number (and proportion) of missing cases, so that the reader can get some idea of how representative the analysed cases are likely to be of the whole sample. (When there is a substantial number of missing cases, it might be even better to describe them: are they typical or untypical of the sample as a whole, and thus is the fact that their answers are not available likely to bias the conclusions? For example, if you were analysing data on views of childbirth and most of the 'missing values' were women, and it further turned out that the women were more likely to be working class than middle class, you might be hesitant about generalizing very far from your results.)

Sometimes it is possible to infer what a value must be from the values on other variables — before analysis, as we discussed in the last section, or once data are keyed in. For example, if we know that someone is employed as a teacher and has very recently started paid employment, we shall probably not do violence to the facts if we code him or her as earning the average starting salary of teachers, even if 'earnings' is a missing value on the questionnaire. A more sophisticated form of inference is possible on some computer packages which amounts to taking an informed guess as to the value of a missing variable on the basis of several other variables which are highly correlated with it. For example, if we know someone's age, occupation and educational background, and in the sample as a whole these three variables are highly correlated with income, then we might be able to substitute an estimate of income for a missing value. We would not want to do this when a large number of cases have missing values, however; it would change the nature of the variable from 'income' to 'estimated income'. The alternative — and normal — practice is to leave 'missing value' cases out of the analysis, but to report on their number and, preferably, their nature in order to show whether there are enough of them, and they are sufficiently non-random, to invalidate the conclusions of the analysis.

5.2 RECODING VARIABLES

We have already spoken of the recoding which may be necessary to correct obvious errors at the pre-analysis stage. This kind of recoding continues into analysis. For example, if when we obtain frequency counts of the variables we find that some cases still bear codes which are not possible according to the coding frame — because of interviewer/respondent error or the error of whomsoever keyed the data in — then we may have to take a reasonable guess as to what the value is likely to be (guessing, for example, that a 3 has been misread as an 8), or, more likely, we may have to recode the case as having a missing value on this variable because the keyed-in code is uninterpretable.

If a variable has a large number of categories and we wanted to present tables, we would normally recode it in order that the tables will make sense to the reader. No-one can make much sense of a table with 20 rows and 20 columns if some of the rows or columns contain very few cases. It is normal to group together categories which have similar meanings (as judged by the purpose of the analysis) in order to present larger numbers and fewer categories. For example, if we wanted a table of 'where you went for your last holiday', we will almost certainly group the rarer countries together as 'other Africa', 'other Asia', etc., rather than showing a large number of destinations visited by only one or two respondents. We might group the whole of the UK together if our main interest is in foreign holidays, or allow several categories for destinations within the UK if it mattered for our purpose where in the UK people took holidays: the precise grouping depends on the purpose of the analysis. It is also common practice, if open-ended questions and the like (e.g. Section 4 in the Appendix) are coded according to a 'representational' principle (see Section 4.4) which lead to a large number of different codes being recorded, to simplify and 'make sense' when presenting tables. Note, however, that each recoding of this or any other kind represents a decision made by the analyst and a manipulation of the data. Recoding is part of the process of *construction* — and also part of the process of laying the underlying structure which is perceived by the researcher open to inspection by the reader.

Similarly, it is routine to group continuous variables, such as age, when presenting tables, so that for people aged 21–80 there are perhaps six rows in a table rather than 60. In the absence of any good theoretical reason to the contrary, we would normally group cases so that each category had roughly equal numbers, or we might try for the shape of a normal distribution, with more cases in the middle categories and fewer in the outside ones. Sometimes, however, theoretical reasons override this tidy practice. For example, in grouping age we would generally arrange for a boundary at 65 for men and 60 for women, because of the normal age of compulsory retirement from paid employment (in the UK, at the time of writing in 1992).

A special case of recoding arises from analyses in which one sub-group of the sample needs to be compared with one or more other sub-groups, as defined by values on some variable. Here we would definitely want to check that there were sufficient cases in each sub-group to ensure that the form of analysis we had planned was valid, and we would combine sub-groups by recoding the variable if numbers were anywhere too small.

A further special case arises in instances when we plan a certain form of analysis and the variables we wish to use are not as yet 'in the right shape'. Recoding to present interpretable tables, as discussed above, might come under this heading, but the most obvious case involves correlational analysis. If we are planning to analyse our data in terms of correlation coefficients, then we need interval or ratio variables, because these are what correlational analysis requires in order to be valid. This may mean rearranging or deleting categories which carry a number which does not fit into an interval or ratio scale. For example, if people were asked whether they lived north or south of London, and some responded that they lived east or west, and these responses were reflected in the coding frame, then some rearrangement would be needed. We might want to count them, with 'Londoners', as 'living at the same latitude as London'; or to scrutinize each location and decide whether they were to count as north of London, south of London or effectively *in* London; or we might want to eliminate them from the analysis by declaring them as 'missing values' on that variable. Whichever strategy was appropriate, *something* would have to be done about them.

ACTIVITY 7

In the *People in Society* survey, a national Open University survey of class location and class attitudes carried out by students on the predecessor to this course (see Abbott and Sapsford, 1987), one measure of educational achievement was coded as follows:

Qualifications attained:

1   None

2   To GCSE/'O' level

3   To 'A' level

4   Above 'A' level but less than degree

5   Degree or higher

6   Other

How might you need to reshape this variable for different kinds of analysis? Think for a few minutes about this, and then see my answer at the end of the unit.

5.3   CONSTRUCTING NEW VARIABLES

An extension of such recoding is to construct new variables, summarizing information from two or more pieces of information which the questionnaire has collected into one new value for purposes of analysis. We might, for example, have asked (a) whether the informant is in paid employment, (b) if so, how many hours he or she is supposed to work, and (c) whether overtime is normally worked, and, if so, how much. From this we could construct a single variable of 'hours worked in paid employment'. It would take a value of zero if the respondent was not in paid employment. If the respondent *was* in paid employment, and overtime was not normally worked, then the variable would be equal to the hours that he or she was supposed to work. If overtime *were* normal, we would want to add on the number of hours of overtime normally worked. This sounds complicated, but most statistical packages can cope with it. It involves arithmetical operations (new variable = old variable A plus old variable B) and some logical branching (if variable A has this value, add such and such to the new variable). Competent statistical packages can certainly do both.

The construction of scale scores from test answers is a case of 'creating new variables'. What happens is that we take the answers to a large number of questions — intelligence test tasks, for example, or personality/attitude items — and add them up or combine them according to some more complicated pattern in order to obtain a single score of the underlying supposed trait or ability. Composite measurement — summarizing several variables with a single index — is another example. In the Plymouth health and deprivation study about which you read in Unit 6, for example, four different Census items were combined to give a single and more interpretable 'Index of Material Deprivation', and another set of Census and health statistics were combined into an 'Index of Health Status'.

ACTIVITY 8

In the *People in Society* survey, one of the questions asked was 'age at which left full-time education'. Some researchers might find this variable of interest in its own right, as representing years of experience of a particular type of stimulus situation. Others, however, would find it more interesting to know how long people stayed on at school *beyond the date when they could legally leave* — using the concept as a measure, not of years of experience, but of commitment to education expressed by staying on instead of leaving (and presumably looking for a job). For a recent sample we could deal with this simply by recoding — people leaving school at 16 or less would be classed as having no years of post-compulsory experience, and one year for every year after the age of 16 would be scored for those who remained at school. Unfortunately, the school leaving age has been raised twice since 1950, from 14 to 15 and then to 16.

Given that the survey also collected information about the age of the respondents, and that we would know in which year a given sample was surveyed, how would you go about constructing a variable of 'years of post-compulsory schooling'?

My answer is at the end of the unit.

5.4 WEIGHTING

A final manipulation which might be needed before you can go ahead with analysing and interpreting your data involves compensation for the nature of certain samples. Sometimes, by accident or by design, your sample turns out not to represent the population in important respects when you compare it with known population figures. By design you might have sampled disproportionately (see Unit 8), collecting larger numbers in rare categories than in others in order to represent the diversity within them properly, even if this means a sample which is not representative of the population in terms of the proportions it contains in that category. By accident, even with random sampling, you might manage to draw one of the 'unlikely' samples, with some category seriously over- or under-represented. If it is important for your research that you are able to talk about proportions in the population, the figures have to be adjusted or *weighted* to eliminate the disproportion. You do this by simple arithmetic, increasing some figures and decreasing others to match the population proportions. Suppose, for example, you were interested in the attitudes of men and women to some proposed social policy, and your sample consisted of 40 per cent women and 60 per cent men, while you knew that women actually form 51 per cent of the population, you might correct the figures by multiplying the 'women' responses by 51/40 and the 'men' responses by 49/60.

Table 3 illustrates the result of weighting in a fictional survey. The first few rows of the table give the number of cases, their distribution 'for' and 'against' on some attitude item, and row and column percentages (the former telling you what percentage of the 'fors' were men, for example, and the latter telling you what percentage of the men were 'fors'). Overall, 55 per cent of the sample were 'for'. Then we weight the data to represent the population better. This makes no difference to the sample size (except for a trivial error due to rounding). It also makes no difference to the row percentages — men and women remain for or against the item in the same proportions as in the unweighted sample. It does make a difference, however, to the actual numbers and the column percentages. Most important, it alters the proportion 'for' the item in the total sample, from 55 per cent to only 52 per cent. (I have used weighting to adjust a tabular analysis, but a sophisticated analysis package will allow you to weight the data directly, so that each case counts for its weighted total — so, in the example, each man would count for 0.817 of a case in every analysis carried out, and each woman for 1.275 cases.)

Table 3 Weighted and unweighted data in a fictional survey

Gender	Actual numbers			Row percentages		Column percentages			Percentage in population
	For	Against	Total	For	Against	For	Against	Total	
				%	%	%	%	%	%
Unweighted data									
Men	80	40	120	66.7	33.3	72.7	44.4	60.0	49
Women	30	50	80	37.5	62.5	27.3	55.6	40.0	51
Total	110	90	200	55.0	45.0				
Weighted data [Weighting factors: men: 49/60 = 0.817, women: 51/40 = 1.275]									
Men	65.4	32.7	98.1	66.7	33.3	63.1	39.6	49.0	
Women	38.2	63.8	102.0	37.5	62.5	36.9	60.4	51.0	
Total	103.6	96.5	200.1	51.8	48.2				

ACTIVITY 9

In the *People in Society* survey, the sample was a quota one, and various biases were apparent in the collection (Abbott and Sapsford, 1987, Chapter 2). Fewer people over the age of 65 were sampled than would be expected from Census or General Household Survey figures, for example; the class distributions were somewhat different from what would be expected nationally (both by own occupation and by head of household's occupation); the distribution of educational qualifications showed more people with high qualifications than would be expected from a national sample (particularly among the women); and there were more women in full-time work than would be expected. The sample also contained more people in middle-class jobs who said they voted Labour than would be expected from opinion polls or general election results, suggesting that the sampling was biased towards people working in the public sector (which is known to support Labour disproportionately — see Heath et al., 1985).

What could you do to correct these biases by weighting the data?

My answer is at the end of the unit.

In conclusion, you now realize (if you did not realize it before) the amount of manipulation and the number of decisions that may be necessary before raw data can be analysed, and you see why we speak in this course of data being *constructed.* Most of this process is invisible to the reader of research; if it were all reported, research papers would be extraordinarily long and extraordinarily tedious to read. You need to be and remain aware, however, of the possibilities for the introduction of bias which exists during this initial pre-analysis stage where researchers are 'working over' the data to try to give a true picture of what their survey shows.

However, you should not leave this unit with the idea that most research results are falsified and merely the result of the researcher's data manipulation. The majority of data sets are recoded, reweighted and 'manipulated' or otherwise 'reinterpreted' in a parsimonious way during data handling and coding. If the design of the research is sound and has no major flaws, results can flow from the data as defined in the precoding and coding frames, with restructuring being confined to a limited amount of recoding and collapsing of variables. This restructuring is mainly undertaken when it will clarify underlying structures and the relationships among variables, *or* permit comparisons to be made with the findings of other researchers or national statistics, *or* allow exploration of interesting ideas which emerge in the course of data analysis or, perhaps, testing of new theory. A variety of constraints, such as limited resources (research assistance, money and personal time) and the need to produce results in the form of papers or reports to deadlines, each impose natural limitations on the amount of data manipulation that can be carried out. The most important limiting factor, however, follows from the motivation for engaging in research at all: why build biases into the research and be anything other than meticulous in the treatment of hard-won data when the object is to contribute to knowledge or understanding of a field or problem?

You can experience some of the latter feeling for yourself through exploring a resource which is provided with this unit, namely the data set which is available on data disk file DOC6. It is a 'real' data set — a subset of data that I collected for an evaluation of two presentations (one short and one long) of an Open Business School course. There are 200 cases (50 men and 50 women in each of the two presentations). The data contain variables on which you can try out your data manipulation skills — for example, recoding to correct respondent errors which were not picked up at the data checking stage and to try to minimize the effects of a badly designed question — and you can see the effects for yourself by looking at how the frequencies and relationships between variables change.

More generally, the data set is a resource for you to explore and use to build up data analysis skills. There are two 'natural experiments' built into the design (short presentation versus long presentation, and men and women students' reactions to two different subjects), and the variables include data about motivations and outcomes and student reactions to the content and 'teaching style', as well as more mundane information such as the respondents' ages and the hours spent on TMAs. (See the information about the survey and the variables in DOC5.) As well as trying out the data manipulation activities that are suggested (in DOC7) as a means of strengthening the skills you have learnt in this unit, you might want to formulate your own hypotheses and test them — either during the course or subsequently — using the various data analysis procedures and techniques that are discussed in the units that follow. As a starter, DOC8 suggests some tables that you might wish to construct and some relationships you might wish to explore later in the course, using, for example, chi-squares, t-tests, correlations and regression analysis.

ANSWERS TO ACTIVITIES

ACTIVITY 3

The errors I spotted on the questionnaire were as follows:

Question 1

Although numbers for answers categories, and also sequential column numbers to indicate locations in the data matrix, have been allocated, the variables have not been correctly identified. All answers have been given a code of '1' and all have been assigned a column number (but, did you spot the gap in the sequence?). If this practice had been followed throughout the questionnaire, it would involve unnecessarily high data-keying costs and also substantial recoding of the data, once they were on the computer, to put them into an appropriate form for producing tables and analysing relationships between variables.

We have to start from scratch, deciding what the variables are and assigning the appropriate codes and column numbers. For example, Question 1 might be divided into nine variables (ignoring possible variables that might be derived from the written-in answers and for which we might like to allocate some spare columns):

Grade of bachelor's degree (variable 1).

Has/has not a post 'A' level qualification (variable 2).

Has/has not an HNC/HND (variable 3).

Has/has not other undergraduate diploma/certificate (variable 4).

Has/has not a postgraduate diploma/certificate (variable 5).

Has/has not a master's degree (variable 6).

Has/has not a PhD (variable 7).

Has/has not a professional qualification (variable 8).

Has/has not other post 'A' level qualification (variable 9).

Variable 1, 'Grade of bachelor's degree', would have seven values (0 to 6):

0   No bachelor's degree indicated; no response.

1   Bachelor's degree, class unspecified.

2   1st class.

3   Upper second.

4   Lower second.

5   Third.

6   Pass degree.

At the data analysis stage, we might want to derive further variables from this variable by collapsing codes, for example:

New variable 1A: has/has not a bachelor's degree:

0   Has not a bachelor's degree (variable 1, code 0).

1   Has a bachelor's degree (variable 1, codes 1 to 6).

New variable 1B: whether has a good first degree:

0   Does not have a bachelor's degree (variable 1, code 0).

1   Has a bachelor's degree, but not indicated to be a first or upper second (variable 1, codes 1, 4, 5 or 6).

2   Has a first or upper second (variable 1, codes 2 and 3).

UNIT 14 WHAT IS DONE WITH DATA

Variables 2 to 9 above would have just two values '0' = no and '1' = yes. You might note that these are conventionally referred to as 'dichotomous' or 'zero/one' variables. We had to divide up these data into so many variables because, in theory at least, it would be possible to have several of the qualifications specified.

In the case of the written-in or specified data, giving details of professional qualifications and other qualifications, all we can pre-code is the presence or absence of the qualification, even though there might be written details. If we were interested in coding the details, this would be a task that would have to be undertaken later when the survey had been completed and the range of answers was known. It would be good practice to allow extra columns for this information at the pre-coding stage.

Question 2

This question poses a real problem. We have a matrix in which there could be several entries in the rows (e.g. for 'Engineering') — and there could equally well be several entries in some of the columns (e.g. postgrad. dip.; master's; PhD). Yet to treat each cell in the column as a zero/one variable would mean a very long data record for each person (expensive to key in) — and at the data analysis stage we would have the problem of creating summary variables for the various rows and columns.

We would consult our clients:

(i) Did they want to represent presence or absence or an entry in each cell? *Or*

(ii) Were they primarily interested in the subject, or combination of subjects, in each column? *Or*

(iii) Were they primarily interested in the row variables — for example, the fact that an informant had a particular qualification or combination of qualifications in Engineering, in Science/maths, etc.?

If the decision were that option (ii) would best represent the clients' interests, we would end up with three variables (the columns), each with categories representing the various subjects and combinations of subjects that were of special interest and with an additional code for 'other combinations of subjects'.

Question 3

The 'BS' score that informants were asked to write in was a three digit score, not a one digit score. Only one column had been allowed, so the solution was to extend the field size of this variable — for example, from (42) to (42–44).

Question 4

Here we have two variables that had been correctly identified as variables — as can be seen in column numbers (43) and (44). However, the scale points have been labelled alphanumerically. For convenience, it is better practice to give them the codes 1 to 5. This allows the data to be analysed more efficiently at the data analysis stage. For example, the alphanumerics 'a' to 'e' would have to be recoded into numerics — for example, '1', '2', '3', '4' and '5' — to permit the calculation of means, correlations and other statistics.

Question 5

There is an obvious problem with the boxes under the heading 'Personal interest': there are boxes to tick but no codes, unless the data keyer is expected to know that the codes are 'H', 'M' and 'L'; that is, as in the column headings. Even if data keyers are given the instruction to do this, there is still a difficulty — no columns have been allocated for these data. Further, as in Question 4, numeric codes would be preferable to letters because the variables are (continuous) scalar variables with values ranging from high to low.

Parts (a) and (b) of the question are all right in theory, in that the pre-coding scheme allocates ten columns for the ten variables: own ranking of Arts, of Science and of each of the other subjects, and the same for the informants' views in respect of employers. It is my bet, however, that the numbers of the cells of the data matrix would not all reflect rankings. Some informants would be sure to get 'ranks' muddled with 'ratings' so that they put in a number between 1 (= rated highly) and 5 (= rated lowly) in the boxes. (This would emerge at the data checking stage when, in the most extreme case, the person checking the questionnaires might see a column of '1's under the heading 'Yourself' instead of a column in which each of the numbers 1 to 5 occurred once; that is, ranking task probably done correctly. The remedy would be clearer instructions, with examples.

Thinking ahead to the data analysis stage, I also wondered whether the variables that the pre-coding would produce were the variables that best fitted the researcher's analysis and report writing requirements. As indicated above, it would produce separate variables for each subject, as for Variable A, below:

Variable A: value placed on Arts by self	**Variable B:** subject most valued by self
0 No ranking	0 No answer
1 Arts ranked first	1 Arts
2 Arts ranked second	2 Social studies
3 Arts ranked third	3 Business studies
4 Arts ranked fourth	4 Science/maths
5 Arts ranked fifth	5 Engineering

Variables like Variable A would be fine if the researcher's chief interest was to relate rankings of the *individual* subjects with other variables; for example, gender and age. However, if the main interest lay in painlessly comparing men and women in terms of the subjects which they (and their employers) valued most, second and least, it would be best to change the format of the question so as to produce variables like Variable B, above.

This could be done quite easily by: (i) giving a subject a key (1 = Arts; 2 = Science, etc.); (ii) replacing the list of subjects in the rows of the question by 'Subject valued most', 'Subject valued second', and so on; and (iii) instructing the informants to enter the appropriate codes in the boxes. However, this change would mean that the new row titles would no longer fit the task in part (c) of the question and it would need to be split off and specified as a separate task with the existing row titles.

ACTIVITY 6

You cannot, of course, do much with such a small sample of responses, but here are some possible frames:

1   Representative (of the areas of research)

Code	Content	Responses
0	No answer	—
1	Science-oriented	3, 5, 7(a)
2	Business/management	1, 4
3	Medical	2, 7(b)
4	Academic	6
5	Other	8

2   Anchored (in the fact that it is a dissertation that was being undertaken)

Code	Content	Responses
0	No answer	—
1	Not relating to a thesis/dissertation	1, 2, 5, 7(b), 8
2	Relevant to a thesis/dissertation	3, 4, 6
3	Not classifiable	7(a)

3   For the hypothesis-guided or theoretical frame, I thought about what I know about MBA dissertations — that they involve research into business or management. So:

Code	Content	Responses
0	No answer	—
1	Relevant by reason of content or field of study	1, 8
2	Relevant in that a thesis or dissertation was prepared	3, 4, 6
3	Relevant in *both* senses	(None in this sample)
4	Relevant in *neither* sense	2, 5, 7(a), 7(b)

ACTIVITY 7

For purposes of tabular analysis, it might be sufficient to use the variable as it stands, provided that numbers were reasonably large in all categories. Alternatively, for some purposes you might want to dichotomize — to split the cases into two categories with respect to this variable. This would be quite simple if what was of interest was whether those surveyed had any qualifications at all; you could split the cases into 'none' (code 1) and 'some' (codes 2–6). If you split them anywhere else, you have problems with code 6 'other', because you do not know at what level these 'others' could reasonably be counted. You would probably have to miss them out by declaring them 'missing values' for the purpose of this part of the analysis. You would certainly have to do so for correlational analysis, unless you could think of some good reason for combining them with one of the other categories, because their numerical value (6) places them higher even than a degree, and this is unlikely to reflect the true state of affairs. (Correlational analysis is discussed at length in Unit 19/20.)

ACTIVITY 8

Given the respondent's current age in years, the year in which the sample was collected and a knowledge of the dates on which the school leaving age was raised, the problem can be tackled by simple arithmetic and a little logic:

1   Current year minus current age = year of birth.

2   Year of birth plus 14 = year in which the respondent could have left school if the minimum leaving age were 14.

3   If that year is before the leaving age was raised to 15, then years of post-compulsory schooling = age at which left school minus 14.

4   If it is after this, but before the leaving age was raised to 16, then it equals this value minus 1.

5   If it was after the leaving age was raised to 16, it equals the value calculated at stage 3 minus 2.

There are two further problems, however — one inherent in the survey and one a matter of logic:

1 The logical problem is that it is possible to score a larger number on this new variable if you left school when it was permissible to do so at 14 than if you left school when you could not do so until 16. Given that the highest category of the 'age at which left school' variable was '18+', someone who left school at 14 could score up to 4, while someone who left at 16 but stayed in full-time education to the age of 21 (to the end of a degree, for instance) could score only 2. It was necessary, therefore, to recode the new variable into only three categories — 0, 1 and 2+. Otherwise there would have been a spurious correlation with age.

2 The second problem was that the question as asked of informants did not ask for exact ages, but for age in bands. The best that could be done with the data, therefore, was to assign each respondent to the mid-point of his or her age-band. This will have introduced a certain amount of unavoidable error.

Thus we can see that what looks simple (I hope) in principle may nonetheless work out as quite complicated in practice. This is why I describe analysis and data preparation as an art rather than a science: they require a good deal of sensitive imagination.

ACTIVITY 9

Most of these problems could be cured by weighting. You would work out 'expected figures' — what proportion of your sample ought to lie in each cell of a complex table defined by age, own class, class of head of household, etc. — from the national data. Then you would work out another table of the observed figures — what proportion of your sample actually did lie in each cell of the table. Dividing the expected figure by the observed figure gives you your weighting factor, the amount by which each case is to be multiplied. (Given that so many variables are involved, you would certainly want to be working on an analysis package which is sophisticated enough to do the weighting for you — for instance, SPSS: Statistical Package for the Social Sciences.)

The political bias is not correctable, because:

1 The survey did not collect 'whether employed in the public sector'.

2 We do not have national figures for voting behaviour by class, head of household's class, age and the other relevant variables in a form in which they could be used to calculate weighting factors.

REFERENCES

Abbott, P.A. and Sapsford, R.J. (1987) *Women and Social Class*, London, Tavistock.

Erickson, B.H. and Nosanchuk, T.A. (1977) *Understanding Data*, Toronto, McGraw-Hill Ryerson.

Farnes, N.C. (1992) 'Life course analysis of students' lives', in Evans, T. and Juler, P. (eds) *Research in Distance Education 2*, Geelong, Deakin University Press.

Heath, A., Jowell, R. and Curtice, J. (1985) *How Britain Votes*, Oxford, Pergamon.

OPCS, Office of Population Censuses and Surveys (annual) *General Household Survey*, London, HMSO.

Runkel, P.J. and McGrath, J.E. (1972) *Research on Human Behavior: A Systematic Guide to Method*, New York, Holt, Rinehart and Winston. (*Note:* this is an advanced text and is considerably more difficult to read than some other texts on methods.)

Swift, B. (1991a) *Teachers into Business and Industry: The Views of Users of the Pack*, Milton Keynes, The Open University, Institute of Educational Technology, Student Research Centre Report No. 56.

Swift, B. (1991b) *B886 MBA Dissertation: Student Perspectives*, Milton Keynes, The Open University, Institute of Educational Technology, Student Research Centre Report No. 46 (restricted circulation).

ACKNOWLEDGEMENTS

Grateful acknowledgement is made to the following source for permission to reproduce material in this unit:

FIGURE

Figure 7: Farnes, N.C. (1992) from 'Life course analysis of students' lives', in Evans, T. and Juler, P. (eds) *Research in Distance Education 2*, Geelong, Deakin University Press; © Deakin University 1992.

APPENDIX

Extracts from Swift, B. (1991a) *Teachers into Business and Industry: The Views of Users of the Pack*, Milton Keynes, The Open University Institute of Educational Technology, Student Research Centre Report No. 56, pp.21–7.

3 OBJECTIVES OF THE PLACEMENTS

The objectives of their placements that the teachers identified (Note: each teacher was allowed to give up to three) were quite varied, ranging from teaching and pupil related benefits to the acquisition of personal skills.

Particular interest was shown in certain topics:

- Looking at industrial and commercial management and organisation
- Observing life outside teaching
- Finding out what teachers can do in and for industry
- Developing links between education and industry
- Developing the school curriculum with material learned from industry and commerce
- Improving ability to help pupils in job placement
- Acquiring particular skills and furthering own professional development

A few of the teachers seemed to be assessing the possibility of a job outside teaching.

The following list, drawn from half the questionnaires, shows the diversity of the objectives for placements. It also demonstrates the extent to which the teachers are able to articulate their objectives for placements — at least with hindsight.

- Application of applied knowledge.
- Apply techniques to classroom teaching.
- Better industrial understanding.
- Bring back experiences into my own teaching.
- Bringing into my control useful ideas — sifting for my own use.
- Build more effective education/business links.
- Career opportunities.
- Change after 17 years in one school.
- Clarify in own mind the relationship between education and work.
- Collect materials to be used as resources in class.
- Comparison of training methods, appraisal and staff development.
- Curriculum development — IT.
- Curriculum enrichment.
- Curriculum planning.
- Dealing with environmental issues.
- Develop ideas for EIU and the National Curriculum.
- Develop industry–education links London/Paris.
- Develop links into school curriculum areas.
- Develop mutual understanding.
- Develop personal understanding.
- Economics of industry.
- Enhancing subject teaching.
- Enterprise in schools.
- Equal opportunities.

Establish links with local community.

Establishing closer school/industry links.

Experience.

Explore possible roles of consultant and ambassador.

Extend knowledge of TIE techniques.

Forge better links with a firm.

Forge links and make relationships.

Gain an insight into management, which can be of use in education.

Gain an insight into a firm as a basis for A level business studies.

Gain career information.

Gain insight into industry.

General insight.

Improve industrial links.

Improve my understanding of industrial life in France.

Inform students of current situation and practices.

Information gathering.

Initiation of school/industry project activities.

Insight for curriculum planning.

Insight into industry.

Liaison.

Links with industry.

Local links.

Look at career.

Look at management structure.

Look at maths used in industry.

Looking at change management.

Looking at how a caring organisation managed time and resources, when limited.

Looking for possible career change (closing school).

Management and organisation within the police.

Management of change.

Management structure observation.

Motivation.

Observe and take part in dealings with customers.

Observe and take part in management structure.

Observe financial structure — LMS focus.

Organisational structures.

Organise students' work experience placements.

Own professional development.

Personal development.

Prepare a pack of resources for use in industry.

Prepare myself for industry-related language teaching.

Professional academic progress.

Professional development and personal experience.

Professional development.

Promoting school/industry interchange.

Pupil enhancement.

Relevance for National Curriculum purposes.

See how industrial management techniques relate to school management.

See how other people function in management situations.

See life outside teaching.

Selling sticky labels.

Specifically geared to improving management skills.

Strengthen school/industry links.

Studying management in industry.

Time management.

To acquire expertise in environmental work.

To acquire materials suitable for classroom use.

To assess current work experience methodology.

To better equip myself to teach Foreign Language at Work.

To construct interesting case studies for my students.

To develop existing links between school and company.

To develop my teaching and management skills.

To enlarge on our own knowledge of the world.

To experience industry.

To experience the day-to-day running of a business.

To experience the extent and level of technology.

To find out how far the school curriculum meets the needs of business.

To find out if or how new technology has affected design and production.

To find out more about the world of work outside school.

To find out what it was like.

To find relevant examples for my students.

To forge permanent links between industrial placement and my school.

To furnish a school/industry link.

To further my own knowledge of industry to help me in planning 6th form course.

To gain an overall understanding of the organisation.

To gain career in media knowledge.

To gain filming/studio management skills.

To gain financial awareness prior to LMS.

To gain greater understanding of police work, in so far as it has a bearing on the life of our students.

To gain insight into the type of skills, practical and academic, that are required.

To gain video editing skills.

To gain wider management perspectives.

To give myself background to teaching business studies at A level.

To identify an area where teachers could help the company on basis of a reciprocal working relationship.

To identify the use of resources available within the placement organisation, with particular reference to National Curriculum cross-curricular issues — e.g. citizenship.

To identify various management strategies which contribute to a successful company.

To improve my career prospects.

To investigate the effect design has on the production of a garment.

To learn about appraisal and career development systems.

To learn about budgeting and running a small business.

To learn from good practice.

To look at industrial management techniques.
To look at methods of staff appraisal.
To look at personnel issues.
To look at the personnel department and its working in a successful company.
To make a link between our school and the chosen business.
To make personal contacts for my work as European Dimension Coordinator.
To observe management styles.
To observe work of police liaison officers.
To offer expertise in school visit organisation.
To see life outside the classroom.
To set up links between industry and the school.
To study police projects currently used in schools.
To transfer management skills from industry to school.
To update knowledge of new developments.
To update my knowledge of electronics and sound technology.
Training policies.
Understanding of education/work transition.
Understanding of management methods and issues.
Understanding the application of quality principles in the context of personnel management.
Up-date qualifications and experience.
Update industrial techniques.
Use of mathematics.
Work as a team.
Work experience contacts and develop visits to company.

4 TEACHERS' COMMENTS ON THEIR PLACEMENT

Two in three of the teachers are well satisfied with what they have gained through their placement: 27% felt they had achieved their objectives almost entirely, and 46% said this was so to quite a large extent. A further 24% said that they had/would achieve them to some extent. Only 4% reported that they had achieved less than they had hoped.

Many teachers used the space at the end of the questionnaire to comment on their placement. The comments give a flavour of the experience of placements and provide useful information and insights. Some identify things that have helped to make the experience particularly useful and others identify problems. This section concludes, therefore, with a sample of the teachers' comments on their experience.

> 'I found it extremely valuable. I made excellent contacts, and as a result have had several meetings with P & O personnel, and as a result agreed on a project which is mutually beneficial.'

> 'Teacher placement should be an integral part of a teacher's professional development and every teacher should experience industry at least every three years. Personally, I would like to undertake a teacher placement every year.'

> 'I thoroughly enjoyed my placement, and personally learned a lot and gained a lot of experience, but no one else has been interested in my school, so I have not had the opportunity to pass on my knowledge and experience. I felt that the management skills were very important. I would like to complete the OU, but unfortunately I will have to pay for

this privilege myself and due to heavy family commitments I cannot afford this.'

'Having now completed teacher placement, I would feel better equipped to do it again, and this time gain more from it. It was a very unknown quantity, and I wasn't sure what to expect or what was expected.'

'An excellent idea which should be broadened. I found it very rewarding and helpful.'

'A fulfilling and profitable experience for both myself and the company. It has led to a much greater awareness of the aims and challenges of both sectors, points of mutual interest, and a mutual appreciation of the quality produced by both.'

'Very useful for preparing 14–16 year old pupils of varying abilities for their own work experience, and for their choice of employment suitable for their skills and interests.'

'The placement was extremely illuminating and I gained much from it that is difficult to verbalise, but has been of use to me personally in school.'

'Excellent idea, but there must be ways of facilitating knowledge/ experience gained through the placement being disseminated to others "back at base". It seems all too often that lecturers and teachers go back full of ideas and enthusiasm, but there is no means of capitalising on this.'

'They are a very useful way of finding out something about industry, but — 1) I would have liked to experience more than one industry, and 2) I found it difficult to make the most of the experience and keep my teaching commitment going, and therefore the pack has not yet been much use.'

'The most rewarding thing was seeing how my pupils were getting on in the outside world.'

'Extremely useful experience: personal development, to help students in teaching: sharing of information with colleagues: updating of business philosophy.'

'I feel that more time could be set aside for follow-up placements or follow-up work, and for teachers involved, some recognisable remuneration for the work involved.'

'Placements seem to highlight the gap which exists between industry and education, and there is a need for far more liaison between the two.'

'In my own case, I was the first in my school to have taken up a teacher placement. The results have been slow, but over twelve months I can see a pattern emerging and changes in style at school happening.'

'My placement was important to me. The school was not interested in the outcomes, except in the possibility of financial benefits.'

'An excellent idea, but it is increasingly difficult to get out of school due to cash limitations on supply cover. Many people in industry may have an out of date idea of present ideas in education — more input here may be useful. We would have liked employees to visit school.'

'I was not impressed by the organisation of the teacher placement. I do not feel that my needs were really considered, but an easy option was chosen. The company were extremely accommodating, but I feel also considered the placement not entirely appropriate and were sorry they could not do more.'

'They should be well arranged and given more support from school management. I was refused time off for the placement this academic year. The unions should insist — no refusals.'

'Will not work unless senior management use ideas and experience gained. This has been obvious from an adviser teacher viewpoint.'

UNIT 15 EXTRACTING AND PRESENTING STATISTICS

Prepared for the Course Team by Roger Sapsford

CONTENTS

Associated study materials		**172**
1	**Introduction: the right figure for the job**	**173**
2	**Frequencies**	**176**
3	**Two-way distributions**	**183**
4	**Simplifying tabular data**	**188**
5	**Introducing a third variable**	**198**
6	**Postscript: the element of chance**	**200**
Answers to activities		**202**
References		**207**
Acknowledgements		**207**

ASSOCIATED STUDY MATERIALS

There is no set reading for this unit, but you might find it useful to run through some of the exercises on the presentation of figures in the NUMERACY disk if you found them difficult earlier in the course.

Some of the activities in this unit will require the use of your computer — mostly using OUSTATS, but you may prefer to use FRAMEWORK to draw graphs, etc. The PLYMOUTH data file, on disk, provides the data for these activities.

1 INTRODUCTION: THE RIGHT FIGURE FOR THE JOB

According to the 1981 Census there were approximately 49,154,700 people in England and Wales on Census night, of whom some 23,873,400 were men. The figures are impressive, but they do not tell us very much. More information is *conveyed*, paradoxically, by sacrificing precision and simplifying the total figure — '49 million' is a more usable concept than '49,154,700'. In terms of components, proportions and percentages are often more useful than absolute numbers; it is more useful to know that 48.5 per cent ('just under half') were male than to know the number in millions — actual numbers may be useful for planning purposes, but percentages are more interpretable and lend themselves more easily to useful comparison. The art of presenting numerical data lies in giving the figures that will convey the desired information in an easily readable form, while still giving enough information for the reader to check the figures and draw conclusions from them other than those presented by the author. This unit is about what you are entitled to expect from such a presentation.

Depending on the audience for the paper or report, different kinds of presentation will be appropriate. Sometimes we are interested in actual numbers, particularly if we have to plan a service; people who plan school provision are less interested in whether the local population of children is going up or down, for example, as in *how many* children will need school places in five years' time. More often, however, a description or a theoretical argument is better served by quoting a summary figure (a mean or median, for example, or a correlation) or a comparative figure (a mean or a percentage compared with the mean or percentage for another interesting group or for the population as a whole). The reader of a report or paper is entitled to expect the figures which are most appropriate for the argument which is being made or the description which is being given. In addition, he or she is entitled to expect sufficient additional detail for the conclusions to be checkable and for obviously relevant further calculations to be feasible. Precisely what is needed will, of course, depend on the target audience of the presentation: planners have different needs from academics, who in turn have different needs from policy makers and the informed general public. However, many presentations of 'applied' research — including most research reports published in journals — will reach all three of these audiences. It is therefore incumbent on the writer(s) to demonstrate the size of 'the problem', to locate it in a relevant context or contexts, to provide enough detail for other researchers to test the conclusions, but to do so in such a way that the main conclusions remain accessible and the evidence interpretable.

This unit has the function, to some extent, of bridging earlier and later discussions in the course. You have already looked at ways of presenting figures, very early in the course, and techniques of presentation and standardization (to render figures comparable with one another) have also been discussed in Unit 6. Unit 14 looked at how data are prepared for analysis. Now this unit covers the first stages of analysis. To this extent the unit acts as revision, consolidating your handling of numerical information. It also looks forward to Block 4, however, and begins to consider how quantitative data are analysed to enable conclusions to emerge from them.

A major example to be used in this unit is the Plymouth study of health and social deprivation, an account of which you have already read in Unit 6. Here we shall be looking at some of the forms of presentation used in the reports of it (Abbott, 1988; Abbott *et al.*, 1992) and the data set which is provided for some of this unit's exercises is extracted from the data set on which these reports were based.

A number of statistical and other technical terms are used in this unit. Most of them you will have encountered earlier in the course, but sometimes they will have been mentioned only 'in passing'. We thought it might be useful to present brief definitions of key terms here, to which you can refer if you need to do so.

A glossary of terms

Bar graph:	see *Graph*.
Cell percentages:	see *Percentages*.
Column percentages:	see *Percentages*.
Correlation:	The systematic linear relationship of two variables. We talk about two variables being *positively correlated* when high values on one variable predict high values on another, and low values predict low values. *Negative correlation* is the opposite — high values on one predict low values on the other, and vice versa. Two variables are said to be uncorrelated — to exhibit *zero correlation* — when the values on one variable do not at all predict the values on the other.
Correlation coefficient:	is a summary of the amount of correlation between two variables. *Correlation coefficients* are constructed to take the value of +1 if there is perfect positive correlation, −1 if there is perfect negative correlation, 0 when there is no correlation, and values in between where some degree of correlation exists but not perfect correlation. (This last situation will normally be the case in social science research.)
Spurious correlation:	is said to occur where two variables are correlated, but not because one has an effect on the other; the effect is due to the fact that both are correlated with a third variable.
Effect:	In statistical jargon, an *effect* is a proportion of variance explained by a variable or by error. More colloquially, we speak of 'an effect' when we have shown a relationship between one or more independent variable(s) and the dependent variable.
Main effect:	the effect of an independent variable, over and above the effects of any other variables.
Interaction effect:	the effect of two variables in combination, over and above their main effects. The effect is shown by the relationship between two variables being of a different degree for different levels of a third variable. For example, ability to run fast might well be attributable to age, weight and the interaction between them: the effect of weight on running speed might be different for children than for adults.
Error term:	The amount of variance still unexplained after all the variables have been taken into account: taken as due to (a) other variables, (b) sampling error, and (c) measurement error.

Graph:	A graphical presentation of data. The main variants are:
Bar graph or histogram:	a graph which presents figures as bars whose height is proportional to what is being measured. Strictly speaking, the term *bar graph* should be used where the variable being measured has natural discrete categories (e.g. male, female), and *histogram* where what is being presented is continuous scores aggregated into categories (e.g. age in five-year bands).
Histogram:	see *Bar graph*, above.
Line graph or graph:	a graph which presents data as a line whose points are defined by the two variables which form the vertical and horizontal axes. For example, a plot of height against weight in a population.
Pie chart:	a graph where the total is illustrated as a circle or 'pie', and figures are shown as segments of the circle ('slices of the pie'), and values are shown.
Index:	A summary variable relating all scores to a comparison point. One common form of indexing is to set one data-point (e.g. a year) equal to 100 and express all other data-points as percentages of it. Another is to set the mean equal to zero and express all other points as deviations from it.
Indicator:	Where a quantity cannot be measured directly, an *indicator* is a variable which is measured which can plausibly be argued to be highly correlated with the desired quantity. For example, scores on intelligence tests are indicators of intelligence; the height of mercury in a thermometer is an indicator of temperature.
Interaction effect:	see *Effect*.
Line graph:	see *Graph*.
Main effect:	see *Effect*.
Mean:	The arithmetical average of a set of figures, obtained by adding them all together and dividing by the number of cases.
Median:	Another form of average, the mid-point of a distribution. This may or may not be close to the mean, depending on whether the distribution is a symmetrical one.
Normal curve:	A distribution of events occurring randomly, with the largest single number of cases at the mean, large numbers of cases close to the mean, and progressively fewer cases as we move further away from the mean.
Percentages:	Figures expressed as though their total were 100.
Cell percentages:	on a table, cell percentages add up to the total of the table: the figure in each cell is divided by the overall total and multiplied by 100.

Column percentages:		percentages based on the totals of the *columns* of a table (down the page).
Row percentages:		percentages based on the totals of the *rows* of a table (across the page).
Pie chart:		see *Graph*.
Proportion:		Figures expressed as though their total were 1.00.
Row percentages:		see *Percentages*.
Spurious correlation:		see *Correlation*.
Suppressor variable:		A variable which has the effect of suppressing the visibility of another variable's effects. For example, mode of transport would suppress the relationship of fitness to speed of travel: bicycles go so much faster than walking that even an unfit cyclist should be able to go faster than a fit walker.

2 FREQUENCIES

The Plymouth study discussed in Unit 6 was one of several local area studies which used census, birth and mortality statistics to build composite indicators of 'material deprivation' and 'health status' and showed that the two were substantially correlated (but less so in rural areas). The unit of analysis was the census ward, so what the analysis does is to correlate the level of material deprivation in a ward with the level of health status in the same ward, across the whole of the Plymouth Health Authority District (which included the City of Plymouth itself, a range of small towns and rural areas in southwest Devon, and a narrow band of more remote rural wards in east Cornwall).

In this section we shall be concentrating on the deprivation data. Table 1 is taken from Abbott (1988) and lists the wards in order of their score on the composite indicator of material deprivation (highest numbers indicating greatest degree of deprivation). We can see that the first ten or so wards have high positive scores, indicating that they are among the most deprived, while the last seven on the list have substantial negative scores, indicating relative affluence. We can also see that the departure from zero (the average, neither deprived or affluent) is greater in the direction of deprivation than of affluence; St. Peter's, the most deprived ward, scores much higher in a positive direction than the most affluent ward, Wembury, scores in a negative direction.

This is probably the simplest of all the ways of presenting data: to list them in some interpretable order. The table does not convey much to the sociological reader, but it was of interest to 'professional' readers of the original report — doctors, health visitors, social workers and the like — who were interested to see where their area ranked in the distribution of deprivation. The research was 'commissioned' in a sense, by the Community Health Council, and the results were intended to inform practice and policy as well as to add something to the sociology of health; the findings have since been used as a basis for funding inner city initiatives. The maps from Abbott *et al.*'s (1992) paper, which were reproduced in Unit 6, do much the same job more graphically, showing the distribution of material deprivation and health status by geographical location so that you can see at a glance where it clusters. The Abbott *et al.* paper chose to emphasize extremes by illustrating the fifth of wards (17, as there are 85 in total) which are most deprived and least deprived and the fifth which have the best and worst health status. Another commonly used mapping technique is to show the whole range, using a form of shading which gets darker, for instance, where the condition to be illustrated is more pronounced.

Table 1 Ranked Material Deprivation Index scores for the wards of the Plymouth Health Authority District

Rank	Name	Score	Rank	Name	Score	Rank	Name	Score
1	St. Peter's	4.16	31	South Brent	0.00	61	Mary Tavy	−0.54
2	Ham	3.32	32	Eggbuckland	−0.01	62	North Petherwine	−0.56
3	Keyham	2.30	33	Altarnum	−0.02	63	Chilsworthy	−0.60
4	Budshead	2.25	34	Bere Ferris	−0.02	64	Stokeclimsland	−0.61
5	Sutton	2.09	35	Ottery	−0.02	65	Milton Ford	−0.63
6	Southway	1.79	36	St. Veep	−0.05	66	Stokenham	−0.64
7	St. Budeaux	1.75	37	Launceston South	−0.05	67	Modbury	−0.64
8	Honicknowle	1.65	38	Salcombe	−0.06	68	Tavistock North	−0.65
9	Efford	1.53	39	Tamarside	−0.09	69	Ugborough	−0.66
10	Maker with Rame	1.01	40	St. Cleer	−0.09	70	Saltstone	−0.69
			41	Downderry	−0.13	71	St. Ive	−0.72
11	Drake	0.96	42	Torpoint	−0.15	72	Marlborough	−0.86
12	Mount Gould	0.96	43	St. Germans	−0.15	73	Tavistock South	−0.86
13	Lydford	0.94	44	Charterlands	−0.15	74	Landrake	−0.86
14	Stoke	0.63	45	Dobswall	−0.18	75	Yealmpton	−0.90
15	Erne Valley	0.49	46	Saltash	−0.25	76	Avonleigh	−0.91
16	Launceston North	0.44	47	St. Dominic	−0.25	77	South Petherwine	−0.93
17	Lansallas	0.32	48	Callington	−0.27			
18	Looe	0.32	49	Estover	−0.28	78	Plymstock Radford	−0.95
19	Morval	0.31	50	Brixton	−0.29	79	Ivybridge	−1.05
20	Lanteglos	0.29	51	Menheniot	−0.30	80	Plympton Erle	−1.17
21	Liskeard	0.28	52	Thrushel	−0.34	81	Buckland Monachorum	−1.18
22	Gunnislake	0.27	53	Walkham	−0.36			
23	Kingsbridge	0.27	54	Compton	−0.40	82	Plymstock Dunstone	−1.19
24	Sparkwell	0.16	55	Shevioc	−0.40			
25	Millbrook	0.11	56	Thurleston	−0.41	83	Burrator	−1.31
26	Calstock	0.08	57	Lyner	−0.42	84	Plympton St. Mary	−1.61
27	St. Neot	0.06	58	Cornwood	−0.50	85	Wembury	−1.71
28	Bickleigh	0.03	59	Garabrook	−0.53			
29	Trelawney (Plymouth)	0.01	60	Newton and Noss	−0.53			
30	Trelawny (Cornwall)	0.00						

(Source: Abbott, 1988, Table 41)

Look back at the maps in Unit 6 if you do not remember them.

Another form of graphic presentation might be to display the census wards not in terms of geographic location but by their location on a variable of interest. Figure 1 (from the 1988 report) shows how the wards of the Plymouth Health Authority District 'stack' in terms of the material deprivation indicator (with the values of the indicator grouped to cut down the number of 'bars'). Again this was of interest to professionals and administrators because it shows in graphical form where their particular areas are to be found along the dimension of deprivation. It also illustrates the shape of the 'distribution' — taller bars in the middle, growing shorter as we move outwards in either direction, but with more wards at the extreme of the 'high deprivation' end than at the other end.

The figure shows much the same information as Table 1 — which wards are extremely different from the mean, and in which direction — but it shows it in a more readily assimilable form. It is a complex display, however, both to read and to prepare. For most purposes something similar can be done without displaying the names of the wards but using a *bar graph* or *histogram*. Figure 2 illustrates what this would look like for the same set of data. It shows the shape of the

		Eggbuckland						
		Altarnum						
		Bere Ferris						
		Ottery						
		St. Veep						
		Launceston S.						
		Salcombe						
	Garabrook	Tamarside						
	Newton & Noss	St. Cleer						
	Mary Tavy	Downderry						
	N. Petherwine	Torpoint	Erne, Valley					
	Chilsworthy	St. Germans	Launceston N.					
	Stokeclimsland	Charterlands	Lansallas					
	Milton Ford	Dobswall	Looe					
	Stokenham	Saltash	Morval					
	Modbury	St. Dominic	Lanteglos					
	Tavistock N.	Callington	Liskeard					
	Ugborough	Estover	Gunnislake					
	Saltstone	Brixton	Kingsbridge					
	St. Ive	Menheniot	Sparkwell					
Ivybridge	Marlborough	Thrushel	Millbrook					
Plympton Erle	Tavistock S.	Walkham	Calstock					
Buckland Mon.	Landrake	Compton	St. Neot		Southway			
Plyms. Dunstone	Yealmpton	Shevioc	Bickleigh	Drake	St. Budeaux			
Burrator	Avonleigh	Thurleston	Trelawney (P.)	Mt. Gould	Honicknowle	Keyham		
Plymp. St. Mary	S. Petherwine	Lyner	Trelawny (C.)	Lydford	Efford	Budshead		
Wembury	Plyms. Radford	Cornwood	S. Brent	Stoke	Maker/Rame	Sutton	Ham	St. Peter's
Score:	−1.00 to	−0.50 to	0.00 to	0.50 to	1.00 to	2.00 to	3.00 to	4.00+
<−1.01	−0.51	−0.01	0.49	0.99	1.99	2.99	3.99	

Figure 1 *The Plymouth Health Authority District: distribution of scores on the Material Deprivation Index (highest numbers indicate greatest degree of deprivation)*
(Source: Abbott, 1988, Figure 2)

deprivation variable as something like the normal distribution you read about in Unit 8 — tall stacks of cases in the middle of the range, sloping off into smaller stacks as we get towards the extremes in either direction. Also, it illustrates the point made in the reports, that the distribution is not symmetrical (the technical term is skewed). There are more census wards far from the mean at the materially deprived end of the variable than at the materially advantaged end, and the worst stand out further from the mean; the very deprived wards' scores are more

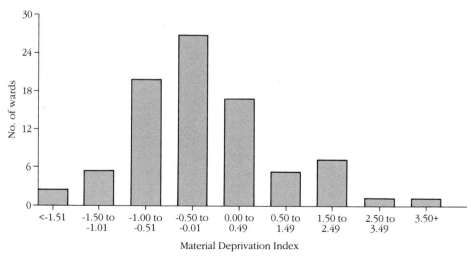

Figure 2 *Bar graph of Material Deprivation Index scores*

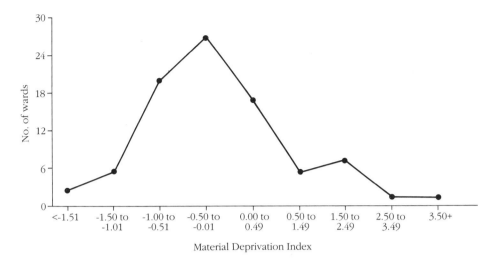

Figure 3 *Line graph of Material Deprivation Index scores*

extreme in the direction of deprivation than the affluent wards' scores are in the direction of affluence.

Figure 3 illustrates the same data display as a *line graph*, treating the variable as a continuously varying one rather than stacking cases by grouped values. Again the underlying shape is quite apparent — the largest number of cases at zero or not far from it, sloping away to very small numbers at the extremes, but with too many cases towards the extreme at the right to make the distribution quite a normal one.

Note that in Figures 2 and 3 the apparent extremity of the skew is partly a question of how the figure is produced: you can make it seem more extreme by increasing the size of the vertical axis, or less extreme by spreading the horizontal axis. For example, in Figure 4 the two graphs both use the data illustrated in Figure 3, but in the one on the left the scale has been manipulated to produce something more akin to a straight line, while in the one on the right the scaling is arranged to produce more marked 'peaks' in the line. The same kind of thing can be done with bar graphs. The temptation is to think of these variants as 'cheating', but the fact is that there is no right way of drawing a graph; you scale it so that it

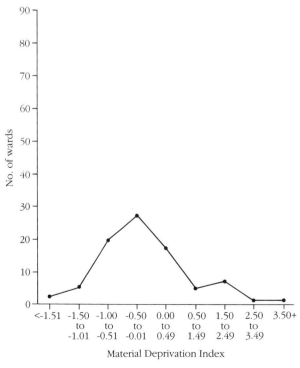
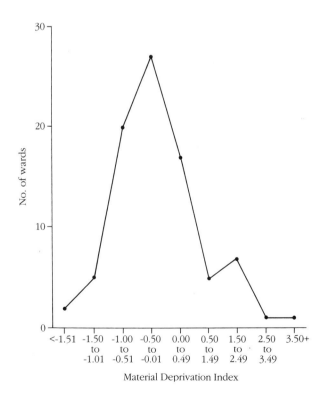

Figure 4 *Effects of varying scale*

makes the point you want it to make. For this reason you should treat the graphic presentations you come across in published reports as illustrations of points, not proof of them; the proof — if proof is possible — lies in the data themselves, not in how they are drawn.

With modern computer graphics packages it is possible to produce much more appealing kinds of pictures than this, and you will find some reports illustrated with three-dimensional bar charts. These are to be avoided, however, because the information they convey may be ambiguous. Of the three bar graphs in Figure 5, for example, in which is it true that the bar to the right is eight times the size of the bar on the left? The answer is, in the first two cases. In (a) the bar on the right is eight times as high as the one on the left, but cross-sectional area remains the same, so the volume is increased by a factor of eight. In (b) each dimension has been doubled, so the volume is again increased by a factor of eight. (So these two are trying to get the same information across, even if they look very different.) In (c) however, *all* dimensions have been increased by eight, so the bar on the right is actually 512 times as large as the one on the left!

Finally, of course, we shall need the actual numbers if we are to be able to do more than just look at the data. Numbers are needed for planning purposes, and also for further analysis; we can draw more detailed conclusions from numbers than from most forms of graphical presentation. Table 2 is a *frequency distribution* of the Material Deprivation Index scores, in arbitrary units of 0.5 standard deviations (normalized scores). It shows, of course, a similar pattern to the graphic presentations — the majority of cases clustered around zero, and a longer 'tail' at the high end of the distribution than the low end.

An important point about the presentation of numbers, incidentally, is that you should *never* 'let the figures speak for themselves'. Wherever a table is presented, there should also be at least a sentence or so saying what you think the table demonstrates. A research presentation is a reasoned argument in which the author's job is to take the reader through, step by step, from the initial premises to the final conclusions. This holds even for what we would normally describe as 'descriptive statistics'. The annual *Social Trends*, for example, reports on the year's statistics and sets them in the context of past years by means of tables and graphs, but it also explains in words what the statisticians see the figures as meaning. (It does not hold for publications such as the volumes of census statistics which simply present tables for a county or administrative area; these are not research reports, however, but the comparatively raw material out of which research reports might be written.)

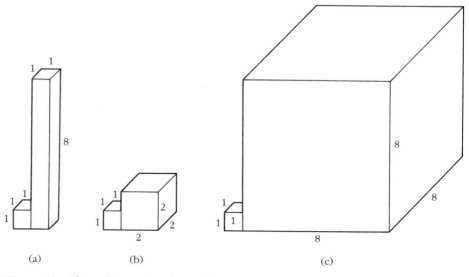

Figure 5 *Three-dimensional graphics*

Table 2 Material Deprivation Index scores in the Plymouth Health Authority District, raw data[a]

Score[b]	Number of wards
<−1.51	2
−1.50 to −1.01	5
−1.00 to −0.51	20
−0.50 to −0.01	27
0.00 to 0.49	17
0.50 to 0.99	4
1.00 to 1.49	1
1.50 to 1.99	4
2.00 to 2.49	3
2.50 to 2.99	—
3.00 to 3.49	1
3.50 to 3.99	—
4.00+	1
Total	85

[a] Derived from Table 1 above.
[b] Remember that a low score denotes affluence and a high score deprivation.

In itself Table 2 is not very informative for the average reader. What other figures would you like to see here, thinking back to the computer familiarization week of the course and to the material on standardization in Block 2?

As a minimum we would normally display percentages in each category; readers are entitled to be told what percentage of the total each figure constitutes, without having to work it out for themselves. For some purposes it might also be useful to show *cumulative* percentages, so that the reader can see at a glance what percentage of cases have a given score *or a lower one* (e.g. less than zero). Table 3 on the next page remedies these omissions.

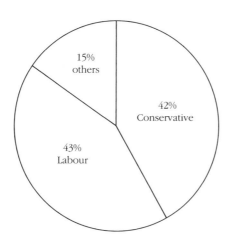

Figure 6 Share of votes in a fictional constituency

Table 3 Material Deprivation Index scores in the Plymouth Health Authority District, percentages

Score	Number of wards	%	Cumulative %
<−1.51	2	2.4	2.4
−1.50 to −1.01	5	5.9	8.2
−1.00 to −0.51	20	23.5	31.8
−0.50 to −0.01	27	31.8	63.5
0.00 to 0.49	17	20.0	83.5
0.50 to 0.99	4	4.7	88.2
1.00 to 1.49	1	1.2	89.4
1.50 to 1.99	4	4.7	94.1
2.00 to 2.49	3	3.5	97.6
2.50 to 2.99	—	—	97.6
3.00 to 3.49	1	1.2	98.8
3.50 to 3.99	—	—	98.8
4.00+	1	1.2	100.0
Total	85	100.0	

Note: percentages may not add exactly to a hundred because of rounding errors; 25.04 would be expressed to one decimal place as 25.0, but four of them would add up to 100.16, which would round to 100.2. The same may happen with the cumulative percentages in the final column; you will notice, for example, that the first two percentages appear to add up to 8.3, but the true total is 8.2.

You can also present percentages graphically, using bar graphs or (to show visually how the different percentages add up to the total) in a pie chart in which the total number of cases are represented as a circle and each percentage is shown as a sector of the circle (or 'slice of the pie'). Figure 6, for example, illustrates a fictional political constituency in which 42 per cent of the voters chose the Conservative Party, 43 per cent the Labour Party, and the rest other parties.

ACTIVITY 1

You get a better grasp on data analysis by doing it yourself than by reading about it.

1 Using the PLYMOUTH data set provided on disk, try producing a frequency table like Table 3, a bar graph and line graph for the score on the Health Index. (The most efficient means is to use OUSTATS.) In other words, carry out the same procedures as above but on a different variable in the data set. (Note that for the Health Index the scores scale in the same direction as the Material Deprivation Index — high scores mean *poor* health.)

2 Now compare your results with the results for material deprivation above, look again at the four maps in Unit 6, and see what you can deduce about the relationship between the two variables.

My answers are at the end of this unit.

3 TWO-WAY DISTRIBUTIONS

When comparing the relationship between the Material Deprivation Index and the Health Index in Activity 1, looking at the maps probably told you more than the other figures. You can see that it is the same wards, by and large, that score low on health and low on material deprivation, or high on health and high on material deprivation. (Remember that both indexes are constructed so that high scores mean poor conditions, poor health.) In other words, there is a manifest correlation between the two variables. We could demonstrate it on a single map by using clever graphics, for example marking wards high on one variable with slanting lines in one direction, wards high on the other variable by lines slanting in the other direction, and seeing which wards finished up decorated with a cross-hatch pattern. It can be shown more directly using a tabular presentation, however:

Health Index	Material Deprivation Index							
	<–1.00	–1.00 to –0.51	–0.50 to –0.16	–0.15 to 0.14	0.15 to 0.49	0.50 to 0.99	1.00 to 1.99	2.0+
<–1.00	Burrator Wembury Buckland Mon.	Yealmpton Tavistock S. S. Petherwine Newton & Noss Garabrook	Cornwood St. Dominic Compton	Tamarside Salcombe		Lydford		
–1.00 to –0.51	Plyms. Dunstone	Stokeclimsland Mary Tavy	Brixton Thurleston	Altarnum Charterlands Ottery	Lanteglos Erne Valley Sparkwell Looe Morval			
–0.50 to –0.21	Ivybridge	Milton Ford Saltstone Landrake Marlborough	Walkham	St. Veep Bere Ferris	Lansallas Kingsbridge Gunnislake			
–0.20 to 0.19	Plymp. St. Mary	Chilsworthy Stokenham St. Ive	Lyner Menheniot Thrushel	S. Brent Bickleigh Downderry Launceston S.	Launceston N.		Maker/Rame	
0.20 to 0.49		Plyms. Radford Modbury Tavistock N. Avonleigh	Estover Dobswall Callington	St. Germans Trelawny (C) Torpoint St. Neot	Liskeard	Mount Gould		
0.50 to 0.99		N. Petherwine	Saltash Shevioc	Trelawney (P) Eggbuckland Calstock St. Cleer		Drake	Southway	
1.00 to 1.99	Plympton Erle	Ugborough		Millbrook		Stoke	Honicknowle Efford St. Budeaux	Sutton
2.0+								Keyham Budshead Ham St. Peter's

Figure 7 Location of wards by Material Deprivation Index and Health Index

using each of the dimensions of a two-dimensional array to stand for one of the variables, and placing cases in some way within the two-way table thus defined.

The most straightforward way, using the Plymouth example, is to name the wards in each cell of a table defined by the two variables, and this is what we did in the 1988 report (see Figure 7 on the previous page). This is a useful form of presentation for professionals who want to see where their particular area falls in terms of the two variables.

More generally useful, however, is a table where numbers replace the names; we can usually do without knowing which particular cases fall where, and the results are much easier to read if tabulated numerically — and this is the only sensible way of proceeding if you have more than a relatively small number of cases — Table 4 illustrates this.

Table 4 Location of wards by Material Deprivation Index and Health Index, raw numbers

Health Index	Material Deprivation Index								Total
	<–1.00	–1.00 to –0.51	–0.50 to –0.16	–0.15 to 0.14	0.15 to 0.49	0.50 to 0.99	1.00 to 1.99	2.00+	
<–1.00	3	5	3	2	—	1	—	—	14
–1.00 to –0.51	1	2	2	3	5	—	—	—	13
–0.50 to –0.21	1	4	1	2	3	—	—	—	11
–0.20 to 0.19	1	3	3	4	1	—	1	—	13
0.20 to 0.49	—	4	3	4	1	1	—	—	13
0.50 to 0.99	—	1	2	4	—	1	1	—	9
1.00 to 1.99	1	1	—	1	—	1	3	1	8
2.00+	—	—	—	—	—	—	—	4	4
Total	7	20	14	20	10	4	5	5	85

(Source: Abbott, 1988, Table 26)

As with Table 3, percentages are a useful aid to the reader. For this reason two more tables have been produced: Table 5 shows percentages by rows (showing what percentage of each category of health status falls in each of the Material Deprivation Index categories) and Table 6 shows percentages by columns (showing what percentage of each Material Deprivation Index category falls within each category of health status). The two kinds of percentages are useful for different purposes. In this case we use row percentages (Table 5) to compare material deprivation categories: we can see at a glance, for instance, that most of the low Health Index scores fall in the first three columns, and all the highest scores in the last column. Table 6, similarly, is useful for comparing Health Index categories.

If the two variables are *correlated* — related in such a way that the score on one of them predicts the score on the other at better than a chance level — then we

Table 5 Location of wards by Material Deprivation Index and Health Index, row percentages

Health Index	Total		Material Deprivation Index							
			<−1.00	−1.00 to −0.51	−0.50 to −0.16	−0.15 to 0.14	0.15 to 0.49	0.50 to 0.99	1.00 to 1.99	2.00+
<−1.00	14	%	21	36	21	14	—	7	—	—
−1.00 to −0.51	13	%	8	15	15	23	38	—	—	—
−0.50 to −0.21	11	%	9	36	9	18	27	—	—	—
−0.20 to 0.19	13	%	8	23	23	31	8	—	8	—
0.20 to 0.49	13	%	—	31	23	31	8	8	—	—
0.50 to 0.99	9	%	—	11	22	44	—	11	11	—
1.00 to 1.99	8	%	12	12	—	12	—	12	38	12
2.00+	4	%	—	—	—	—	—	—	—	100
Total	85	%	8	24	16	24	12	5	6	6

(Source: Abbott, 1988, Table 26)

Table 6 Location of wards by Material Deprivation Index and Health Index, column percentages

Health Index	Material Deprivation Index								Total
	<−1.00	−1.00 to −0.51	−0.50 to −0.16	−0.15 to 0.14	0.15 to 0.49	0.50 to 0.99	1.00 to 1.99	2.00+	
Total	7	20	14	20	10	4	5	5	85
	%	%	%	%	%	%	%	%	%
<−1.00	43	25	21	10	—	25	—	—	16
−1.00 to −0.51	14	10	14	15	50	—	—	—	15
−0.50 to −0.21	14	20	7	10	30	—	—	—	13
−0.20 to 0.19	14	15	21	20	10	—	20	—	15
0.20 to 0.49	—	20	21	20	10	25	—	—	15
0.50 to 0.99	—	5	14	20	—	25	20	—	11
1.00 to 1.99	14	5	—	5	—	25	60	20	9
2.00+	—	—	—	—	—	—	—	80	5

(Source: Abbott, 1988, Table 26)

Look at the two tables and make sure you see what I mean, scanning *down* Table 5 row by row to see where the large concentrations of cases, in percentage terms, fall in each row, and doing a similar scan *across* Table 6 column by column.

---

should expect the large percentage figures to 'move' diagonally across the table as we scan down (Table 5) or across (Table 6). In other words, low scores should predict low scores — the largest percentages should be high in the columns at the left-hand side of the table — and as we move across the mean of the distribution and out to the other extreme the large percentages should 'move' towards the middle of the row or column and then away in the other direction. This does indeed appear to be the case in these tables. In Table 5 we can see a degree of correlation — by and large the larger percentages are in the lowest deprivation categories in the first two columns, around the middle (with some variation) in the middle of the table, and towards the bottom of the table as we reach the right-hand columns. Table 6 shows the same.

Two-way distributions can also be presented in a number of ways using bar graphs: see Figures 8, 9 and 10. Figure 8 preserves information about the absolute numbers — the height of each bar increases with increased totals on the variable along the bottom — and shows how those numbers are 'shared out' in each bar according to the categories of the other variable. Figure 9 does the same but loses information on absolute numbers in favour of percentages; all the bars are the same height, which makes it easier to see where a category of the other variable becomes proportionally more or less common. Figure 10, which compares the incidence of certain major diseases between a 'bad' inner city ward and an affluent country area, shows how a similar job can be done by stacking the bars side by side. Which is the most appropriate to use will depend on the point you want to make. Line graphs can also be used in similar ways.

Incidentally, tables do not have to record just figures or percentages adding up to a total. The tabular format can be a very good way of presenting a range of information in compact and interpretable form. Table 7, for instance, compares the best and the worst wards in London and in Plymouth on four 'deprivation' variables. The figures in the body of the table are not percentages of the column or row, but the percentage of people or households in each ward who fulfil the conditions of each variable.

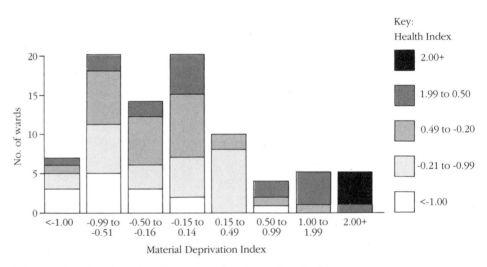

Figure 8 Health Index by Material Deprivation Index

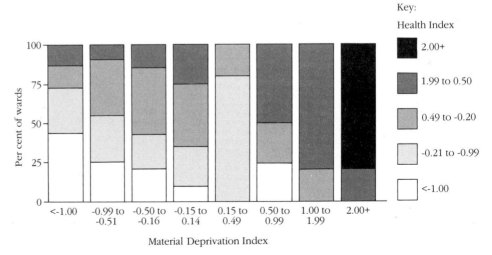

Figure 9 Health and Material Deprivation Indexes (%)

Table 7 A comparison of deprivation indicators for the Plymouth Health Authority District and the Greater London Council. The table compares the best and the worst five wards overall, in each district

Wards	Unemployed adults, %	Overcrowded households, %	Households not owner-occupied, %	Households with no car, %
		Worst		
GLC				
Tower Hamlets, Spitalfields	22	28	97	80
Tower Hamlets, St. Mary	20	17	95	74
Brent, Carlton	22	10	98	77
Kensington & Chelsea, Golborne	19	13	93	74
Tower Hamlets, Shadwell	17	14	98	71
Plymouth Health Authority				
Plymouth City, St. Peter's	19	6	84	68
Plymouth City, Ham	17	8	55	52
Plymouth City, Keyham	14	5	52	56
Plymouth City, Budshead	14	3	76	51
Plymouth City, Sutton	14	3	60	59
		Best		
GLC				
Bromley, Biggin Hill	3	2	10	8
Sutton, Woodcote	5	1	15	7
Sutton, S. Cheam	3	1	9	11
Croydon, Selsden	3	1	7	14
Havering, W. Cranham	3	1	4	12
Plymouth Health Authority				
Plymouth City, Plymstock Radford	7	2	22	29
South Hams, Ivybridge	5	2	23	19
Plymouth City, Plympton Erle	6	1	22	20
Plymouth City, Plymstock Dunstone	6	1	20	21
Plymouth City, Plympton St. Mary	5	1	10	18

(Source: Abbott, 1988, Table 1)

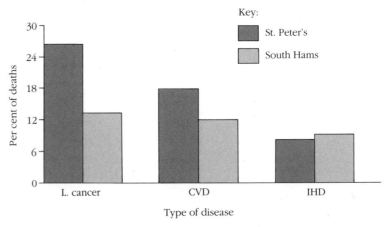

Figure 10 Deaths from lung cancer, cerebrovascular disease and isohaemic heart disease in St. Peter's and South Hams
(Source: Abbott, 1988, Figure 5)

ACTIVITY 2

By way of practice, use the PLYMOUTH data set provided on disk to construct a tabulation of the Material Deprivation Index by the Health Index, and illustrate it with bar graphs and/or line graphs as appropriate. What may be inferred from it?

My answers are at the end of this unit.

4 SIMPLIFYING TABULAR DATA

Tables which you construct yourself, or which are constructed by a researcher to make a point, should be clear, simple and easy to read. The other kind of table with which you may come into contact is just the opposite — a storehouse of data, rich in material but very difficult to disentangle. An example is reproduced as Table 8. It is an extract from the Office of Population Censuses and Surveys (OPCS) Historical Tables of the decennial Census, giving the size of the population recorded by the Census, by a range of other information, for the years from 1861 to 1981.

Table 8 Population present on Census night, England and Wales, 1861–1981 (thousands), age by marital status by gender

Notes:- (1) The divorced were not separately identified in censuses before 1921.
(2) 'Not stated' age and marital status groups have been eliminated by distributing them over the stated age and marital status groups.
(3) *For the years 1881 and 1891 the numbers have been estimated from data for 10-year age groups between the ages of 25 and 64 and the age group 65 and over.
(4) †The 0-14 age group for 1891 has been adjusted to counteract a tendency of certain enumerators to confuse the ages of males and females in the completion of a new type of enumeration book introduced at that census.
(5) ‡For the year 1901 the numbers have been estimated from data for 10-year age groups between the ages of 25 and 84.

Age last birthday by marital status by sex		1861	1871	1881*	1891*†	1901‡	1911	1921	1931	1951	1961	1971	1981
a		b	c	d	e	f	g	h	j	k	l	m	n
Males													
All ages	Single	5,987.9	6,777.3	7,828.2	8,723.9	9,566.9	10,334.0	9,949.4	9,910.8	9,202.3	9,738.2	10,398.8	10,529.8
	Married	3,428.4	3,883.4	4,376.9	4,851.5	5,611.4	6,495.8	7,475.1	8,489.8	10,994.9	11,812.9	12,432.9	12,088.8
	Widowed	360.0	398.2	434.8	485.0	550.3	615.8	642.3	718.9	739.0	658.2	665.9	677.5
	Divorced							8.5	13.5	79.4	94.5	185.3	577.3
0-14		3,587.7	4,108.0	4,728.5	5,079.4	5,265.3	5,531.0	5,284.9	4,808.6	4,948.5	5,424.1	5,942.4	5,160.8
15-19	Single	952.8	1,078.7	1,262.3	1,459.5	1,603.1	1,651.7	1,720.8	1,704.7	1,328.5	1,604.9	1,661.5	2,069.0
	Married	5.1	6.0	5.9	5.6	4.4	3.2	6.9	4.8	6.7	17.0	34.6	22.6
	Widowed	0.1	0.1	0.1	0.1	0.0	0.0	0.1	0.0	0.0	0.0	0.0	0.1
	Divorced							0.0	0.0	0.0	0.0	0.0	0.2
20-24	Single	666.5	730.2	864.4	1,004.9	1,216.6	1,288.1	1,190.8	1,463.3	1,087.7	989.7	1,186.0	1,387.3
	Married	191.6	219.2	245.5	240.4	254.2	213.1	255.9	234.6	338.5	443.9	686.7	449.7
	Widowed	2.1	2.5	2.5	2.1	1.8	1.4	1.5	1.2	0.6	0.2	0.4	0.5
	Divorced							0.2	0.1	0.5	0.5	2.9	11.5
25-29	Single	295.2	330.8	385.1	476.6	598.1	716.7	597.7	766.6	567.3	425.6	414.9	576.4
	Married	431.1	502.8	586.5	625.9	722.1	731.9	733.9	855.0	1,050.4	1,015.1	1,180.6	1,037.9
	Widowed	8.0	9.6	9.8	8.7	8.1	7.2	7.6	6.6	2.9	1.1	1.2	1.3
	Divorced							0.9	0.8	5.3	4.1	15.4	55.9
30-34	Single	149.3	171.4	192.2	239.0	294.2	374.9	296.4	312.3	287.1	262.7	202.0	312.5
	Married	499.3	559.5	631.3	722.6	847.0	985.0	968.4	1,105.7	1,209.4	1,227.6	1,233.8	1,441.5
	Widowed	13.1	15.4	16.7	16.3	16.4	16.0	15.1	13.4	6.1	2.7	2.2	2.9
	Divorced							1.5	1.9	11.3	8.6	22.3	90.9
35-39	Single	90.6	96.7	112.9	140.9	180.2	234.8	207.6	175.5	216.4	213.8	156.3	177.7
	Married	482.0	524.4	609.5	700.8	829.7	1,001.6	1,041.8	1,086.8	1,389.9	1,383.2	1,226.0	1,292.9
	Widowed	17.7	19.7	22.5	23.9	24.5	25.0	22.4	18.5	10.8	6.2	4.1	4.2
	Divorced							1.5	2.2	15.4	13.0	23.4	83.9
40-44	Single	71.6	71.9	82.5	95.4	125.9	159.5	167.2	139.4	180.0	160.1	158.4	133.1
	Married	455.1	492.1	561.3	618.5	738.0	881.2	1,023.5	1,060.4	1,445.6	1,309.1	1,275.9	1,187.4
	Widowed	24.3	26.0	29.1	31.7	33.8	34.3	31.1	27.3	17.5	10.5	8.6	7.2
	Divorced							1.3	2.2	14.8	14.1	23.9	77.5
45-49	Single	48.7	50.1	54.0	66.5	88.0	117.5	144.6	130.0	152.1	151.2	154.4	123.1
	Married	376.5	426.9	460.8	536.7	627.7	763.3	972.2	1,014.9	1,365.8	1,397.1	1,354.6	1,146.2
	Widowed	28.1	30.0	32.7	39.0	44.2	45.3	44.4	39.7	26.9	19.6	18.1	12.8
	Divorced							1.0	2.0	11.6	15.8	24.7	68.4
50-54	Single	40.0	43.7	45.5	52.5	66.1	87.7	111.2	119.6	113.7	139.9	123.5	132.0
	Married	317.5	374.1	399.0	449.3	515.3	621.7	800.3	936.4	1,154.8	1,386.2	1,238.8	1,167.1
	Widowed	34.7	38.0	41.3	47.8	54.8	58.9	58.7	58.7	41.1	34.3	28.1	25.2
	Divorced							0.8	1.6	8.3	15.0	21.6	58.5
55-59	Single	26.8	30.3	31.1	34.3	43.4	59.5	83.1	102.8	84.2	120.5	118.0	129.7
	Married	235.9	276.5	307.8	329.6	393.2	479.5	626.5	803.8	944.8	1,224.8	1,247.8	1,187.1
	Widowed	36.3	39.1	43.0	49.3	60.8	69.0	71.4	79.8	55.4	51.7	48.2	46.2
	Divorced							0.6	1.1	4.9	10.9	19.7	47.8
60-64	Single	24.3	27.0	28.8	30.7	37.0	47.6	60.4	78.0	74.2	86.9	104.6	100.0
	Married	193.7	217.7	254.8	264.1	300.3	348.0	455.8	600.1	779.6	931.1	1,134.9	1,010.9
	Widowed	47.6	50.0	57.0	62.1	73.1	81.6	84.6	99.2	81.7	71.7	75.3	63.4
	Divorced							0.4	0.8	3.3	6.5	15.3	33.4
65-69	Single	15.0	17.1	18.7	19.7	22.4	32.1	42.2	55.5	65.5	60.0	82.0	89.1
	Married	117.3	139.5	158.8	178.6	188.7	243.3	309.4	409.0	601.5	664.6	868.3	904.2
	Widowed	43.2	48.8	54.1	61.4	71.2	90.5	97.5	112.9	111.6	91.0	103.6	99.0
	Divorced							0.3	0.5	2.1	3.2	9.4	24.7
70-74	Single	10.5	12.0	12.1	13.5	14.6	19.0	24.1	32.1	50.1	45.6	48.2	68.5
	Married	73.4	87.2	92.8	108.9	112.7	136.6	168.1	233.7	403.3	440.1	522.6	675.4
	Widowed	44.5	50.7	53.4	62.8	68.2	81.3	88.1	110.4	136.7	112.3	116.9	127.9
	Divorced							0.2	0.3	1.1	1.6	4.2	14.8
75-79	Single	5.4	6.0	6.5	7.2	7.6	9.0	11.9	15.4	30.7	30.8	25.6	43.7
	Married	34.0	39.2	43.5	49.6	53.8	60.6	79.4	103.6	212.8	242.9	272.8	376.8
	Widowed	32.4	36.9	39.9	44.9	51.6	57.9	67.2	85.0	130.5	114.7	109.5	127.7
	Divorced							0.1	0.1	0.6	0.8	1.7	6.7
80-84	Single	2.4	2.6	2.7	2.9	3.3	3.6	4.5	5.3	12.1	15.8	13.8	18.5
	Married	12.4	14.4	15.5	16.6	19.4	20.9	26.2	32.8	73.1	99.7	115.9	141.6
	Widowed	19.4	21.6	22.9	24.3	29.4	31.9	36.3	45.5	79.4	88.9	86.8	92.4
	Divorced							0.0	0.0	0.2	0.2	0.6	2.1
85 and over	Single	1.0	0.9	0.9	1.0	1.1	1.4	1.7	1.7	4.0	6.6	7.2	8.4
	Married	3.5	3.9	4.0	4.5	4.7	5.9	6.7	8.2	18.9	30.4	39.6	47.6
	Widowed	8.5	9.7	9.8	10.8	12.2	15.5	16.3	20.7	37.9	53.1	62.9	66.6
	Divorced							0.0	0.0	0.1	0.1	0.2	0.8

Notes:- (1) The divorced were not separately identified in censuses before 1921.
(2) 'Not stated' age and marital status groups have been eliminated by distributing them over the stated age and marital status groups.
(3) *For the years 1881 and 1891 the numbers have been estimated from data for 10-year age groups between the ages of 25 and 64 and the age group 65 and over.
(4) †The 0-14 age group for 1891 has been adjusted to counteract a tendency of certain enumerators to confuse the ages of males and females in the completion of a new type of enumeration book introduced at that census.
(5) ‡For the year 1901 the numbers have been estimated from data for 10-year age groups between the ages of 25 and 84.

Age last birthday by marital status by sex		1861	1871	1881*	1891*†	1901‡	1911	1921	1931	1951	1961	1971	1981
a		b	c	d	e	f	g	h	j	k	l	m	n
Females													
All ages	Single	6,044.3	6,825.6	7,897.5	8,901.2	9,835.3	10,629.8	10,591.5	10,414.1	9,201.1	9,242.0	9,513.1	9,359.5
	Married	3,489.0	3,948.5	4,438.0	4,916.6	5,717.5	6,630.3	7,590.0	8,603.6	11,092.0	11,860.5	12,487.6	12,202.5
	Widowed	756.7	879.2	999.0	1,124.3	1,246.4	1,364.8	1,621.8	1,782.5	2,319.0	2,527.8	2,773.0	2,908.8
	Divorced							8.2	19.2	130.2	170.4	292.9	810.5
0-14		3,562.4	4,094.0	4,740.1	5,092.8	5,280.4	5,519.9	5,215.2	4,711.7	4,743.0	5,160.4	5,633.4	4,895.6
15-19	Single	944.7	1,060.8	1,246.3	1,456.7	1,613.1	1,661.5	1,743.9	1,693.8	1,308.6	1,475.1	1,476.9	1,911.9
	Married	29.7	34.6	32.4	28.9	25.4	20.1	31.1	31.1	60.4	103.5	140.5	90.2
	Widowed	0.3	0.3	0.2	0.2	0.1	0.1	0.2	0.1	0.1	0.1	0.1	0.2
	Divorced							0.0	0.0	0.1	0.0	0.0	0.5
20-24	Single	643.4	686.0	809.0	980.9	1,196.6	1,266.5	1,237.2	1,332.1	776.9	607.0	737.2	982.0
	Married	321.2	361.3	402.0	414.4	447.9	404.1	459.8	461.0	719.8	833.6	1,107.2	795.6
	Widowed	4.7	5.5	4.9	3.8	3.8	2.5	5.8	2.1	1.6	1.3	1.6	1.9
	Divorced							0.3	0.2	1.9	1.9	9.2	31.3
25-29	Single	307.6	333.9	376.2	488.5	614.0	704.6	664.2	702.1	358.9	219.7	209.7	323.6
	Married	511.5	584.7	672.6	734.0	866.5	906.4	921.0	1,014.4	1,273.4	1,168.7	1,337.6	1,236.1
	Widowed	15.7	18.7	17.9	16.6	15.7	12.2	34.0	10.2	9.0	3.8	4.0	4.4
	Divorced							1.1	1.5	12.8	8.0	27.9	91.0
30-34	Single	168.1	182.0	199.9	257.7	327.1	405.7	394.5	403.3	228.1	162.2	110.7	163.0
	Married	528.7	598.3	671.2	759.7	914.6	1,067.0	1,059.5	1,188.9	1,293.6	1,297.7	1,259.1	1,545.2
	Widowed	28.3	33.4	34.1	32.3	32.0	28.7	64.3	26.7	22.0	8.8	7.7	9.0
	Divorced							1.3	3.1	20.9	13.9	33.6	124.9
35-39	Single	110.0	118.0	131.8	162.6	222.3	284.5	300.5	313.0	224.2	159.1	97.0	95.1
	Married	485.1	536.6	613.0	700.8	834.8	1,016.4	1,089.3	1,147.4	1,404.4	1,422.7	1,231.6	1,326.1
	Widowed	39.2	45.9	51.6	52.8	53.8	50.9	80.7	56.1	39.4	21.2	15.3	14.7
	Divorced							1.4	3.6	22.8	22.6	32.5	113.7
40-44	Single	83.1	90.5	102.1	119.8	160.2	208.1	247.1	260.0	243.0	149.3	108.9	76.7
	Married	443.4	485.2	551.9	605.9	714.8	873.5	1,035.1	1,074.7	1,383.2	1,325.1	1,293.2	1,189.6
	Widowed	56.6	64.0	72.4	75.7	78.2	76.0	94.7	96.1	59.6	42.1	32.8	26.7
	Divorced							1.2	3.4	21.6	26.2	33.4	100.8
45-49	Single	58.4	67.6	74.3	89.7	116.0	164.4	208.8	229.2	245.9	173.1	123.9	78.1
	Married	355.1	404.1	443.4	505.9	590.6	728.3	919.1	1,002.2	1,259.6	1,361.8	1,355.1	1,132.7
	Widowed	64.0	74.4	86.2	98.9	106.7	106.8	115.1	133.2	92.9	82.5	68.3	50.1
	Divorced							0.9	2.8	17.3	27.6	36.4	83.2
50-54	Single	48.1	57.2	61.8	72.2	89.1	125.0	165.9	201.6	225.5	201.5	123.8	92.5
	Married	286.8	337.5	367.0	415.4	471.4	571.7	730.2	894.4	1,111.2	1,280.3	1,210.3	1,150.7
	Widowed	79.5	94.2	107.5	122.6	132.2	137.8	146.3	167.4	156.9	138.9	118.5	101.2
	Divorced							0.7	1.9	13.2	25.0	32.8	69.6
55-59	Single	33.6	40.5	46.8	53.4	68.0	90.7	131.7	169.9	206.8	210.2	147.7	107.1
	Married	202.4	237.0	266.3	289.9	339.7	418.2	542.0	708.6	891.4	1,073.6	1,151.3	1,132.5
	Widowed	79.0	94.8	111.3	127.6	147.4	161.5	174.8	201.3	227.0	217.1	212.6	190.0
	Divorced							0.5	1.3	8.4	19.0	30.3	61.5
60-64	Single	32.2	35.8	41.5	44.3	53.1	69.5	102.5	136.5	187.4	195.5	173.4	106.9
	Married	154.8	175.6	205.0	217.9	249.7	290.1	375.4	504.6	691.6	830.2	982.1	922.6
	Widowed	103.7	116.7	140.5	153.8	177.4	183.2	202.5	236.9	319.4	323.0	330.2	283.7
	Divorced							0.3	0.8	5.6	13.0	25.1	48.6
65-69	Single	21.0	24.6	28.8	34.2	38.6	53.0	74.7	109.7	161.7	176.6	177.0	124.9
	Married	90.2	104.1	117.4	132.9	145.0	187.1	236.8	319.1	500.1	571.5	702.6	761.9
	Widowed	89.8	107.2	124.8	145.3	163.7	200.9	225.0	263.4	383.8	404.5	440.2	432.8
	Divorced							0.2	0.4	3.1	7.3	16.6	38.6
70-74	Single	16.3	18.1	20.1	24.9	27.9	38.8	52.5	77.3	131.6	145.8	150.8	136.6
	Married	51.3	56.9	61.0	73.0	75.3	97.2	122.4	168.9	308.2	345.4	419.0	523.3
	Widowed	85.3	99.2	110.5	134.7	147.7	180.7	201.4	247.8	395.3	447.2	507.4	537.2
	Divorced							0.1	0.2	1.6	3.7	9.0	25.8
75-79	Single	9.1	9.6	11.2	13.7	16.7	21.8	31.1	44.1	89.0	105.6	116.5	123.0
	Married	20.6	23.4	25.3	28.3	30.9	37.6	50.0	66.0	141.3	170.2	200.7	268.4
	Widowed	59.1	66.9	75.9	89.6	103.8	123.1	152.9	185.5	318.2	402.4	454.7	537.0
	Divorced							0.0	0.1	0.7	1.6	4.0	13.5
80-84	Single	4.6	5.0	5.4	6.6	8.5	10.7	14.9	20.5	47.0	64.3	75.8	81.3
	Married	6.5	7.5	7.7	8.1	9.3	10.4	14.7	18.2	43.2	60.8	75.0	97.7
	Widowed	34.4	38.8	41.5	47.2	58.9	66.7	83.2	103.5	190.9	274.8	337.8	408.9
	Divorced							0.0	0.0	0.2	0.5	1.6	5.4
85 and over	Single	1.9	2.1	2.2	2.9	3.6	5.2	6.6	9.3	23.5	36.4	50.6	61.4
	Married	1.6	1.7	1.6	1.7	1.8	2.3	3.4	4.0	10.5	15.1	22.4	29.9
	Widowed	17.1	19.4	19.6	22.8	25.1	33.8	40.9	52.2	102.9	160.2	241.8	310.9
	Divorced							0.0	0.0	0.1	0.2	0.6	2.3

(Source: OPCS, 1982, Table 5)

As a source of information Table 8 reminds me of the comments of one A-level examiner in years past about students who entered everything they knew about a topic and left the examiner to pick the winning combination. Before a table such as this can be used as part of a logical argument it has to be simplified. Let us unpick this one, little by little, and see what can be made of it. We will assume for the purpose of the exercise that we are interested in marital status by gender, and particularly the balance of married to single people. (We will ignore age for the time being.) The first thing to do is to extract the totals and record them as a table. This is done in Table 9 on the next page, and illustrated in Figure 11.

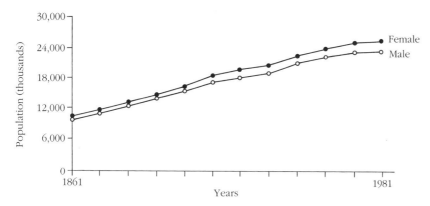

Figure 11 Population, 1861–1981, by gender

This is still a mass of numbers, difficult to interpret, though we can at least see that the numbers go up from left to right. Table 10, however, shows another useful way of presenting time-series data such as these — indexing. What you do is to take a given year — in this case the first one on the table — and set this equal to 100. Then you can express all subsequent years' figures as a percentage of the chosen year's total, which makes it easy to see how much the figures have risen or fallen over the time period. It also makes it easy to compare rates of increase for the different lines of the table.

As we noted earlier, of course, the degree to which the line graph makes two lines look similar or dissimilar is under the control of the person who draws it, not dictated by the data. Figure 11 makes the two lines look broadly similar, though they are clearly not identical. We could make them more similar, or less similar, by expanding or condensing the scale. Another trick would be to 'break' the scale, as in Figure 12. Here the break at the bottom of the vertical scale indicates that a large portion has been omitted; this allows us to use a much larger scale for the portion which is not omitted, exaggerating the slope of the lines.

Table 9 Population size by gender and marital status, 1861–1981 (thousands)

	1861	1871	1881	1891	1901	1911	1921	1931	1951	1961	1971	1981
Total	20,066.3	22,712.2	25,973.4	29,002.5	32,527.8	36,070.5	37,886.8	39,952.4	43,757.9	46,104.5	48,749.5	49,154.7
Single	12,032.2	13,602.9	15,725.7	17,625.1	19,402.2	20,963.8	20,540.9	20,324.9	18,403.4	18,980.2	19,911.9	19,889.3
Married	6,917.4	7,831.9	8,814.9	9,768.1	11,328.9	13,126.1	15,065.1	17,093.4	22,086.9	23,673.4	24,920.5	24,291.3
Wid./div.	1,116.7	1,277.4	1,432.8	1,609.3	1,796.7	1,980.6	2,280.8	2,534.1	3,267.6	3,450.9	3,917.1	4,974.1
Males:												
Total	9,776.3	11,058.9	12,639.9	14,060.4	15,728.6	17,445.6	18,075.3	19,133.0	21,015.6	22,303.8	23,682.9	23,873.4
Single	5,987.9	6,777.3	7,828.2	8,723.9	9,566.9	10,334.0	9,949.4	9,910.8	9,202.3	9,738.2	10,398.8	10,529.8
Married	3,428.4	3,883.4	4,376.9	4,851.5	5,611.4	6,495.8	7,475.1	8,489.8	10,994.9	11,812.9	12,432.9	12,088.8
Wid./div.	360.0	398.2	434.8	485.0	550.3	615.8	650.8	732.4	818.4	752.7	851.2	1,254.8
Females:												
Total	10,290.0	11,653.3	13,333.5	14,942.1	16,799.2	18,624.9	19,811.5	20,819.4	22,742.3	23,800.7	25,066.6	25,281.3
Single	6,044.3	6,825.6	7,897.5	8,901.2	9,835.3	10,629.8	10,591.5	10,414.1	9,201.1	9,242.0	9,513.1	9,359.5
Married	3,489.0	3,948.5	4,438.0	4,916.6	5,717.5	6,630.3	7,590.0	8,603.6	11,092.0	11,860.5	12,487.6	12,202.5
Wid./div.	756.7	879.2	998.0	1,124.3	1,246.4	1,364.8	1,630.0	1,801.7	2,449.2	2,698.2	3,065.9	3,719.3

(*Source: derived from OPCS, 1982, Table 5*)

Table 10 Population size by gender and marital status, 1861–1981 (index figures)

	1861	1871	1881	1891	1901	1911	1921	1931	1951	1961	1971	1981
Total	100	113	129	145	162	180	189	199	218	230	243	245
Single	100	113	131	146	161	174	171	169	153	158	165	165
Married	100	113	127	141	164	190	218	247	319	342	360	351
Wid./div.	100	114	128	144	161	177	204	227	293	309	351	445
Males:												
Total	100	113	129	144	161	178	185	196	215	228	242	244
Single	100	113	131	146	160	173	166	166	154	163	174	176
Married	100	113	128	142	164	189	218	248	321	345	363	353
Wid./div.	100	111	121	135	153	171	181	203	227	209	236	349
Females:												
Total	100	113	130	145	163	181	193	202	221	231	244	246
Single	100	113	131	147	163	176	175	172	152	153	157	155
Married	100	113	127	141	164	190	218	247	318	340	358	350
Wid./div.	100	116	132	149	165	180	215	238	324	357	405	492

(Source: derived from OPCS, 1982, Table 5)

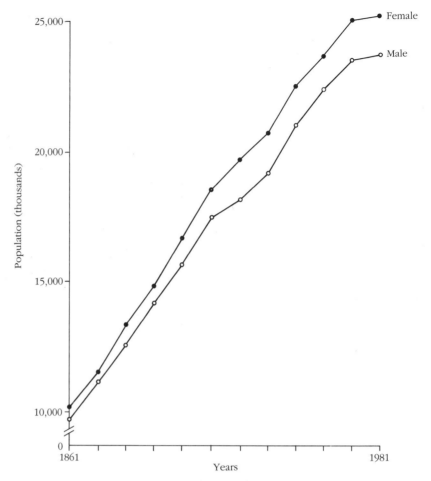

Figure 12 *Population, 1861–1981, by gender: Figure 11 with an expanded vertical scale*

You can see that total population has increased steadily from 1861 to 1981, and that males and females have risen at about the same rate (the final index figure in the 'total' row is similar for males and females). Rates of increase are not the same for different marital status rows, however. The increase in the married population has been far more substantial than the increase in the single population, and the increase in the widowed/divorced population has been greater still (substantially more so for females than males). This does not give us an explanation of *why* the changes have occurred. (Increased divorce rates may be one explanation; the greater average age of the population is another; the tendency of women on average to outlive men would be a third.) It does show us fairly clearly, however, what is to be explained.

Then, having looked at totals, we can begin to explore the ways of looking at the figures. Table 11, for example, expresses the figures as percentages of their appropriate totals — a fairly obvious thing to do, allowing us to compare across rows without being distracted by the absolute levels of the figures. This gives us the scale of the changes. Among men, the single and married groups account for all bar five per cent of the population, while among women some fifteen per cent are widowed or divorced (but they still constitute a minority of the female population). These percentages differ a fair amount from the 1861 percentages, however.

Table 12 gives the ratio of males to females in each line — the number of males divided by the number of females. Table 13 gives the ratio of single people to married people, similarly. Any of these might be 'the right table for the purpose', depending on precisely what was to be argued from the figures. You can see just how rich in information a 'storehouse' table such as the OPCS table can be — we have not yet even considered the information on age in the body of the table! — and how necessary it is to process the information and simplify it if the reader is to understand anything from it at all.

Table 11 Marital status as a percentage of total, by gender, 1861–1981

	1861	1871	1881	1891	1901	1911	1921	1931	1951	1961	1971	1981
Total	100	100	100	100	100	100	100	100	100	100	100	100
Single	60.0	59.9	60.5	60.8	59.6	58.1	54.2	50.9	42.1	41.2	40.8	40.5
Married	34.5	34.5	33.9	33.7	34.8	36.4	39.8	42.8	50.5	51.3	51.1	49.4
Wid./div.	5.5	5.6	5.6	5.5	5.5	5.5	6.0	6.3	7.5	7.5	8.0	10.1
Males:												
Total	100	100	100	100	100	100	100	100	100	100	100	100
Single	61.2	61.3	61.9	62.0	60.8	59.2	55.0	51.8	43.8	43.7	43.9	44.1
Married	35.1	35.1	34.6	34.5	35.7	37.2	41.4	44.4	52.3	52.9	52.5	50.6
Wid./div.	3.7	3.6	3.4	3.5	3.5	3.5	3.6	3.8	3.9	3.4	3.6	5.3
Females:												
Total	100	100	100	100	100	100	100	100	100	100	100	100
Single	58.7	58.6	59.2	59.6	58.5	57.1	53.5	50.0	40.5	38.8	38.0	37.0
Married	33.9	33.9	33.3	32.9	34.0	35.6	38.3	41.3	48.8	49.8	49.8	48.3
Wid./div.	7.4	7.5	7.5	7.5	7.4	7.3	8.2	8.7	10.8	11.3	12.2	14.7

(*Source: derived from OPCS, 1982, Table 5*)

Table 12 Ratio of males to females, by marital status, 1861–1981

	1861	1871	1881	1891	1901	1911	1921	1931	1951	1961	1971	1981
Total	0.95	0.95	0.95	0.94	0.94	0.94	0.91	0.92	0.92	0.94	0.94	0.94
Single	0.99	0.99	0.99	0.98	0.97	0.97	0.94	0.95	1.00	1.05	1.09	1.12
Married	0.98	0.98	0.99	0.99	0.98	0.98	0.98	0.99	0.99	1.00	1.00	0.99
Wid./div.	0.48	0.45	0.44	0.43	0.44	0.45	0.40	0.41	0.33	0.28	0.28	0.34

(*Source: derived from OPCS, 1982, Table 5*)

Table 13 Ratio of single to married, by gender, 1861–1981

	1861	1871	1881	1891	1901	1911	1921	1931	1951	1961	1971	1981
Total	1.74	1.74	1.78	1.80	1.71	1.60	1.36	1.19	0.83	0.80	0.80	0.82
Males	1.75	1.75	1.79	1.80	1.70	1.59	1.33	1.17	0.84	0.82	0.84	0.87
Females	1.73	1.73	1.78	1.81	1.72	1.60	1.40	1.21	0.83	0.78	0.76	0.77

(*Source: derived from OPCS, 1982, Table 5*)

UNIT 15 EXTRACTING AND PRESENTING STATISTICS

ACTIVITY 3

Now see what you can do with Table 14, which is also from the 1981 Census. We will use the England and Wales part of the table; the information for separate countries may be interesting for other purposes, but we do not need it here. Construct tables to show:

1. The family type of household in which children live.
2. The size of families in which children live.
3. Whether there is a difference in kind of household by number of children in the family or size of household.

Comment on your results. My answers are at the end of this unit.

Table 14 Private household families and dependent children, 1981

All families	All married couple families	Married couple family — Number of dependent children in family						Size of family by number of persons not in family
		0	1	2	3	4	5 or more	
a	b	c	d	e	f	g	h	

ENGLAND AND WALES

								All households with one family with child(ren)
81,809								2 persons
278,915	237,384	100,333	137,051					3 "
305,761	290,140	35,223	45,965	208,952				4 "
113,198	107,726	6,111	16,402	18,948	66,265			5 "
34,872	33,083	1,090	3,442	6,204	6,093	16,254		6 "
9,030	8,552	152	594	1,242	1,671	1,497	3,396	7 "
4,210	3,982	32	130	374	584	692	2,170	8 or more persons
827,795	680,867	142,941	203,584	235,720	74,613	18,443	5,566	All families
1,143,857	1,002,579		203,584	471,440	223,839	73,772	29,944	All dependent children in families

								Households with all persons in a family
64,332								2 persons
253,714	222,657	93,225	129,432					3 "
288,713	277,137	32,952	43,130	201,055				4 "
105,982	102,012	5,663	15,388	17,769	63,192			5 "
32,469	31,148	1,022	3,240	5,827	5,704	15,355		6 "
8,217	7,881	136	548	1,121	1,554	1,376	3,146	7 "
3,772	3,614	29	118	342	531	634	1,960	8 or more persons
757,199	644,449	133,027	191,856	226,114	70,981	17,365	5,106	All families
1,051,732	953,925		191,856	452,228	212,943	69,460	27,438	All dependent children in families

								Households with one person not in a family
15,992								2 persons
23,267	13,528	6,641	6,887					3 "
15,717	11,990	2,126	2,674	7,190				4 "
6,642	5,241	421	927	1,079	2,814			5 "
2,120	1,697	55	189	335	343	775		6 "
702	581	12	41	112	105	96	215	7 "
379	319	3	12	28	47	52	177	8 or more persons
64,819	33,356	9,258	10,730	8,744	3,309	923	392	All families
84,251	43,972		10,730	17,488	9,927	3,692	2,135	All dependent children in families

								Households with two or more persons not in a family
1,485								2 persons
1,934	1,199	467	732					3 "
1,331	1,013	145	161	707				4 "
574	473	27	87	100	259			5 "
283	238	13	13	42	46	124		6 "
111	90	4	5	9	12	25	35	7 "
59	49	–	–	4	6	6	33	8 or more persons
5,777	3,062	656	998	862	323	155	68	All families
7,874	4,682		998	1,724	969	620	371	All dependent children in families

ENGLAND

								All households with one family with child(ren)
77,036								2 persons
262,173	222,956	94,321	128,635					3 "
288,495	273,721	33,296	43,330	197,095				4 "
106,450	101,261	5,755	15,477	17,768	62,261			5 "
32,846	31,162	1,041	3,248	5,854	5,759	15,260		6 "
8,503	8,051	143	551	1,177	1,572	1,421	3,187	7 "
4,009	3,789	29	121	355	547	661	2,076	8 or more persons
779,512	640,940	134,585	191,362	222,249	70,139	17,342	5,263	All families
1,077,925	943,988		191,362	444,498	210,417	69,368	28,343	All dependent children in families

(Source: OPCS, 1984, Table 17)

5 INTRODUCING A THIRD VARIABLE

As a reader of a report or article you can be faced with a table or some other way of presenting figures and find the point that it makes quite convincing. None the less there may be more for the writer to do in order to make a convincing case and/or to make the most of the available data. Quite often two variables are related, but allowance needs to be made for some third variable (or more than one). The reader needs to know that some obvious explanation has been considered, and to see evidence that it may be rejected. Otherwise, he or she may not be in a position to accept the writer's arguments.

- There may, for example, be *spurious correlation* between two variables because both are related to a third: in other words, the causal relationship is with the third variable, not between the two under examination. The example of this most beloved of statisticians is a series of Dutch statistics showing a positive correlation between the number of storks nesting in a series of springs and the number of human babies born at that time. (Both were related to the state of the weather some nine months previously!)

- A third variable may simply be *more important*, in causal terms, than the explanation being put forward. For example, many attempts have been made to identify parents likely to be violent to their children in terms of their psychological characteristics. However, far more of the variance in the behaviour seems to be contributed by their material circumstances — poverty, unemployment, overcrowding, lack of resources, etc. This tends to mean that any effect of psychological variables is, simply, swamped by the large effect of material circumstances.

- There may be an *interaction effect* between the supposed cause and some third variable. For example, the likelihood of reaching a senior management position (at the time of writing) is related, among other things, to gender and to the social class of origin. Either alone shows some correlation with the thing to be explained, but both together are enormously more predictive. Moreover, the effect of class differs by gender: in many studies the class of eventual job is more affected by class or origin than level of education for boys, but somewhat less so for girls.

There are sophisticated statistical techniques for dealing with such questions. However, a fair amount can be done simply, through tables. This section of the unit looks at examples of each of the effects listed above, mostly using 'made-up' figures (because it is easier to make the point if the figures are specifically designed to make it) and tries to suggest to you what to look out for when reading this kind of analysis. The basis of the technique involves splitting a table into two sub-tables, to show the effect of the third variable.

As a case of *spurious correlation*, let us consider a fictional study of the use of flashing lights to ameliorate toothache. Over a period of months a dental receptionist is instructed to send one patient out of two to the dentist for examination in the normal way — turning them over to the dentist if he or she is there, or waiting with them until the dentist arrives. On the other hand, alternate patients are conducted by the receptionist to a special room where he or she settles them in a chair and switches on stroboscopic lights, explaining this as a new therapy for pain; then, after five minutes, the receptionist takes them to the dentist. (Sometimes the receptionist is not able to stay with them, if another patient arrives during the five minutes.) At the end of each treatment the patients report on the degree of pain they were feeling on arrival at the dentist. Table 15 shows the results of the study. (As you can see, the allocation to treatment or control does not work out perfectly even in fictional studies! We have 440 'treatment' cases, whereas the design should have yielded 500.)

Table 15 The effects of light therapy in dentistry (fictional data)

Degree of pain reported	Total patients	Effect of treatment (i.e. light therapy)		Effects controlling for receptionist's time with patient			
				receptionist stayed with patient		receptionist did not stay with patient	
		treatment	none	treatment	none	treatment	none
	1,000	440	560	400	100	40	460
	%	%	%	%	%	%	%
Severe	48	34	59	30	32	70	65
Mild	52	66	41	70	68	30	35

The first block of the table is looking for main effects of treatment (i.e. irrespective of the receptionist's presence or absence), and it suggests that there is quite a respectable effect: only a third of the treatment cases report severe pain, compared with nearly 60 per cent of the control cases. The two blocks on the right, however, separate out cases with whom the receptionist stayed (most of the 'treatment' cases, but also nearly a fifth of the control cases) from those with whom she or he did not stay (approximately four fifths of the control cases, but also 40 people in the treatment group). From these figures we can see that the apparent effect of the treatment is almost certainly spurious, and that the determining factor is whether the receptionist stays with the patient. Alternatively, we might have found — with slightly different figures — that most of the effect was contributed by the receptionist staying with the patient but that there was still a small effect of the treatment even when this effect was controlled for. In other words, there could be a genuine effect of the treatment, but swamped by the effect of a more important variable.

Our example of a third variable being *more important* comes from *Rival Hypotheses* by Huck (1979), an intriguing collection of research studies and alternative ways of interpreting results. Huck's example is a study of women students' halls of residence, in a period when some still imposed a time by which students were required to be back in hall, while others had relaxed this requirement. Huck looked specifically at a college of 787 women, 371 of whom were required to observe 'dormitory hours' while the rest had parental permission to ignore the closing hours. Scores on academic tests were compared at the end of the first academic term. Obviously there was a risk that the two groups differed on initial academic ability, given that allocation to one group or the other was not random, but the researchers allowed for this in their statistical analyses. After initial ability had been controlled in this manner, there was no difference between the two groups in their performance at the end of the first term. The researchers conclude that time restriction has no effect on academic performance. As Huck points out, however, it is very likely that the girls whose parents did not relax the restrictions were ones considered likely to perform badly if not supervised, and that the reason their initial academic performance (based on high-school grades) was as good as the others was because their parents had supervised their hours while they were at high school. In other words, there could well be a genuine difference between the two groups in likelihood of gaining good academic grades, but it is suppressed by the limitations imposed on their social lives.

For an example of an *interaction effect*, we can turn to some real results on the pay-off of education in terms of salary, by gender. Table 16 shows data from the 1980–84 responses to the Open University's People in Society Survey (see Abbott and Sapsford, 1987). Among other things, the survey recorded gender, whether or not the respondents were in full-time employment, how much they were earning, and their educational qualifications. In Table 16 the level of earnings has been dichotomized at the overall mean into 'low' and 'high', and educational qualifications have been dichotomized into 'O level or less' or 'higher than O level'.

Table 16 The pay-off of education, by gender

Education	Total			Males			Females		
		low wages	high wages		low wages	high wages		low wages	high wages
O level or less	%	62.9	37.1	%	44.2	55.8	%	82.3	17.7
Greater than O level	%	31.2	68.8	%	15.9	84.1	%	46.8	53.2
N =		4,632			2,307			2,325	

(Source: Open University's People in Society Survey, responses for 1980–84)

Overall there is a marked association, as you would expect, between level of education and amount earned: nearly two thirds of people with lower-level qualifications fall in the low-wage column, but less than a third of those with higher qualifications. Looking at males and females separately we find a similar pattern, with a much larger proportion of the less educated than of the more educated earning low wages. We can also see that the overall level of earnings is markedly lower for females than for males. Thus we have identified two main effects — the dependent variable (earnings) is predicted separately by two independent variables: level of qualifications, and gender. However, we have also noted an interaction effect — an effect of one of the independent variables on the other, changing the extent to which it predicts the dependent variable. In this case, the relationship of qualifications to earnings is not the same for men as for women; there is an interaction between gender and qualifications in the prediction of earnings.

ACTIVITY 4

Now try your hand at three-way analysis, verifying a point made in Abbott et al. (1992) about the predictability of health status from material deprivation in urban and rural areas. In Activity 2 you prepared a table of health vs. material deprivation overall. Now, using the PLYMOUTH data set on disk, construct tables of the relationship between the two separately for rural and urban areas.

My answers are at the end of this unit.

6 POSTSCRIPT: THE ELEMENT OF CHANCE

Finally, we should note in reading other people's data or in presenting our own that the observed difference between two groups may not necessarily be due to a real difference between them; it may be a product of the way in which the figures were collected. In the fictional dentist experiment above, for example, the 'treatment' and 'control' groups differed in the amount of attention they received from the receptionist, and this turned out to be part of the explanation of the results. In the fictional study this was something the researchers measured and were therefore able to examine. However, it might not be measured, and (as you can see from Table 15) it is not randomly divided between the treatment and the control groups and therefore constitutes a source of systematic error not controlled by random allocation to groups.

When looking at trends in population size since 1861, from the Census, we need to be very sure that the figures were collected in the same way from decade to decade. In one respect they were certainly *not* collected in the same way: before

1921, divorced people were not represented separately, which will have consequences for the married/single comparison in Table 13. Systematic bias of this kind is always likely to creep in, and identifying and eliminating it is much of the business of validity of measurement. As we saw in Units 5 and 6, identifying ways in which statistical series change their definitions or their ways of measuring or collecting data over time is an important part of the analysis of 'secondary sources'. Otherwise differences between years which are in fact a product of changed measurement technique will be taken as real changes in the social world in need of an explanation.

Further error is likely to be introduced where the figures are samples from larger populations, as they usually are, because a sample represents its population only within a margin of error, even if properly drawn. As we saw in Unit 8, even the best of samples is not necessarily a perfect representation of its population; it just stands as high (and precisely estimable) a chance of being so as possible. You have already met the concept of sampling error in Unit 8, and in Block 4 you will learn how to capitalize on it to calculate the *statistical significance* of differences. For now, let us merely note that we cannot have great confidence in any of the differences between groups which have been illustrated in this unit. We have not tested whether they are big enough, in relation to their sampling errors, to be unlikely to have come about by chance alone.

ANSWERS TO ACTIVITIES

ACTIVITY 1

1 The frequency distribution of the Health Index should look something like Table 17.

Table 17

Score	Number of wards	%	Cumulative %
<−1.51	4	4.7	4.7
−1.50 to −1.01	10	11.8	16.5
−1.00 to −0.51	13	15.3	31.8
−0.50 to −0.01	17	20.0	51.8
0.00 to 0.49	20	23.5	75.3
0.50 to 0.99	9	10.6	85.9
1.00 to 1.99	8	9.4	95.3
2.00+	4	4.7	100.0
Total	85	100	

The two graphs should look similar to those shown in Figure 13.

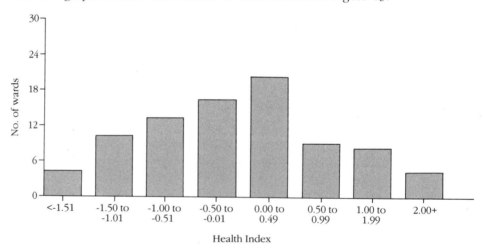

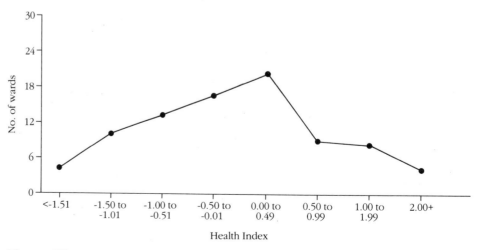

Figure 13

2 The frequency tables and graphs give us a good idea of how each variable is distributed, but nothing at all about the relationship of the two variables. We can get an idea of this from the maps, however, noting that it tends to be the same wards which are high on each variable or low on each variable.

ACTIVITY 2

The table might look like Table 18.

Table 18

Material Deprivation Index	Health Index			
	<−1	−0.99 to −0.01	0.00 to 0.99	1.00+
Total	14	30	29	12
	%	%	%	%
<−1	21	7	3	8
−0.99 to −0.01	71	60	62	8
0.00 to 0.99	7	33	28	17
1.00+	—	—	7	67

Percentages the other way, or even the raw figures, would have shown much the same in this case. We can see that the correlation is by no means perfect — there is a spread up and down each column — but the tendency of high values to go with high ones and low values with low ones is quite clear.

For those who like graphic illustration, something like Figure 14 might make the point.

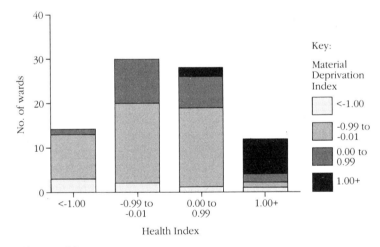

Figure 14

ACTIVITY 3

1 The first question, what kind of household children live in, can be answered from a simple frequency distribution of selected totals (Table 19). Each figure is the total in the left-hand column of one of the blocks of rows — though I have moved the overall grand total from first place to last.

Table 19

Type of household	Number of children	%
All members in family	1,051,732	91.9
1 not in family	84,251	7.4
2+ not in family	7,874	0.7
Total	1,143,857	

2 The size of family in which children live, similarly, is given by a frequency distribution (Table 20). The figures come from the left-hand column of the first (top) block of rows.

Table 20

Size of household	Number of families	%
2	81,809	9.9
3	278,915	33.7
4	305,761	36.9
5	113,198	13.7
6	34,872	4.2
7	9,030	1.1
8+	4,210	0.5
Total	827,795	

Note: you want the total of families, which is what the figures add up to, not the total of children.

3 'Difference' questions tend to call for two-way tables (Table 21). (Note that from this particular storehouse table we can answer questions about numbers of dependent children only for married-couple households.) The columns of Table 21 each represent a block of rows from Table 14, and the rows of Table 21 are the bottom figures, within a block of rows, from each of the 'number of children' columns — the row which gives the total number of children.

Table 21

Number of children in family	Type of household		
	all in family	1 not	2+ not
Total children	953,925	43,972	4,682
	%	%	%
1	20.1	24.4	21.3
2	47.4	39.8	36.8
3	22.3	22.5	20.7
4	7.3	8.4	13.2
5+	2.9	4.9	7.9

UNIT 15 EXTRACTING AND PRESENTING STATISTICS

A common mistake would be to use number of families rather than number of children, which would give a rather different table (Table 22). Table 22 is the same as Table 21 except that I have used the next to bottom figures — the number of families — instead of the bottom one.

Table 22

Number of children in family	Type of household		
	all in family	1 not	2+ not
Total families	511,422	24,098	2,406
	%	%	%
1	37.5	44.5	41.5
2	44.2	36.3	35.8
3	13.9	13.7	13.4
4	3.4	3.8	6.4
5+	0.1	0.2	2.8

You get the 'total' row by subtracting the families with no children from the total 'married couple' figures. Failing to do so would be another mistake, as this exercise is all about children, and would yield yet another different table (Table 23).

Table 23

Number of children in family	Type of household		
	all in family	1 not	2+ not
Total families	644,449	33,356	3,062
	%	%	%
0	20.6	27.8	21.4
1	29.8	32.2	32.6
2	35.1	26.2	28.1
3	11.0	9.9	10.5
4	2.7	2.7	5.1
5+	0.8	1.2	2.2

So we can see that virtually all families — around 90 per cent — have 1–3 children, but the proportion with 4+ children increases as the number of non-family adults increases. Where all the adults are in the family, nearly half of the families have 2 children. As the number of non-family adults increases, this proportion drops to not much more than a third.

UNIT 15 EXTRACTING AND PRESENTING STATISTICS

ACTIVITY 4

The overall table, from Activity 2, looked like this.

Table 18 (from answer to Activity 2)

Material Deprivation Index	Health Index			
	<−1	−0.99 to −0.01	0.00 to 0.99	1.00+
Total	14	30	29	12
	%	%	%	%
<−1	21	7	3	8
−0.99 to −0.01	71	60	62	8
0.00 to 0.99	7	33	28	17
1.00+	—	—	7	67

Splitting it by rural and urban areas, we get the following table (Table 24). (Numbers were so small in some columns that I have added adjacent columns together to give a better base for percentages, turning each block of the table into a dichotomy.)

Table 24

Material Deprivation Index	Health Index			
	urban		rural	
	negative	zero or positive	negative	zero or positive
	%	%	%	%
Negative	78	36	74	75
Zero or positive	22	64	26	25

A table as crude as this shows very clearly that there is a strong relationship in urban areas but virtually none in the rural areas. So splitting the original table by a third variable — in this case presenting separate tables for the urban and the rural wards — enables a hidden relationship to emerge.

REFERENCES

Abbott, P. (ed.) (1988) *Material Deprivation and Health Status in the Plymouth Health District*, Department of Applied Social Science, Polytechnic South West, Plymouth.

Abbott, P. and Sapsford, R. (1987) *Women and Social Class*, London, Tavistock.

Abbott, P., Bernie, J., Payne, G. and Sapsford, R. (1992) 'Health and material deprivation in Plymouth', in Abbott, P. and Sapsford, R. (eds) *Research into Practice: a Reader for Nurses and the Caring Professions*, Buckingham, Open University Press.

Huck, S.W. (1979) *Rival Hypotheses: Alternative Interpretations of Data-based Conclusions*, New York, Harper & Row.

Office of Population Censuses and Surveys (1982) *Census 1981: Historical Tables 1861–1981*, London, HMSO.

Office of Population Censuses and Surveys (1984) *Census 1981: Household and Family Composition, England and Wales*, London, HMSO.

Office of Population Censuses and Surveys (annual) *Social Trends*, London, HMSO.

ACKNOWLEDGEMENTS

Grateful acknowledgement is made to the following sources for permission to reproduce material in this unit:

FIGURES

Figures 1 and 10: Abbott, P. (1988) *Material Deprivation and Health Status in the Plymouth Health District*, © Dr Pamela Abbott, Department of Applied Social Science, University of Plymouth.

TABLES

Tables 1, 4, 5, 6 and 7: Abbott, P. (1988) *Material Deprivation and Health Status in the Plymouth Health District*, © Dr Pamela Abbott, Department of Applied Social Science, University of Plymouth; Table 8: Office of Population, Censuses and Surveys (1982) *Census 1981: Historical Tables 1861–1981*, Reproduced with the permission of the Controller of Her Majesty's Stationery Office; Table 14: Office of Population, Censuses and Surveys (1984) *Census 1981: Household and Family Composition, England and Wales*, Reproduced with the permission of the Controller of Her Majesty's Stationery Office.

UNIT 16 THE POLITICS OF OPERATIONALIZATION

Prepared for the Course Team by Roger Sapsford and Pamela Abbott

CONTENTS

Associated study materials		**210**
1	**Introduction**	**211**
2	**Operationalizing concepts**	**213**
	2.1 Achievement	213
	2.2 Potential	216
	2.3 Social class	223
3	**Politics and measurement**	**230**
	3.1 Intelligence and the politics of race	230
	3.2 Social class and the politics of gender	235
	3.3 Intelligence, achievement and the politics of class	239
4	**Politics, ideology and research 'style'**	**243**
5	**Conclusion**	**248**
Answer to activity		**250**
References		**250**
Acknowledgements		**254**

ASSOCIATED STUDY MATERIALS

Offprints Booklet 3, 'The results of the survey', by Pamela Abbott and Roger Sapsford.

Offprints Booklet 3, 'The technical problems of assigning a class to women', by Pamela Abbott and Roger Sapsford.

Reader, Chapter 10, 'The value of quantitative methodology for feminist research', by Toby Epstein Jayaratne.

1 INTRODUCTION

This unit is about the concepts the researcher brings to a research project and the methods of measurement he or she uses. As we have seen throughout the course so far, research reports do not just 'report' their results, as if these were something unproblematically collected; data collection always involves some element of inference, and a research report always has to establish the credibility of its results — to put forward an argument to justify why we should take the reported findings as supporting the conclusions that are drawn.

This is particularly the case when the research is focused on the kind of generalized variable which is in no sense amenable to direct measurement or observation. We cannot directly measure attitudes, or general ability, or even temperature. What we have to do is to find *indicators* which we *can* measure directly — what people say they believe, or what particular tasks they are able to do, or the height of a column of mercury in a glass tube — things we feel we can report with confidence, because little or no inference appears to be involved in their measurement. We then have to produce a convincing argument that these measurements may indeed be taken as valid indicators of the more abstract and conceptual quality about which we wish to speak. We start in this unit with the technical question of *operationalization* — how such 'measuring instruments' are constructed.

This is not the main focus of the unit, however, but preliminary ground which you need to cover in order to come to grips with the rest (and a useful revision and extension of ideas you have met in Units 11 and 14). The aim of the unit is to cover not just how instruments are constructed and validated, but how they are used and what assumptions are implicit in them. We are concerned, not so much with the instruments themselves, as with the concepts which they express and with the way these function to shape the direction of research and the nature of research conclusions. Thus our examples are mostly complex concepts which are expressed in complex measuring instruments — intelligence, achievement, personality, social class. The points we want to make about them, however, also hold true for much simpler concepts, and for concepts used in participant observation and 'unstructured' interviewing, as much as for the sort of highly structured research which calls for measuring instruments to be constructed. Ultimately, all research stands or falls by the way that the researcher *conceptualizes* the field of study: in the design of the study; in the way that measures are defined and measuring instruments constructed; in how the data are coded or clustered or segmented for analysis; and in the choices the researcher makes, when analysing and writing up, about what is important and what sense to make of it. The influence of any one of these four elements may differ from project to project, but all four are crucial influences on the final document(s). What we are pointing out in this unit is the extent to which ethical and political *assumptions* are built into the design of research, the ways in which data are collected and the use that is made of them.

Section 2, then, looks at how measuring instruments for abstract concepts are constructed and validated (how we make them, and how we can try to show that they do measure what they are supposed to measure). We look first at the abstract but comparatively uncomplicated idea of 'achievement' and how we can measure what people have achieved, at school for example, by means of 'paper and pencil' tests. We go on to the more difficult concept of 'potential' and to look at the measuring instruments that have been devised to assess intelligence (potential for intellectual achievement) and personality (potential for one or another kind of behaviour or reaction). Finally in this section, we look at 'social class', a conceptual way of locating people within social hierarchies, and how researchers have gone about constructing measures of this.

These are very commonly used concepts in research, but our interest is not just in these particular concepts — we want to use them as examples of how any 'abstract concept' might be measured. Having looked at how concepts are operationalized in a positivistic way, as though scale construction and the selection of measures could be divorced from the social world, we go on in the next sections to locate our particular examples in their social and historical context. Our concern becomes to see what the tests or scales were constructed *for*, how they have been used and what views of the world are implied in their use.

Section 3 stands back from the measures themselves, therefore, to examine (a) to what uses they have lent themselves, and (b) what kinds of theory underlie them or are implicit in them. We look at the use of intelligence tests for purposes which would now be regarded as racist or at least discriminatory in a pejorative sense — to declare some people unfit to be citizens, and indeed to exclude immigrants of certain nationalities. We look at the invisibility of gender in European and North American class theory up to the mid-1980s, treating this not as a curious historical fact but as symptomatic of the way that certain ideologies dominate even academic thought. We look at the use of concepts of intelligence and achievement, and of the whole paraphernalia of measurement that goes with them, to help reproduce a particular type of social order and a set of taken-for-granted beliefs about the world. We look, in other words, not just at the research, as something neutral and scientific, but at the researchers in their social context and the role of research ideas in maintaining and interpreting that context.

Finally, in Section 4, we look briefly at the suggestion sometimes now made that ideological perspectives on the social world are reproduced, not just by what we measure or how we measure it, but by the overall 'style' in which we conduct research and what it takes for granted about the nature of the social world. Just as a test or a set of questions or a form of observation may be seen, not just as measuring or collecting data on a concept, but also as embodying 'taken-for-granted' facts about the social world, so too can a whole style of research. Questions are raised about the normal relationship of researchers to researched, about the ownership of data and about the status of knowledge and expertise. The fact that we normally take the answers to these questions for granted makes them no easier to answer once the questions have been raised and made explicit.

In other words, we look at the *politics* of research. This unit is part of a 'strand' running through the course, from Block 1 via Unit 10 at the end of Block 2 and culminating in the final unit, which looks reflexively at the research process, its social context and its social consequences. Our particular focus here is on the way in which researchers' concepts about the proper ordering of the social world and the proper solution of social problems can be supported in their results because they were implicit in the way the research was conceptualized — and in the *tradition* within which it was conceptualized. We shall look at what is taken for granted as true about the world in particular research perspectives — so plausible that it needs no assertion — and how the very fact that propositions appear to be taken for granted which may be argued to be in the interests of some people and not others exposes the *ideological* nature of these beliefs. (In our critique of ideology we shall undoubtedly betray our own 'taken-for-granted' assumptions; it really *is* impossible not to take *something* for granted. You should look out for these assumptions while reading the material.) We shall look at how research ideas are grounded in particular *discourses* (sets of frameworks within which we understand and make sense of the conceptual world), pointing out that these discourses have historical origins and have been taken up and used by some people to the potential disadvantage of others. These are *political* questions — and by 'politics', here, we mean not the public disputation between political parties, or the government of countries, but the way in which inequalities of power are expressed and reproduced in social structures and ideologies. Our aim is not to attack particular lines of research, but to reinforce the point made in Block 1 that research cannot, ultimately, be divorced from politics. Knowledge is power, and the power to determine what shall count as knowledge is a very substantial power indeed, and one that is much more likely to be possessed by the researcher than the researched.

2 OPERATIONALIZING CONCEPTS

In this section we shall start with the technical problems of operationalization: what techniques people have used to construct 'measures' of the concepts they want to explore which can be used in empirical data collection. We begin with a conceptually easy example (though not without its problems, as we shall see), and move on to conceptually more difficult operationalizations. All the examples involve the construction of measurement scales, but the problems of operationalization are by no means confined to these.

2.1 ACHIEVEMENT

'Achievement at arithmetic' is a good concept with which to start this discussion, because it is conceptually comparatively simple. There may be dispute about the skills children should attain at school, and about particular forms of global testing at particular ages, but few teachers would doubt their own ability to assess whether children have learned their arithmetic. We appear straightforwardly to *measure* whether children can do arithmetic, by setting them tests and seeing how they score. In fact, however, the tests are still only *indicators* of achievement. We set children a range of problems to solve and calculations to carry out, but these are *particular* problems, and what we observe directly is only that the children can produce correct answers to these problems. We make an *inference* from these correct scores to a generalized concept of achievement — that the children have learned what we have been teaching them — when we use these scores on particular tests as an indicator of the overall level of their attainment. In other words, there is an implicit *argument* positioned between the test scores and the conclusions about arithmetical achievement — that the test does indeed measure achievement at arithmetic. Clearly, not just any series of items will do — we have to be able to argue that they are appropriate indicators of arithmetical competence. (In this and subsequent sections we shall be discussing 'paper and pencil' tests, where people answer written questions. Precisely the same principles would hold, however, if we were setting people tasks to do, or observing their ordinary behaviour, in order to measure some quality or quantity.)

One kind of test is conceptually straightforward, and that is the test aimed at certifying that the child has reached a given absolute standard. If you have been teaching long division, say, and want to assure yourself that the children have learned it, you set long-division problems and see whether the children can do them. If they can (but with a few careless mistakes, perhaps) then they pass; if they cannot, they need to be retaught. This kind of test is called a *criterion-referenced* test, because it assesses whether those who take the test have reached a certain criterion.

Tests which are used to grade children and assign them a 'standard' — a rank-order or position with respect to other children of their own age and/or other ages — are a little less straightforward. If you were devising an arithmetic test for a given age-band, you would assemble a large set of items (questions) appropriate to the age and get children to try them. Using the results, you would select from them a smaller test by:

1. Making sure that you had a range of items of different facility (difficulty) — some items that most children could do, some that only half could do, and some that only a few could do.

2. Deleting items which failed to *discriminate* between children — items which all or virtually all children could do (unless you wanted to leave a few in to reassure the weaker performers), and items which no child could do. (Eventually we shall want to show that the test discriminates between children good

or bad at arithmetic; in the first instance, however, we have to show that it makes *any* discrimination.)

The resultant test should be as short as is compatible with testing the full range of ability and should locate children in a hierarchy from the best to the worst at arithmetic. There are several more stages of checking to be gone through, however, before the argument for taking the test as a good measure of achievement becomes strong enough to be acceptable.

First, it would be necessary to check the stability or *reliability* of the test — whether it gave consistent results or was subject to large amounts of random variation. There are two ways of doing this: the 'test–retest' method and the 'split halves' method. In the former, you would retest the same children a little later (after long enough for them probably to have forgotten the answers they gave the first time). In the latter, you would construct a double-length test and see how well random halves correlate with each other. (A more sophisticated variant is to consider the correlation of each item score with the test score as a whole — so the concept of 'reliability' can be related to that of 'unidimensionality', which is discussed later in this sub-section.) If the test–retest procedure or the split-half procedure placed the children in the same order on both sets of scores, then the test would be judged entirely reliable. If it placed them in a completely different order, you might decide that the answers were random and the test of no value. Most tests will lie between these two extremes, but you obviously want one which is as reliable as possible, one that gives the same hierarchy of achievement for the same children on different occasions (provided the children themselves have not changed in the interim). The reliability of tests is usually assessed in published reports by quoting the *reliability coefficient* — for example, a correlation between test and retest. To be acceptable, reliability coefficients need to be high — 0.8 or even 0.9 would be the kind of level that testers would be seeking. For some purposes we accept correlation as low as 0.7, particularly in tests of adults, where it is often difficult to represent the full range of abilities and there are therefore technical reasons why the correlation may be lower. However, we have to acknowledge in doing so that the test is not very stable — that a non-trivial proportion of the score is contributed by random variation, so that two scores from the same person will seldom be identical. (You get 'proportion of variance explained' by squaring the correlation coefficient, so a reliability coefficient of 0.7 is explaining only 49 per cent of the variance in the test results.)

Secondly, you would want to demonstrate that the test did indeed measure what you were trying to measure, in this case arithmetical achievement — that it was a valid test. One way to do this would be to exhibit the items used in the test and argue that they obviously cover what is required — *face validity*; this is a weak form of argument, however, boiling down as it does to: 'Well, the test certainly *looks* as though it ought to be a valid measure!'. If you already knew the children's level of achievement it would be relatively simple to produce more convincing evidence — you would have to show only that the test placed the children in the same order as their true achievement level did. Generally, however, we do not have absolute knowledge, but only other ways of assessing achievement, so in practice we validate either:

1 Against some other written test of achievement — last year's examination, for example — which has the obvious problem that achievement level may have changed since then in some children but not others, or more commonly:

2 Against teacher's assessment of their achievement — which is not an absolute measure, but just another kind of measuring instrument, and one which is seldom tested for reliability even, let alone validity.

(This process of comparing a new test against an existing measure is called *concurrent validation*.) If the new test produces grossly dissimilar results to the existing measure, we are likely to consider it a poor indicator of achievement. If it produces results which are similar but do not give quite the same result in some cases, we may want to argue that it is actually a better test than the existing measures. Whichever, you can see that a process of *argument* is involved in citing test results; their validity as evidence is not automatically accepted but has to be justified.

Another way of strengthening the test's claim to be a valid measure might be to demonstrate *unidimensionality* — that all the items correlate with each other quite highly, so that the test as a whole is measuring the same thing as each separate item is measuring. Indeed, you might have taken this principle into account at the stage of constructing the test, discarding those items that did not correlate with the others but placed the children in a different order from the majority of other items. Note, however, that the appeal to unidimensionality rests on a theory: that what is being measured is and should be expressible on a single dimension. It assumes that 'achievement in arithmetic' is a single dimension, and that someone good at addition should also be good at multiplication or division. If you believed that doing addition was something quite different from doing long division, and different again from doing multiplication — so that children might be good at one but bad at the others — you would probably devise different tests for the different operations. If you needed an overall test, however, that assessed achievement over the range of operations, it would not be a unidimensional test but one that fairly represented all the different operations — several *different* subjects combined into one test paper.

A final point on validity, at this time, is that the whole argument rests on agreement as to how the test is to be marked. This is fairly simple when testing achievement at arithmetic, where there are agreed right answers and a fairly small range of methods for getting to them. An achievement test in English language might be more difficult to construct and justify, because different teachers will disagree as to what the important elements are — grammar and punctuation, 'style', ability to reproduce material taught in the classroom, ability to bring in material from outside the classroom, comprehension of written material, creativity, and so on. It is unlikely that three teachers would rate the work of a class of children in quite the same order, and equally unlikely that three teachers would agree entirely on the validity of a particular test, if they knew precisely what it was aiming to measure.

If you were constructing tests for general use, once you had demonstrated reliability and validity you would need to apply them to large random samples of the appropriate population, to obtain *norms*. In other words, you might want to know how well the average seven-year-old, eight-year-old, nine-year-old and so on did on the tests, and what the typical spread of cases was around these means. This would enable a particular school to find out whether its seven-year-olds, for example, were achieving as well as the national average, or worse, or better.

ACTIVITY 1

There are also other forms of 'comparison with the norm' which become possible once age-related norms for tests have been collected. Can you think of any? Make a note of your response before you continue.

The major use to which age-related norms are put is to estimate an 'age' for individual children on the quality that is being measured — in this case, an 'arithmetic achievement age'. If a child's performance lies at the seven-year-old average for the test, we could say that he or she 'had an arithmetic achievement age of seven'. We could compare this with the child's actual age to get an idea of individual standing relative to the country's children as a whole — a child of seven with an achievement age of eight is doing well, and one of eight with an achievement age of seven is doing badly. We could even combine the two ages into one figure — an 'achievement quotient' — to show how the child is doing in percentage terms, by dividing the achievement age by the chronological age and multiplying by one hundred. Then a child of eight with an achievement age of seven would have an achievement quotient of 7/8 x 100 = 87.5, a child of seven with an achievement age of eight would have a quotient of 8/7 × 100 = *c*. 114, and a child of eight with an achievement age of eight would, of course, have a quotient of 100. Both these strategies allow comparison of children, not just with the norms for their own age, but with children of other ages.

The use of quotients — single scores calculated from two 'age' figures — has gone out of fashion to some extent in the research literature because they tend to mean different things at different ages. More common now is the use of 'standard scores' with an age group's mean set at 100. These resemble quotients in form but are more like the standardized scores discussed in Unit 6. You will still find quotients in older research papers, however, and they are still used by organizations dealing with a restricted range of abilities (e.g. MENSA). Moreover, the basic idea is still live in educational practice: we still speak of a child of ten as 'having a reading age of eight, or fourteen'.

2.2 POTENTIAL

Section 2.1 looked in some detail at how researchers (and teachers) can measure what children are achieving in class. We described this as a relatively simple concept to operationalize; there may be political differences about the appropriate-

Multiplication

A	213 ×2	332 ×3	433 ×2	313 ×3	212 ×4
	111 ×5	233 ×3	221 ×4	444 ×2	343 ×2
B	202 ×2	101 ×5	301 ×3	403 ×2	102 ×4
C	106 ×2	204 ×3	103 ×4	105 ×5	207 ×2
	308 ×2	206 ×4	107 ×6	109 ×5	209 ×4
	407 ×2	108 ×5	308 ×3	207 ×4	305 ×2

D Find the product of   Multiply
  1 109 and 3   1 209 by 3
  2 405 and 2   2 434 by 2
  3 108 and 4   3 205 by 4
  4 307 and 3   4 108 by 6
  5 109 and 6   5 107 by 5

Figure 1 *A self-assessment test in arithmetic*
(Source: Newton and Smith, 1978, p.50)

ness of global testing, but few people doubt that it is possible to test achievement and few people dispute the kind of test that is appropriate. Researchers face more complex problems, however, when they need to measure more problematic hypothetical characteristics, ones which are theory-rich but whose measurement is by no means obviously or easily achieved. In this section we look at two such sets of concepts which have played a large part in psychological theory and research — concepts of intelligence and concepts of personality.

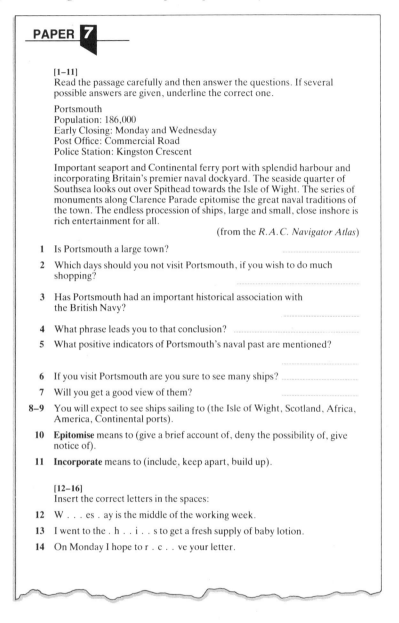

Figure 2 *A self-assessment test in English*
(Source: Thomas and Thomas, 1988, p.40)

Intelligence

Intelligence tests are constructed in much the same way as achievement tests, by compiling a large bank of questions, obtaining answers to them from a range of people, keeping those questions which appear to discriminate between people, and then going on to validate the test (discarding items which do not discriminate between people of high or low intelligence as otherwise determined). Rather different kinds of items are required for the test, however, because we are trying to measure not achievement but the *ability* to achieve, independent of whether the achievement has yet occurred.

The first systematic intelligence test, developed in France in 1905 by Alfred Binet (Binet and Simon, 1905), aimed to distinguish children who were incapable of learning from those who had simply been badly taught. It was built as a diagnostic instrument rather than as an expression of theory, and it concentrated on 'general knowledge' — testing understanding of the surrounding culture and its day-to-day realities — coupled with conceptual tasks such as devising a systematic search pattern for a lost item. The test was brought into the USA in the second decade of the century by Henry Goddard, Robert Yerkes and Lewis Terman and soon became widely used for the identification of children who would now be said to have 'learning difficulties' but who were then termed 'mental defectives' in the USA — particularly those children whose difficulty was only mild (in the IQ 70–80 range) and otherwise hard to detect. An Americanized version of the test, the Stanford–Binet, was devised and published by Terman in 1916. Revised versions of this instrument are still in use, but a wide range of different tests of intelligence have been constructed from a variety of theoretical bases. Such tests have undergone two major kinds of change since their introduction into the English-speaking world.

Form M **Average Adult, 7**

7. * **Essential Differences** (Same as S.A. II, 3)

Procedure: Say, "*What is the principal difference between ...... and ......?*" Repeat for each item.
   (a) Work and play.
   (b) Ability and achievement.
   (c) Optimist and pessimist.

Score: 2 plus. See scoring standards, pages 400 ff.

8. **Binet Paper Cutting**

Material: Six-inch squares of paper.

Procedure: Taking one of the sheets, say, "*Watch carefully what I do. See, I fold the paper this way* (folding it over once in the middle), *then I fold it this way* (folding it again in the middle, but at right angles to the first fold). *Now I will cut out a piece just here*" (indicating). Cut out a small triangular piece from the middle of the side which presents but one edge. Leave the folded paper exposed, but pressed flat against the table. The fragments cut from the paper should be kept out of sight. Indicating the $3'' \times 3''$ square in the booklet say, "*Make a drawing here to show how this paper would look if it were unfolded* (opened). *Draw lines to show where the paper would be creased and show how and where it would be cut.*" If S. omits either the creases or the cuts, repeat, "*Draw lines to show where the paper would be creased and show how and where it would be cut.*"

Score: The test is passed if the creases in the paper are properly represented, if the holes are drawn in the correct number, and if they are located correctly, that is, both on the same crease and each about half way between the center of the paper and the outside. The shape of the holes is disregarded.

Figure 3 *Extract from the Stanford–Binet Intelligence Test, Form M (Source: Terman and Merrill, 1937, p.180)*

The first of these came about with the growth of the mathematical technique of *factor analysis* in the 1920s and 1930s. Factor analysis is a technique for understanding and simplifying the intercorrelation between test items. In the previous section we talked about unidimensionality and the desirability of having all the items of a test correlating highly with each other if the test purports to be measuring a single dimension. Factor analysis effectively fits models to the correlated data, to see whether the same pattern of variance could be obtained with a much smaller number of items or 'factors', without much loss of information — in other words, if all the items which were highly correlated were counted as being aspects of a single item rather than as separate items. As developed by English psychologist statisticians such as Charles Spearman (1904, 1927) and Cyril Burt (1927, 1940), factor analysis was used to try to construct tests which would measure a single factor of 'general intelligence', and such unidimensional tests turned out to be capable of construction. Factor analysis is now a standard part of intelligence test construction, used to identify and discard items which do not correlate adequately with others and as a guarantee of unidimensionality. Given that the theory of intelligence posits intelligence as a single dimension — that is, it suggests that people good at one kind of intellectual task should also be good at others — the results of factor analysis are put forward as support both of the concept and of the tests that measure it. This is an example of *construct validation* (which will be referred to again later) — using the fact that a test behaves as theory says it should as evidence that it constitutes a good measure.

The second major change, less dramatic but possibly even more important, has been that more thought has gone into the kinds of questions that are asked. The items which Binet used would *not* now, for the most part, be acceptable in intelligence tests, because they are too dependent on cultural knowledge and not totally independent of schooling. More and more effort is put into devising questions which can be answered by people of all social classes, whatever their level of achievement at school, and by people from other cultures who have had a different kind of experience and a different kind of schooling. The task is not an easy one, and ultimately, it is suspected, one which can never be perfectly achieved. The 'Draw a Man Test', for example, which consists quite simply of telling a young child to draw a picture of a man, and capitalizes on the kinds of drawing that children of different ages typically manage, was hailed as a breakthrough in culture-free tests, because it was not even dependent on knowledge of language. However, when its proponents tried to use it in fundamentalist Muslim countries, whose religion forbids portrayal of the human form, the fact that it was not suitable for every culture became clear! (It has been replaced by the 'Draw a House Test' — but houses differ in their form from country to country.) However, more and more ingenuity goes into trying to frame questions which test people's ability to reason without requiring either a stock of knowledge or previous training in techniques.

ACTIVITY 2

As an example of an item which can be discredited as requiring knowledge rather than just reasoning, take the following number series and see if you can complete it:

2, 2, 3, 2, 2, 2, 1.25, 2, 2, 2, —

As a hint: the sequence would have been difficult for, but within the grasp of, someone who was a child in the 1940s or 1950s. It was already becoming difficult by the 1960s and would be very difficult indeed for anyone born after about 1965. Our answer is at the end of the unit.

Thus two forms of validation have been built into the test. *Face validity* is important for intelligence tests, in the negative sense that the items must not be seen as depending for a correct answer on schooling or knowledge. Given that intelligence is posited as a unitary quality — *general* intelligence, not specific mental

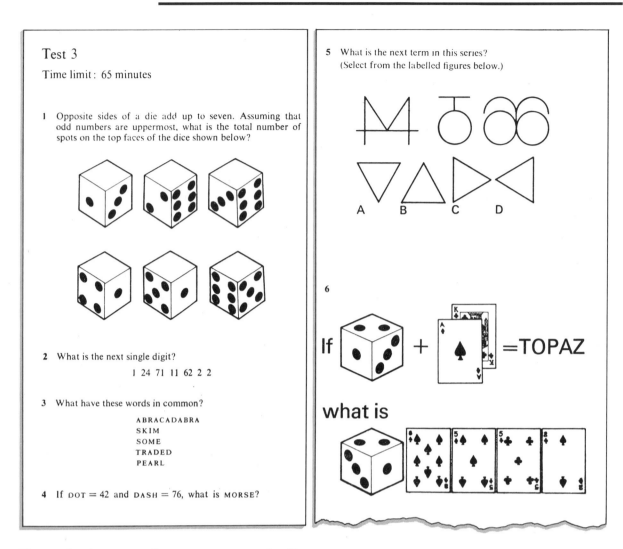

Figure 4 *An extract from a more recent intelligence test*
(Source: Sullivan, 1978, pp.124–5)

abilities — it is important to demonstrate *unidimensionality*, which is where factor analysis is useful. *Reliability* will also have to be demonstrated, of course — that the tests give consistent results for the same person on different occasions. Beyond this, however, it is necessary to show that this unidimensional, reliable, apparently valid test does indeed measure intelligence. Two strategies are available for demonstrating this:

1 *Concurrent validation*, discussed in the last section, means showing that a new test produces the same results as an accepted existing test; this is how many new tests would be validated. Clearly, however, this was not available as a stratagem for validating the original tests.

2 Stronger as a stratagem is *predictive validation*. Here we specify what people who score high or low on the test should or should not be able to do, and see if the prediction holds true. If what we have is a test of intelligence, for example, then people who score highly on it should be able to do difficult crosswords, solve mathematical puzzles and work out complex practical problems. All things being equal, they should do better at school than people who have the same kind and amount of schooling but who have lower intelligence test scores. If these predictions are borne out, then we have quite strong arguments for our test being a valid measure of intelligence.

In a wider sense we sometimes talk about *construct validation*. This indicates that our theoretical construct is sound by showing that a viable test of it can be constructed. If it were not possible to construct a test whose high scorers were good at a range of intellectual tasks, at school work and so forth, then we might doubt whether it was sound to talk about 'general intelligence' at all. Conversely, if people who scored high on the test and did well at intellectual tasks also turned out to be the best at mechanical tasks, at sports and physical endurance, we might reasonably doubt whether what we were measuring was general *intelligence*: 'general *ability*' would seem a better description. In technical terms, what we are looking for is *convergent validity* — that the test correlates well with other measures with which theory says it should correlate; and *divergent validity* — that it does not correlate well with measures with which theory says it should *not* correlate.

Once we have a validated test we can proceed in just the same way as was discussed, in Section 2.1, for achievement tests. Data are collected on large random samples, to establish age-related population norms. From these are derived the familiar concepts of 'mental age' and the 'intelligence quotient' or 'IQ'.

Our discussion here makes the validation of intelligence tests seem a simple matter, but it is, in fact, far from simple. Particular problems reside in the great dependence of test constructors on factor analysis:

1. Factor analysis is a technique for describing data, not a technique for making decisions about them. In particular, the number of factors to be extracted is not dictated by the analysis but determined by the analyser. Sometimes it is quite clear that a data set can be best described by extracting a single factor, but sometimes two- or three-factor solutions may be equally possible. Psychologists who have posited intelligence as made up of two different kinds of ability — verbal and spatial/mathematical — have been able to use factor analysis to construct and validate their tests.

2. The technique is very dependent on the way that cases are sampled to obtain the data. If your sample is homogeneous — consisting of only a narrow range of abilities — then a one-factor solution is very likely to emerge. With a wider range of abilities represented in the sample, solutions which extract more than one factor become increasingly likely. One criticism of early intelligence theorists is that they based their findings on samples which did not exhibit much range of abilities.

3. Perhaps most important of all, factor analysis shows only which variables are correlated; it is the analyst who determines what the factors shall be *called*. This is why construct validation is so important — demonstrating, for example, that what the test measures is intelligence (*reasoning* ability), not some wider and more general kind of ability or skill.

More generally — and it is a point we shall need to bear in mind for later in the unit — the theory precedes and underlies the test. The unitary nature of general intelligence was not discovered from factor analysis of answers to tests; the existence of the concept was the reason why the factor analyses were done in the first place. That such a test can be developed adds plausibility to the concept — it would be of very dubious status if it proved impossible to operationalize it — and the increased plausibility of the concept lends credence in its turn to the test. The test can be taken as a valid measure of what it purports to measure, however, only in the light of the theory; without its theoretical underpinning it would make no sense whatsoever.

Personality

An even less readily measurable or perceptible concept in psychology has been the concept of personality, but if personality theory is to be amenable to research then indicators of 'dimensions of personality' have to be found. The problem is handled in just the same way as it would be for tests of achievement or intelligence such as have been discussed above. A dimension has to be defined, items accumulated which probably look 'on the face of it' to have some relationship to the defined dimension, answers obtained from samples of people, items discarded which do not appear to discriminate between people, and the revised test checked for reliability and validated in some way to demonstrate that it does indeed measure what it purports to measure. Christie and his colleagues, for example, hypothesized a dimension of 'Machiavellianism' — that people would differ in their enduring tendency to manipulate the behaviour of others. Sentences were constructed which did or did not express Machiavellian sentiments and people were invited to choose between them, yielding a 'Machiavellianism score'. Retest investigated reliability, and the test was validated by the predictive method, seeing if it gave a useful prediction of who would use Machiavellian strategies in an interactive game (see Christie and Geiss, 1970).

Beyond 'single-trait' tests such as this, people have also attempted to construct 'inventories' which will provide reasonably complete descriptions of mental state. The usual procedure is just the same — to accumulate a large bank of questions about what people believe, think, feel and do; to obtain answers from samples of people; to discard items on which people do not differ; and then to construct a multi-dimensional test which purports to measure a number of dimensions along which people can be located. A range of methods has been used for doing this, from the 'criterion-referenced' approach, discussed briefly in Section 2.1 in relation to achievement testing, to the factor-analytical approach typical of intelligence test construction.

ACTIVITY 3

How might you go about constructing a personality inventory (a) by criterion-referenced methods, and (b) factor analytically? Think of tests you know which have been constructed by the one route or the other. Alternatively — if you are not familiar with psychological tests — look back at the discussion of the methods above and think about how you might proceed.

An example of the criterion-referenced construction of a personality inventory is the MMPI (Hathaway and McKinley, 1940) — the Minnesota Multiphasics Personality Inventory, an instrument which is now quite old but still in general use. What the testers did was to assemble a very large batch of attitude, personality, belief and behavioural statements — over five hundred, in the full version of the inventory. For the construction of the initial scales, these were administered to groups of psychiatric patients who were diagnosed as having or not having some particular mental trait or condition, and the scores on items which were consistently answered one way by those having the trait, and the other by those not having it, were added together as 'Scales'. Among the earliest scales to be constructed were the Hypochondriasis Scale (McKinley and Hathaway, 1940) and the Depression Scale (Hathaway and McKinley, 1942). Reliability was checked by retest, and predictive validity by administration to different groups of patients — and also by collecting national norms from the general population and showing that the scores they produced were mostly much lower than those produced by the diagnosed group. Factor analysis played no part in the original construction, but data from the MMPI have subsequently been factor analysed, and most of the original factors have been shown to be adequately unidimensional (Comrey, 1957a,b, 1958). Other researchers have constructed further scales from the same inventory of items for their own purposes. The Ego Strength Scale (Barron, 1953), for example, which predicts success in therapy (Taft, 1957; Gottesman, 1959), was constructed in the same way as the original scales, by contrasting patients judged to succeed in therapy with unsuccessful cases. The Social Introversion Scale (Drake, 1946; Drake and Thiede, 1948) was validated against other accepted measures of the trait (that is, *concurrently* validated).

By contrast, the 16PF — Cattell's 16 Personality Factor Inventory — depended on factor analysis for its construction from the outset. After preliminary research, Cattell (1946) took a large number of adjectives from the dictionary, descriptive of personality, and asked people to describe other people on them, using a numerical rating scale. Factor analysis boiled down their replies to sixteen factors which between them could account for most of the variance in the many hundreds of adjectives used, and the factors were named according to their most obvious loadings (the items that contributed most to them). Reliability was checked in the usual way, and studies using self-rating and behavioural measures were used to offer validation evidence for the naming of the factors. The factors were not independent of each other but correlated: a score on one factor was sometimes predictive of scores on others.

Cattell's work is essentially descriptive in its aims — it uses factor analysis to 'discover' the structure of personality data. By contrast, Eysenck (1947) used factor analysis to build tests which conformed with theory. Positing that personality — tendencies to behave/react in certain ways — can adequately be described by the two factors of extraversion/introversion (broadly, though it is in fact a complex theoretical notion, the extent to which the person is dependent on reinforcement from outside the self or able to supply his or her own reinforcement) and stability/instability-neuroticism (variously interpreted as stability of temperament/behaviour or liability to display symptoms of mood disorder), he obtained responses to a large number of questions selected on the basis of the theory and used factor analysis to select those items which appeared to be useful measures of one or the other trait. (The traits are theorized as being independent of each other, and Eysenck used a form of factor analysis which ensured that this should be the case.) Reliability was established by retest, and validity by predictive laboratory experiments and by successful predictions about the nature of 'extreme populations' such as the inmates of prisons and patients in psychiatric hospitals (though some of the latter kinds of prediction have since been brought into doubt by further research on prisoners' and psychiatric patients' personalities — see Heskin *et al.*, 1973, 1977; Crookes, 1979; Sapsford, 1983). Interestingly, further factor analysis of the scores on Cattell's sixteen primary factors yields 'higher order factors', two of which are reasonable approximations to Eysenck's two primary factors. Eysenck (1970) has since found that a third factor, 'psychoticism' (liability to display symptoms of thought disorder), was necessary for a complete account of the variance, and the three factors go to make up the test now known as the Eysenck Personality Inventory.

2.3 SOCIAL CLASS

A third concept at which we might look moves us away from the territory of psychology and starts us on the measurement or description of social structure and the location of individuals within it, the home ground of sociology. Social class is probably the most common descriptive variable encountered in sociological and social policy research, and its measurement is to a large extent taken for granted. It is a common way of distinguishing between people or groups, not only in 'theoretical' research (e.g. into class sentiments or class action), but also in diverse areas of applied social research — health, education, poverty and social welfare, crime and its 'treatment', and many others. Theoretical arguments may be pursued as to which is the most appropriate for any given purpose, but on the whole the measurement of class is not treated as problematic.

However, social class is another 'invisible concept', like intelligence and achievement, and what we have to work with is not direct measurement but indicators of the underlying concept. Variables such as class press the philosophical position known as 'realism', which we have adopted by and large in this course, to its limits. That is, real people stand in real relations of dominance and subordination, advantage and disadvantage to one another, but the concepts we use to describe these relations do not, one might argue, 'exist in the real world'; they are our ways of trying to simplify the detail of the real world and detect meaningful patterns. (People stand in a potentially infinite number of different real relations to each other; to single out one subset of relations in this way as coherent and important is to impose a construction on reality.) Thus, while not doubting that it is a real world that is being described and that true description is the aim, researchers may nonetheless argue about the most useful way of describing it, almost as though the *utility* of a concept were all that mattered.

Social class and its measurement form a useful example in the current discussion because the concept is not only an abstract and theoretical one, but informed by *different* and often conflicting theories. There are a number of different ways of classifying social class in common use, influenced by different theoretical perspectives and constructed for different purposes. They have in common, however, that the basic 'building blocks' are people's occupations: an individual's social class is determined by his or her occupation. Occupations are then aggregated into groups which are said to be similar in socio-economic terms to form social classes. There have been three basic and influential clusters of ideas which have affected how class is measured; we might label them crudely 'the Marxist', 'the Weberian' (or 'the sociological') and 'the official' (the Registrar General's and other scales derived from this). The third of these is more concerned with constructing a hierarchy of social and economic prestige than with operationalizing sociological or political/economic theory.

For the Marxist school, for the purpose of classification, class is defined by the relationship of individuals and groups to the means of production. Those who own capital are capitalists, in the simplest version of the theory, while all others have only their labour to sell and are workers. The theory has become more elaborate to accommodate the growing middle class of managers, administrators and technical experts — people who do not own the means of production, but who frequently stand in an 'ownership relation' to it and control workers on behalf of capital or help with their control and management. Key questions have been the extent to which these classes do indeed share interests in the way that theory says they should, the extent to which they are aware of shared interests or are fragmented by other factors, and the extent to which they undertake common action. Marxist conceptions of class underlie most theoretical discussions of the topic in the European tradition, but the class of 'owners' is so small and so well protected from public scrutiny that it does not lend itself to large-scale survey research — and, indeed, it differs so much from the bulk of the employed population in its economic situation that any who did occur in a survey sample would probably be readily identifiable as individuals merely from the pattern of their answers. Most sociologists, including Marxists, have been more concerned to make distinctions among the non-owning classes, and they see managers, professionals and small businesses, as well as the 'owner' class, as materially advantaged even if few of them dispose of capital in any significant sense and many of them stand in a fundamentally wage-labour relationship to the sources of their advantage (see, for example, Westergaard and Rexler, 1975).

The boundary between middle class (white collar) and working class (manual and routine service occupations), and whether it is permeable, has been a common target of research in the last thirty or forty years. In many ways, this owes less to Marx than to Weber, who focused interest on the way in which classes maintained their boundaries and privileges at the expense of people outside them and on the hierarchy within classes in respect of market position (i.e. the 'going rate' for a given type of labour — including conditions of work and 'fringe benefits' as well as straightforward monetary reward). Some research has been done using scale measures of social class based on the concept of economic interests and relationship to the means of production, but strongly influenced by the concept of internal hierarchies; perhaps the most notable in recent years being the analysis of the 1983 British General Election by Anthony Heath and his colleagues (1985). Looking at class relationships to party preference, Heath *et al.* devised a 'scale' of social class which they hoped reflected to some extent the economic interests that ought to be shared within classes and to differ between classes. Their way of formulating the problem is to suggest that:

> ... broadly speaking, wage labourers have different interests from those of the self-employed or from those of salaried managers and professionals. Their incomes may overlap, but the conditions under which

they earn that income differ quite markedly ... It is the competitive position of different groups in the labour market which provides the basis for their differing values and political principles.

(Heath *et al.*, 1985, p.14)

In theoretical terms, this reflects a Weberian rather than a Marxist view of class — class as determined by labour market position, but influenced by the Marxist view that classes share interests which are distinct from those of other classes. The classification scheme in which these principles are expressed works as in Table 1. It is not a totally new form of classification, but a rearrangement of an existing scale, the Hope-Goldthorpe Scale, discussed below.

Table 1 The social class scale used by Heath *et al.*

	Men	Women
Salariat	30	23
Routine non-manual	11	46
Petty bourgeoisie	10	4
Foremen and technicians	11	2
Working class	38	25
	100%	100%

(Source: Heath et al., 1985, Table 2.5, p.23)

Other scales set out in an explicitly Weberian way to measure social status, or prestige. The Hall-Jones Scale (Hall and Jones, 1950), for example, was constructed by taking a list of job titles and inviting a sample of people to rank them in order 'as to their social standing'. From the resultant data a six-point ordered scale was derived. A similar but more elaborate exercise was carried out in the construction of the Hope-Goldthorpe Scale (Goldthorpe and Hope, 1972, 1974), used for the 1971 Oxford Mobility Study — subsets of a long list of occupational categories were ranked by a large sample of respondents and aggregated into a point scale. This has also contributed, in modified form, to recent political analyses (Heath *et al.*, 1985) and to the most recent of the large-scale mobility surveys, the Scottish Mobility Study (Payne, 1986a,b). Goldthorpe would argue that the Hope-Goldthorpe Scale is compatible with a Marxist framework, and it certainly follows the European tradition of conceptualizing society as broken up into broad, bounded classes — groups with shared interests which are different from or even opposed to those of other groups — but he would also acknowledge a strong Weberian influence. For example, he conceptualizes his scale as a hierarchy, but with a number of parallel groups in the middle which differ in market position but not in any significant way in their relations to the means of production.

Among the 'official' scales the most widely used is the Registrar General's categorization of social class, used in the Census and a number of other government sources. This first appeared in the Registrar General's Annual Report for 1911, where it was used as a tool for analysing differential infant mortality rate and described as 'designed as far as possible to represent different social grades' (Registrar General, 1912). It has continued since then, changing from time to time to reflect changes in the labour market and in our understanding of class; the last major revision was in 1971, when the 'routine skilled labour' class (III) was subdivided into 'manual' and 'non-manual'. The classification broadly reflects popular views about occupations which 'go together' in terms of the kinds of people who finish up in them, their interests and habits and their 'implied social position'. Length of time in formal education is heavily reflected in the classification, and the professions (doctors, lawyers, clergy) outrank journalists, personnel managers and even members of Parliament.

Table 2 The Registrar General's social class scale (showing the economically active population, 1981, Great Britain)

Social class		Economically active (10% sample census)	
		Men	Women
I	Professional, etc., occupations	84,862	10,004
II	Intermediate occupations	332,132	199,247
III(N)	Skilled occupations — non-manual	173,840	381,647
III(M)	Skilled occupations — manual	537,545	79,759
IV	Partly skilled occupations	250,671	207,598
V	Unskilled occupations	94,568	66,766
Armed forces and inadequately described		79,053	42,867
Total		1,552,671	987,888

(Source: OPCS, 1984, from Table 17, p.548)

A related scale is the Social Grading Schema of the Market Research Society (classes labelled A, B, C_1, C_2, D, E), which is explicitly based on the Registrar General's Scale, but with an additional 'class' to include those with little or no income (those who are, for example, unemployed, state pensioners, or permanently sick or disabled), and with some modifications to reflect differential purchasing power and purchasing behaviour. Though fairly widely used in social research, its main purpose is to construct groups which are homogeneous with respect to buying power and shopping behaviour. Its most powerful use has probably been in the analysis of television viewing behaviour and newspaper readership in order to determine where and when advertisements can be placed to greatest effect, though in recent years there has been some trend here away from overall aggregate classes and towards targeting advertising at groups more precisely defined in terms of age, income and tastes. This scale has also been used in many of the studies of British elections and voting behaviour. When used for purposes of social analysis it can sometimes distort the results because of its quite deliberate reflection of income and life-style at the expense of other factors. It is not the most useful class schema, for example, for the analysis of voting behaviour, as Anthony Heath has demonstrated in the most recent of the British election studies at the time of writing (Health et al., 1985).

For the sake of completeness, we might also mention briefly the other 'class' measure used in Census and other governmental data, Socio-Economic Groupings (SEGs). These form a seventeen-point categorization scheme, roughly but not entirely hierarchical in nature, which differentiates more finely between groups likely to have different life-styles, levels of prestige and experiences of the labour market — 'people whose social, cultural and recreational standards are similar' (CSO, 1975). These are sometimes used (see, for example, Payne, 1986a) where a more detailed breakdown of occupation seems desirable and the hierarchical ranking of all cases is not of overwhelming importance.

These are the main systems of social class categorization in common use; there are many more, not described here, which have been used from time to time. They differ a fair amount in their theoretical orientation, and also in the way they are interpreted; British and European class theory, for example, tends to put greater stress on the bounded nature of classes and the divide between middle/white-collar and working classes, while theorists in North America conceive of class more as a continuous graded scale. Overall, the different scales show a large amount of agreement as to where they locate particular occupations, but there are differences, particularly in the middle of the scales, which make one scale more

Table 3 The Registrar General's classification of socio-economic groups (showing the economically active population, 1981, Great Britain)

Socio-economic group	Economically active (10% sample census)	
	Men	Women
1 Employers and managers in central and local government, industry, commerce, etc. — large establishments	84,757	20,483
1.1 Employers in industry, commerce, etc. — large establishments	562	127
1.2 Managers in central and local government, industry, commerce, etc. — large establishments	84,195	20,356
2 Employers and managers in industry, commerce, etc. — small establishments	135,597	42,637
2.1 Employers in industry, commerce, etc. — small establishments	37,419	12,722
2.2 Managers in industry, commerce, etc. — small establishments	98,178	29,915
3 Professional workers — self-employed	14,367	1,380
4 Professional workers — employees	70,235	8,610
5 Intermediate non-manual workers	113,711	142,206
5.1 Ancillary workers and artists	101,259	130,548
5.2 Foremen and supervisors — non-manual	12,452	11,658
6 Junior non-manual workers	147,398	368,732
7 Personal service workers	17,846	120,173
8 Foremen and supervisors — manual	55,945	6,630
9 Skilled manual workers	409,101	39,198
10 Semi-skilled manual workers	210,799	102,795
11 Unskilled manual workers	90,589	66,504
12 Own account workers (other than professional)	83,013	18,002
13 Farmers — employers and managers	10,534	1,196
14 Farmers — own account	10,370	1,347
15 Agricultural workers	19,356	5,128
16 Members of armed forces	24,296	1,808
17 Inadequately described and not stated occupations	54,757	41,059
Total	1,552,671	987,888

(Source: OPCS, 1984, from Table 17, p.548)

suitable than another for a given theoretical or practical purpose. One thing they have in common is that they are sloppily constructed by comparison with scales of achievement, intelligence or personality. Much thought goes into the theory behind their derivation, but very little effort goes into validation at the construction stage; rather, researchers determine which jobs shall go where 'from the armchair' on the basis of theory and commonsense knowledge about the labour market and the social world. The exceptions to this critique are the Hall-Jones and Hope-Goldthorpe Scales, which were constructed on the basis of empirical work into the prestige of occupations and the order in which people actually did rank them (though the Hall-Jones construction exercise was methodologically inept — for a brief but insightful critique see Coxon *et al.*, 1986).

Validation evidence for all the scales is not lacking, however. There is little *differential* validation of one scale against another, except for a little in the field of political analysis (Heath *et al.*, 1985), but, overall, there is considerable validation of the concept of class. The scales are good predictors, as they should be and as has been shown in studies too numerous to list here, of income, education, housing, other aspects of life-style, political and voting behaviour, the jobs and education achieved by the sons and daughters of the man whose class is being measured (as we shall see in Section 3.2, women have frequently been ignored in the sampling), the class of origin of the wife he marries, and very many other aspects of attitude and behaviour. As we saw in the paper by Abbott *et al.* (1992) on health status and material deprivation, which you read earlier in the course, social class correlates with material deprivation and therefore also predicts health status. Predictively, therefore, the scales stand up well to critical examination. There are four major problems with them, however:

1 The scales correlate very well with many of the aspects of behaviour, attitude and circumstance which they are required to predict, and all these aspects correlate well with each other. Under this circumstance — known technically as *multi-collinearity* — it is not always easy to know what can reasonably be seen as causing what. Sometimes a variable can be a very useful predictor because it 'summarizes the variance' of a number of others, without itself being a reasonable candidate for causal influence. The best predictor of whether a young person is likely to be criminally convicted in the future, for example, is how often he or she has been convicted in the past. Now, it seems reasonable that having twenty previous convictions should be a good predictor of the twenty-first — the previous convictions measure the extent to which the person is committed to a criminal life-style and/or his or her inefficiency and likelihood of being caught. No-one except an extreme behaviourist psychologist, however, would argue that having one previous conviction predisposes people to another in itself, or that two previous convictions predispose to a third, even though this is what the figures suggest. More likely is that the number of previous convictions is acting as an indicator of aspects of attitude, circumstance and life-style which do have a causal connection with likelihood of committing offences and being caught. In the same way, 'social class' may sometimes be a surrogate for income or material state, as we argued in the health paper, rather than a causal variable. This would not affect its value as a predictor, but it would limit the extent to which research findings were useful for class theory.

2 A second problem is the assumption of linearity built into the scales. Many of them (e.g. the Hall-Jones Scale, the Hope-Goldthorpe Scale and the Socio-Economic Groupings of the Census) do not assume continuity between all classes but have groups in the middle which are different but not necessarily 'higher' or 'lower'. All, however, embody an overall assumption of progression from the lowest class to the highest, and this is not an empirical discovery but an inbuilt *assumption*. There is, in fact, evidence that many people do not have a simple linear conception of social class, and indeed that many people do not use the concept at all in their daily lives in terms of the overall structuring of society (Kahl, 1957; White, 1970; Coxon *et al.*, 1986). Where scales have been tested for unidimensionality by formal means, they have often not exhibited it (e.g. McDonald, 1972).

3 Thirdly, all the scales necessarily work by aggregating occupations together into groups on the basis of perceived similarity, but it is not always clear that the similarity is as great as is sometimes supposed. Within the middle classes, for example, it is not clear that professions such as medicine and the law, commercial sectors such as banking, insurance and advertising, and public-sector professional

occupations such as university lecturing or the civil service necessarily have a great deal in common, in their life-styles or their attitudes or the possibilities of intergenerational social mobility into them. It is well documented, for example, that public-sector white-collar employees display a different voting pattern from other sectors of the middle class (Heath *et al.*, 1985; see also pp.41–5 of Payne, 1986a, for a discussion of problems in the conceptualization of the middle class). The 'aggregation problem' is certainly very acute for women's jobs, with occupations as disparate as air hostess and café waitress being aggregated into the same class by most scales despite the very different life opportunities which they represent (see Prandy, 1986).

4 Finally, there is a problem about the population to which the commonly used scales of social class may validly be applied. All the scales mentioned above were developed to describe *men's* jobs, and most class and mobility theory has been about the location and mobility of men; women — particularly married women — have not been seen as having a personal position in the class hierarchy at all, but only an indirect one through the class position of their husbands. However, the evidence is that women do have class sentiments (see, for example, Abbott and Sapsford, 1987a) and that their class-related attitudes and behaviours are to some extent independent of those of their husbands and fathers. Nor are their socio-economic circumstances necessarily identical to those of the men in whose households they live. These factors face class theorists with substantial problems — both theoretical and practical — which will be discussed in Section 3.2.

A GLOSSARY OF TERMS USED ABOUT VALIDATION

We thought it might be useful if we summarized, at this point, some of the major technical terms that are used about the process of validating tests (trying to show that they do indeed measure what the researcher claims they measure).

- *Reliability*: a basic requirement of a test which purports to measure stable attributes of persons, or any other measuring instrument, is that it should give the same results over reasonably short periods of time.

- *Face validity*: having the *appearance* of measuring what is desired, looking appropriate.

- *Concurrent validity*: placing the sample in the same order as an existing test or measure.

- *Predictive validity*: successfully predicting the order of a sample on a subsequent test or task which can be seen as a valid indicator of the quality being measured.

Note that the last two of these shade into each other in the case where a test is validated against a set of measurements which were available at the time when the test was constructed but were not used for its construction — for example, last year's examination results. It is probably better to restrict the use of 'concurrent validation' to cases where a test is validated against another test because it produces results similar to an existing one.

- *Construct validation*: the simultaneous development of concepts and measures, or treating a test as valid because the results from it behave as theory says they should.

All of the above are aspects of construct validation. Other relevant aspects of it are:

- *Unidimensionality*: where a test purports to measure a single trait, one form of validation is to show that the items do indeed all appear to be measuring the same thing, by examination of inter-item correlation or by factor analysis.

- *Convergent validation*: showing that the test correlates with other variables with which theory says it should correlate — for example, that measures of intelligence correlate with academic performance.

- *Divergent validation*: showing that the test does not correlate with other variables with which theory says it should not be correlated — for example, that intelligence tests do not correlate with class, 'race', gender, etc.

3 POLITICS AND MEASUREMENT

We have looked in Section 2 at the concepts of attainment, intelligence and social class — as wide-ranging examples of the kinds of concepts which social scientists and educationalists use — from the point of view of how they are operationalized into workable measures for research use. In this section we shall be looking more at the part which the concepts themselves have played in research and the use that has been made of them in social practice. Sometimes, as with intelligence testing and 'race', the politics of their use is crude and, with hindsight, obvious. Sometimes a political use of concepts which has the effect of reinforcing an existing inequality may masquerade as a technical problem or be correctly derived from an underlying theoretical position which itself conceals an ideology, as in the way that women were ignored until quite recently in British and American class theory. Sometimes a whole area of research and theory seems to adopt a natural and inevitable way of analysing social relations because it reflects and is shaped by (but also reinforces and shapes) the structure and norms of the society in which it has arisen. This section uses the same three examples as Section 2 to explore the issue of the political and ideological basis of research arguments.

3.1 INTELLIGENCE AND THE POLITICS OF RACE

The concept of intelligence and intellectual ability as central to 'getting on' in a meritocratic society is a taken-for-granted part of our everyday way of thinking. Intelligent children do well at school and get the 'good' jobs. In this way an assumed natural ability, intelligence, justifies the class hierarchy. As Kamin points out: 'The interpretation of IQ data has always taken place, as it must, in a social and political context, and the validity of the data cannot be fully assessed without reference to that context. That is in general true of social science ...' (Kamin, 1977, p.16).

Intelligence tests are often portrayed as relatively neutral instruments — acknowledged to be imperfect and influenced by achievement, schooling and social background, but *in principle* neutral measures of an underlying quality. However, their origins are political, and they embody the assumptions of particular periods of history.

The 'theory of intelligence' — that individuals 'possess' natural ability, in different quantities — predates intelligence testing. In the mid-nineteenth century, after a period during which the 'moral panics' were mostly due to fear of insurrection (with the memory of the French Revolution not so very far in the past), greater attention came to be paid to the notion that the 'national stock' was deteriorating physically and morally. Following a number of military and imperial 'shocks' —

the defeat of Gordon at Khartoum at the hands of a supposedly inferior people, the poor physical condition of working-class army recruits at the time of the Boer War, the increasing influence of Germany and the USA in areas of manufacturing and marketing which had been seen as a British preserve — concern began to be expressed about the physical and mental state of the nation's children and adults, especially in the working class. This concern was heightened by the realization that, while the middle class and the 'respectable' working class were limiting family size, the 'disreputable poor' continued to have large numbers of children. The science of the day began to suggest that a nexus of conditions — physical unfitness, 'mental inferiority', 'pauperism', prostitution, insanity, crime and delinquency (to use the terms of the time) — all had a common cause in the deterioration of genetically transmitted abilities and were concentrated in a 'residuum' of lower-class people who bred children who inherited their undesirable characteristics and contributed nothing to the common good. In imperial Britain the concepts of race and nation were closely intertwined, and people of low intelligence (the 'feeble-minded') came to be seen as 'the enemy within', no less threatening than the Empire's military and economic rivals. (It is no accident that Down's Syndrome, one form of learning difficulty, was originally conceptualized as 'mongolism', with the suggestion of regression to a 'lower racial form', nor that the ideas of Lombroso on criminality as a form of genetic regression held the scientific imagination for so long.)

The first IQ test in 1905, as we saw above, was designed to pick out those children who were considered unteachable from those who were just badly taught, and it was a relatively pragmatic and untheorized object. It came into a social and intellectual world which was very ready for it, however — a world in which the identification of 'defectives' and the monitoring and control of their rate of breeding was seen as of very great importance; the world of eugenic science aimed at the improvement of the race by scientific means, encouraging the fit to breed and preventing the unfit from breeding. The first promise of the test, to North American and British eyes, was that it at last provided a way of identifying 'borderline defectives', those with a level of intelligence not much below the norm but who were, in the eyes of eugenicists, fast and irresponsible breeders and therefore liable to pollute and dilute the national stock, the gene pool: '... in the near future intelligence tests will bring tens of thousands of these high-grade defectives under the surveillance and protection of society. This will ultimately result in curtailing the reproducing of feeble-mindedness and in the elimination of an enormous amount of crime, pauperism and industrial inefficiency' (Terman, 1916, pp.16–17).

The need for a way of separating out and dealing with those who should be discouraged from breeding is most readily associated with the propaganda work of the Eugenics Education Society and its successor organizations, most of which were firmly behind the proposition that mental defect was hereditary and therefore could be passed on and amplified by interbreeding. Their opponents, however, presented a position which might have been ideologically opposed but which was rooted in the same discourse. Writers such as J.B.S. Haldane (1933, 1935, 1938) and L.S. Penrose (1933) argued very cogently that inequalities between people were caused not so much by inheritable character as by environmental pressures, and they advocated the improvement of the lot of the poor rather than control of fertility and breeding as a way of improving the 'national stock'. Environmentalists such as Haldane still had a great deal of use for a test which would pick out the able from the less able irrespective of schooling, however; it was by this kind of means that class origin was to be overcome and the best promoted to positions where their talents could be used — the creation of a meritocratic society. The Fabians, trying to develop a programme for the scientific management of population and social life, could also find substantial use for tests which claimed to pick out the best of the nation's youth for higher education, irrespective of class. So could organizations such as the Workers' Education Association whose aim was to make education more widely available to working-class people who could make use of it.

By 1908 Binet's test had changed its function and was being used not just to screen out 'defectives' but to rank-order 'normal' children in terms of their intellectual ability (see Binet and Simon, 1908). Cyril Burt, later to have a great influence on the shape of schooling for all children in London, was first appointed by the London County Council in 1913 to identify 'defective' children for transfer out of the ordinary schooling system (as opposed to those who were merely backward and in need of remedial teaching). By 1915, however, he had set up a comprehensive programme for the testing of children of all abilities in London County Council schools. As he said in the introduction to the book which first promulgated an Anglicized and standardized form of the Binet-Simon test: 'No appeal is more often addressed to the psychologist than the demand for a mental footrule. Teachers, inspectors, school medical officers, care committee visitors, the officers of the juvenile criminal courts, all have long felt the need for some such instrument' (Burt, 1921, p.1). Thus intelligence tests had developed from (a) a tool for identifying those who were unable to benefit from normal schooling because of their low intelligence, to (b) a tool for selecting out and controlling those same 'defectives', to (c) a tool for rank-ordering children and enabling inherent ability to be fostered.

Another group who welcomed the tests for eugenic reasons were the officials responsible for immigration control in the USA, where the problem of 'contamination of the national stock' was seen as even more severe than in the UK. The USA seemed, to the eugenic scientists of the time, to be facing a double threat — from within, and also from outside. Within the boundaries of the USA, as in the UK, eugenicists identified pockets of 'bad stock' where it was claimed that the inbreeding of 'degenerates' was spreading the disease of mental deficiency, pauperism, prostitution and crime — see, for example, Dugdale's study of the Jukes (1877), or Goddard's of the Kallikaks (1912). Immigration was the other problem, for it was firmly believed that 'races' differed in their innate ability. It was claimed that borderline mental deficiency:

> ... is very, very common among Spanish-Indian and Mexican families of the Southwest and also among negroes. Their dullness seems racial, or at least inherent in the family stocks from which they come ... the whole question of racial differences in mental traits will have to be taken up again. ... The writer predicts that when this is done there will be discovered enormously significant racial differences which cannot be wiped out by any scheme of mental culture.
>
> (Terman, 1916, pp.91–2)

When the same methods of investigation were applied to the different kinds of European who were attempting to migrate to the USA, it turned out that white Northern Europeans of protestant stock stood at the peak of the intellectual pyramid, and other (e.g. Mediterranean) nationalities some way behind them. This gave a scientific method, and a scientific justification, for regulating immigration to preserve the quality of the population. Official control over immigration began with an Act of 1875 barring 'coolies, convicts and prostitutes', but 'lunatics' and 'idiots' were added to the list in 1882, 'epileptics' and 'insane persons' in 1903, 'imbeciles' and 'feeble-minded persons' in 1907, and 'persons of constitutional psychopathic inferiority' in 1917 — demonstrating, among other things, the changes which were occurring in psychological terminology:

> There arose a public clamour for some form of 'quality control' over the inflow of immigrants. This at first took the form of a demand for a literacy test; but it could scarcely be doubted that the new science of mental testing, which proclaimed its ability to measure innate intelligence, would be called into the nation's service. The first volunteer was Henry Goddard, who in 1912 was invited by the United States Public Health Service. The intrepid Goddard administered the Binet test and supplementary performance tests to representatives of what he called 'the great mass of average immigrants'. The results were sure to prod-

uce grave concern in the minds of thoughtful citizens. The test results established that 83 per cent of the Jews, 80 per cent of the Hungarians, 79 per cent of the Italians and 87 per cent of the Russians were 'feeble-minded'. By 1917 Goddard was able to report ... that 'the number of aliens deported because of feeble-mindedness ... increased approximately 350 per cent in 1913 and 570 per cent in 1914 ... This was due to the untiring efforts of the physicians who were inspired by the belief that mental tests could be used for the detection of feeble-minded aliens'.

(Kamin, 1977, p.31)

The same tests, and others developed later, were very widely administered within the USA during and after the First World War, often as part of military selection or induction procedures, and it is their results which provided the first 'scientific evidence' for the alleged racial inferiority of Americans of African origin, something which was not of concern at the time but has since been elevated to a major scientific and political controversy. Reanalysing these data in his book *A Study of American Intelligence* (1923), Carl Brigham (then an assistant professor at Princeton) demonstrated that around 40 per cent of draftees of Eastern European origin scored no better than these, and developed a theory of races which paralleled and borrowed from what was being written in Germany at the time. He distinguished between people of 'Nordic', 'Alpine' and 'Mediterranean' origin, characterizing Nordics as rulers and aristocrats and Alpines as peasants and serfs. These ideas were widely taken up for a time, and they naturally allied themselves with the same sort of gratuitous anti-semitism that characterized similar writing in Germany: 'we have no separate intelligence distributions for the Jews ... [but] our army sample of immigrants from Russia is at least one half Jewish ... Our figures ... tend to disprove the popular belief that the Jew is intelligent ... he has the head form, stature and colour of his Slavic neighbours. He is an Alpine Slav' (Brigham, 1923, p.190).

The major point we are trying to make is not just that the tests were used for political purposes, but that their use was in fact scientifically illegitimate — a fact that was pointed out at the time but which had little impact in the contemporary political climate. The employment of intelligence tests for this purpose was grounded in the discovery that certain populations — whom we might characterize crudely as 'non-WASP' (white Anglo-Saxon Protestant) — tended on average to score less than 'native' Americans (by whom the proponents of the tests would have meant white settlers, not 'American Indians'); the differences were of the order of up to ten or fifteen score points, or one standard deviation. The plain fact is, however, that the tests of the time were not sufficiently precise for a difference of this order to be meaningfully attributed to genetic inferiority (nor are current tests), for a number of reasons:

1. Although some attempt was made to overcome the problem, there can be little doubt that those for whom American English was not a first language were at a disadvantage with these tests. The work on army recruits used a specially constructed 'non-verbal' test for those who were functionally illiterate in American English, but little attempt appears to have been made to demonstrate that its scores were comparable with those on verbal tests, and those who were functionally illiterate in American English will have included a disproportionate number of people from impoverished homes, including immigrants and citizens of African origin.

2. The items of which the tests were made up were selected as representing the familiar and common-sense world — but the familiar world of British and white North American people, not of Mexicans or Spaniards or Greeks.

3. The whole notion of test-taking, as we shall see, is tied up with a certain kind of approach to schooling. Those who came from other cultures may well not have learned this particular skill. (Few modern-day testers put the effects of practice at 'intelligence tests in general' at less than ten to fifteen score points.)

4 The best marks on tests go to those who are fundamentally motivated towards individual competition and keyed up to show themselves at their best (without being disruptively over-anxious). This state of mind, and the rules of the 'game' which demands it, are characteristic of people in advanced capitalistic societies and much less characteristic of those in peasant ones.

5 Tests generally have a time limit within which the items have to be completed. This expresses and draws on a cultural norm of getting things done in a set time, which is much more common in advanced industrial societies, where time dominates the day's activities, than in non-industrial societies, where precise timing has less meaning.

In other words, the observed differences are as likely as not to be cultural, due to environment and upbringing rather than innate condition. Beyond this, the use of the tests for this purpose betrays the political stance of the scientists who advocate it, if only by their use or misuse of evidence. Sometimes the misuse is wilful. Brigham, for example, somehow managed to cling on to a 'racial' theory of intelligence even in the teeth of evidence that immigrants who had been in the USA some while scored no worse than 'native' Americans. Sometimes the misuse is more subtle, but in our opinion it still constitutes misuse. The tests of the 1930s showed a gender difference, for example. This was not hailed as a great discovery, but identified as a fault in the tests at a time when gender differences were not acceptable in this respect and eliminated by reselection of items. When a 'racial' difference is found, however, it is hailed as a great discovery. Both reflect the politics of the time; it was not acceptable for girls to be less intelligent than boys, but eminently acceptable for immigrants and people of African origin to be less intelligent than other citizens.

ACTIVITY 4

Spend a few minutes thinking about what you have just read. Is the racism which has been displayed by intelligence testers — the tendency to cling to lines of argument even against evidence or valid criticism, and the use of tests to the deliberate disadvantage of people of certain ethnic origins — avoidable, do you think, or is it inherent in the tests? Make a note of your response before you continue.

It certainly still seems to be true that the concept of intelligence lends itself particularly well to the identification of supposed genetic differences between races, and the faults of the tests are all too easily forgotten. (Jensen, 1972, 1973, offers a more recent example of a similarly sized difference in mean scores being interpreted as a genetic deficiency.) In principle, however, culture-fair tests are possible (though it has yet to be shown that they are achievable in practice), and certainly a culture-fair attitude among testers and test constructors is something which they themselves often seek. A great deal of effort has been expended on attempts to build tests which are not dependent on language or culturally common knowledge, and some theorists of intelligence do show an awareness of a 'culture of test-taking'. Thus one might be inclined to think that the problems of measuring intelligence are partly problems of measurement (and ultimately soluble) and partly attributable to misuse by administrators and officials (though with the encouragement of scientists).

However, the point remains that the concept of intelligence emanates from a particular period of history in response to the perceived problems of that period. Historically, its development has been much bound up with inequalities of race and, as we shall see in Section 3.3, class. Whether the concept would have been thought useful in a history where these particular inequalities were not crucial elements of social structure remains open to question. The need for the test, the concepts out of which it grew and the perceived social problems which these concepts addressed grew up together to yield the tests and the concepts which we now employ. These concepts and this way of looking at people are now more or less taken for granted, part of the 'cultural stock of knowledge'. Whether present-day psychologists who have grown up with quite different perceived problems would have found a need for such tests and such concepts, if they were not already a strong part of the discipline's 'knowledge', is not something we can readily determine.

3.2 SOCIAL CLASS AND THE POLITICS OF GENDER

In Section 2 we looked at the measurement of social class and the different and sometimes conflicting lines of 'grand theory' which underlie it; we described it as an interesting case for precisely this reason. It is of methodological interest also, however, for the opposite reason — that all the theories converge to express basically the same model of society, which gives them all basically the same 'blind spots'. In this section we shall consider the way in which theory and research on social class have tended to exclude women from consideration as equal citizens or members of 'public society'.

Social class theory starts with an examination of people's material circumstances — their relations to the means of production and/or to the labour market — and broadens out to explore people's beliefs about the social order, their actions taken as a consequence of the social order, and, on occasions, their resistance to current forms of social order. As expressed in the major social class scales which we examined in Section 2.3, it rests on an implicit model of the social order as being dominated by work; a person's social class is totally determined by occupation. A man has a career, or a steady job, or a succession of jobs. He rises by his own efforts, and eventually (or quite soon, in the case of working-class men) he reaches the ceiling above which he is not going to be able to rise. The starting point for a career is the class of the father, and much social class research has been about social mobility — when and under what circumstances it is possible to rise above your father's class and whether we live in an open society or in one in which the advantages of the father are jealously guarded and passed on to the sons.

Implicitly, there are groups of people who do not have a class position in society — they are not bound up in the network of labour market relations that direct, sustain and locate the rest of us, because they are not in paid employment. Those who are permanently sick or disabled, or those people unable to get paid employment, for example, have a class of origin but in one sense do not have a current class position; in this implicit model they are parasitic on a work economy. People who are often in prison have little connection with the class system because the range of jobs available to them tends to deteriorate with repeated incarceration until they are employable only in the kind of casual and unsocial labour which others will not do. People who are often unemployed, or unemployed for a long time, also fall out of the class system. This broad perspective on the social order is seldom made explicit, but it is acknowledged in the Social Grading Schema by the residual category 'E' which includes the long-term unemployed, disabled people, state pensioners and others with little or no spending power. Most of the other scales, including the Registrar General's, leave them out altogether; the scales apply only to those who are 'economically active'.

We should note, first, that this model of society is culturally and historically specific; it is not a universal truth, but a local contingency. The concept of unemployment as a separate and structural phenomenon is very recent — first elaborated in Britain in its present form as recently as the 1890s, when the concept of a 'right to work' was transmuted into a concept of full employment (Kumar, 1984). The notion of wage labour was itself still a confused one in nineteenth-century Britain. Craft patterns of payment to a 'master' who then sustained apprentices and labourers, and agricultural patterns of payment made mostly by provision of housing and food with a money payment often made only at the end of the year, survived alongside the more modern pattern of a straightforward payment of money for time. The notion of a career or steady job developed in the nineteenth century, and before that a very different conception of working-class labour may have been in place:

> ... the eighteenth century labourer was a 'pluralist' as far as occupation was concerned. Where one occupation went cold and slack on him, he could often resort to another. There was a continuum from the fully mixed in which a man might be equally dependent upon two occupations, through the seasonally mixed in which he might be employed in one or other of two occupations, depending on the time of year, to the tending of a garden which added usefully but in a strictly collateral way to the family's comfort. Manufacturing and mining activities were often inextricably mixed with agricultural ones.
>
> (Kumar, 1984, p.195)

The other group — around 50 per cent of the adult population — whom classical class theory takes as having no direct relationship to the class structure, is made up of women. The 'model', which has men in careers or steady and continuous jobs, has women tied primarily to home and family, and in paid employment outside the home only as an additional activity or an unfortunate and stark economic necessity. Only single women not living with parents have been treated by the majority of researchers and official surveys as having a class in their own right; others are classified according to 'the class of their household', which is the class of the husband's or father's job. Very few of the major British mobility surveys have paid much attention to the social mobility of women, and few have even bothered to sample women. The Oxford Mobility Study (Goldthorpe *et al.*, 1980; Halsey *et al.*, 1981) had no women in its sample. The Scottish Mobility Study (Payne, 1986a,b) surveyed the wives of its male sample but did not collect an independent sample of women (for an account of the data on the wives, see Chapman, 1984, 1990). The Irish Mobility Study (Hayes, 1987; Hayes and Miller, 1989; Miller and Hayes, 1990) again samples women only by reference to a primary male sample — the wives and sisters of the sampled men. The Essex Mobility Study (Marshall *et al.*, 1988) was the first national purpose-built study in Britain to sample both genders equally. Studies of aspects of class other than mobility have tended to ignore women even more blatantly; it was normal in the 1960s and 1970s to have to turn to the footnotes to tables to see if an article on factory life or class sentiment included women in the sample, and sometimes even then it was not possible to determine if women had been included (see Siltanen and Stanworth, 1984).

The absence of women is partly an oversight — they have not occurred to the authors as important. Partly it is sometimes a matter of convenience, as measuring the social class of women in their own right is not an easy technical task, as we shall see. Partly it is justified by questions of resource and the need to present data comparable with earlier studies which also omitted women. (Treating women as 'unimportant' in these ways betrays a model of what matters in society, of course.) Partly, however, it is deliberate and springs from a model of society which regards women as of only peripheral importance to social class theory. Up to the Second World War, only a relatively small minority of married women had paid employment outside the home, and women might be regarded as homemakers and mothers rather than as active participants in the public sphere. This is no longer the case, and yet the stereotype has continued to have a major influence on class theory and class research until very recently.

The first extract associated with this unit, which is reproduced in Offprints Booklet 3, outlines the results of a survey of women's work and their class-based attitudes, and the significance of these. The data are taken from five years of a national survey carried out by Open University undergraduate and MSc students on the research methods courses which preceded this one. There are faults with the data, because a quota-sampling design was adopted for reasons of time and resource and there was some tendency on the part of the students to pick people like themselves when filling quotas by age, gender and social class. Particularly, the women in the survey are, on average, better educated than the norm, more likely

UNIT 16 THE POLITICS OF OPERATIONALIZATION

to be in full-time employment and less likely to be in routine non-manual occupations than one would expect from a random national sample. There are also fewer people over the age of 60 than there should be to represent the national population faithfully. The strength of the survey was that it sampled women in their own right, rather than omitting them or sampling only the wives of the male sample, and so was one of the first mobility studies in this country to provide usable data on the mobility and class sentiments of women.

The extract begins with a brief discussion of the nature of the labour market for women. It moves on to consider questions about the possibilities for social mobility which have been important in class theory and the answers which previous surveys have given to them; it shows that some of these 'well established' conclusions about the nature of British society do not hold up if we take women as well as men into account, and that omitting women from the analysis seriously distorts our understanding of the labour market. Finally, it looks at class attitudes and images and considers whether the understanding of the social order which women have is fundamentally different from the way in which men understand it.

READING

You should now read the first extract by Pamela Abbott and Roger Sapsford, entitled 'The results of the survey', which is reproduced in Offprints Booklet 3.

Thus we can see that the tendency to omit women from class research may have led to a distorted view of the social order. More than this is involved, however: what is interesting is not just that false conclusions have been reached, but *why* they have been reached. What is asserted is that the sociological theories of class, on which the class-measuring scales are based, embody a set of common ideological propositions. A common and self-fulfilling belief of our society is that paid employment is more important for men than women, that a woman's place is in the home and her proper employment child-rearing and housekeeping. Women are said to be less committed to the labour market than men. Social class research has been so imbued with these propositions that it has tended to take them entirely for granted and not even to subject them to testing. (Where they *have* been tested they have been proved false; most women are now in paid employment for most of their employable life, and there is no evidence that they are less committed to it than men — see Martin and Roberts, 1984). Thus when scales have been devised, it has been seen as important to represent *men's* employment in a usefully analysable way; scales have not been devised to represent *women's* employment with equal utility.

To represent women's class position usefully, however, poses a number of technical problems:

1   Very many women take time out of the labour market at some point during their working lives, to have and raise children, and during this period they have no paid employment to act as a class indicator. (The same problem faces us in trying to assign a class to unemployed men, or to male prisoners and long-term hospital patients, but these are minorities among the male population.)

2   Because of these 'breaks', a woman's job may not represent her true standing — she may have taken work of a relatively less demanding nature, or part-time work, because it fits in with the exigencies of child-minding, and she will very likely have forfeited opportunities for training and promotion.

3   This being so, her own feeling about the class to which she belongs *may* be less influenced by her current job than a man's would be, and more influenced by her husband's job, her educational level, and/or her father's class (Abbott and Sapsford, 1987a).

4   There is also the problem that the scales devised to discriminate between men's jobs do not discriminate well between women's jobs — as we have seen, they tend to 'bunch' a very large proportion of women in a single category of clerical/secretarial/personal services work (a category in which men are comparatively rare), and jobs which yield very dissimilar life chances finish up classified under the same category. Women who are classified by the conventional scales as being in the same occupational class may have very different jobs in very different settings, may meet and marry different kinds of people and may have different kinds of benefits to pass on to their children. (The same is true of men, but the conventional scales discriminate between different kinds of men's jobs to a larger extent than they do between women's.)

A variety of attempts has been made, for different purposes, to provide an adequate classification of women's social class, and the second extract associated with this unit, in Offprints Booklet 3, reviews some of these.

READING

At this point you should read the second extract by Pamela Abbott and Roger Sapsford, entitled 'The technical problems of assigning a class to women', which is reproduced in Offprints Booklet 3.

ACTIVITY 5

From your reading of this extract by Abbott and Sapsford, what problems do you see with trying to use scales such as Roberts' City Grading Scale or the preliminary Surrey Scale? Spend a few minutes thinking about this.

The major problem with these approaches, clearly, is precisely that the scales are for women only. They would be useful for work comparing groups of women, but they could not be used for research comparing men and women or to examine the labour market as a whole. The alternative approach is to attempt a classification of *households* by occupation, which would eliminate the problem of classifying women who are not in paid employment. This, of course, is Goldthorpe's approach and that of conventional sociology, but they have classified all households by the occupation of the senior male and taken no account at all of women's employment. The simplest modification of this is known as the *dominance principle* (Erikson, 1984), whereby the class assigned to a household is that of the highest class of full-time jobs within it — generally that of a man, but not necessarily always. (This is the position that Goldthorpe has now adopted — see Goldthorpe and Payne, 1986.) A more elaborate schema was the one worked out by Heath and Britten (1984) which takes account of whether one or both partners is in full-time employment. Schemata such as these have been found more predictive, than husband's class alone, of, for example, the extent to which households provide their own services or buy them 'on the market' (Pahl and Wallace, 1985).

ACTIVITY 6

Look back at this kind of schema, in the extract you have just read. Again, what problems do you see with it?

This kind of classification has been used with some success to predict class-related attitudes and behaviours. Because it takes account of wife's employment as well as husband's, it can distinguish between the social circumstances of people with one or two incomes coming into the household. However, there are interesting problems that it cannot be used to tackle: for example, whether there is a class/

employment basis to differences between husbands' and wives' attitudes or behaviour. It may also be argued that it does not represent faithfully the way that people themselves see their class; for example, women in paid employment seem perfectly capable of distinguishing between their own class and that of their family (Hammond, 1987). Problems such as these, it has been argued, bring into question the whole accepted basis of the measurement of class: they raise 'the question of how useful it is to regard occupation as a straightforward index of social class, a question which arises initially with women but may be relevant to men if career change and/or periodic unemployment becomes a norm' (Payne and Abbott, 1990a, p.173).

Difficulties of measurement, however, or even doubts about aspects of class theory, should not distract us altogether from the central point of this section of the unit, which is to show in practice how an accepted ideological position can become incorporated into a branch of social science theory and totally distort its results and conclusions. As we have said, it is often the practical problems of measurement which alert us (by the process of construct validation) to serious shortcomings in our theory:

> ... we are suggesting that the problems we experience in attempting to incorporate women into mobility studies, or indeed to study the social mobility of women at all, are not restricted to women. They are also problems that arise in studying men, but their importance has either been less obvious ... or they have been disregarded as 'minor issues' ... We want to conclude by stressing that while we feel that women's social mobility is an area of sociological interest in its own right, in practice we can only make sense of women's and men's social reality when we study both together.
>
> (Payne and Abbott, 1990a, p.174)

This echoes the point made at the beginning of Block 2: it is generally possible to make sense of results on one group only by contrasting them with the position of an obvious other, and we cannot make sense of results at all if we study a part of a population and assume without justification that this part can be taken as standing for the whole. To do so may be to reinforce an ideology, which is one way of engaging, unwittingly, in politics. That we can escape ideology altogether is too much to hope for, but we can at least do our best not to build it unthinkingly into our methodology.

3.3 INTELLIGENCE, ACHIEVEMENT AND THE POLITICS OF CLASS

So far in Section 3 we have examined (in Section 3.1) the patent use of research concepts and their operationalized measures for political purposes. (We should note that it is the existence of the operationalized measure which makes the political action possible; if there were no way of measuring intelligence, groups could not be segregated or excluded on the basis of it.) We have also looked at a subtler way in which theory can fail to be neutral politically, by examining how gender inequalities have been 'scientifically' reinforced by sociological theories of class and the research associated with them. (This is not to say that sociology has a major impact on gender inequality, but that it failed to question its own assumptions in this matter and thereby lent the existing situation its support.) We found that this was not just a political question but had implications for questions of fact; a whole society can be misdescribed if we ignore a substantial group of its population. Now we return to the measurement of intellectual potential and actual attainment, to look at an aspect of the way that research is grounded in politics which is more subtle still.

We have noted, above, that intelligence tests have been used for political purposes, though the politics of their use is perhaps not necessarily inherent in their theory and construction. Achievement tests, by comparison, appear politically neutral; they simply test whether a form of teaching has 'taken' and a content been 'delivered'. The 'culture of test-taking' may distort results — people from some backgrounds may be more determined to show themselves capable than others — but this appears a fairly minor factor and one for which allowance might be made in cross-cultural comparison. There is a sense, however, in which both kinds of test play their part in the essentially political processes whereby a form of society reproduces itself. Both can be seen as elements in a *discourse* that is prevalent in our society — a discourse that defines people as necessarily having a place on a continuum of intelligence. Even if intelligence tests are not used, people are judged and classified on this criterion, and the attributed intelligence of a child is used to define the type of education to which he or she is to be exposed.

DISCOURSE VERSUS IDEOLOGY

There is considerable confusion about the terms 'discourse' and 'ideology'. As it is used in this unit, an 'ideology' might be described as a coherent set of propositions about what people and/or social institutions are like and how they ought to be — generally presenting to one group of people that certain behaviours are in their own interests and concealing the fact that they are also (or more!) in the interests of another and more powerful group. The term 'discourse', on the other hand, is used to mean the general framework or perspective within which ideas are formulated. Thus the view that it is natural, necessary and right that mothers should put their children's and other dependants' interests before their own and should want to devote their major energies to home-making and child-rearing is an ideological position — it presents a certain form of domestic and work organization, which is in the interests of men, as also in the interests of women and the natural and inevitable way in which women should view their lives. The ideology is framed within a discourse which defines certain terms — mother, child, family — in ways which make some conclusions easy and natural to make and renders others apparently paradoxical or difficult to defend. The proposition that adult females should have the same rights at work and obligations at home as adult males looks reasonable on the face of it, for example, and the proposition that it is *not* a mother's duty to put her children's interests before her own is more difficult to defend — yet both make the same statement, framed within different discourses. Note, however, that this account is too simple, because it pretends that what is at stake is the words by which we describe things. The ways in which we live and relate to each other and the aspects of our lives we take for granted are even more important components of both concepts.

As we have seen, intelligence testing grew up in reaction to fears about people who are seen as inherently 'feeble-minded', who would pass on their 'defect' to their offspring. The introduction of mass schooling further stoked the fires of alarm, by making it possible to count the size of the group of children who were physically indistinguishable from other children but apparently unable to benefit from schooling, and posing this group as an administrative problem with which the authorities had to deal. It sharpened the definition of 'feeble-mindedness' by the mere fact of setting up standards for learning, which some then failed and by that failure defined themselves as feeble-minded. For efficiency's sake there was a need for a diagnostic test to do what the doctors could not do — identify the feeble-minded child *before* he or she had struggled through schooling and failed to profit from it. It was the devising of such tests — what eventually became known as IQ tests — that first gave psychology a stake in this area and legitimated the claims of psychologists to expertise in it. Binet originally denied that the test he devised in 1905 was suitable to anything other than this specific administrative task, but by 1908 it was being used to calibrate the development of 'normal' children, and the concept of the intelligence quotient as a measure standardized for chronological age was developed two years later. The measurement of intelligence as a routine way of identifying potentially able pupils took a little longer to become established, but eventually it became a standard feature of the schooling system.

Schools became an important part of the state/societal mechanism for maintaining order and work discipline as the UK became increasingly an industrial society. Schooling which had previously been denied to working-class children began sometimes to be available, in one form or another, during the eighteenth century, but without evidence of an intent to gather up and socialize an entire social class; this was distinctively a nineteenth-century phenomenon. The factory system undermined the traditional family to some extent — the family of agriculture or cottage industry, with children socialized into production at home — and the traditional skills that might have been learned at home became increasingly inappropriate in an era of rapidly changing methods. Schools came to be seen as necessary, therefore, for the teaching of new skills (including basic literacy and numeracy). More important to those who were active in establishing schooling for working-class children, the school was a medium of socialization — including gender differentiation. It taught 'habits of industry' and accustomed male children to the discipline necessary for factory work while giving female children the skills needed for domestic labour. It accustomed children to systematic, routine and often dull work and brought them to regard it as a normal part of life. It was also a chance to convey the moral precepts of the work ethic, directly through instruction or indirectly by example. In other words, it was a site of power in the sense in which Foucault (e.g. 1982) often uses the term — a place where people can be moulded into understanding the world in the way in which the shaper wants them to understand it and behaving habitually in accordance with that view of the world. Schools may inculcate critical enquiry, but while doing so they also set the parameters of the society within which this inquiry is to take place.

This is not to suggest that schooling became some kind of monolithic repressive mechanism, aimed at the working class. Indeed, the same period was one of working-class struggle *for* education and to have access to schooling. Education was not just something imposed from above; its value was well realized by working-class people, and there was considerable individual and collective striving to make it more available to working-class children. Education became a major means of upward mobility for working-class children and made a wide range of occupations available to them which would previously have been beyond their reach. However, none of this changed the basic structure of the society: it may have changed the accessibility of various places within the structure — changed the likelihood of particular people filling particular positions within it — and constructed thereby a fundamentally more open society, but the broad pattern of social structures and social relations remained unchanged.

Perhaps even more important, both for mobility and for the preservation of the social structure, education became a site of classification — a mechanism whereby emerging adults could be assigned their 'place in the scheme of things'. Testing is inseparable from our concept of schooling; one important function of schooling is the rank-ordering of children with regard to their abilities, by teachers' informal reports and by public examination. More insidiously, school plays a part in assigning some children to the higher-grade occupations and others to lower ones by a process of self-shaping. Perceiving themselves to succeed or fail in the tasks which schools set them and which are necessary for the successful completion of public examinations, which in turn are necessary for the acquisition of higher-grade employment, children come to think of themselves as able or less able, suitable or not suitable for the higher reaches, successes or failures. This process may occur even in schools which have a conscious rhetoric and policy of encouraging all children: despite all the efforts of teachers, some children succeed in the system and some fail. It is in the nature of the schooling system that children have to be located on a 'success–failure' dimension. Studies such as Paul Willis' *Learning to Labour* (1977) may give us the clue as to how the process can occur: working-class boys, Willis argues, may come to reject the concept of schooling and form an 'anti-school culture', a culture of masculinity learned from their home environment which is curiously appropriate for their subsequent labouring employment. This culture rejects as 'cissy' the skills and abilities — reading, writing, academic success — that the school values, and it may be embraced by those whom the school classes as intelligent as well as those whom it labels unintelligent. This 'cultural set' may not be encouraged by the school — indeed, teachers may fight against it — but schools tolerate it in a way in which other kinds of rebellion might not be tolerated.

We should note, moreover, that the process of education is not a politically neutral one, because middle-class children are at a natural advantage over working-class children in the 'schooling game' — they come into school 'knowing the rules', or at least some of them. Middle-class children are more familiar from a very early age with the objects and procedures which are relevant to schooling — books, pencils, reading, counting, drawing — and tend to be more firmly encouraged by their parents to use these objects and procedures. Middle-class parents tend to worry more, and to more effect, about how their children are labelled at school, to interact with teachers more to ensure their children's advantage, and to have the resources to supply additional schooling when a child seems not to be 'thriving' during the regular school day. They also tend to have more freedom to direct their children to one school or another according to the standing of the school, and more knowledge or access to knowledge on which such decisions can be based.

The developments of 'intelligence testing' in the first two decades of the twentieth century opened up the way to further stratification and the direction of children to types of school 'consonant with their needs and abilities' rather than just according to their parents' ability to pay. By about 1925 the division of schooling into 'academic' and 'vocational' was well advanced, and intelligence tests were well established as an important way of determining which track should be followed. The process reached its most visible form in the tripartite system of grammar, technical and secondary modern schooling which most Local Education Authorities established following the Education Act 1944; here intelligence testing came into its own as a 'scientific' means of selecting 'the best children' independently of their parents' ability to pay. (There is certainly evidence that it acted in a more 'class-fair' manner than, for example, headmasters' recommendations, but nonetheless a middle-class child of the same measured ability was some five times as likely as a lower working-class child to finish up at grammar school — see Douglas, 1964.) We appear to have retreated from such selection into the proliferation of 'comprehensive' schools, but vocational tracking still occurs in school practices (streaming and setting), in the nature of the curricula and in the nature of the examinations for which children 'of different abilities' are entered. (Indeed, the same might be said of primary schools, despite the comparative prevalence of mixed-ability classes.)

Achievement testing acts similarly to intelligence testing to differentiate, classify and assign pupils. The examination (and continuous assessment is included in this concept) provides documentation on the person and his or her abilities; it turns him or her into a 'case', a subject to be assigned to a category. The outcome of school practice — differential curricula, examining, profiling, testing — is therefore to produce a well-divided and ordered society. It does not necessarily preserve the status quo in the sense that only the children of advantaged parents finish up in advantaged positions — though there is a strong element of this — but it does tend to maintain the general shape and hierarchical nature of the society within which it is set. The existence of these divisions and the importance of 'correct' allocation to them is the justification for a whole range of professional experts — teachers, lecturers, educational psychologists, sociologists of education. They in their turn have a stake in what these divisions shall be and some measure of power in determining what sorts of people shall finish up in each of them.

School tests and examinations may be seen as arising out of and at the same time reinforcing and reproducing a particular discourse or way of viewing people and their social relations — a discourse which is inherently typical of, and adaptive for, capitalist forms of social organization. Individuals are posited as truly individual rather than social, making their own decisions and 'naturally' in competition with each other. They are seen as variously endowed, and it is this endowment which is seen as determining where they will finish up in the power hierarchy (but the fact that social background — class of origin — is part of this 'endowment' tends to be glossed over). The individual in turn is seen as made up of — 'possessing' — qualities which are measurable and which enable us to compare one individual with another. In the early forms of this discourse, the concern is with physical and, to a lesser extent, moral qualities; in later forms it centres on psychological qualities — mental abilities, emotional tendencies, degrees and kinds of motivation, the extent of types of learning, and so on. During the period of industrialization a new 'knowledge base' grew up around this increasingly dominant view of human nature — what eventually became the disciplines of 'individual' and 'social' psychology. Terms developed in which to describe the human subject, and concepts developed in these terms, which allowed the measurement of the subject's 'interior state'.

This leads us to the most important feature of the discourse, that it is mostly aimed at the *management* of the individual. Mostly it posits human beings who are perfectible or changeable or curable, by manipulation of their qualities or attributes. At the same time it assigns them their place in society by reference to these qualities or attributes. Thus the activity of testing, however scientific in its form, is far from politically neutral. It may form a ladder by which the able few transcend their class position, but for the majority it reproduces the structure of society unchanged.

To say this is not necessarily to criticize it or declaim it as unjust, but to identify one of its functions, as an institution which permits upward mobility but tends on the whole to maintain the stability of the social system. It is nonetheless worth bearing these functions in mind, however, when carrying out or assessing research into schooling or the testing of children; we should not suppose that work in these areas is ever quite politically neutral. Indeed, the same point may be made of a much wider range of research topics — the criminal justice system, health, community care, income maintenance — all of which are rooted in existing social institutions which generate and are maintained by particular discourses, particular models of what people and the social order are like and what may be taken for granted about them.

4 POLITICS, IDEOLOGY AND RESEARCH 'STYLE'

We have looked in the previous section at how theory, concepts and operationalized measures can embody ideologies or discourses — models of the world and of how questions about it are legitimately framed. Thus a line of research can be so imbued with a particular (unacknowledged) world view that its conclusions must fall within that world view and reinforce or validate it. In this section we shall look, not at particular theories which inform particular research programmes, but at the whole way in which research is conducted. It has been argued, as we shall see, that the 'stance' which is adopted in research itself expresses (and serves to validate) a particular model of how the social world is and should be.

It has been argued that to adopt one research style or 'instance' in preference to another is an implicitly political act, because research styles are not neutral or interchangeable: they embody implicit models of what the social world is like or should be like and of what counts as knowledge and how to get it:

> Methods and methodology are not simply techniques and rationales for the conduct of research. Rather they must be understood in relation to

specific historical, cultural, ideological and other contexts ... when one ponders the questions — what methods will I use in my study? or, why was a certain method used for a given study? — these are not simply technical issues ...

(Reinharz, 1983, pp.162–3)

In this final section of the unit we shall explore a common criticism of 'conventional' research as this criticism has been developed by feminist scholars and researchers, among others. We should point out that the critique is by no means specific to feminism; elements of it have been expressed over the last 20 years by researchers in a number of quite disparate disciplines.[1] Nor are we arguing in this unit that there is a distinctive 'feminist research methodology' — and, indeed, we take rather different positions from each other on this issue.[2] Feminist scholarship is one place, however, where issues of politics and power in research have been particularly sharply developed, and the discussion which follows owes a great deal to it. Two concepts of power will be involved in our discussion of this scholarship: the direct power of the researcher over those researched, and the power of the researcher to 'set the agenda' of the research and declare and disseminate the results.

READING

Think about the Reinharz quotation above and marshal your ideas about what form such an argument might take. Then, for one author's version of a feminist argument, read the first part of Chapter 10, 'The value of quantitative methodology for feminist research' by Toby Epstein Jayaratne, in the Reader — that is, the introductory paragraphs and the section on 'Feminist criticism of the quantitative research process and quantitative analysis'.

You should note that there are two separate (though related) issues involved in the argument as Jayaratne expresses it. First, there is the criticism of quantitative research which conceives of itself as 'scientific', objective, value-free — the criticism of positivism which you met in Block 1. Feminists (and others) have argued that such research does not discover what the social world is like, but rather imposes its own conceptual schema on to the social world. A case in point would be the social mobility research briefly discussed in Section 3.2 above, which *declared* women unimportant both for examining rates of social mobility over time and for theorizing about social mobility (rather than *discovering* that they were unimportant). Sociological theory defined women as dependent on male heads of households and therefore outside the concerns of class theory. Conversely, accepting that the social differences between men and women were natural (biological) and inevitable, sociology did not see sexual divisions as an area of sociological concern and defined the work that women did in the domestic sphere as of no sociological interest. Thus when Anne Oakley wanted to start research on housework in the late 1960s, for example, she found it very difficult to find a supervisor and have the topic accepted, because housework was seen quite simply as something trivial, not something which constituted any sort of sociological problem. It was a very common experience of women sociology and psychology students in the 1960s and 1970s (and often still is today) to find a disjuncture between 'experience of the world ... and the theoretical schemes available to think about it in' (Smith, 1974, p.7); large areas of their lives and much of what really concerned

---

[1] For a developed version emanating from humanistic psychology, for example, see Reason and Rowan (1981) — particularly the articles by Heron, Rowan, Reason and Parlett.

[2] For recent contributions to the debate, see Hammersley (1992) and the replies by Ramazanoglu and Gelsthorpe in the same journal issue.

them were declared non-existent, trivial, peripheral, not on the agenda for research or theory.

Feminists and others have argued that methods whose strength lies in the testing of theory are not suitable tools for research intended to *develop* new theory. Quantitative research is designed to obtain answers to researchers' questions; it does not yield an understanding of people's lives in depth nor, generally, leave space for them to indicate what *they* regard as the important questions. Quantitative methods typically isolate 'variables' for study, independent of the context in which they make sense and the sense which is made of them in that context: 'Concepts, environments, social interactions are all simplified by methods which lift them out of their context, stripping them of the very complexity that characterises them in the real world' (Parlee, 1979, p.131). Such criticism led to a call for relatively unstructured, qualitative methods which will 'take women's experience into account', explore the basis of women's everyday knowledge, let women 'speak for themselves' without the prejudgement and prestructuring of prior theory.

Positivistic science itself may reasonably be seen as expressing a discourse, a model of what truth is and how it is to be ascertained. The 'rules' of the scientific discourse are that disputes are settled on the basis of evidence and logic — evidence in the form of careful, repeatable measurements whose relevance to the dispute can be readily justified, and logical argument from that evidence to a conclusion. These are the dominant 'rules of truth' in our current culture — the 'respectable' grounds on which arguments may be won. To say that something expresses a discourse is not to say that it is wrong; everything expresses some discourse, is framed according to some set of rules. The force of the scientific discourse, however, is to divert problematic issues from the arena of political debate — to 'depoliticize' them. 'Science' is not just a body of knowledge acquired for its own sake, but the basis of techniques which are used to solve problems. By accepting that certain kinds of issue are amenable to scientific solution — 'matters of fact' — we empower experts both to act on our behalf and ultimately to determine what our 'best interests' are. A part of the control which this establishment of expertise exerts is achieved:

> ... by taking what is essentially a political problem, removing it from the realm of political discourse, and recasting it in the neutral language of science. Once this is accomplished the problems have become technical ones ... the language of reform is, from the outset, an essential component, ... Where there [is] resistance or failure ... this [is] construed as further proof of the need to reinforce and extend the power of experts.
>
> (Foucault, 1982, p.196)

The second criticism which feminists (and others) have raised is that much research is exploitative and oppressive — that it consists in a researcher with power controlling and manipulating 'subjects' for whom a better term might be 'objects'. (This criticism is not confined to quantitative research; conventional participant observation research and 'unstructured' interview studies also come under fire.) Jayaratne points out that the process of research has been likened by some feminist scholars to the process of rape: 'the researchers take, hit, and run. They intrude into their subjects' privacy, disrupt their perceptions, utilize false pretences, manipulate the relationship, and give little or nothing in return. When the needs of the researchers are satisfied, they break off contact with the subject' (Reinharz, 1979, p.95). This research is criticized for the way it exercises power over its 'subjects'. A further criticism, however, might concern the power of the researcher to determine what is important in the situation, what needs researching, what the problem is. Here again the 'conventional' researcher has near-total autonomy and those who are researched may have little input (particularly in quantitative research).

These two criticisms have led some feminists and other researchers to call for fully collaborative research and the displacement of 'the researcher' from the control of the research process — or even, sometimes, for the abandonment of research in favour of participation in social action. As Maria Mies argues in the Reader chapter you read during your work on Block 1:

> The vertical relationship between researcher and 'research objects', the *view from above*, must be replaced by the *view from below* ...
>
> ... the hierarchical research situation as such defeats the very purpose of research: it creates an acute distrust in the 'research objects' ... It has been observed that the data thus gathered often reflect 'expected behaviour' rather than real behaviour ...
>
> [However,] Women, who are committed to the cause of women's liberation, cannot stop at this result. They cannot be satisfied with giving the social sciences better, more authentic and more relevant data. The ethical–political significance of the view from below cannot be separated from the scientific one ...
>
> The contemplative, uninvolved 'spectator knowledge' must be replaced by *active participation in actions, movements and struggles* ... . Research must become an integral part of such struggles.
>
> (Mies, 1983, in Hammersley, 1993, pp.68–9)

READING

Now read the rest of Jayaratne's article and see what she herself is proposing. Does it avoid the two criticisms outlined above?

What Jayaratne is proposing is a 'compromise position'. Broadly, she supports the value of qualitative data, but she advances quantitative methods as useful for testing propositions, as 'objective' in the sense that they are less open to challenge on the grounds of personal bias in interpretation, as covering a wider range of informants quickly, and therefore as more convincing to policy makers. It is insufficient, after all, that the results of feminist research be plausible to feminists, or indeed to the wider academic community; if they are directed at a change of policy, then they must also be plausible to politicians, administrators, local government officers, head teachers, industrialists and others of similar standing. For example:

> ... suppose that a researcher is interested in why some women find it difficult to return to work ... A quantitative researcher might ask respondents to indicate the importance of various reasons ... Quantitative analyses could produce statistical evidence that most women feel that lack of good jobs is the most important reason ...
>
> A qualitative researcher exploring the same issue might ask women why it was difficult to return to work. Many reasons might be given and analysis without quantification might indicate that poor job possibilities was a major one. However, the analysis would be more subject to debate and thus personal judgment ...
>
> (Jayaratne, 1983, in Hammersley, 1993, p.118)

(Note also, on the next page of the article, the example of sexual harassment.)

This position, or one slightly modified from where Jayaratne leaves it, would be quite compatible with the first of the two lines of criticism. There is no reason why quantitative methods should not be used as sensitively and openly as qualitative ones, providing the basic qualitative work has already been done. In Jayaratne's example, people's attitudes and commitments would need to be explored in a less structured way, beforehand, if researchers' theoretical conceptions were not to be imposed in place of the informants' opinions and attitudes. Once this has been done, however, it is quite possible to derive a list of reasons from the data and get a wider sample of women to say which they think is the most important. It is probably this question of the 'wider sample', however, which gives quantitative research its plausibility, not the fact that it counts heads. Very few researchers would actually do an 'unquantified' analysis even of qualitative data: we would be saying that *most*, or *more than half*, or *some*, or a *few* of the sample came up with a given reason. Better still, we would probably say what percentage of the sample came up with it — to know that 51 per cent of the sample, or 99 per cent, came up with a particular reason is more informative than just knowing that a majority did so. Using qualitative approaches we would not, however, be able to argue convincingly from the proportion of the sample giving a response to the proportion of the population likely to give it, because we would be unlikely to have a sample that was plausible as representing the population well. Survey techniques 'do representation' better and are therefore more convincing in this respect.

An alternative, of course, would be to educate policy makers to the value of qualitative research, and, indeed, such research is much more acceptable to them now than it would have been a decade or so ago. Indeed, it might validly be argued that Jayaratne is mistaken about the influence of such research on policy. Politicians in Britain now generally accept that policies of community care place a heavy and often unacceptable burden on 'informal carers', who are mostly women. The research in this area has mostly been qualitative in nature, and its influence has to a large extent been grounded in the immediacy and power with which qualitative accounts are able to convey the 'feel' of a situation to the reader — the experience of caring for a dependent relative twenty-four hours a day, seven days a week, fifty-two weeks a year. Qualitative research certainly appears to have some impact at the level of individual practitioners. Much of the research on women's experience of childbirth has been qualitative in nature, and the changes that have occurred in medical practice over the last fifteen years suggest that it has influenced even doctors, a group notoriously resistant to any research whose results cannot be cast in terms of numbers.

We are not sure that Jayaratne comes to grips with the second criticism at all. She sidesteps it to some extent by pointing out that the object of feminist research is to benefit women and arguing that research which is convincing to policy makers is more likely to bring about benefits. Her idea of research is 'conventional' rather than 'collaborative', however. She has a researcher interested in a problem who goes out to do research on informants, not a researcher sharing on equal terms the tasks of doing research and bringing about a social change that the other participants want brought about. (Again, we should note that this second criticism is not confined to feminists, though we have used a feminist example to illustrate it, but may be found among a wide range of different kinds of researcher.)

ACTIVITY 7

What problems do you see with the 'collaborative' approach to research? Spend a few minutes thinking about how it could be put into operation and what the implications would be for the researcher and the research.

Four problems occur to us:

1. We are inclined to think that adoption of a fully collaborative stance as an ethical imperative would abolish research into 'theory' and the use of research as an aid to scholarship and the development of ideas. If researchers are to avoid 'using' people for the researchers' purposes and confine their attention to helping to solve participants' problems, then all research becomes applied research. It is not clear, even, whether the researcher can initiate the research, or whether he or she has to wait to be 'commissioned'.

2 The adoption of a fully collaborative stance probably abolishes the role of researcher altogether. If the researcher is in no 'privileged' position — has no particular say in the planning of the research, no particular 'ownership' of the data, no special rights to use the material for, for example, publication — then it is difficult to see what he or she brings to the situation other than technical knowledge. Now, one may argue that researchers make their name and their living from studying the problems and miseries of others, and that the abolition of the role would be no bad thing, but one has to be clear that this *is* one possible consequence of this line of argument. We cannot take an authoritative position on this issue; as academics, we find it difficult to argue for the abolition of the academic role.

3 Most important of all, it is not clear that full power sharing is possible, even in principle. In the extreme version of the collaborative stance, all participants are to be equal, and the researcher's knowledge gives him or her no special position but has to be shared. 'Informed consent', in this position, involves the sharing of knowledge and experience so that all participants have the same power of understanding. Arguably, however, this would mean putting all participants through the same history of academic and research training and experience as the researcher has undergone, which is impractical and would not be desired by the participants. To the extent that it is not done, the power of knowledge necessarily remains with the researcher.

4 There is also the question of whom the researcher is collaborating with and who has given 'informed consent'. Research often involves several groups, where interests may not be the same; collaborating with one group may even reinforce power relationships, even if the research is intended to benefit all groups involved. For example, collaborative research with social workers into their practice still leaves the clients as research 'objects'.

We raise these objections not to decry the collaborative stance — we think that those who advocate it have alerted us to some very important ethical considerations, and that research should be strongly influenced by them — but to suggest that there are no easy answers to ethical and political dilemmas, in research as in most walks of life.

Returning to Jayaratne's article, we should note — remembering the discussion in Block 1 — that even the 'social policy' position which she adopts is a departure from straightforward realism and accounting research successful to the extent that it makes credible claims to having discovered truths. If the main aim of research is influencing public policy, then it must be judged on its utility, not its truth. In Jayaratne's terms, research is valuable to the extent that it influences policy, and this must be the main basis of evaluation. Our own position, and the position adopted on the whole throughout this course, would be that a particular article or book or presentation might be judged effective or ineffective according to whether it has desired effects on its target audience, but that the question of the truth or falsity — the credibility — of the conclusions is a prior and, in some ways, a more important one.

5 CONCLUSION

In this unit we started with how concepts are expressed within research studies and research reports, and that is also where we have finished, but considerable conceptual ground has been covered in the process. In Section 2 we looked at how four 'concepts' of increasing conceptual complexity are operationalized in quantitative research: achievement, intelligence, personality and the structural variable of social class. For this purpose we took it for granted that these four variables 'exist' in some sense which is difficult to define but unproblematic, and that the problems lay in how to measure them. In Section 3 we looked at the background, history and usage of three of the variables to examine how the concepts have grown up, not as academic abstractions but as ways of describing the social world for particular purposes. We discovered that social construction is an aspect of their 'existence': that they arise from certain theories or ideologies or discourses/world models and incorporate the assumptions implicit in their origins. The 'grand abstractions' of social science are not 'existent things', but ways of describing and abstracting from and characterizing the real 'existent things' — people and their social relations — and the notion that they might be constructed for a purpose, and deliberately or unwittingly incorporate theories about the social world, should come as no surprise. In Section 4 we looked at our own usual way of conceptualizing research as an activity and found that even here taken-for-granted assumptions about the nature of the social world and the proper ('natural', 'inevitable') way that power and knowledge are distributed are built into the way the enterprise is conducted and can shape the outcomes.

In other words, in looking at research papers or conducting your own research you need to be sensitive to the 'taken-for-granted'. Taken-for-granted ways of conceptualizing a problem area (or even taken-for-granted ways of conceptualizing aspects of social behaviour as 'belonging' to certain problem areas) shape how the problem is formulated, which restricts what can conceivably come out as results of any study undertaken. (Even more interesting, perhaps, is the way that disciplines and applied areas declare some questions to be 'real' problems and others as peripheral, trivial or 'not on the agenda'. Some selection *has* to be made — not everything can be researched — but we have shown that the omissions sometimes add up to a systematic exclusion of some set of interests or points of view.) The question as to the kinds of people who do and should appear in the sample, again reflects a model of the social world with respect to the problem which has been formulated, as does the method of data collection adopted, the form of analysis chosen and even the form in which we choose to promulgate results and conclusions. In a sense, this is not a criticism, because it is a general statement about all conceivable research projects and all conceivable research reports. It is not possible to work in a vacuum; at the same time as some aspects of a situation are problematized, others must be taken for granted. However, an important aspect of the conduct of research, and an even more important aspect of reading research reports, is thinking about precisely what has been taken for granted and how it affects the conclusions.

The point has also been made that the use of existing and accepted methods of research, grounded in the 'knowledge base' of a discipline, may sometimes amount to taking sides in a potential dispute. We have used social class as an example of how gender issues may be prejudged, and intelligence and attainment as examples of implicit and (sometimes) unconscious prejudgement of issues related to 'race' and social class. It is inevitable that most research will proceed along established lines and within established paradigms — we cannot for ever question *everything* — and it is true that to use '*un*conventional' methods and theoretical bases is equally to take sides. We need where possible, however, to identify what is being taken for granted in the methods we use and the disciplinary knowledge in which they are grounded.

This unit has used a fairly small range of examples — research into social class, intelligence and achievement — to make its points. The overall 'message', however, is that all research can be viewed from this kind of perspective and is open to this kind of critique. A major debate in research on the criminal justice system, for example, has been the ways in which social class is ignored or hidden or taken for granted in its analyses. Research on families, health and community care is rightly, some would say, attacked for the way in which it tends to take for granted a particular set of relations between the genders and across the generations. Feminist research into the position of women is attacked for its tendency to ignore the important dimension of ethnic origins. It is always a relevant form of critique to uncover the buried assumptions taken for granted by a piece of research, if only to show that they make no difference to the credibility of the conclusions — that a relevant political issue is not prejudged by the methods employed.

ANSWER TO ACTIVITY

ACTIVITY 2

The numbers represent the number of items of a denomination of pre-decimal English currency which go to make up the next largest item, before farthings were abolished.

  2 farthings make a halfpenny

  2 halfpennies make a penny

  3 pennies make a threepenny piece

  2 threepenny pieces make a sixpence

  2 sixpences make a shilling

  2 shillings make a florin

  Adding another sixpence makes a half-crown

  2 half-crowns make a crown (not in general circulation and minted only for special occasions, but legal tender)

  2 crowns make a ten-shilling note

  2 ten-shilling notes make a pound note

  5 pound notes make a five-pound note.

REFERENCES

Abbott, P., Bernie, J., Payne, G. and Sapsford, R. (1992) 'Health and material deprivation in Plymouth', in Abbott, P. and Sapsford, R. (eds) *Research into Practice: A Reader for Nurses and the Caring Professions*, Buckingham, Open University Press.

Abbott, P. and Sapsford, R. (1987a) *Women and Social Class*, London, Tavistock.

Abbott, P. and Sapsford, R. (1987b) 'The results of the survey', in Abbott, P. and Sapsford, R. (1987a) (extract reproduced in Offprints Booklet 3).

Abbott, P. and Sapsford, R. (1987c) 'The technical problems of assigning a class to women', in Abbott, P. and Sapsford, R. (1987a) (extract reproduced in Offprints Booklet 3).

Barron, F. (1953) 'An ego-strength scale which predicts response to psychotherapy', *Journal of Consulting Psychology*, vol. 17, pp.327–33.

Binet, A. and Simon, T. (1905) 'Methodes nouvelles pour le diagnostic du niveau intellectuel des abnormaux', *L'Annee Psychologique*, vol. 11, pp.191–244.

Binet, A. and Simon, T. (1908) 'Le developpement de l'intelligence chez les enfants', *L'Annee Psychologique*, vol. 14, pp.1–94.

Brigham, C.C. (1923) *A Study of American Intelligence*, Princeton, NJ, Princeton University Press.

Burt, C. (1921) *Mental and Scholastic Tests*, London, London County Council.

Burt, C. (1927) *The Measurement of Mental Capacities*, Edinburgh, Oliver and Boyd.

Burt, C. (1940) *The Factors of Mind*, London, University of London Press.

Cattell, R.B. (1946) *Description and Measurement of Personality*, London, Harrap.

Chapman, A. (1984) *Patterns of Mobility Among Men and Women in Scotland, 1930–1970*, unpublished PhD thesis, Plymouth Polytechnic.

Chapman, A. (1990) 'The mobility of men and women', in Payne, G. and Abbott, P. (eds) (1990b).

Christie, R. and Geiss, F.L. (1970) *Studies in Machiavellianism*, New York, Academic Press.

Comrey, A.L. (1957a) 'A factor analysis of the MMPI hypochondriasis scale', *Educational and Psychological Measurement,* vol. 17, pp.568–72.

Comrey, A.L. (1957b) 'A factor analysis of the MMPI depression scale', *Educational and Psychological Measurement,* vol. 17, pp.573–7.

Comrey, A.L. (1958) 'A factor analysis of the MMPI psychaesthenia scale', *Educational and Psychological Measurement,* vol. 18, pp.91–8.

Coxon, A.P.M., Davies, P.M. and Jones, C.L. (1986) *Images of Social Stratification: Occupational Structures and Class*, London, Sage.

Crookes, T.G. (1979) 'Sociability and behaviour disturbance', *British Journal of Criminology,* vol. 19, pp.60–6.

CSO (Central Statistical Office) (1975) 'Social commentary: social class', *Social Trends,* no. 6, pp.10–32, London, HMSO.

Douglas, J.W.B. (1964) *The Home and the School*, London, MacGibbon and Kee.

Drake, L.E. (1946) 'A social IE scale for the MMPI', *Journal of Applied Psychology,* vol. 30, pp.51–4.

Drake, L.E. and Thiede, W.B. (1948) 'Further validation of the social IE scale for the MMPI', *Journal of Educational Research*, vol. 41, pp.551–6.

Dugdale, R.L. (1877) *The Jukes: A Study in Crime, Pauperism, Disease and Heredity*, New York, Putnam.

Erikson, R. (1984) 'The social class of men, women and families', *Sociology*, vol. 18, pp.500–14.

Eysenck, H.J. (1947) *Dimensions of Personality*, London, Kegan Paul.

Eysenck, H.J. (1970) *The Structure of Human Personality*, London, Methuen.

Foucault, M. (1982) 'The subject and power', in Dreyfus, H. and Rabinow, P. (eds) *Michel Foucault: Beyond Structuralism and Hermeneutics*, Brighton, Harvester.

Gelsthorpe, L. (1992) 'Response to Martyn Hammersley's paper "On feminist methodology"', *Sociology,* vol. 26, pp.213–18.

Goddard, H.H. (1912) *The Kallikak Family: A Study in the Heredity of Feeble-mindedness*, New York, Macmillan.

Goldthorpe, J.H. and Hope, K. (1972) 'Occupational grading and occupational prestige', in Hope, K. (ed.) *The Analysis of Social Mobility*, Oxford, Clarendon Press.

Goldthorpe, J.H. and Hope, K. (1974) *The Social Grading of Occupations*, Oxford, Clarendon Press.

Goldthorpe, J.H., Llewelyn, C. and Payne, C. (1980) *Social Mobility and Class Structure in Modern Britain*, Oxford, Oxford University Press.

Goldthorpe, J.H. and Payne, C. (1986) 'On the class mobility of women: results from different approaches to the analysis of recent British data', *Sociology,* vol. 29, pp.531–53.

Gottesman, I.I. (1959) 'More construct validation of the ego-strength scale', *Journal of Consulting Psychology,* vol. 23, pp.342–6.

Haldane, J.B.S. (1933) *Science and Human Life*, New York, Harper.

Haldane, J.B.S. (1935) *Human Biology and Politics*, London, British Science Guild.

Haldane, J.B.S. (1938) *Heredity and Politics*, London, Allen.

Hall, J. and Jones, D.C. (1950) 'The social grading of occupations', *British Journal of Sociology*, vol. 1, pp.31–5.

Halsey, A.H., Heath, A. and Ridge, J.M. (1981) *Origins and Destinations: Family, Class and Education in Modern Britain*, Oxford, Oxford University Press.

Hammersley, M. (1992) 'On feminist methodology', *Sociology*, vol. 26, pp.187–206.

Hammersley, M. (ed.) (1993) *Social Research: Philosophy, Politics and Practice*, London, Sage (DEH313 Reader).

Hammond, J.L. (1987) 'Wife's status and family social standing', *Sociological Perspectives*, vol. 30, pp.71–92.

Hathaway, S.R. and McKinley, J.C. (1940) 'A multiphasic personality inventory (Minnesota) I: construction of the schedule', *Journal of Psychology*, vol. 10, pp.249–54.

Hathaway, S.R. and McKinley, J.C. (1942) 'A multiphasic personality inventory (Minnesota) III: the measurement of symptomatic depression', *Journal of Psychology*, vol. 14, pp.73–84.

Hayes, B.C. (1987) 'Female intergenerational mobility within Northern Ireland and the Republic of Ireland: the importance of maternal occupational status', *British Journal of Sociology*, vol. 38, pp.66–76.

Hayes, B.C. and Miller, R.L. (1989) 'Intergenerational occupational mobility within the Republic of Ireland: the ignored female dimension', *Women's Studies International Forum*, vol. 12, pp.439–45.

Heath, A. and Britten, N. (1984) 'Women's jobs do make a difference', *Sociology*, vol. 18, pp.475–90.

Heath, A., Jowell, R. and Curtice, J. (1985) *How Britain Votes*, Oxford, Pergamon.

Heskin, K.J., Bolton, N., Banister, P.A. and Smith, F.V. (1977) 'Prisoners' personality: a factor-analytically derived structure', *British Journal of Social and Clinical Psychology*, vol. 16, pp.203–6.

Heskin, K.J., Smith, F.V., Banister, P.A. and Bolton, N. (1973) 'Psychological correlates of long-term imprisonment II: personality variables', *British Journal of Criminology*, vol. 13, pp.323–30.

Jayaratne, T. (1983) 'The value of quantitative methodology for feminist research', in Hammersley, M. (ed.) (1993) (DEH313 Reader).

Jensen, A.R. (1972) *Genetics and Education*, New York, Harper and Row.

Jensen, A.R. (1973) *Education and Group Differences*, New York, Harper and Row.

Kahl, J.A. (1957) *The American Class Structure*, New York, Holt, Rinehart and Winston.

Kamin, L. (1977) *The Science and Politics of IQ*, Harmondsworth, Penguin.

Kumar, K. (1984) 'Unemployment as a problem in the development of industrial societies: the English experience', *Sociological Review*, vol. 32, pp.185–233.

McDonald, K.I. (1972) 'MDSCAL and distances between socio-economic groups', in Hope, K. (ed.) *The Analysis of Social Mobility*, Oxford, Clarendon Press.

McKinley, J.C. and Hathaway, S.R. (1940) 'A multiphasic personality inventory (Minnesota) II: a differential study of hypochondriasis', *Journal of Psychology*, vol. 10, pp.255–68.

Marshall, G., Newby, H., Rose, D. and Vogler, C. (1988) *Social Class in Modern Britain*, London, Hutchinson.

Martin, J. and Roberts, C. (1984) *Women and Employment: A Life-time Perspective*, London, HMSO.

Mies, M. (1983) 'Towards a methodology for feminist research', in Hammersley, M. (ed.) (1993) (DEH313 Reader).

Miller, R.L. and Hayes, B.C. (1990) 'Gender and intergenerational mobility', in Payne, G. and Abbott, P. (eds) (1990b).

Newton, D. and Smith, D. (1978) *Practice in the Basic Skills: Mathematics 2*, Edinburgh, Collins.

OPCS (Office of Population Censuses and Surveys) (1984) *Census 1981: Economic Activity — Great Britain*, London, HMSO.

Pahl, R. and Wallace, C. (1985) 'Household work strategies in economic recession', in Mingione, E. and Redclift, N. (eds) *Beyond Employment*, Oxford, Blackwell.

Parlee, M. (1979) 'Psychology and women', *Signs,* vol. 5, pp.123–33.

Payne, G. (1986a) *Employment and Opportunity*, London, Macmillan.

Payne, G. (1986b) *Mobility and Change in Modern Society*, London, Macmillan.

Payne, G. and Abbott, P. (1990a) 'Beyond male mobility models', in Payne, G. and Abbott, P. (eds) (1990b).

Payne, G. and Abbott, P. (eds) (1990b) *The Social Mobility of Women: Beyond Male Mobility Models*, Basingstoke, Falmer.

Penrose, L.S. (1933) *Mental Defect*, London, Sidgwick.

Prandy, K. (1986) 'Similarities of life-style and occupations of women', in Crompton, R. and Mann, M. (eds) *Gender and Stratification*, Cambridge, Polity Press.

Ramazanoglu, C. (1992) 'On feminist methodology: male reason versus female empowerment', *Sociology,* vol. 26, pp.207–12.

Reason, P. and Rowan, J. (1981) *Human Inquiry: A Sourcebook of New Paradigm Research*, Chichester, Wiley.

Registrar General (1912) *Annual Report for 1911*, London, HMSO.

Reinharz, S. (1979) *On Becoming a Social Scientist*, San Francisco, CA, Jossey Bass.

Reinharz, S. (1983) 'Experiential analysis: a contribution to feminist research', in Bowles, G. and Klein, R.D. (eds) *Theories of Women's Studies*, London, Routledge and Kegan Paul.

Sapsford, R. (1983) *Life-Sentence Prisoners: Reaction, Response and Change*, Milton Keynes, Open University Press.

Siltanen, J. and Stanworth, M. (1984) *Women and the Public Sphere: A Critique of Sociology and Politics*, London, Hutchinson.

Smith, D. (1974) 'Women's perspective as a radical critique of sociology', *Sociological Enquiry,* vol. 44, pp.7–13.

Spearman, C. (1904) 'General intelligence objectively determined and measured', *American Journal of Psychology,* vol. 15, pp.201–93.

Spearman, C. (1927) *The Abilities of Man*, London, Macmillan.

Sullivan, M. (1978) *Use Your Intelligence*, Glasgow, Fontana.

Taft, R. (1957) 'The validity of the Barron ego-strength scale and the Welsh anxiety index', *Journal of Consulting Psychology,* vol. 21, pp.247–9.

Terman, L. (1916) *The Measurement of Intelligence*, Boston, MA, Houghton Mifflin.

Terman, L.M. and Merrill, M.A. (1937) *Measuring Intelligence: A Guide to the Administration of the New Revised Stanford–Binet Tests of Intelligence*, London, Harrap.

Thomas, H.H., revised by Thomas, A.J. (1988) *English 1 Progress Papers: Pupils' Book*, Walton on Thames, Nelson.

Westergaard, J.H. and Rexler, H. (1975) *Class in a Capitalist Society: A Study of Contemporary Britain*, London, Heinemann.

White, H.C. (1970) *Chains of Opportunity*, Cambridge, MA, Harvard University Press.

Willis, P. (1977) *Learning to Labour*, Farnborough, Saxon House.

Yerkes, R.M. and Foster, J.C. (1923) *A Point Scale for Measuring Mental Ability*, Baltimore, MD, Warwick and York.

ACKNOWLEDGEMENTS

Grateful acknowledgement is made to the following sources for permission to reproduce material in this unit:

FIGURES

Figure 1: Newton, D. and Smith, D. (1978) *Mathematics 2 (Practice in the Basic Skills Series)*, Collins, an imprint of HarperCollins Publishers Ltd; Figure 2: Thomas, H.H. (1951) (revised by Thomas, A.J., 1988) *English 1: Progress Papers, Pupils Book*, Thomas Nelson and Sons Ltd; Figure 4: Sullivan, M. (1978) *Use Your Intelligence*, HarperCollins Publishers Ltd.

TABLES

Table 1: reprinted from Heath, A., Jowell, R. and Curtice, J., *How Britain Votes*, copyright © 1985, p.23, with permission from Pergamon Press Ltd, Headington Hill Hall, Oxford OX3 0BW, UK; Tables 2 and 3: Office of Population Censuses and Surveys (1984), *Census 1981: Economic Activity — Great Britain*, reproduced with the permission of the Controller of Her Majesty's Stationery Office.